The Evidence of Things Not Seen

*By the same author (*fiction)*

MOUNTAINEERING IN SCOTLAND
ROCK CLIMBS: GLENCOE AND ARDGOUR (*guidebook*)
UNDISCOVERED SCOTLAND
THE SCOTTISH HIMALAYAN EXPEDITION
THE STORY OF EVEREST
FIVE FRONTIERS*
THE SPURS OF TROODOS*
MAELSTROM*
HIGHLAND LANDSCAPE
THE CRAFT OF CLIMBING (*with J.E.B. Wright*)
DARK ROSE THE PHOENIX*
THE HEBRIDES
COMPANION GUIDE TO THE WEST HIGHLANDS OF SCOTLAND
THE REAL MACKAY*
THE ISLANDS OF WESTERN SCOTLAND
THE SCOTTISH HIGHLANDS
THE CURLING COMPANION
ROB ROY MACGREGOR – HIS LIFE AND TIMES
SCOTLAND'S MOUNTAINS

HONOURS & AWARDS

1950: Mungo Park Medal, RSGS (for Himalayan explorations)
1954: Literary Award, USA Education Board
(*for The Story of Everest*)
1966: OBE (for contributions to mountain literature and exploration)
1975: Hon Doctorate, D.Lit., University of Stirling
1991: Hon Doctorate, D.Lit., University of Strathclyde

The Evidence of Things Not Seen

A Mountaineer's Tale

W. H. MURRAY

FOREWORD BY HAMISH MACINNES
POETRY BY ANNE B. MURRAY

Vertebrate Publishing, Sheffield
www.v-publishing.co.uk

The Evidence of Things Not Seen

W.H. Murray

Vertebrate Publishing
Omega Court, 352 Cemetery Road, Sheffield S11 8FT, United Kingdom.
www.v-publishing.co.uk

First published in Great Britain 2002 by Bâton Wicks, London. This digital edition first published in 2020 by Vertebrate Digital, an imprint of Vertebrate Publishing.

Cover image: Murray in the Menlung Chu. Photo: Murray Collection.
Back cover image: W.H. Murray. Photo: Murray Collection.

This book is a work of non-fiction based on the life, experiences and recollections of W.H. Murray. In some limited cases the names of people, places, dates and sequences or the detail of events have been changed solely to protect the privacy of others. The author has stated to the publishers that, except in such minor respects not affecting the substantial accuracy of the work, the contents of the book are true.

A CIP catalogue record for this book is available from the British Library.

ISBN 978-1-912560-82-0 (paperback)
ISBN 978-1-912560-81-3 (ebook)

Produced by Vertebrate Publishing.

Contents

Acknowledgements

I wish to thank Professor Donald B. MacIntyre for permission to quote from his funeral address in my epilogue and for conferring on matters both serious and humorous. My thanks also go to Dr Euan A.M. MacAlpine for letters from his archives, to Dr Robert Aitken and to Hamish MacInnes for writing the Foreword.

Many others have helped with photographs or advice including help while writing the book: Tom Weir, John Tyson, Michael Ward, Douglas Scott, Gordon Stainforth, Peter Hodgkiss and the executors of the late, well-known Glasgow portrait photographer J. Stephens Orr. The individual photographers are all credited near their entries.

The late Tony Colwell, a senior editor of Jonathan Cape, gave me valued advice at a crucial stage; Betty Patey gave me permission to use Tom's verse.

Thanks also go to Alastair Robertson and Jack Webster for permission to quote from their work, and Marcia Newbold for granting use of the letters of her father (Geoffrey Winthrop Young) in Appendix III.

Others who have helped include John Bowles (National Library of Scotland), Jeff Connor, Sarah Bojard (Royal Photographic Society), Roy Humble, Sir Edmund Hillary, Des Rubens, John Lyall and Jack Ashcroft.

I would also like to thank Jennifer MacMillan for help with typing and deciphering and Julie Campbell for being a wise sounding board.

A.B.M. 2002

WINTER NIGHT – GLEN COE

The hills lie
White on the sky
Moon cold and still.
And I
Spraying frost
From the bound, gagged grass
Listen for life.
But sound is lost
Held
Fastened to ice.
Stars move
In themselves
In the sky
Throwing sparks
To fire smothered snow
Blazing below
While I
Ringing night
From the close barred earth
Search for keys
Listen for life.

Foreword
by Hamish MacInnes

I first met Bill Murray on an icy February night in 1947 in the car-park of the Royal Hotel, Tyndrum. I was with a group of climbers travelling back to Glasgow in a mountaineering club bus. Around, the snow-covered hills and moors were bathed in moonlight. A car drew up with a group of SMC types including George Roger whom I knew. He introduced me to Bill and we stood together gazing at the mountains. I was immediately struck by his presence which seemed to have a spiritual quality. Indeed, as I learned later, he had spent time in a Benedictine monastery. He seemed to me, as a young and impressionable climber, to convey the image of a frugal, contemplative eagle.

As an avid consumer of climbing literature I had already devoured Bill's articles in the magazine *Open Air in Scotland. Mountaineering in Scotland* had just been published and this book captivated me, as it did thousands of climbers throughout the land. Bill had a magical gift of encapsulating a scene in a way we all felt, but could never express. Acknowledged as one of our greatest descriptive writers, he involves all who read him. For an ambitious climber it was his ability to get quickly to the centre of the action that I found particularly inspiring.

Bill was a free spirited adventurer, who could visualise sermons in stones and prose in the clarity of a mountain stream. I often wondered if his choice of Geoffrey Winthrop Young's poem 'Knight Errantry' for the preface of *Mountaineering in Scotland* was inspired from within the confines of a prison camp:

'There is a region of heart's desire
free for the hand that wills'

It was during his prisoner-of-war years that he took up meditation, a practice which he continued all his life. This was reflected in his writings which often had a mystical quality.

> 'May it not be possible, by some practical method to help one's mind to grow in awareness of beauty, to develop that faculty of perception which we frustrate and stunt if we do not exercise? The answer is that growth may be given to the spiritual faculty as

> simply as growth and health are given to the body by awakening it from slumber, and providing nourishment and then by giving hard exercise. In this work there is no static position: one goes on, or one drops back. Therefore, and above all – persist.'

On the double traverse of the *Aonach Eagach Ridge* of Glen Coe with Donald McIntyre in February 1947 he describes the scene as they linger on the summit of Meall Dearg awaiting dawn's first light:

> 'We knew, as surely as men know anything on earth, that the implacable hunter had drawn close … One's ear caught the ringing of his footstep: and one's eye gleams like the flashing of a shield.'

In a strange way Bill's earlier mountain life appears entwined in the theme of 'Knight Errantry' – the urge to search and appreciate, the need to proclaim through his writings. Tom Patey – also a gifted writer – took up the theme in his 'Ballad of Bill Murray':

> 'In that Tournament on Ice, Death or Glory was the price
> For those knights in shining armour long ago –
> You must forage for yourself on that ghastly Garrick's Shelf
> With every handhold buried deep in snow.'

In the post-war years Himalayan exploration became one of Bill's driving passions. With Douglas Scott, Tom Weir and Tom McKinnon he took part in the Scottish Himalayan Expedition in 1950, a small time venture, big in achievement, run on the 'old pals' principle pioneered by Longstaff, Shipton and Tilman, all of whom Bill admired. As well as bagging three virgin peaks and attempting several others, they succeeded in getting through the Girthi Gorge to connect two great trade routes across the Himalaya to Central Asia.

In 1951, having organised the expedition from Loch Goil, he was with Ward, Shipton, and others in what was to prove to be the crucial Everest reconnaissance prior to the first ascent. This was followed by fascinating explorations around Cho Oyu, Menlungtse and Gaurisankar. In 1953, with John Tyson, there was the circumnavigation and exploration of the Api/Nampa range which included a dangerous foray into Chinese-occupied Tibet.

Bill's contribution to the conservation of the environment was vast. He was a latter-day John Muir; in fact he was a founding trustee of the John Muir Trust. He has influenced important allies who wield big sticks; Al Gore, when US Vice President, quoted Bill in his powerful conservation treatise *Earth in the Balance*. He is an admirer of Bill's work. A large portion of Bill's latter years was devoted to conservation. This inevitably had a price tag of endless debates sandwiched by tedious journeys to faceless meetings, as alien to his natural instincts as falling off a difficult pitch. We all owe him a debt of gratitude for this dedication to our environment.

I have been fortunate enough to have repeated most of Bill's Scottish climbs over the years, during a period in time when giant strides in mountaineering were made. Techniques in winter climbing allowed older routes, many of which Bill and his mates had pioneered, to be completed faster and in relative safety.

The 'ice crowned castles' of Bill's career, such as the stubborn *Garrick's Shelf* on Buachaille Etive Mor, stand the scrutiny of time. Not many mountaineers of this new millennium would relish scaling that glassy rampart wall of Crowberry Ridge with the bare trio of necessities – an antiquated ice axe, nailed boots and a hemp rope that resembled, when frozen, a steel hawser – though Bill had, on that climb, taken a slater's hammer, an indicator of the technical developments that were to follow. 'Those were the days my friends … '

My second encounter with Bill was just prior to his departure to Everest in 1951. I had just returned from National Service in the Austrian Tirol and was fired with irrepressible enthusiasm for steep rock and ice. I wanted to hear first-hand from Bill about this ambitious project. My motorcycle shuddered to a halt outside his house at Loch Goil and Bill came out to greet me. He was as always keener to listen and find out what you had been doing than talk of his own exploits, but bubbling underneath was his passion for the hills which was contagious … always urging one to get out and up there. I had a slight tinge of conscience over the visit and never mentioned it to my friends in the Creagh Dhu. They were the product of the Clydeside shipyards who lived hard and climbed hard and to whom the 'toffs' of the Scottish Mountaineering Club were aliens. My sense of adventure was obviously greater than my loyalty!

Bill's tendency to play down his role in events is illustrated in an incident in the French Alps in 1948 when he was involved in a terrible accident with John Barford and Michael Ward when all three ended up in a bergschrund after a long fall. Bill, with his large rucksack still on his back, became jammed in the mouth of the 'schrund. Below in the murky depths he could see Barford, who was dead, and below again was Ward, still alive, wedged between the icy walls. With superhuman effort Bill managed to get down to the ice ledge on which Barford lay and eventually managed to extricate Michael, who had lost his memory and like Bill had fractured his skull. He was disorientated and weak and could contribute little to his extraction from the 'schrund.

I mention this incident, for in later years Bill was Patron of the Glencoe Mountain Rescue Team and took an interest in new innovations and techniques. I used to look forward to his visits. After one protracted annual dinner,

Bill voted to return to Loch Goil in his trusty Morris Traveller rather than take up my offer of a bed. Nosing his way up through the snow-covered Glen Coe gorge on his journey home he was stopped by the police. They asked him where he was going on such a night at such an ungodly hour. He told them, and added he had been with me at the rescue dinner and was hoping to get back home.

'Well Mr Murray, any friend of Hamish is a friend of ours' one replied, 'you take care … '

Bill, who had an impish sense of humour, used to relate this story with glee.

We will all miss Bill yet he is still with us – his writing, as if carved from the living rock, will be remembered by mountaineers as long as there are mountains to climb. Both mystic and prophet, he saw things we didn't and could scan the future to visualise a bigger horizon.

Bill met Anne when descending from the winter hills. It was a chance meeting between a writer and a poet, a match if not made in heaven, certainly on the mountain slope. It was inevitable that they should meet again and share their lives together. Anne, reserved, with the sharp focus of a poet and Bill embracing his philosophical concept of the Sadhu. Writing on the advent of spring her verse seems appropriate for Bill:

Belonging not to the dark
But to me
But at night
The tree has gone
And on the wrong side of the window
Tapping the brittle glass
It is I, now
Who have to seek that other side of night.

THE EVIDENCE OF THINGS NOT SEEN

'In this book I write little of childhood days but much of manhood's experience of mountains, war, and the art of writing. In selected incidents I have traced a long life to give one man's impression of his world.'

W.H.M. 1995

'We have to act as best we know and surrender the fruits: be not attached, but learn to accept the consequences of all acts serenely.'

W.H. Murray

After Bill's death in 1996 I continued the editing of his book as he would have wished and as we discussed.

In consultation with the publisher it was agreed to expand sections dealing with pre-war Scottish ice-climbing and the 1950 Scottish Himalayan Expedition. Bill had dealt with these subjects only briefly as two of his books covered them thoroughly.

We felt that the reader of this book would want a fuller description and accordingly the highly evocative 'Garrick's Shelf' chapter from *Mountaineering in Scotland* has been included plus six chapters abridged from his vivid and acclaimed 1950 expedition book.

Some of Bill's interesting letters from army, prison camp and the Himalaya have been included adding immediacy and detail to descriptions 'recollected in tranquillity'.

The poems chosen by the author for inclusion in the book are mine, and the amusing verse is from Tom Patey's 'Ballad of Bill Murray'.

Photo captions and some informative footnotes have been supplied by the publisher.

Anne B. Murray, 2002

Early Years

1 Twists of the Thread

The child by instinct can be wiser than the man. He picks up at birth the thread spun for him by the Fates, accepting without murmur its inter-twisted good and ill. I lacked a father, yet never felt short-changed. He had been killed at Gallipoli in the Dardanelles Campaign of 1915, when I was two. I never knew him. The realisation of loss came years later, but never did I feel wronged.

He and my mother were Scottish. I was born at Liverpool, where my father had been posted (from Broxburn, West Lothian) as HM Inspector of Mines for Lancashire and North Wales. My thread still had two good strands. My mother Helen, aged thirty-two at my birth, was a woman of resource. Unbounded courage and two children had made her ready to fight. In 1915, she took me and my sister back to Glasgow, where our paternal grandparents lived, and saw us properly schooled, civilly brought up, and launched on life not consciously impaired. The second strand was my sister Margaret; she was five years older than I – and that was later to bring me no small benefit.

A first sense of deprivation came to me on entering my teens; inevitably so, for too much had then to be learned alone – always the hard way, the long way. My mother told me of my father's talents: how able in mathematics (at which I was inept); how skilled in music, for he could take up any instrument, play well, and sing with good voice (I seemed to be tone-deaf and sang out of tune); how gifted in the arts of drawing, painting and wood-carving, which I could see with my own eyes to be true (but no such arts were mine when I tried); how boldly strong he was in skating and climbing, for the great frosts of the late 1890s came in his teens, when he used to skate ten miles up Loch Lomond from Balloch to Rowardennan, weaving his way through the dozen islands, then climb Ben Lomond and skate back (whereas I could not skate at all, for the long frosts were no more). My admiration for my imaginary father was boundless, but he wasn't there to give any practical lead. My lack of abilities left me adrift, as if rudderless on wide and windy seas.

Margaret and I owed everything to our mother's fighting instinct. Her first act of battle on our behalf was fought against three government ministries: the Home Office, the War Office, and the newly formed Ministry of Pensions. She sought to extract funds for our schooling. Senior civil servants turned deaf ears. They had a war on their hands. Undeterred, she persisted vigorously. That she finally wrung this concession out of them has amazed me all my life. In accepting responsibility for her children's schooling, they boiled down her choice for me to either Fettes in Edinburgh or Glasgow Academy. She chose the Glasgow school, feeling that if sent away from home I would feel deprived of her love.

Our mother had set up home on the west side of Glasgow, together with her mother and unmarried sister. For this family of five, she organised annually – as soon as the war had ended – the most splendid summer holidays. These always lasted, at least for the children, a full two months in remote, unspoiled country – the islands of Lismore and Arran or on the wildland coasts of Donegal, or Kintyre, or the Solway Firth. These idyllic places gave endless and diverse adventure to town-reared children, and certainly bred in me a love of wild land, if not yet high land.

We lived for these long holidays. A glamorous excitement invested the very preparations, when big hampers stood in the hall for some ten days of June, gradually packed before our 5 or 6 a.m. departures by horse-drawn cab to railway station or shipping dock. We regretted over the years the advent of unromantic taxis, but no disappointments ever marred our farther journeys. They stick in mind to this day: my first storm at sea, aged six, on a passage to Ireland when the ship began to pitch and roll and a seaman screwed down the portholes with a laconic 'Dirty nicht the nicht,' which quelled my rising fears of a capsize; followed by next day's blue skies, when we trundled in pony and trap along the cliff tops of Donegal's north coast to a white cottage on its brink; or two years later, in a gathering storm on Appin's shore, my mother browbeating a ferryman into sailing his lugger across Loch Linnhe to Lismore. I met another boy there, and with him climbed high into an old oak to hide in its canopy, and to smoke our first cigarette from a two-penny packet of Woodbines. The smoke inflicted more than the storm – my life's first dizzy head. Trivial events, being each child's first experience, figure as long in memory as important later ones. I can hardly see a broad, sandy beach without reliving my first, dangerous racing games on the Solway Firth, when my sister and I aged twelve and seven would fly for our lives across mile-wide sands, the tide at our heels flowing 'fast as a galloping horse'. If we miscalculated and failed to give ourselves a long enough start, we would find ourselves marooned on some low and tiny islet, faced with a wearisome wait or a wet self-rescue.

My sister was naturally more adventurous than I, a difference more heavily marked when she crossed the gulf of puberty. On holiday in Arran, she and her new-found boyfriends climbed their first mountain, Goat Fell. I was not a whit interested. It looked (from distance) a highly remote lump of land, not for me.

Glasgow Academy brought me a brief devotion to Rugby football. Its former pupils then supplied, year in year out, a quarter of Scotland's national team. Wanting to be one of them, I felt mortified at my lack of a Scottish birthplace, which meant irrational debarment, irrelevant too as I soon found on reaching my teens. Although tall, I was and always would be far too light in weight for first-class rugby. Often asked what I wanted to be, I had no idea. I devoured books. By the time I was thirteen I had read twenty-five of Scott's *Waverley* novels, admittedly skipping the first 100 pages to get at the action, and most of R.L.S. and Alexandre Dumas. My boyhood heroes were all fictional, especially D'Artagnan of *The Three Musketeers* or Buchan's Richard Hannay, or Ewan Cameron of *The Flight of the Heron*. My school friends and I were divided by this difference, that they read as little as they could, and I as much as I could. They loathed writing essays. I enjoyed them. But writing as a career? Even I knew it impractical for a school-leaver.

My sister was meantime reading English Literature and Philosophy at Glasgow University. Her brain was quicker than mine and more subtly sensitive. I won endless benefit from her and her visiting boyfriends, since all were older than I. They unburdened their eagerly active minds at evening ceilidhs at our new home in Jordanhill. They came for music and talk. Principally talk. My sister had picked them well. Their talk was of ideas, no subject barred, ranging all over human life. I, fascinated, was thrown a line across the maturity gulf. Involuntarily, I had my reading lifted from Scott to Shakespeare and Shaw, from Dumas to D.H. Lawrence, from Broster to James Joyce (smuggled in from Paris), and so on across other aspects of literature. My more staple diet remained, of course, the common thriller.

Amid the growing multiplicity of books to which my attention was drawn, those discovered by myself in my late teens more effectively broadened my mind. They were not the latest from Paris, but the earlier from Greece – Plato's *Republic and Dialogues*. His writings on the reality of abstract ideas – good, beauty, truth, unity and justice – at first stretched my mind as if on a rack, but by degrees of familiarity over the years became as heavily bracing as hill winds off the Cairngorm plateaux. They enlarged all concepts of life and purpose. I owed any such rewards, initially at least, to my sister's example. Although good at games, she liked to think as well as play.

I began to dream again of writing, but again dismissed the notion. I could not hope to emulate authors of the quality I read. I had to earn a living. Had my father been alive, he would certainly have packed me off to university, there to study for some profession. Instead, I left school for an office job in the Union Bank of Scotland, where after four years' study of accountancy, law, economics, stocks and foreign exchange, I duly qualified as a member of The Institute of Bankers. Banking gives sterling service to the community; it can become an absorbing subject for anyone with a flair for its higher practice. But the flair was not mine. I had no vocation. The plain fact was that I wanted to write, and write I did, my short stories earning the customary flow of rejection slips.

Providence and the Fates share this endearing feature: intervention in all lives to bring the best out of bad situations. My own grandfather, for example, had been prospering as a young man in wool manufacture, when he lost all his money invested in the City of Glasgow Bank – an unlimited company. It crashed in 1878. Now ruined, he won fulfilment of his real talent, for music. Starting at the Anderson College, where he taught advanced music classes, he became Music Inspector for the Board of Education, then Conductor of The Glasgow Choral Union, from which he and Hugh Roberton took the leading part in founding Glasgow's Orpheus Choir. His musical talent had passed to his eldest son, but not to his grandchildren. My own salvation was offered in ways quite different, each set up by 'circumstance', but the choice left always to me. The first turning point appeared in 1934.

2 Siren Song

It does seem strange that I, bred and schooled in Glasgow, had been unaware of mountains, except as a backdrop to a lowland foreground, until I was out of my teens. My change of focus came with all the suddenness of a conversion in faith. When nineteen and lodging at Maclay Hall (a Glasgow students' residence) I overheard the Warden talk at table of his traverse of An Teallach in Wester Ross – clouds lifting off a high and rocky mountain ridge, sun-shafts lighting a glen deep below – and my attention was gripped. Here was a wildland of the skies, to me unknown and waiting for exploration, yet unlike the moon or Mount Everest, immediately accessible.

I made no move. I knew no one who climbed mountains. A year later in April 1934, I at last bestirred myself and went to the nearest I knew by name, the Cobbler at Arrochar. Approaching by train on the West Highland Line, I thought the cloudless day perfect for the job. The first sight of my first mountain across the blue waters of Loch Long jolted me wide awake. It rose from the shore in one abrupt swell of grassy hillside, uncluttered by so much as a tree, up to a snowfilled corrie crowned by three big tusks Their black rock sprang sheer out of a dazzling white hollow. I could see no good way on to the central summit, but felt hopeful of getting close by a wide snow gully to its left-hand side. I had no boots, but snow in my short life had been soft stuff, not icy. I was wearing walking shoes, and with these could probably stamp out a way. I had never even heard of an ice axe.

I stepped off the road on to the Cobbler and gaily went up. Soon I was delighting in the simple breathing of sharp and sunny mountain air, in the personal choice of my own way at every turn, in the new sense of freedom from all rules. In the very uncertainties of it all was fun. I reckoned that I could always turn back if I met real trouble. One thing I had not reckoned on, when I reached the snows of the upper corrie, was the ice-hard plating on its flanks. By dint of an hour's agonised toe scraping, with its growing awareness of dire penalties to pay should I slip, and the still worse threat in any attempt at retreat, I learned the hard way of the need of proper tools for the real enjoyment of climbing. I shed my innocence, as always, with the suddenness of the fly caught in the web.

The Cobbler's lesson, if salutary, was not the most important of the day. That came at the rocky summit. I looked across hill ranges, sparkling white or blue shadowed, receding to the distant rim of an arctic plateau. It looked as if it must stretch on forever. I had never dreamt that my own country held wild land so vast. I recognised on the instant that every peak had to be known. A man of twenty-one enjoys a god-like assumption of immortality. This day I saw with a pang of dismay that life is short and the hill ranges long. There was no time to be lost. First impressions being the lasting ones, it was my good fortune, when I ventured into the Cairngorms, to see them whole – in the sense that I walked the full breadth from Tay to Spey. I walked alone, so at once grasped two vital facts: that here were 2,000 square miles of mountains in which my whole being could revel, free of all the cares of the world; and second, that here no mistakes were allowed. The paradox holds the secret of the mountains' call. Delight and danger. They impose a discipline: a need to stay alert, alert to weather, to one's footing, to time of day, the shape of the hill and the right route. A need for self-possession. The Cairngorms won my respect without giving me a beating, for I walked in June. The sun smiled across the expanse of the Capel Mounth; rainstorms chased me off Lochnagar and north to the Don. My first top was Ben Avon.

The vastness of the Ben Avon plateau astonished my innocent eyes. It sprawled for miles, snow drifts lay deep, fantastic tors epitomised wilderness. In many a twelve-hour day thereafter, I found the long walks through the Rothiemurchus pines into Glen More (then impassable to cars), Glen Einich and the Lairig Ghru, so full of change and beauty that I never grudged the time they took. On the plateaux above them, those immense deserts of stone never wearied the eye as I thought they might. Spectacular corries carved their flanks, cliffed and rimmed white by cornices, or sunk so deep like Loch Avon, or cupped so high like that of Angel's Peak, that always the great scale gave a lift to the spirits. Height too I felt in a purity of air unique to the Cairngorms – at 4,000 feet like nectar of the gods, to be drunk deep.

True as such words are, they can be sudden nonsense if it snows and blows. Next May, a friend and I were caught by blizzard on Cairn Toul. Arctic cold combined with hurricane to bring on the dreaded chill factor. Despite our windproof shells and layers of inner wool, the cold had bitten down to our bones before we gained Braeriach. The 'white out' of spindrift had long since lost us any sight of the ground, daylight was ebbing, and any mistake in our bearings would have finished us. Luck was ours. We glissaded into the Lairig Ghru as darkness fell. There had been no margin of safety. We had escaped only by getting our compass work right – always dicey in a white out.

Another day in May, another year, found another friend and me swimming in a lochan of deep sea green under the cliffs of Lochnagar. Warm air poured upwards in visible waves, streaming and shivering in sunlight against the grey face of the rocks. We lay in sparkling water and chose our line up the cliff. Cairngorm days bring endless surprise: fear, exhilaration, suspense, idyllic ease – one can never tell what next, save that here is flying.

My instant reaction to mountains had proved constant – to know and explore. A second need, to climb rock and ice, grew naturally out of the first, a freedom to be won: but I felt scared of trying to join a club. I had been meeting walkers on the hills. They assured me that rock climbers, unlike us, were fearless, held danger in contempt, were physically close to gorillas, and with bulging biceps able to haul themselves up long ropes, and to grip with their toes a ledge at chin level and stand up. A reading of George Abraham's *British Mountain Climbs* (1909) partially dispelled that nightmare, but climbers had still to hold on the rope their companions who fell off high above. I felt weak not only at arms and shoulders, but now at the knees too.

When courage was at last screwed up, I joined the Junior Mountaineering Club of Scotland (JMCS).

Before I had time to know any of its members, I found an unexpected companion in Archie MacAlpine. I had first met him when I was a boy of fourteen, and he an undergraduate at Dental College in Glasgow. His interest, therefore was not in me, but in my sister Margaret, whom in following years he wooed and won. At that first meeting in Kintyre, where my sister and I were on holiday, he arrived at Skipness by sea after rowing from the Clyde around the Kyles of Bute and Ardlamont Point – a distance of sixty miles – hands not even blistered. I was impressed. His thatch of fair hair, matched by eyes of Viking blue, seemed most appropriate for a university oarsman, shelves loaded with the silver cups he'd won. After he had set up practice at Ibrox and married my sister, he became concerned for her brother's sanity. I had found mountains. This to him was a puzzlement. What on earth was the point of sweating up hills? Margaret, scorning the safety-first trends of the time, encouraged him to try. I persuaded him to think of Glen Coe,[1] to which I had not yet found my way. I owned no car but he did – and a new road had been opened that very year across Rannoch Moor. The trumpet call of Glen Coe was sounding in my ears. One September morning of 1935, we rounded that last bend of the Rannoch road and for the first time saw the huge rock cone of Buachaille Etive Mor lift high out of the moor. Our breath was taken from us. We stopped the car. Every detail of the cliffs showed clear and sharp – to our eyes unclimbable.

We found the easy way up from Glen Etive. Archie, not yet fit, dubbed the trudge laborious, but his attitude changed on reaching the summit screes, where we could walk in delight to the cairn. He needed just one look over that wild, far scene to be hooked, just as I had been the previous year on the Cobbler. Spurred by curiosity, we climbed down to the top of the North Buttress, and chanced to see three rock climbers starting up the Crowberry Tower. They were members of the Scottish Mountaineering Club, to which we

1 Climbers have tended to refer to Glencoe which is actually the title of the village at the end of Glen Coe – the glen itself. The latter title is invariably used henceforth.

could not aspire. Their ease of movement made our impossible cliff look feasible, even for us if led. Now doubly hooked, Archie filled in his application form for the JMCS.

A few weeks later, its members took me in hand. On a drizzly November morning I was led up my first rock climb, the *Spearhead Arête* of Ben Narnain. I can remember that day as if I were still on the climb – the awareness of airiness, the high angle, the fingertip feel of coarse rock, then the lightness that comes of self-abandonment. Life, it seemed to me, had just begun.

The five years that followed, and many of their best mountain days, I later described at length in my first book, *Mountaineering in Scotland*. The particular advantage I now have in looking back on them is that great age comes like a hilltop in time from which early years appear in true perspective.

I and my fellow climbers of the 1930s had been too close to the First World War and its aftermath to realise our position, or to guess at our deprivations. These latter, I now know, were of two kinds. The first was our lack of inherited climbing standards. Since those days, each new generation has been given standards by their seniors, and received techniques by example, taken them for granted, and used them (even if unconsciously) as a springboard for higher achievement; each has had that boost and made good use of it. In the 1930s we did not have it. There was no springboard. For winter work we started from scratch; for summer rock, from a level set around 1900, the year of the Abrahams' *tour de force*, the *Crowberry Direct*, since when little advance had been made.

Our cut-off had been caused by the huge depletion in the nation's manpower relative to a small population. There was no young leadership left. This stemmed both from long casualty lists and from a sapping of psychic vigour by trench warfare. The few who had survived that ordeal had a bellyful of risk and rough living. They wanted no more of it. Mountains were there as always for enjoyment, not for battle, and certainly not for competition or any nerve testing beyond modest rock climbing. 'An expert with strong arms' might aspire to Severe routes after many years. Winter was for walking, varied by occasional snow gullies like the Central Gully of Beinn Laoigh.

My contemporaries and I had been war babies or born close before or after. We entered uncritically a social environment newly and strongly biased against more risk to life. Therefore the second brake on us was this all-pervading safety code. World wars do have a double effect on mountaineering. First they stop it and by drain of life delay resumption; but second, in compensation, they rouse in freed youth an urge to climb exploratively. When we came to mountains we had to find them for ourselves, and this had one great gain – our untold delight in such a vast field for adventure, untrammelled by company of elders and betters. The mountains were ours. We were free to do as we willed. It never occurred to us, distracted as we were by the heady joys of climbing, that our performance was handicapped by an unnatural generation gap – one so deep and wide that we could not imagine that some of our predecessors might have achieved standards beyond our own. In this youthful arrogance, our generation was at least no different from any other.

We had this excuse, that in the 1920s climbing in Scotland had to all appearance died. There had been no strong renewal like that in the Lakes or Wales. Nor was any great example set like the opening up of Clogwyn Du'r Arddu by Pigott and Longland, which seemed in effect to light a fuse, exploding the latent energies of England's rock climbers. Nothing of that high order brought life up here. The best new rock climbs were by English summer migrants, birds of passage mostly alighting in Skye. We were grateful to them for routes on Sron na Ciche like Mallory's *Slab,* Pye and Shadbolt's *Crack of Doom,* and Holland's *Cioch West.* A 'Severe' was the acme of climbing achievement.

The slow advance in relation to what was happening in the Lakes and Wales had multiple reasons. Climbers were few. A novice to get company in the 1920s had to join a club. There were three: the Scottish Mountaineering Club, the Cairngorm Club, and the Ladies' Scottish Climbing Club. Only a small minority of their members were still climbing rock, mainly in the SMC.

One would be lucky indeed ever to know them. Few of the new generation were able to qualify for the SMC. The deadlock was seen by a small group of its members. They founded the JMCS in 1925, open to all men of seventeen years, and left to themselves in the hope that self-responsible young would thrive and revitalise Scottish climbing. Ten years later the hope was justified.

Other clubs were forming in Glasgow: in 1929, the Ptarmigan Club; in 1930, the Creagh Dhu of Clydebank, which made little mark before the Second World War, but won fame after it; and in 1933, the Lomond Club. All three tended to localise their activities in the Southern Highlands.[2]

Services of real value were given by the SMC in this period: their building of the Charles Inglis Clark Memorial Hut close below the cliffs of Ben Nevis at 2,200 feet, and their publication of guidebooks to the Cairngorms, Skye, and Ben Nevis – the latter made possible by the hut's presence.

Ben Nevis rises to 4,406 feet at the head of Loch Linnhe, which occupies the southern part of the Great Glen – a crystal fault that splits Scotland from the North Sea to the Atlantic. Those happy few who enjoy gales, rain and blizzard will enjoy the Ben: it lies full in the track of North Atlantic storms. In shape like a sperm whale, afloat on a sea of peaks spreading 14,000 square miles, it rewards persistent wooers with days that stay long in mind for one grim reason after another, alleviated by days so clear that the Antrim Hills can be seen from its summit 120 miles south-west. Its cliffs face north-east and are Britain's biggest.

2 With the notable exception of *Raven's Gully,* on Buachaille Etive Mor, which was climbed by a Ptarmigan/Creagh Dhu party led by Jock Nimlin in 1937 and amongst the hardest climbs in the country at that time. *Editor*

They lift out of the glen of the Allt a'Mhuilinn in a two-mile arc 2,000 feet high. Unlike the pink granite mass of the mountain, the cliffs are lavas, mainly a grey andesite, formed 350 million years ago in a cauldron subsidence. The rock is hard-baked and sound. The CIC Hut, built out of the Ben's granite was conceived in memory of the Club's dead in the Great War, the money for the building was given by Dr William Inglis Clark and his wife Jane whose son Charles had been killed in action in 1918. Jane had been the founder and first President of the Ladies' Scottish Climbing Club in 1908 and William, the Scottish Mountaineering Club's President throughout the War. They gave the hut a splendid site under the great array of deeply carved ridges, buttresses, and pinnacles which tower overhead, above lingering snow fields. When the hut was officially opened by Jane Inglis Clark in 1929 it saved years in the cliffs' exploration.

The SMC had within itself three other means of renewal: its biannual journal, and two top-class climbers in Dr J.H.B. Bell and Dr Graham Macphee, each placed where he could do most good: Bell as editor of the *SMC Journal*, and Macphee as editor of the Nevis guide.

Everyone's activities were hampered by the state of Highland roads, which were bad and narrow. The old road to Glen Coe across Rannoch Moor, metalled in broken stone, went higher than now on the Black Mount, where every snowfall blocked it. A minority of the new climbers owned cars, and these mostly second-hand. They had no heaters and were refrigerators in winter. Travel was slow and fraught with West Highland troubles. Oil sumps cracked on the crown of the road, springs burst on the potholes, water froze in radiators. Having no money, I bought a motor bike for £8 – a 500cc Norton – which achieved 80 miles per hour across the new Rannoch road. One snowy winter cured me of that. Second-hand cars were cheap. I paid £30 for an oil-eating Austin Seven, which otherwise ran like a Rolls Royce until the door handles fell off. At such prices one could afford to climb farther afield than Arrochar.

Since the only hut was halfway up Ben Nevis, we made much use of hotels in winter. Clachaig Inn charged 5 shillings [25 pence] for supper, bed and breakfast, and the rats in the wainscot lent atmosphere, Kingshouse and Inverarnan, 7/6 pence [37½ pence] rising to 9/6 pence [47½ pence]. Inverarnan in Glen Falloch virtually became a winter base for the JMCS. When we ran out of money, as often happened, or were saving up, we camped, or literally hit the hay at Danny's Barn at Altnafeadh in Glen Coe. On good weekends we camped in high corries or up on the mountain tops. A spin off from Everest expeditions had been the production of high-altitude tents (£6), eiderdown bags £2.10.0, [£2.50], and windproof anoraks and breeches. No one wore tweed jackets. A three weeks' camping holiday in Glen Brittle cost £10 for two weeks all in. It was a golden age, and even felt like it at the time. Good snow years come in cycles. We had an unbroken run.

PRE-WAR CLIMBING IN SCOTLAND

3 Rocks and Climbers

To Archie MacAlpine I now owed a new impetus to both our mountain careers: a chance to team up with two of the club's leading rock men, Bill Mackenzie and Kenneth Dunn.

On summer rock, Mackenzie was one of the six best leaders in Scotland. On mixed winter rock and high-angle ice, he had no rival in Britain. His natural athletic talent extended to ball games; he played off scratch at golf, and football too at near professional standard. In May 1936, the JMCS held a meet in Glen Coe, from which I was absent (in the Cairngorms). Archie MacAlpine and Margaret pitched their big tent, which we called 'the canvas palace', at Coupall Bridge in Glen Etive. It proved so popular in heavy rain that a camp bed broke under the weight of parked bodies, two of them Dunn and Mackenzie.

Mackenzie blurted, 'Archie, we'll climb in the glen the week after next.'

'Sorry,' said Archie, 'I can't do that. I always climb with Bill Murray.'

'Bring him along,' said Mackenzie.

I had longed for such good chance, but as a novice felt most diffident when we camped in Glen Etive two weeks later. Mackenzie that evening took us to the short roadside chasm west of Altnafeadh. His frame was wiry, hair black, manner incisive, and speech brusque; yet he was a great bringer-on of the young and inexperienced, scorning their natural fears. He picked out a hard, near vertical rib and went up unroped, not without trouble. I managed to follow.

At the top he looked me in the eye and barked, 'What else have you done?'

I hesitated, 'Well, *Curved Ridge* and the Cobbler by –'

'Done *Crowberry Direct*?'

'No – maybe in twenty years if I keep at it ...'

He withered me with a glance. 'We'll do it tomorrow,' he snapped.

With four words he snatched us out of the last century. As in summer, so in winter, he had me in no time leading hard rock fouled up with snow and ice, confidence boosted high by finding I could stay on the stuff. Thereafter, Mackenzie, Dunn, MacAlpine and I formed a team that held together for four years of unbroken climbing, winter and summer. We had the advantage – a great one in winter – of being the only team that consistently climbed together, met weekly, and planned in advance where and how we would strike.

One thing about mountaineers that first astonished me was their improbable appearance. The hard men took no trouble to act up. They stayed their natural selves. When Dr Graham Macphee came to give a talk to the JMCS, he was turned out resplendent in pinstripe trousers and creamy spats, whereas Dr Bell dressed in rags. Another was George Williams, who had newly made the first ascent of Rannoch Wall on Buachaille, yet was slightly built with beautifully wavy hair and spectacles. I had been expecting muscle men, and their rarity cheered me. An exception was Kenneth Dunn, our strong-arm man, whom I came to prize as a car companion, for I ran the tyres of my Austin Seven down to the canvas, and when punctures resulted he could lift the whole side of the car clear off the ground to save time jacking. Although he had passed from Fettes to law school, and from sailing to mountains – and now was a budding solicitor, he had high talent as car mechanic, learned from his own bitter experience of second-hand jobs. He once got my old Austin home from a remote glen by mending its rotor arm with a bit of elastic garter. Resourcefulness on the road was matched by the same on rock. With Dunn one could feel safe and relax. None of us, not even the blunt-spoken Mackenzie, were able to ruffle his built-in geniality.

One block to a quicker advance than we made was a happy one. Unexplored crags abounded. Even Ben Nevis, Glen Coe and Skye held them in plenty; still more so the Cairngorms and the North and West Highlands. There were no 'exhausted' cliffs demanding ever harder routes. With so much ground inviting exploration, easier routes were naturally taken first. We felt no pressures, no interest in the aid climbing starting in Germany, other than the natural urge shared by all to climb harder as skills are won. This need was felt much more emphatically in winter, because ice was such a variable quantity, and its presence fickle. Every chance had to be taken to master it. Otherwise we felt at leisure. The keynote was exploration, our climbing free of competition in the new sense of that word. We took the original sense, 'to strive with' others, not against. The rocks and the elements gave all the opposition wanted. The rule had one exception – the Macphee/Bell feud on Ben Nevis.

Our standards were not felt to be cramped by our gear. Boots with narrow welts had arrived early in the thirties, and tricouni and clinker edge-nails gave as good a grip as vibrams (moulded rubber soles from Italy, 1935), often better, and always better in winter. Nails more quickly taught a precise placing of the foot and neatness in movement. Our clothing was adequate. Tweeds, long gone, had been replaced by good wind-proofs, spin-offs from Arctic and Everest expeditions. Manilla ropes (hemp), although heavier than present day nylon, put us at no disadvantage, since we used no artificial techniques. Our first important act was to lengthen our ropes and use waist belays. (Before the first war, rope-belays had been given direct across rock, if given at all, and in the 1920s given over the shoulder.) When I first climbed rock and turned for advice to the *SMC General Guide* (1933), I found that Raeburn recommended eighty feet for a party of three, which after they had tied on allowed barely thirty-five feet between each man. His rule imposed such low standards of climbing that we at once doubled the length, and soon trebled it. Raeburn's words still baffle me. At the time they gave me a wrong impression that Raeburn could not have climbed to high standards in winter, hence my neglect of his records and our omission to learn from them.

This simple lengthening of our ropes opened up the rocks in alluring ways. It fetched us out of the chimneys and gullies – the more obvious routes – testing power-to-weight-ratios rather than nerve control. It took us away from the ridges which, though airy and open, are narrowly defined, making little demand on judgement or route selection. Instead it compelled us to appraise the great walls, slabs and faces. Leaders were by now accustomed to accepting long run-outs of 120–150 feet at high angles without any protection, reinforcing the maxim 'a leader does not fall'. An example is the Rannoch Wall of Buachaille Etive Mor. To everyone it seemed at first sight impossibly steep. We were intimidated. The first move was made in 1934 by George Williams of the SMC. He made a top-rope survey of Route One, then climbed it with Graham Macphee. The event gave a needed shake to the younger men. They promptly repeated the climb and followed that with *Agag's Groove* in 1936, led by Hamish Hamilton of the JMCS. Had he been ten minutes later, he would have lost the climb to Bill Mackenzie, who made the second ascent with Dunn and MacAlpine. These were two bold leads. As seen from below, they were fly-on-a-wall routes, and the leaders did not know in advance that they were easier than they looked. Routes of the kind multiplied thereafter.

The acceptance of long run-outs on exposed faces had been one of the main contributions to English climbing made by Colin Kirkus and his friends between 1930 and 1934. It directly influenced Williams' lead, but only indirectly those of the JMCS, who were at this stage out of touch with Welsh and Lakeland example.

The new generation of Scots now fell out with the old. A pillar of the pre-war school came to berate us, urging with passion in his voice that we abandon slab-and-wall climbs. They were 'unjustifiable' (a much-used term of abuse in the 1930s), implying an irresponsible disregard for human life-values. Worse, they were Germanic (the early attempts on the Eigerwand were in progress, exciting the strictures of the *Alpine Journal*). Our reaction was outspoken on-the-spot revolt. 'Our' means here, the several leading climbers and their teams. The main body of Scottish climbers held to the past. Theirs was a most frustrating influence – frustrating because we spoke different tongues. They had not had our new experience of the rocks, and we had not yet found a way to express ours to them.

On high-angle walls and slabs, as on hard ice climbs, the exposure and the move were problems that gave us a peculiar sense of elation – a kind of abandonment to Providence. We did not think of it in these terms – we felt only a sense of release. The elation imparted to our climbing the very skills needed: balance, lightness of touch, hands held low when possible, faith placed in the friction of the foot and the carriage of head and body, all giving certainty of movement. No tuition required. Thus all was made safer than it looked. Reliance on balance, not muscle, might seem to an onlooker to impose greater strain on the nerves, frightening to anyone not accustomed to self-mastery, when in truth it was only a matter of building up confidence by practice. Since we failed to communicate, our elders watched in dismay or moral disapproval. We were giving the sport a bad name.

During these early years I had rapidly learned that the human race is composed of just two distinct species, those who climb mountains and those who don't. All light and wisdom lay with the former. The latter dwelt in darkness. I am astonished how long this conviction lasted in face of the mountain climate and the company I kept. Having become a 'fanatic' (of winter rock and ice), I tended to have friends of eccentric character (minds not running in orthodox grooves). I have already mentioned three. I found a fourth one April day in 1937 at the CIC Hut on Nevis. The scenes that spring to mind there, are those that give a lift to the spirits on black nights: the first sight of the hut's beckoning light far up the glen of the Allt a'Mhuilinn: the warm, welcoming fug when the door swings open; the steaming mugs of rum punch, the brewing of which was always the first move on arrival; and the coal fire in the big iron stove. And such was the scene when Mackenzie, MacAlpine and I arrived that night to be welcomed by a short, stocky man with a bald head and wicked grin. This turned out to be Dr J.H.B. Bell. He had with him three English climbers, Henson, Dick Morsley, and Percy Small. They were up to make the first ascent of Green Gully.[1] They banished our night's cold with mugs of hot soup before a blazing fire. I then had my first lesson on the follies of volunteering when Bell sent me out to the burn to fetch a bucket of water for the rum punch. After digging through feet of interminable snow, I found the burn frozen solid. My principal lesson came the following morning, when I watched Bell make his party's breakfast.

Oatmeal, sausages, kippers, tomato soup, peas and beans all went into the porridge pot. As a practical chemist, he was imbued with the truth that a meal was a fuel intake, therefore its separation into courses was an auld wife's nicety, and not for climbers. He later persuaded me to share his burnt toast, on the grounds that charcoal was a bodily need. He expounded equations of chemical change to show how charcoal absorbed the troublesome gases of stomach and gut to our mutual benefit. Bell, when cook, could talk one into eating almost anything. But not even that toughest of characters, Dick Morsley, had a palate tough enough for Bell's porridge. After one spoonful, he strode to the door and flung his plateful out on the snow. The fuel mix certainly worked for the others.

1 At that time Raeburn's and Phildius's 1906 ascent of the gully was not generally known.

They not only climbed Green Gully, but next year the English members[2] returned and climbed its neighbour, Comb Gully, the best ice climb on the Ben up to the war.

The hut for me was a school of further education. Its eight bunks were the best sprung and most comfortable on which I have ever slept. One could lie there on a winter's night and watch the iron stove glow red hot in the dark. Especially was this true if Archie MacAlpine were present. As fire stoker, he had the genius of Satan himself. Perhaps inspired by the latter after a heady brew, he once stoked the stove to an unprecedented redness, forgetting that he had put his blankets into the oven to warm. When this was shortly discovered, Mackenzie and I basked in a glow of moral righteousness, the more keenly enjoyed for its rarity, while MacAlpine pondered whether to confess the blankets' incineration to the hut's custodian, or to claim more plausibly that Bell had eaten them for breakfast.

Bell and I having met, we corresponded much and began to climb together from 1938 onward. I appreciated his manner of dealing with hard rock. Needless to say, he had a quick eye for a new route, and at close quarters a keen nose for the best line. His climbing style did not have the smoothly flowing grace of the textbook ideal. Apart from his expertise in every kind of hard move, which he made with an India-rubber-like suppleness, he had two notable styles of attack at the crux of a climb. He never dilly-dallied, or spent time on hesitant, tentative moves. He stood back, took quick stock, and then if the rocks were near vertical, took his holds decisively and went up with a vigour that positively emanated out of him. If the rock was slabby and holdless, and always when wet, he took to his stocking soles and went on to the rock with delicate tread, catlike in its implication 'I know where I'm going'. He could make his chosen line on severe or unknown rock look like a foregone conclusion. His strong point was this decisiveness: vigour of mind pairing with vigour of body. He was fallible like us all, but never came off his holds.

In our more adventurous climbing we were given much encouragement by Bell, who was at the same game himself. He had recently climbed the 1,000-foot *Basin Route* on Ben Nevis, the first of his Very Severe series on the Orion Face of North-East Buttress. Editors of climbing journals are more influential than they generally realise, for they move learners rather than pundits, and a man's best climbs are done when he is young and relatively inexperienced, not when old and wise. Bell was (to us) an exception to that rule. Being over thirty, he should to our eyes have seemed ancient, his life done. Instead, we found him ageless, superior to us all on summer rock, though not on winter. His company was stimulating, for he was always a learner himself, seeking new ways. He never opposed the use of pitons, and sent Sandy Wedderburn with

2 With Henson being replaced by F.G. Stangle.

two Jugoslav aidmen to *Slav Route* near *Zero Gully*. Their first nailing of the Nevis cliffs in 1934 pleased Bell, who hoped it might infuriate Macphee. Bell wanted to put Macphee's guidebook out of date, and climbers arriving at the hut always had the immediate excitement of opening the Climbs Book to read what new thing had been done, tried, or repeated.

His editorship of the *SMC Journal* coincided most fortunately with the renaissance of Scottish climbing. He had generosity of mind and width of interest, whether in people, events, or ideas. His talk covered the full spectrum from the earthy to the metaphysical. His friendships had equivalent range. He suffered no exclusions. This open-minded quality was basic to his mountaineering and that of his own contribution – seventy new routes, of wide-ranging, diverse character and unequalled standard. His choice showed no exclusions. Their influence was made vital by his deliberately seeking out the most active young climbers of the day, both men and women, and inviting them to join his rope at weekends. He made the various new climbing groups known to each other, and linked them by airing their ideas. He kept all abreast of events, at the same time presenting articles that related Scottish conditions and practice to those of the greater ranges. In short, he tried to keep us all in balance, and succeeded by personal example in broadening exploration to remoter areas than Glen Coe and Ben Nevis.

Likewise, he broadened our ideas about climbable rock. That clean, sound rock is alone worth attention does seem a natural preference. It came close to becoming gospel until Bell's critical comments aroused second thoughts. I have recorded in earlier books the terse words with which he converted me: 'Any fool can climb good rock, but it takes craft and cunning to get up vegetatious schist and granite.' When we realised the vast amount of such rock in Scotland, his new testament gained prime importance. His creed had the same effect in Scotland as Menlove Edwards' in Wales. If Bell's rock was loose as well, so much the better.

His enthusiasm for bad rock was sometimes enough to chill the blood of the orthodox. Here is Bell in a seventh heaven of delight, writing of *Hesperides Ledge*, a climb on the Comb of Ben Nevis:

> 'It is a steeply inclined, curving shelf and is a perfect garden of mossy and lush vegetation ... there are several exceedingly delicate corners with a most precipitate drop on the right. The vegetation is loosely anchored, the rocks are rather loose, and there are practically no positive holds ...'

He might have added: 'Don't throw the holds away, there are no others.'

When he could feel at home on rocks like that, Bell, not surprisingly, did congenial company. On the other hand, he never disdained safe and Moderate or Easy climbs. He produced many. His catholic tastes came as a bonus to the average climber, providing routes that all could enjoy.

His enthusiasm for dicey rock persuaded me to explore and climb Clachaig Gully (1,700 feet), neglected since George Abraham's attempt of 1900. The changing attitudes to dubious rock yielded a rich harvest from Torridon southward. Despite his own words, Bell's most important climbs were on sound rock, on routes like his *Orion* series on Nevis, the *Spillikin* on Buachaille, the *Eagle* and *Parallel Buttresses* of Lochnagar, and the *Labyrinth* of Creag an Dubh-loch. I joined him for the *Parallel Buttress* in 1939, when he banged two pitons into the tower's crux for direct aid. This was the first time that Scottish rocks had been so abused. I did feel a qualm. They were not strictly necessary: after taking them out, I was able to follow in nails without using a further pull on the rope.

Macphee, like Bell, had powerful influence between the wars. The two were extreme opposites, like cat and dog: Bell small and sturdy with a strong Fife accent, one of the toughest men I ever met, never mincing his words; Macphee big and broad with a gentlemanly drawl and quizzical tone – yet able to pull up on one arm to chin the curtain pole in the CIC Hut. He drove Bentleys, fortunately, since he had to drive 700 miles each weekend to Fort William. Bell's influence was the more broadening, because wider ranging; Macphee's restricted to Ben Nevis, because saddled for five years with his guidebook to write. Published in 1936, it hastened all later development. Until then, the Nevis cliffs were little known, apart from main features, to a degree that can hardly now be grasped. Macphee spread enlightenment.

Apart from these few SMC men, rock climbing was in the hands of the young in half a dozen clubs. The JMCS was the most effective. Ten years old in 1935, it grew to over 200 members. After finding their feet and taking bearings, they made new routes all over Scotland from 1936, but notably in Glen Coe, where H.I. Ogilvy raised the Rannoch Wall standards. J.B. Nimlin made one of his rare visits in 1937 to climb *Raven's Gully*, one of the hardest climbs in the glen up to the Second World War. To the new clubs already mentioned were added the Etchachan Club of Aberdeen (1939) and several others, but none as yet contributed to new climbing. All were important, for all were tapping new sources for recruits, hitherto drawn somewhat exclusively from professional and business classes. Their day was to come in the late 1940s.

The JMCS was meantime one exception to the general rule. Formed earlier than the others, and larger in numbers, its members in ten years first re-established old winter standards, then between 1936 and 1940 helped to push them higher. They had no time (granted early impediments) to better Bell's and Macphee's summer rock work before the second war broke out. Their most distinctive contribution to Scottish and UK climbing was not in summer, but in winter.

4 Renaissance: 1930s

The total neglect of winter climbing in the 1920s cannot be blamed entirely on the First World War. Any enthusiasm that might have survived it was damped down by a ten-year cycle of mild weather. In the thirties, hard winters returned – continually blocking the old Glen Coe road at the Black Mount until the new one opened. No inspiration came from Raeburn's records. They had been lost. For example, the SMC guide *Ben Nevis* (1920) said only this of his Green Gully climb (not named as such):

> 'Raeburn made an icy ascent (of the Comb) on 2 April 1906, which although not on the arête yet led to the summit of the Comb. The climb was almost entirely on snow and ice.'

This sounded to us like one of those vague, indefinite routes of a bygone age. In March 1934, a revival was heralded by Pat Baird of the JMCS. He led a Cambridge party up the *SC Gully* of Stob Coire nan Lochan in Glen Coe. His trumpet was muted. A too short, dully-written note in the *SMCJ* mentioned a seventy-foot ice pitch, but failed to alert the Glasgow young. He made no other route.

The event that fired our aspiration came next year. An article in *SMCJ* written by George Williams described Graham Macphee's lead in March up *Glover's Chimney* on the west side of Tower Gap. They had started late from the hut. Macphee spent two hours' single-handed cutting on the first ice pitch and ran out 135 feet of line to reach a stance. A traverse over icy slabs led back to the gully, where after two short ice walls they felt in need of food – and found that Macphee on leaving the hut had picked up fire-lighters in mistake for the packed sandwiches. The sky was darkening, conditions bad, eighteen inches of loose snow had to be cleared to reach and cut the ice in the bed. In two hours more, Macphee reached the foot of the final chimney. Williams' account continued, as if casting a fly for our minds:

> 'By this time it was nearly dark. The sky was overcast but there appeared to be still a little light, probably diffused moonlight. The condition of the final chimney made it extremely severe. The leader had to clear every hold and most of them were iced.

> A chockstone pitch in the chimney nearly proved impossible, but, despite the exhausting work which had gone before, Macphee was quite equal to the situation. I could now but dimly see him as he moved slowly and steadily upwards. Now and then when clearing holds of ice his ice axe struck bare rock, I could see sparks fly out. Above the chockstone the conditions, instead of easing off, became harder. The entire chimney was sheeted with ice and there was no place where the leader could take a proper rest, much less to which he could bring me up. He had now run out over 100 ft. of line, and the situation was very sensational. It was a thrilling experience for the second and third, straining their eyes in the darkness, watching the leader's figure dimly silhouetted against the sky as he got nearer to the Tower Gap ...'

Having read the words, we bolted the bait. We knew that more in abundance lay all around. We had already taught ourselves one-handed cutting on high angle ice (65–90°) by much practice on iced boulders, then on short climbs like the *Upper Couloir* of Stob Ghabhar in the Black Mount, the *Arch Gully* of Stob Coire nam Beith, and the *Gardyloo* of Ben Nevis. We were ready for bigger things. The leaders of the movement were Bill Mackenzie, Hamish Hamilton, Douglas Scott, Tom MacKinnon, and myself, all from the JMCS Glasgow and all in our twenties, and Macphee and Bell from the SMC. Jock Nimlin was one other. I knew of no one else.

Bill Mackenzie was the best ice man of that time (better than Bell or Macphee).

The new era opened in February 1936 when Mackenzie and Dunn were joined by Hamish Hamilton for the winter ascent of *Crowberry Gully* – a climb of 1,000 feet, twice as long as *Glover's Chimney* and harder. They knew nothing of Raeburn's ascent at Easter 1909 (Easter is normally too late for good ice in Glen Coe). Having still much to learn, they used full size axes and took twelve hours.

All ice axes had straight picks. Their length had been reduced to 31–32 inches, weight two pounds, but they were too unwieldy for prolonged, one-handed cutting above the head. Wrists grew red hot and forearms ached. The shaft could be near to unmanageable in chimneys or other confined space. The first man to act on the new need was Douglas Scott. He had one made by a Glasgow blacksmith (a pick with a short shaft and with this repeated the *Crowberry*. When Mackenzie and I saw the new tool, we realised that slater's hammers would be the right length and weight (fourteen inches and one pound nine ounces). Price – ten shillings [50p]. All we needed to do was cut off the side claw – perfect then for the job. Lighter picks could be had, but

I proved them of no use, because at very high angles, where the ice coating thinned on the rock, and holds grew tiny and balance delicate, we would be forced to cut from the wrist, not the elbow, so there had to be weight in the axe head to get the chips out. If the pitch were long and the ice hard, the blood ran out of the axe arm, so that we had to be equally skilled with either hand; even so, the arms tired before the top was reached, which is why long pitches took an hour and even longer to lead, while followers froze. There was then very great temptation, which we all felt, not to cut the last handholds but just strike the pick into the frozen snow above and pull up. Fatal practice with a straight pick. Hamish Hamilton thus peeled off the top of a big pitch in the *Crowberry* when his pick slipped out. He survived (and at least saved the rest of us from that trap ever after). It never occurred to anyone that a drop-head axe might be the answer.

After the *Crowberry* and *SC* Gullies, we moved on to the big ridges and buttresses of Ben Nevis, Glen Coe, and elsewhere. Mixed rock and ice gave the most interesting of all routes, endlessly worth repeating: they could change out of recognition not just from year to year but week to week. Since we were out on the climbs every weekend without fail, we encountered many freak conditions never recorded in pre-war years. Examples were the North Buttress of the Buachaille, normally free of ice, now congested across its great breadth with blue and green bosses that could not be turned to either side; or *Observatory Ridge* buried deep under sugary powder, glazed rock beneath, and *Zero Gully* to which we escaped, the same. Here we learned that night climbing was perfectly feasible if each man had a head torch, provided the route were known, or well defined, as in *Zero*. Our fear of the dark there ended. The inexhaustible variety certainly cut down much new route seeking – hence far more good climbing was done than might appear from records of the time. Yet we had an eye to new climbs from the start, which further blackened our bad reputation, for although Macphee, being old and wise, could be excused his *Glover's Chimney* and midnight return, we could not, being young and of no name.

Our blackest affront was a first winter attempt on Crowberry Ridge in December 1936. Mackenzie, Dunn, MacAlpine and I ran into verglas at dusk on the upper rocks of *Garrick's Shelf*, could find no exit to the crest, then were hit by blizzard and spent fourteen hours getting down – no pitons. Daybreak saw us safely back at Coupall Bridge. While waiting for the frozen ropes to thaw, we were met on the road by a rescue party. Each of us received before long a well-earned written rebuke from our club's committee, damning our route as unjustifiable. Desist, said they. The important results were three. First, we thereafter carried slings, snap-links and pitons to secure withdrawals. Second, we now knew early December to be too early for climbs of that kind. Third, we had learned the need to be humble while ignoring our elders' advice, and to start earlier with a smaller party. Next March, Mackenzie and I climbed *Garrick's Shelf* in five hours using through leads. It was then a natural ice trap with the crux 500 feet up at a small pinnacle near the top. Front point crampons there would have been no help. The climb remained Scotland's hardest ice route until after the war.[1]

In the course of all this winter work, Archie MacAlpine used to be a most valued member of our rope. Whatever ills befell, he could make us laugh. His sense of humour was backed by two other gifts: a mimic's ear (he used to catch to perfection Macphee's drawl or Bell's Fife accent), and what he called 'a fly-paper memory' which allowed him to retain without effort an inexhaustible fund of good stories. These were real talents. One may sometimes hear of a good storyteller having his listeners rolling in the aisles, but only once in my life have I seen this literally happen – when Archie spoke at a JMCS dinner in Glasgow. He gave a simple recitation of Longfellow's 'Wreck of the Hesperus', delivered as if by an upper crust English gentleman, slightly sozzled. The result was so hilarious that members could hardly keep upright in their seats, and some did in fact have to throw themselves on to the floor. I have never seen the like again, for he would never give a repeat performance, despite all urgings. On mountains, the worse conditions became, whether on cliffs, or in wet tents, or in bleak bothies, he never failed to lighten the fix we were in. Although a top-class performer on rock and ice, he would rarely consent to lead, yet would climb without hesitation any rock or ice that Mackenzie or I were able, even with much difficulty, to find a way up or down. We could rely on his seconding to the limit.

Bell, that same year of 1937, climbed his two best ice routes – *Green Gully,* where he shared the lead with Jack Henson from England, and the 1,000-foot *Centre Post* of Coire Ardair on Creag Meaghaidh, led by C.M. Allan, who turned the big pitch (150 feet) by an hour-long and exposed upward traverse on green ice at 72°. To save time cutting handholds, he used an ice-pick as dagger in one hand and a small hatchet for step-cutting in the other. His hair-raising technique won no converts. Although Bell climbed on every kind of winter rock, his routes were by timing and character less influential than those of Mackenzie – or Macphee before him.

In 1939, Mackenzie and I made another route on ice-bound rock in Glen Coe – *Deep-Cut Chimney* on Stob Coire nam Beith. Successive thaws and frosts had glazed it heavily. We were never tempted on such routes to use crampons, which then had no front points. We kept them for glacier travel in the Alps and Norway. In Scotland, no one found them worth their weight. On open slopes we enjoyed fast cutting up or down when needed. On iced rock or

---

1 Described as 'a prototype of the modern ice climb' by Tom Patey (*AJ* 1960) and Chris Bonington (*The Climbers*, 1992 – a TV series). [See full account of the ascent in the following chapter.]

on pure ice pitches, boot nails were far better. They gave quicker, neater movement often allowing good use to be made of brittle ice, which crampon-spikes would have shredded. They also allowed delicate manoeuvring, like changing feet on a sloping hold without handhold (for example, the crux of *Garrick's Shelf*) or other balance moves, impossible in clumsy crampons. Our tricouni-nailed soles gave a non-slip grip on hard snow, and allowed too an occasional 'miracle' to be pulled off on thin, brittle ice that ought to have peeled off the rock. I used to call such moves levitation for want of a better word – nothing so crude as a step-up, but rather a float-up, with no weight placed anywhere so far as humanly possible. It worked well if we hit top form, and on mixed climbs (iced rocks) got Mackenzie and me up some nasty places.

Ice-work remained an art for the next thirty-five years, and a most satisfying one it was, physically more exacting than summer rock and mentally more stimulating. One had to plan ahead and engineer the way several moves in advance. I have rarely enjoyed anything in life more than cutting up a long, high-angle ice pitch where balance was delicate. The craft used varied according to the quality of the ice – black, white, green, blue, brittle, and watery – they each had their quirks, which had to be learnt until one could tell them apart at a glance and cut accordingly, each needing different treatment to save time or provide the kind of hold wanted. Our long axes still had a share of the work, for walls often bore a plaster of tough white snow – ice with a glazed surface, in which finger holds could be cut faster with the axe after bursting the crust with the pick. We had a great store of such lore, which made ice absorbingly interesting for the leader, however slow compared with the crude present.

Our rock and ice work was enlivened by our rejection of slings and snaplinks for intermediate protection on very severe routes. Run-outs of up to 150 feet were accepted without mutinous thought, even in bad weather. Full-weight rope could not therefore be used – too great a drag on the leader. We preferred line of 1 to 1 1⁄4-inch circumference. When it stiffened from wet or frost we called it piano-wire. In very hard frost it could often not be untied until we reached shelter. Our use of pitons for no more than belay-pins remained an unbroken rule in winter.

Bell and I came close to sinning in 1939. A direct route was still waiting to be done in the *Centre Post* of Coire Ardair. We went there in March to try. When we met the day before in Glen Spean, I found that Bell had brought a bag full of brass curtain rods, which he said we could use to nail the big pitch. He had ringed the tops and filed the bottoms. Tubular pitons, he had correctly discovered, gripped better in ice.

'We can use tension if we have to,' said he. I inwardly quailed, knowing he might want me to lead. I had never practised tension and wondered about brass. (In tension climbing, the leader ties on to two ropes, drives in a piton above his head, clips a rope to it with a snap-link, and his second man tensions that rope while he climbs up a step or two and repeats the process with the other rope.) Relief came in the morning when we found insufficient ice in the gully. I still had forebodings for the following winter, when battle must be rejoined, but was saved by the outbreak of war.

In the winters of 1939 and 1940, I climbed much with Gordon Donaldson and Douglas Laidlaw, both in their late teens. I thought them our two most promising mountaineers. We reconnoitred *Point Five* and *Zero* Gullies on Ben Nevis (as Mackenzie had too), but always stone-fall or powder-slide turned us away. Donaldson then spotted those long snow-and-ice routes of alpine type on the Coire Leis face of the North-East Buttress. I sent Tom Patey there in 1957, when he climbed *Cresta* (900 feet). These were our last recces or perhaps gestures of hope in a future. But we dared not think of that. War swallowed us up.

We knew only that in the last five years Scottish climbing had been re-founded.

5 The Winter Ascent of *Garrick's Shelf*

To give a flavour of the often eventful nature of winter climbing in Scotland in those pre-war years I have selected my account of our *Garrick's Shelf* attempt and climb from *Mountaineering in Scotland*:[1]

It is the custom of mountaineers to set on record their most successful climbs, but to say nothing of their reverses. The custom is an unfortunate one; there can be no doubt that one may sometimes gain more genuinely valuable experience from defeat than from the most brilliant series of first ascents. This consideration persuades me to set down in writing an unsuccessful attempt, on 13 December 1936, to make the first winter ascent of the Crowberry Ridge by way of *Garrick's Shelf.*

With this high task in view, Mackenzie, Dunn, MacAlpine and myself assembled at Inverarnan on the night of 12 December. The following morning we drove north to Coupall Bridge in Glen Etive where we discovered that once again Dunn had forgotten his boots. He drove that seventy miles to Inverarnan and back like a rocket, and we finally set out for the Buachaille at 10.30 a.m.

The hour was now late, yet we adhered to our original plans, although a defeat high up at dusk on a rock-snow-ice climb could hardly be contemplated with equanimity. However, the route was well known to us and we felt confident of success. We were all in excellent physical condition, exceptionally well equipped, and yearning for a first-class climb. These factors overcame our good judgement. The morning was cloudy, with the wind in the west-southwest. New snow had fallen overnight but was not lying in sufficient depth seriously to impede our progress to the foot of *Crowberry Gully,* where we encountered a short difficult pitch that whetted our appetite for bigger and better things. Never was an appetite destined to be more harshly glutted.

1 In the current guidebook the climb is titled 'The Shelf', the Garrick's prefix now sadly dropped denying the climb its evocative name. Alan Garrick and D. Biggart (actually Harry MacRobert) claimed the route in May 1923 but Murray recorded the 1920 first ascent by J. Wilding and Fred Pigott in his 1949 guidebook. Harry MacRobert and Arnold Brown had an earlier winter 'adventure' on the route in April, 1910, very similar to that described in Murray's account. Luckily they started earlier and were also defeated by the short final pitch, making their escape in daylight. Nowadays, with modern equipment, the climb is graded Difficult in summer and Grade 4 in winter. *Editor*

We now left the gully and moved up the lower rocks of Crowberry Ridge, where we traversed a ledge of steeply shelving snow on its northern wall. This movement brought us under the first big pitch of *Garrick's Shelf.* Here we found a cave large enough to accommodate the whole party, and we hastily gulped down our second breakfast before roping up.

The construction of *Garrick's Shelf* is peculiar. It is a narrow trough running up the northern wall of the Crowberry Ridge, parallel to the *Crowberry Gully.* The shelf itself, which is punctuated with steep pitches, terminates in precipitous rock some 250 feet below the crest of the ridge. This last section, difficult in summer, ends in a steep scoop that debouches on the Crowberry Ridge near the base of the Tower.

We found the rocks well plastered with snow, but ice was present only in small quantity – too small quantity, as we discovered later. The snow-covering on steep rock was not sufficiently frozen to hold, and had to be cleared away as we advanced. Our progress was much hindered by fierce blasts of wind from the south-west, which swept down the *Crowberry Gully* and the shelf, bearing great clouds of powder snow that completely filled all the holds after each of us had passed upwards. Woollen gloves froze to the holds, and were sometimes difficult to disengage.

Four hours of continuous climbing on the shelf found us at the top of the fourth pitch, at a height of some 2,700 feet. At this point I took over the lead from Mackenzie, who retired to the end of the rope for a rest. Henceforth the order on the rope was myself with Dunn as second man, then MacAlpine and Mackenzie. The shelf now began to narrow and steepen, while the snow was thinner and in worse condition than ever. The sun had already set, and the upper reaches of the shelf were pervaded by a grey and gloomy twilight. The need for haste had become urgent, yet the next fifty feet of plain, straightforward gully occupied no less than twenty minutes. The difficulty lay simply in persuading the snow to hold. There was no danger of its avalanching.

Garrick's Shelf now ended and merged in the steep face of the final rocks. On our right, the shelf fell perpendicularly into the depths of *Crowberry Gully*; on our left rose the vertical wall of the Crowberry Ridge; before us the rocks swept up steeply for sixty feet to a small, rectangular tower. This tower was sheathed in black ice and fog crystals. It lent distinction to the place.

Our first problem was a narrow crack set in a corner and packed with snow. My first two attempts on it failed, but a third and more determined effort proved successful, and I climbed the crack by the lay-back method to a small ledge. The time was now 4.30 p.m. The usual route into a square recess at the base of the tower was unjustifiable, on account of its skin of thin ice, and I therefore made an attempt to force the rocks on the left. After a great deal of manoeuvring for position, an outward-tilting mantelshelf plastered with firm snow lying on ice was laboriously overcome. For a moment the position looked promising; on the left only a short wall barred the way to the easier rock leading past the tower to the crest of the ridge. But my first movement to the left would of necessity be made without handhold, a down-and-out strain being placed upon the feet, the foothold being a sloping slab coated with verglas.

I reported my position and the party consulted. The time was now a quarter to five; the weather was rapidly deteriorating; to retire now would spell immediate benightment with the whole of *Garrick's Shelf* below us. On the other hand, only six feet of rock barred the leader from almost certain triumph. The decision we had to make was a grave one. Should or should not that next, very dangerous step be taken? We decided that it should not, and I retired.

Across the black chasm of *Crowberry Gully* the wall of the North Buttress was now growing steadily dimmer in the gathering darkness; already the rising storm was roaring across the upper rocks of the Crowberry Ridge. Snow was falling steadily, and this was reinforced from time to time by sheets of drift snow, hurled upon us from the rocks above. The situation appeared to be sufficiently desperate, but the party had climbed too long in combination to entertain any doubt of a satisfactory issue. We carried with us 330 feet of rope, a torch, spare batteries, and sufficient food. We resolved therefore to continue to climb downwards rather than bivouac.

The descent of the steep section in the snow gully to pitch four was less hazardous than we had expected. The first three, secured by the rope, enjoyed a comfortable passage. They cheerfully urged me to slide, and trust them to field me if need be. I declined, and the party moved down in strictly text-book style to pitch four. A wide square-cut chimney, all three walls of which were vertical, now presented an interesting problem largely complicated by its invisibility. The solution taxed us for two hours, but we finally dug out a spike of iced rock, from which the others roped down, belayed from above. Having seen Dunn safely down and well established, I followed a thought too gaily. For the fixed rope somehow rolled off its hitch above. Down I went with a rush, conscious only of one fat blue spark where a boot-nail struck bare rock. A split second later I landed astride Dunn's shoulders. He was strongly placed, safe and solid as rock itself, and by grabbing my thighs stopped a farther fall. The party was working now at such a high pitch of concentration that we gave the incident not a thought until later.

We were by this time enveloped in darkness. The snow on the shelf and on the surrounding rock could be dimly discerned as a dull grey mantle, far too obscure to afford any indication of the route. We progressed slowly by torchlight. Creeping circumspectly down the shelf over snow and broken rock, we descended as much as 150 feet in one and a half hours. Above the uproar of the wind and the flail of careering snow could be heard some unusual noises which, had we not known each other better, must have sounded suspiciously like profane language. At 9 a.m. we reached an open corner at the top of pitch three.

Here we were unable to rope down. There was no rock-belay, and the snow was too unsound to take an axe-belay, but we contrived a good anchor by jamming our axes in an angle of rock. Thus protected we climbed in turn down steep snow to a point near the base of a rockface. A distinctly tricky traverse to the right then led, after one and a half hours, to soft snow below the pitch. We could not afford to leave an axe behind us, so I went down without a fixed rope. I was coached over the traverse in brilliant style by Dunn, who employed the effective though inhuman device of ruthlessly skewering his victim with the spike of an axe.

We were now back in the trough, hard against the wall of the Crowberry Ridge, and descended very slowly to a short chimney that we failed to remember climbing on the way up. A little disconcerted, we climbed down from axe-belays and found ourselves in a narrow cave festooned with giant icicles. This cave was the most comfortable spot on the whole route, and we felt loath to leave it. I hailed the place with great joy, and after ejecting the rest of the party urged disingenuously that any haste in accomplishing the next section would be most unadvisable. From the narrow recesses of the cave I could speculate as to what was happening below, while I watched, with a certain measure of perverted pleasure, the swirling snow pour in hissing cascades over the roof and down the shelf, where my more energetic companions would literally get it in the neck.

Time sped on. For over an hour there had been a great deal of shouting below and singularly little movement. But at long last a faint call from Dunn summoned me downwards. Sixty feet below, we all congregated on what appeared to be a broad horizontal ledge on the wall of *Crowberry Gully*. An eighty-foot rope had been fixed round a spike on the wall itself and Mackenzie, after prospecting the route at the far end of the ledge, had just announced that farther advance was impossible. He was faced, or seemed to be faced, with a bottomless abyss. We had lost the route.

A good twelve hours had now elapsed since our last meal, and the thought of the party turned to hot soup and roast pork. With freezing fingers we then extracted from our rucksacks the handfuls of sodden crumbs that had formerly been jam sandwiches. We reviewed our position as we ate, and came to the conclusion that we were now above *Garrick's Shelf*, on a ledge ending in a cul-de-sac. The torch-beam was therefore directed downwards toward the *Crowberry Gully*. After some prospecting a lower route was pronounced practicable.

Our principal concern was whether the fixed rope would reach to the foot of the pitch. Mackenzie, belayed by the others, set off downwards; he went leftward down steep snow, and then swung into the mouth of a vertical shallow chimney. A long period of suspense followed. In half an hour there was still no movement of any kind from below. The party above gradually became aware that it was being kept waiting – a feeling never absent during the entire descent – and wrathfully enquiring howls were directed downwards. Several minutes later a muffled 'What?' drifted upwards, followed after a while by 'Yip!' – whatever that might mean. We gave it up.

Quite suddenly a shout of triumph assured us that our proper route had been regained below pitch two: the vertical chimney was, indeed, on pitch two itself. In half an hour we were all down. The fixed rope refused to run round the spike and was left behind. A further hour of vigilant toil took us all to a big outcrop of rock which presented a rectangular face to the lower regions of *Garrick's Shelf*. Immediately below us was the last great step in the shelf. We edged carefully round the right-hand corner of the outcrop, and near its base discovered an excellent spike-belay. The snow here was firm but excessively steep, so we stood face-in during the hours that followed.

Our plan was to attach a thirty-foot loop round the spike, to rope down on 120 feet of rope, which we fervently hoped would reach the foot of the shelf, and to secure the first man down with 100 feet of line. This 250-foot maze of rope and line was thereupon possessed by an evil spirit and became tangled in the darkness. The whole shelf resounded with the most powerfully expressive oaths known to man. Incredible delays occurred. Violent bursts of wind-driven snow still came lashing down the shelf, unendingly, and the last battery in the torch was fading. By wriggling our toes continuously during these halts we contrived to avoid frostbite.

At four o'clock in the morning everything was ready. One by one we roped down a narrow chimney on the flank of an overhanging bulge. This was appallingly difficult, for the rope declined to run, and our descent resolved itself into an exhausting struggle against friction. The torch was now out of action, so a fitting climax was provided by an awkward left-hand traverse round the bulge from the chimney, a movement that we made unroped, and which led us into the cave below the shelf. Upon reaching the foot of the chimney, I found myself unable to persuade the now obstinately vicious rope to run through the loop. I left it behind, with emotions closely akin to pleasure. When at length I joined the party in the cave, I at once remarked in the bearing and attitude of my companions a striking complacency, the source of which was speedily betrayed by the crumbs adhering to their now incipient whiskers. Thus gorged, these callous people had yet no scruple in demanding bites at my one remaining apple, on the pitiful plea that all their own food was finished.

We roped up on a hundred feet of line. The absence of a torch was a serious handicap, and we experienced no little difficulty in the traverse along the Crowberry wall, where drift snow had piled up on the ledge at a high angle. Shortly afterwards we gained the lower part of the *Crowberry Gully*, where we found our difficult pitch of the previous day miraculously transformed into an easy scramble, but on leaving the gully we unfortunately lost all trace of the usual line of descent.

An hour of prospecting, both up and down, resulted in our finally defying orthodox tactics by committing ourselves to the mercy of an unknown gully, which led us with unexpected ease to the moor. The latter imparted some wholehearted if concluding kicks, and we were all, at one time or another, immersed up to the thighs in bogs. We reached Coupal Bridge at dawn, safe and sound, if not precisely hale and hearty. We had been out for rather less than twenty-one hours, of which fourteen had been spent on the descent.

The moral of this is only too plain. It is one appreciated by none so well as by the party most closely concerned. But our defeat had in no way discouraged us in our determination to make a second attempt under more favourable conditions, when the shelf would he more heavily plastered with ice. By the end of March such conditions obtained and the route was climbed in its entirety.

THE FIRST WINTER ASCENT

An early start, a small party, good snow and ice, these were essential conditions for a winter ascent of *Garrick's Shelf.* The last consideration delayed our second visit until March blizzards had been followed by a fortnight of sun and frost.

On 28 March 1937 Mackenzie and I arrived at Kingshouse on a perfect morning. A streamer of white mist ringed the Buachaille, whose upper snows were pink in the rising sun. We reached Crowberry Ridge to find that, from top to bottom, *Garrick's Shelf* was masked in glinting ice – the longest ribbon of clear ice we have ever seen. The ropes we had left behind on defeat were still visible, the cores of transparent pillars two feet thick. We roped up and agreed to lead alternately. We went hard from the start.

In two hours of fast and furious cutting we climbed 400 feet, passed over four very difficult ice-pitches, and arrived at twelve noon below the crux. This pitch had shrunk to fifty feet. Once again the moderate summer slabs to the left of the pinnacle were glazed and impossible. We attacked to the right on rocks overlooking *Crowberry Gully*. Here, too, the ice was thin, axe-cut holds to the square recess under the pinnacle were painfully minute. Our escape from the recess, made on the pinnacle's right-hand edge, was unusually delicate. Splayed out on this bulging corner, we had to change feet on a small sloping hold without handhold, and with a long drop below into *Crowberry Gully*. The pitch was Very Severe and occupied two hours.

We then arrived in a broad groove which hung over the gully beyond the pinnacle. The groove was choked by an ice-fall of a 150 feet, twice bulging in fifty-foot pitches, which tried the leaders severely; for the ice was inclined to be brittle and belays poor. At 3 p.m. we debouched on the crest of Crowberry Ridge – a sensational arête arrayed in sharks' fins of translucent ice, which we shattered regretfully. Deterred from direct ascent of the Tower by ponderous snows, we traversed southward into D Gully and won the summit at 4 p.m.

Our climb is not one I shall ever repeat in like conditions. It became too exacting. But our day's route led us through snow and ice scenery of deathless beauty. This lives strong in the mind, while physical pains and trials, the so-called realities of defeat and victory, have long been forgotten.

FORTUNES OF WAR

BUACHAILLE ETIVE MOR – WET SPRING EVENING

Before me
Glides
The moonscape of Rannoch

A moor moving
Wide from the mist

Undulating
To silver.

Against its shore
Placed and sculpted

The morning mountain

Lifts
In evening.

Buachaille Etive Mor ...

Starker than any nightfall
This risen mountain;

Outline of cliffs
Black, grey

Tiers towering
Angled and cracked

Vertical patterns
Carving the hill;

Scatter of stones
Firmed on the face

Boulder fields fixed
In their long ago fall –

Splurged snow
Shrinking in to itself

Lines merging
Scoring the dusk

Buachaille Etive Mor
Fading

Linear
Brittle

A pencilled out hill
Thin on grey sky

Vanishing
Insubstantial

In the rain cloud's thicket;

A faded out
Fallen out
Hill –

An Evening
Emptied

As the smirr and beat of rain
Sweep Buachaille and Rannoch
Into the dark

6 The Home Front

I drove slowly that Sunday morning, north over the Rannoch Moor toward Glen Coe. A shroud of low mist covered its empty desert. Only the blunt arrowhead of Buachaille Etive Mor loomed, appropriately black, through curtains of drizzle. My eyes searched the moor for the white dot of Kingshouse Inn. At 11.30 I drew up to the door and hurried into the kitchen. Mrs Malloch, its West Highland owner, was standing by the window, fitting a curtain.

'Well, if it is not you, Mr Murray!' she exclaimed. 'Mr Chamberlain has declared war on Germany, just a few minutes ago! The Nazis could be over tonight to bomb Kinghouse, so I am fitting a curtain for the black-out.'

It was 3 September 1939. It must be hard for anyone born in Britain during the last half century to realise how it must feel on the outbreak of a world war. Cataclysmic is the word. To me and everyone I knew at the time, mobilisation spelled the ruin of everything we most valued in life. At least that was what it seemed when I arrived at Kinghouse.

I had come alone. My instinctive reaction was to turn to the mountain that had given most to me – the Buachaille. So I walked across the moor in a smirr of rain and climbed the Crowberry Ridge to the summit. I remembered many days and nights on this mountain – the beauty and brilliance of moonlight, ice glinting, the climbing hard. I remembered the stillness and the music of silence when it seemed to merge with the mountain and the beauty of creation.

I had been lucky in my mountain days, had found in difficult climbing an aptitude for concentrating and focusing my mind on the challenge ahead. I could work out the moves and then, in balance, follow them through gently and lightly, untrammelled by fear and enjoying the airy exposure. The rock had a beauty and simplicity akin to that of ice in winter. Were those days over? Days of inner and outer exploration. Days of joy and friendship ...

I spent a full hour on the top – and came down as slowly as I knew how. Every rock and stone seemed familiar to me.

This gloom of my inner self was ignorant – not an ignorance of future and material catastrophes, of which I guessed all too rightly, but rather a failure to learn the lesson I ought to have learned by now from experience: that Providence can turn even dire adversities to benefit. It was one of many other things that had still to be driven home to me by war. Men usually question the reality of Providence and the Fates, professing to call their operations luck. Since these operations occur much too coincidentally in real life to be called luck, I choose instead to give the right name to the right cause.

I made a reluctant conscript. By April 1940 I could delay no longer. First, I went up to Ben Nevis with Gordon Donaldson and climbed *Observatory Ridge*, then came straight down to Fort William, where I registered for military service with the Argyll and Sutherland Highlanders. The RAF might have seemed a natural choice, but for my schoolboy experience with Jim Mollison, an old boy of Glasgow Academy, who later made the first solo flight to Canada in his Puss Moth. He had taken me up in this open biplane, then terrified me with stunt flying. It put me off all thought of the RAF.

In June, I joined the Argylls at their Regimental HQ, Stirling Castle, and was posted to their training station at Tillicoultry, close beneath the Ochils. Nissen huts housed several hundred recruits. Two things there startled me. First was the low physical standard of Britain's young men. The Argylls had a fairly equal intake of Scots and English; with rare exception they were unfit to fight, by which I mean unexercised. In a stand-up fight, most might have floored me, but in walking or running or any other test of endurance they were surprisingly inferior. The physical training now given them by the Army was the best thing that could have come their way. Three months was the minimum needed for the fitter ones and six months for all others. And that latter is what they got.

The second surprise was the poor food and its destructive cooking. All vegetables were boiled until tasteless and nauseating; and meat cooked until tough and flavourless – mostly boiled liver with its inevitable cabbage, which left me with long-lingering revulsion to both, not cured till later years of starvation. Quartermasters bought liver in huge quantity as the cheapest meat on the market – from which, it is alleged, they could make most on the fiddle.

After each evening meal, we were still hungry, but free to walk out in Tillicoultry. I was often joined there by Bell, who worked nearby at Alloa. After a long walk on the Ochil tops, we used to share a high tea of bacon and eggs at the Eagle Inn. He was kind to me, daily giving me company for some real exercise and conversation.

I was not a good soldier, and much surprised when quickly promoted lance corporal. To win free of cabbage and liver, I tried for a commission. My Commanding Officer (CO) sent me for interview on 8 July before a regimental committee at Stirling Castle. As I climbed the steep road up the castle rock, the August history of the place began to seem incongruous with my lowly mission, for the massive walls perched on top had been built by Scotland's kings in the first millennium. I had premonition of playing a part in some comic opera by Gilbert and Sullivan. After passing through the great gate, I was ushered – for once not marched – by the regimental sergeant major (RSM) to an inner chamber, where I saluted my inquisitors. They sat around a broad table

– an elderly triumvirate in Sam Brownes, chests ablaze with medal ribbons. Obviously retired, they had been roped in to perform national duties. The stage was set; my own role, the clumsy-booted clown in ill-fitting battledress, trying to hide his guilty conscience and shifty eye.

The chairman waved me to an empty chair. All watched how I took it.

'Murray,' he barked, scenting blood, 'why do you want a commission?' The suddenness, the incredulity of voice, were framed to elicit truth. But the sober truth was one thing I dared not confess. My hackles rose to cover confusion.

'To serve my country as best I can, sir.'

My inquisitors' eyes brightened just a shade. I had jumped the first hurdle – and now took the second in my stride.

'What school?'

'Glasgow Academy, sir.'

'Ah! you joined their Officers' Training Corps?'

'Yes, sir.'

But after that promising start my prospects plunged to an abyss.

'You won promotion out of the ranks, we hope?'

'No, sir.'

'But you did attend summer training camps?'

'No, sir.' I sensed a stir of disapproval.

'Well then, what games do you play?'

'I used to play rugger, sir.'

'Used to? In your school's first fifteen?'

'No, sir. Just in practice games. I could never make the grade for a school team. Not any.'

'Now, that's a great pity. What other games?'

'None, sir.'

'None! Come, man, you must have played cricket?'

'Hardly ever, sir – never in a team – no good at ball games.'

'What! No team games?'

'No, sir.'

I sensed the atmosphere dim to black night. My grim inquisitor threw me a last, tentative line.

'Boxing! Maybe you boxed?'

'No go there either, sir.'

'So it comes down to this – you took no worthwhile exercise?'

'I did walk, sir.'

Three sharp stares impaled me. Was I winding them up?

'Walked!' 'Walked?' – derisively – 'Where did you walk?'

'On mountains, sir. I climb rock and ice.'

Their dark eyes took light. 'You mean with ropes and axes?'

A stream of questions followed. They knew nothing at all of mountains, apart from old press reports from Mount Everest – had all the misconceptions that once had been mine. But that didn't matter. They had been so plainly relieved to find any subject that made me talk, that only then did I realise that such had been the only object of the exercise. In the arrogance of my youth, I had misjudged them. Hence it was not school, or Officers' Training Corps, or rugger, or cricket that won my commission, but mountains, and no frills. That thought pleased me. Maybe the British Army was not as bad as its rations, but second thoughts amended the too hasty conclusion. The Army was desperate to recruit officers. It had been losing them in quantity through spring and summer in Norway, Dunkirk, and the Middle East.

In early September, I was posted to an Officer Cadet Training Unit at Dunbar in the Lothians. Here we lived in commandeered hotels, stripped to barrack status. Food and exercise were at last adequate. Field exercises in attack and defence were taught well; even enjoyably. Weapon training was markedly deficient. The more lasting impression was made by parade-ground drill under apoplectic regimental sergeant-majors. Their vitriolic tongue-lashings were of course an act; for a few days a convincing act; after which we realised what was happening. Our main trouble then was to keep straight faces. Unhappily, a tiny minority never saw through the sergeant-major act and was driven to revolt under merely verbal abuse. Such men were returned to unit.

Sergeant-majors off duty were relatively mild-mannered men, good at their job, which was not just to 'put the buggers through it', but to instil quick obedience through high standard drill and, no less important, to weed out the men who lacked control of temper under stress. They succeeded. I would hesitate to say they entirely succeeded with me, for I was still left with a firm tendency not to accept orders blindly, but to question content for sanity (unless on trivialities like parade-ground drill *per se*).

I was commissioned in December 1940 and posted to the Highland Light Infantry. Their headquarters was at Maryhill Barracks in Glasgow. Not a kilted regiment, its officers wore tartan trews for dress uniform. Our active lives were lived in battledress. At this early stage of the war, we dined at Maryhill in regimental splendour, on food and service that no five-star hotel could rival. The circulating port at the meal's end was accompanied by airs on the pipes – a small price to pay for escaping boiled cabbage and liver.

One of my first, ungrateful actions was to apply for transfer to the mountain commandos. I ought to have known better, for I was now well aware of the 'never volunteer' rule. The War Office will normally dash your hopes if it can. But I thought I was safe. The CO of the Scottish Commandos, then in course of forming, was Sandy Wedderburn of the SMC. He had power to requisition personnel, and his requisition of me had been passed to the War Office.

The calm of Army life at Maryhill was suddenly disturbed by the blitzkrieg on Clydebank. On the nights of 13 and 14 March, 1941, the German bombers came in waves, each attack a long eight hours. My mother was living at Jordanhill, close to Clydebank's fringe. The Luftwaffe was here combining the mass bombing technique used on Coventry with the incendiary attacks they had used on London. Just three miles to my south-west, the night sky was lurid with the light of explosions and fires and weaving searchlights. The long-drawn thunder seemed unending. In the early hours of the 14th I could take no more and walked out of the barracks through a now chaotic city to the fringe of its desolation – 40,000 houses had been hit, a thousand people killed, unknown thousands injured. The lit sky of night had changed to a daylight dark under clouds of smoke and dust. I discovered my mother and aunt unharmed in their terrace house. Windows had been blown in, a door unhinged, slates scattered, but otherwise all was well. They had spent the nights lying under the dining room table, listening to the scream of 'grand pianos' (the common name for falling bombs). To my great relief, both were calm and talking rationally. No tears. Women in emergencies can be no less steady than men, and no less able to look after themselves.

7 North Africa

I returned to Maryhill, to be told by my CO that he'd posted me to the 2nd Battalion Highland Light Infantry (HLI) in the Middle East. It was a battalion of regular troops rather than territorials, now in action against the Italian Army in East Africa. In short, the HLI had been taking casualties in Eritrea, and were not disposed to let suitable cannon fodder like me slip through their fingers. Although I didn't know it just then, Wedderburn's requisition order lay on my CO's desk, while he replied to London that I was embarking for Egypt and could not be recalled. He gave me a week's leave, with orders to report at Greenock on sailing date, when I should board the P&O liner *Orcades*. All this I did, not knowing the truth until two months later, when I received a letter from Wedderburn – a letter which had travelled on the same convoy as mine.

The convoy was the war's biggest, and the Home Fleet was deployed for its defence. We sailed at midnight, heading out for mid-Atlantic, where the merchant ships and liners from ports of the UK and Canada mustered for the long voyage round the Cape of Good Hope. Our shepherds gave spectacular displays in wild weather, the destroyers cutting like knives through mountainous seas, their hulls barely visible through white spray, weaving in and out among the great ships scattered in all directions farther than eye could see. The bigger battleships were never seen, for they stood far out beyond the convoy's fringes, guarding the main body and directing the faster destroyers. These greyhounds gave us the real show of power, moving always at full speed whatever the weather. From mid-Atlantic we closed in on Africa's west coast, where the battle-fleet turned back to home waters, leaving our vast convoy to destroyer-escort.

The most luxurious days of my war were those on the *Orcades*. (She was later torpedoed in the Indian Ocean.) She had been commandeered at short notice and not yet stripped as a troopship. Newly and lavishly stocked with food and drink for her normal Australian passage, she sailed complete with stewards. We enjoyed her superb services for a full two months. Always there are snags to military bliss. As a second lieutenant I was given 'command' (supervision) of thirty men, plus a sergeant and corporal. Consternation was mine when I read their conduct sheets. The men were the scrapings of their units' barrels. All except the non-commissioned officers (NCOs) had served recent sentences for a wide variety of crimes – arson, assault, burglary, rape and lesser offences. Their home units wanted rid of them. They were troublemakers.

At first, all was peace. Our luxury cruise came as happily to them as to me. I met them each morning at boat drill. While the NCOs allocated light fatigue duties, I saw that their persons, uniforms and berths were kept spick and span. Entertainments were laid on at night, but decks were too crowded for play by day. Soon, too much spare time and duty-free drinks led to brawls. NCOs were struck or given insolence. My orderly room became a daily court, dispensing reprimand for minor offences, and for the major, confinement in the ship's hold. In tropical weather that made an effective deterrent. I kept to reprimand as far as I could and to my surprise discovered a natural talent, provided I rehearsed inwardly – like my former RSMs. Culprits visibly wilted. That was just what was wanted, but it made me uneasy. Could I really be as nasty as that? The NCOs' pleased grins salved my conscience a little. But I did wonder.

In mid-April we docked for three days at Cape Town to take in stores. Before I left home, a friend in the RAF, George Roger, had warned his sister in Cape Town of my coming. She, Mrs Hollingdale, invited me to stop overnight and to climb Table Mountain next day.

'What,' she asked me, 'would you most like for a first meal ashore?'

I had answered jocularly, 'A plateful of roast pork crackling' (a delicacy not tasted for two years). Her laughter whetted my appetite when I sat down at table, for there it was, piled on my plate to a small mountain, crisp and delicious. We climbed Devil's Peak in the morning, and walked on to Table Mountain where we had the wild-land and skies all to ourselves. I felt deep relief to be free of the crowded ship, and the crowded bars of Cape Town. We came down to bathe at a sandy beach. A few hours' peace is no brief or passive benefit. Reinvigorating joy lasts long.

The next month's voyage – more than 6,000 miles round and up Africa's south and east coasts – brought one strange event. In the Red Sea a soldier died. Within the hour, vultures flew out from the coast of Sudan, and kept circling the ship until the body was buried at sea. The convoy being widely spread far out from land, how could these birds have known of one man's death below decks? I never understood the incident, nor heard it explained.

We disembarked at Suez in a mid-May heat wave. I was sent to Ismailia, on the canal, there to await the return of the 2nd HLI, which was still in action 1,200 miles south in Eritrea. I spent nearly a month waiting, learning my first lesson that a soldier 'on active service' spends most of his life sitting on his baggage. When at long last something does happen, he has hectic cause to regret it. Meantime, I had two quicker lessons to learn.

Egyptian heat, to a body long acclimatised to Scottish cold, seemed too much to endure. The nearest hilltops west of the canal looked cool in clear morning air, and a lot closer than they were. By the time I came on to their summit ridges I knew my mistake. The loose rock and stone were reflecting the noonday sun tenfold. I returned to base camp in the late afternoon consumed with thirst, and going straight to the bar downed an iced John Collins. Third lesson: never treat dehydration with alcohol. My temperature shot up. I had heat exhaustion; i.e. my skin had stopped sweating. I had to be rushed to hospital and wrapped in wet sheets. Thereafter I took my exercise swimming in the Bitter Lakes.

Idling at Ismailia, we all felt remote from the desert war. Wavell's brilliant campaign had early this year driven the Italian armies far out of Egypt's Western Desert and 500 miles into Libya. But he had then to supply an expeditionary force of 60,000 men in defence of Greece, which meant that he could do no more than hold Libya's eastern province of Cyrenaica. This had allowed a German general named Rommel to come into Libya with a newly formed Afrika Korps. Rommel had forced Wavell to draw back to Egypt's frontier, 400 miles to our west. But Tobruk in Libya stayed in our hands and was strongly held. The threat it posed to Rommel's rear had made his further advance impracticable. We in Egypt felt no real sense of threat, not even at the fall of Greece in late April – for the Army of the Nile had then been powerfully reinforced by the return of its armies from Greece and Eritrea, and now from home too by the latest convoy.

Late in May, sudden threat was renewed: airborne invasion of Crete. Within two weeks, the German paratroopers had taken the island.

THE WESTERN DESERT

My battalion arrived back from Eritrea early in June. I joined it at a desert camp outside Cairo. The 2nd HLI was a crack battalion, having seen continuous action over twenty-one years in India's North-West Frontier, and then in Palestine and North Africa. In Eritrea it had suffered heavy losses in the battles for Addis Ababa and Asmara; therefore the CO, Lt Colonel Thorburn, and his officers, were glad enough to have me and another two subalterns, even if conscripted civilians. At first I did not register how high their standards really were. Unlike home units, they put no emphasis on parade ground drill. Their quick discipline came on wider fronts.

Having newly come out of battle, the officers were most relaxed in their own mess, casual in dress and of easy manner. Most wore 'brothel-creepers', desert shoes with thick crepe soles, neckerchiefs with bush-shirts and shorts, and hair not cropped close. Some had pet dogs. All were most friendly. None wore the solar topee with which I'd been issued by an out-of-date home establishment. Khaki bonnets were quite enough protection from sun (or the Glengarry with dress uniform). Relaxed as their attitude was, they had a wary eye for untried subalterns from civvy street. I could see the same quizzical light in the eyes of my platoon, when I first met the men and tried to memorise thirty names. I liked them. Most were tough Glasgow or Highland characters, mixed with one third English. I read their conduct sheets with a sense of relief, and could see that unlike privates of home regiments they had no disposition to belittle their officers. They gave them respect as men who had led them well in battle. But I had not led them and they were wondering how I'd be when I did. I wondered too.

The HLI was brigaded with two Indian battalions, Gurkhas and Garhwalis, in the 10th Indian Division. No sooner had I joined them than Crete fell. We received drafts from our evacuated army, and heard at first hand the efficient tactics of enemy paratroopers, armed with Tommy guns and backed by tanks, in overrunning the ground. Our .303 rifles began to seem an anachronism, like bows and arrows. We had no submachine-guns. The Sten gun had not yet arrived, and our Brens were too easily jammed by dust – clumsy too and heavy for troops moving and fighting on foot.

In late June we moved west to the Libyan frontier at Hell-Fire Pass (Halfaya), the scene of Wavell's victory last year. This was true Western Desert country: rock thinly sanded and covered in short green scrub on its broad coastal fringe, becoming ever sandier southward. We occupied a tented 'box' ringed by minefields. Apart from flies, I liked the desert, especially at dawn when the huge sun-disc lifted up from the horizon, the cool stillness then, the vastness of blue skies – nine-tenths of all we could see – and above all the starlit sky at night. Even the occasional dust storm, choking and coating us head to foot, was to me, as a new boy, interesting.

Senior company commanders had leisure to hunt gazelle. Their jeeps, like the gazelles, could travel at 50 mph in short bursts over the hard-baked and bumpy ground. The chase appeared to be fun, success rare. But this sport was not for subalterns, who had to work. New ones like me had to apply themselves to navigation skills. Compass-work over flat desert seemed child's play after mountain country in mist, but the prismatic compass had small practical use in desert devoid of landmarks and over the long distances to be covered in trucks whose metal fouled the magnetic bearings. Maps were like sea charts, blank sheets apart from the coastline. I had to learn how to read the stars and to navigate by them at night, and how to use the sun compass by day. This latter work proved invaluable, literally a lifesaver.

Used in conjunction with the jeep's mileage clock, the sun compass was simply a gnomon centred on a metal compass dial, and mounted just forward of the windscreen. The shadow falling on the dial's rim could be set for north, then adjusted to show the bearing wanted for each leg of the 'line of march'. Every ten minutes the dial had to be turned slightly by hand to allow for the earth's own spin. All this might seem chancy to a high degree. The shadow was never seen on the chosen line except momentarily, but to one side or the other according to ground humps, and swerves to avoid hillocks, or soft sand-like swamp, or other obstacles like derelict tanks. These innumerable minor changes in direction cancelled each other out. The end result was so accurate that I could scarcely believe it. But for this training, I should never have kept my nerve when I came to long-distance patrol work out of a brigade-box ringed by invisible minefields. Return had to be made exactly at the right gap. That crucial test still lay ahead.

8 To Iraq and Cyprus

We were getting ready for action against Rommel when Germany invaded Russia. Our battalion had started moving west when we received sudden orders from Wavell: to detach from our brigade and move 1,000 miles east to Iraq. German paratroopers had landed on the Kirkuk oil field. We had to winkle them out and were given ten days to do it.

Churchill, we heard, foresaw a pincer movement by three German Armies, breaking simultaneously south through the Caucasus to Palestine, east through Greece and Crete, and west from Libya to Egypt, thus to roll up the whole Middle East. The parachute drop on Kirkuk looked like a preliminary and needful reconnaissance of its oil reserves.

IRAQ

After a hectic day or two 'bombing up' – taking in fuel, food and ammunition – the HLI crossed the canal at Kantara into Sinai. We sped north to Palestine. From now on every man had to sleep on top of his rifle. Sentries gave no sure protection. Beyond Jerusalem we swung east through Jordan into the Syrian Desert. Here the ground became hard and stony, at first well-covered in scrub. Heavy dew fell at night. We pitched no tents, but slept under the stars, I in my down sleeping bag (not an army issue). Soaked by morning, it dried fast at the fiery sunrises.

We were now moving in battle formation. The desert was infested with armed bands following the break up of the French-Syrian Army. Our several companies drove widely deployed in line abreast far beyond sight. The clouds of dust rising from the multitude of wheels obscured each vehicle from all others, therefore a rearguard was essential to pick up any who fell out with engine or puncture troubles. My platoon was this rearguard appointed because I, as the newest subaltern, was the most expendable. My trucks, widely spread, had to lie a few miles back to allow the battalion's dust to settle, and to see where rescue might be needed. We had no radio communication. Since my own jeep had to lie back farthest of all, my station posed that ancient riddle of Juvenal: Who is to guard the guardian? If anyone hit real trouble it would be me. And sure enough, about 250 miles into the desert on our third day, the jeep's engine stuttered and died. My rearguard disappeared into the distance. By the time its dust had settled, the desert was empty. At the end of a couple of hours, my driver had failed to find the fault. A vulture appeared high overhead. Our canvas water bottles had as always been left hanging from the jeep's outside body to keep cool by evaporation – the metal was almost too hot to handle – so we moved them back into shadow. Water might soon be our direst need. As if in emphasis, the vulture dropped lower and began to circle hopefully. By late afternoon I was reconciled to benightment as the least of our looming misfortunes. The driver, near to despair, dismantled and cleaned the carburettor for the third time – and the engine fired! We were off. At dusk we drove into the old fort of Rutba. This square, whitewashed building stood alone amid thousands of square miles of barest desert. Its commander dispensed tea. He had no way of communicating with an HLI on the move, but assured us that if we failed to find them, a search would be made by an aircraft from Lake Habbaniyeh, about 200 miles east.

'If you break down again,' said he, 'do NOT shoot the vulture. It's the only one we have. Remember, a lone truck is hard to spot from the air. The vulture is the pilot's one sure guide.'

We pressed on, and some hours after dark found the battalion bedded down for the night. No one had been much bothered about us. Two days later, we passed through Habbaniyeh, where our battalion reverted to single file for the passage through Baghdad. Its pro-Nazi people stoned us in the streets. They had known of our coming: therefore so too had the Germans at Kirkuk, who had by now been airlifted back to Russia. Our last hundred miles became a more leisurely drive. We found the oil plant undamaged. The Germans were clearly hoping to return in force on the conquest of Russia.

We enjoyed a pleasant couple of months at Kirkuk. Our tented camp at the grassy outskirts lay near the oil company's club-house and big open-air swimming pool. Melons were plentiful. We always had one side-tabled in our company's mess-tent, where we fed it daily with gin through a cork-size hole cut in its top. When the spirit had percolated through the whole fruit, it was judged ripe – and delicious. Field exercises took up our time, but were not overdone. Our CO was a sane man. Meantime, Wavell had been given a new command in India, and Auchinleck taken his place in Cairo. He recalled us in early September, with orders to rejoin our brigade at Hell-Fire Pass. An attack on Rommel was now imminent.

CYPRUS

On the day we passed through Alexandria, our brigade was ordered to Cyprus. Task: to forestall an expected German jump to Cyprus from Crete and Greece, preparatory to their invasion of Palestine.

A destroyer shipped us out in late September. We landed at the port of Famagusta, ringed two miles by sixteenth-century walls. The HLI occupied the great Venetian fort on the sea front, my own company being billeted in Othello's Tower at the deep water brink – the very site of Shakespeare's play. The walls, immensely thick, gave a cool and spacious interior; on their outer face providing me with some excellent rock-climbing. I put in much practice in occasional free hours. My men thought me loopy.

In the House of Commons Churchill acclaimed our arrival: 'Cyprus,' he intoned, 'has been heavily reinforced.' Our brigade was in fact the only force on the island, apart from a few RAF Hurricanes. It was a bluff. Would it work? We ardently hoped it would, bearing in mind the fate of Crete, survivors of which were now in our ranks.

Our principal duties were coastal patrols to forestall German attempts to land men, stores, or ammunition from U-boats, or to drop them by air. Cyprus had been a British colony since 1914. Relations between Cypriots and British were good; the country people friendly and hospitable. I knew that at first hand, since my own patrols called in at houses round the coast, where we were welcomed, and often invited to share food with the families. Instead, we gave them some of our own rations. It was different in town, where our leisure hours were at night. Friction arose when our men flocked to the Famagusta bars. They found cheap brandy and wine – and met the Cypriot women. Greek and Turkish males resented the competition. We had casualties from knifings, but still more from venereal disease. No man was allowed out at night without free issue of a condom. Despite which, casualties grew ever higher as the months passed by.

The winter weather grew cold and wet. Since leaving Egypt, we had changed from tropical gear back to battledress, and even to great coats. Snow fell on the high tops. The island had two mountain groups, the Kyrenians along the north coast, and the Troodos group to the south-west, rising to 6,400 feet. The Troodos had snow-cover and good skiing during December and January, for which no time could be allowed.

The 2nd HLI observed annually two traditional celebrations: St Andrew's Night on 30 November, and Hogmanay. While both were for me memorable, the greatest was St Andrew's Night. The officers' mess always ran a party, to which were invited the English officers of the Indian and Nepali battalions. Its feature was the preparation of Atholl Brose to the CO's special prescription.

Into a barrel went oatmeal and whisky, left to steep for forty-eight hours but continually stirred in daylight hours. The oatmeal was then cast out (reserved for the RSM's morning porridge), while to the remaining brew were added a third of its own volume in French brandy, a bottle or two of Drambuie, and sufficient cream to give the whole, after long final stirrings, a mellow cream colour.

Our guests arrived at 6 p.m. for an ostensibly simple cocktail party. No games were played or ceilidh laid on. Just affable talk. After initial drinks, the

Atholl. Brose was served. It was quite delicious. It went over so smoothly that it seemed innocuous. Second, third and still more servings inevitably followed. But the officers of the HLI, being either experienced or like me warned, held back on this deadly brew. Our guests duly fell like ninepins. In the background, our batmen had wheelbarrows lined up and ready. Our guests were loaded on and wheeled to their waiting jeeps for return to unit.

A few days later we had the news of Pearl Harbour. With Japan in the war and the US fleet knocked out, prospects for the future looked grim. We felt that we had better make the most of our Christmas and Hogmanay festivities. They could well be our last. They were especially for the NCOs and other ranks. Turkeys and pigs had long since been bought in by our quartermasters. Each company had been fattening its own stock on full army rations and leftovers. At Christmas dinner, the officers served the men. At Hogmanay, the men were allowed out on the town to all hours, while the officers celebrated more quietly in their own mess – and the more senior in Nicosia. I, as the most junior, was appointed duty officer for the night.

My most important duty was to make the rounds of the sentry posts on Othello's Tower. I chose midnight and found every post empty. The sentries had banked on my neglect to make the round. I would not have believed this possible in a regular battalion. On the other hand, we were all aware that any chance of a German attack on Cyprus had vanished. In Cyrenaica, the Eighth Army had broken Rommel's front, lifted the siege of Tobruk, taken Benghazi, and advanced 400 miles to the Gulf of Sidra – albeit with heavy tank losses. In Russia, the German armies were bogged down for the winter. Cyprus had become a safe place to be this Hogmanay. But that was no excuse. Battalion discipline had been sapped. I reported to my company commander. I could see the steel come to his eye. He had a quick word with his command sergeant major (CSM) and we all three jumped into a jeep and drove fast to Famagusta. Our company was known to favour a particular dance hall and bar. We went in, and found battle about to break. On one side of the wide hall were ranged the HLI, on the other hand the Cypriots, all with raised bottles or chairs and each about to advance on the other. An intimidating sight.

My company commander did not hesitate. Striding to the middle of the floor, he turned his back to the Cypriots, faced the HLI, and barked one word: 'Out!' There was an ugly silence. No one moved. He stood stock-still. Seconds passed. Then one NCO, more sober than the rest, stepped forward, turned to the door, and walked. The rest slowly followed. We waited till the last man was away. Meantime the CSM was out on the street, ensuring that his men did not vanish.

Next day, we wondered how the CO would handle his problem. Court-martial the whole guardroll? By elapse of time we had our answer. The whole incident was 'forgotten', as if it had never been. Behind the scenes, the NCOs were 'chastened' (grilled to cinders) by the RSM. Parade ground drills re-doubled. But that was all. I thought the blind eye decision by our CO wise in the circumstances. During the New Year, most of those young soldiers would die in action.

Spring comes to Cyprus in February. I was just beginning to enjoy the new warmth, the sea air, and the sun on the mellow walls of Othello's Tower, and to revel in my early morning dives into blue, deep water from its platform base – when orders came from Cairo. We were to embark immediately for Egypt, there to rejoin the Eighth Army, now under command of General Ritchie. Our recall came as a great relief to Col Thorburn, for the HLI was suffering thirty per cent casualties from venereal disease – although none above rank of lance corporal. The other ranks would not take sensible precautions. Long before us other units had had the same experience. The Navy forbade shore leave to all hands.

Early in March, a destroyer shipped us back to Alexandria. We moved at once to a Western Desert base, and by rota were granted a few days' leave to Cairo. A long lull had come to the desert fighting while both sides took in reinforcements after their very heavy losses in the November-December offensives. The British had seized enormous booty, but Rommel was getting in more guns and armour than our Middle East HQ realised. Cairo gave us all our last fling before battle, and I made the most of it at the best hotels – Shepheard's and Mena House at the Pyramids. Needless to say, I climbed the Great Pyramid of Gizeh, about 450 feet and no harder than the *Curved Ridge* of the Buachaille, rode camels, and followed the full course of a peace time tourist.

9 The Battle of the Cauldron

Back to the Desert, we moved into Cyrenaica to rejoin the 10th Indian Division. Our brigade lay in a big box west of Hell-Fire Pass and heavily ringed by minefields. We were once more on action rations, probably the same as in the First World War: bully-beef and ships' biscuits, tinned cheese, apple jam, tea and a quart bottle of water per man per day. Throughout April, my platoon and I were frequently out on patrol by day and night. There were daily skirmishes on a wide and deep front, while armour units on both sides, in company with their own batteries of artillery, jockeyed for position and probed each others' defences.

On one daylight patrol of thirty miles, with an escort of two Bren gunners and a sergeant, I saw on the horizon some unusual shape and diverged off course to investigate. It was a grounded Hurricane. We approached most warily, fearing a German decoy. The pilot emerged from under a wing, waving frantically. We moved in and took him aboard. He had run out of petrol!

I set a new course back to base, then asked how on earth he'd allowed himself to make such a mistake. He said he'd been near the end of his day's range when he spotted a Jerry ambulance column out west, heading for Benghazi. He could not resist giving chase, then came down low and made several runs back and forth, machine-gunning.

'They were all out of their trucks,' said he jubilantly, 'trying to get clear or get under them. Fun while it lasted! By the time I broke off and made height, the fuel had run out.'

I heard this tale with such revulsion that I felt stricken. Speechless, I thought to ditch him then and there – fit meat for the vultures. I might have done so had I been alone. German ambulance wagons, like our own, were clearly marked with the International Red Cross on their roofs. I glanced at my sergeant. His face was set in a hard mask. I concentrated on navigation and spoke not a word till we made camp. I came near to wishing we'd miss the gap in the minefield. As usual, we made no error. When I passed the pilot over to Battalion HQ I made a full verbal report to the adjutant. I never heard if any action followed. The RAF, I knew full well, did not gun or bomb ambulances, but every arm of the Services has its psychopaths. They should be cut out when found.

A day or two later, I was sent out on night-patrol. A late aircraft reconnaissance had spotted an unidentified tank squadron just ten miles out. They could be raiders, planning to hit us at first light. I took with me my sergeant and a full platoon section, moving in halfway by truck, then on foot under a crescent moon. Over the last mile we closed in on our target very slowly, and over the last few hundred yards crawled – until we could see the tanks' hulls black against the night sky. It was now close to midnight. The squadron lay in tight laager. We inched forward, fearing at every move to hear a sentry's challenge. I whispered to my sergeant, telling him to stay with the section and not move while I went in alone, but to clear out fast if he heard a shot or a shout, and to warn HQ. I squirmed forward, yet found no sentry. My eye caught the red glow of a cigarette near the base of a tank. My ear caught the murmur of a voice. My conclusion was that no enemy squadron would dare to lie up so close to our division without putting out sentries. It must be British. The rest I had to do alone. I stood up. No challenge. I walked to the nearest tank, grenade in hand. Someone got to his feet.

'Hello,' I said, 'are you British or Jerry?'

An English voice answered, 'OK, OK – where are you from?'

I replaced the grenade's pin and said 'HLI on patrol. Can I speak to your CO?'

This unmilitary casualness seemed to be typical of British armoured units; a mixture of old cavalry and new Desert Rat qualities. They knew their desert so thoroughly that to them it was home. It took a lot to ruffle their equanimity. They truly did know what they were doing, or not doing. As it happened, this particular squadron may not have known. They were newly out from England.

Batteries of artillery were also scattered across the desert at this time. Their isolated operations were part of Ritchie's skirmishing tactics, and we infantry had often to send them men on detachment for temporary defence. This was dangerous work. Rommel too was using similar raiding parties, operating at long range like sea-pirates, using every trick to penetrate and destroy. Some of his raiders were small infantry groups in captured British trucks, trying to slip inside our own defences. I had one very narrow escape in May. Rommel had launched a rapid attack, still aiming to reach Suez while German armies tried to break through the Caucasus. His main armoured force was held for a while by the Free French at Bir Hacheim, about seventy miles south-west of Tobruk, but his smaller units were raiding far eastward. My platoon had provided one section, armed with Brens, to give a few days' protection to a battery lying several miles to our west. After a day or two, I and a senior subaltern went out to them with rations. As our truck drew close, we saw that the ring of twelve-pounder guns was already being approached by another truck, identical to ours, unmistakably British, therefore allowed into the ring's open centre without challenge, as we were too. But that truck was packed with German tommy-gunners. They jumped out and let rip. Under the hail of sudden fire, our driver swung the truck round and by sheer speed of reaction escaped. The battery, taken at its own unprotected centre, had lost all chance of defence. My platoon section was lost with it. There was nothing we could have done. Our escape seemed miraculous. It should not have been possible.

General Ritchie now launched his own armoured attack. This battle of the tanks flowed back and forth during the last week of May. The desert looked in a state of chaos, each side deeply penetrating the others' widely scattered positions, or swirling round them to inflict heavy mutual losses, especially around a British-held territory known as the Cauldron, east of Bir Hacheim.

My brigade waited, interminably waited. We slept light on the open scrub beside our packed baggage, each officer with his own small unit, watching the stars or lightly dozing, always listening. Unluckily I heard some of my own men briefly discussing me, and caught the words, 'He's the kind who gets killed first' – which did not help me to sleep. I felt affronted. They were wide of the mark, I assured myself. All my rock-and-ice days had instilled survival attitudes – those long run-outs of rope without protection had trained me to act by calculation, not impulse and within my abilities for the day. In moments of self-confidence I could leave myself narrow margins. But the rule was, climb safe. I felt without ambition to win a Victoria Cross.

At last the call to action came. Our brigade officers were summoned to a pep talk by one General Maine, commanding our division. An attack was to be made next day on Rommel's panzer divisions, now in position somewhere near the Cauldron. Dawn would be preceded by a four-hour artillery barrage, followed by an infantry attack on the enemy armour. We were to get in close and disable as many of their Mark IV tanks and eighty-eight millimetre guns as we could, by placing grenades on the driving sprockets, which engage the tracks. Our own tanks would follow on behind for the kill.

General Maine added, 'I want no prisoners. The only good Germans are dead Germans.'

That final exhortation was in clear breach of the Geneva Convention. I and my fellow officers had no intention at all of obeying it. Its probable cause was Rommel's personal domination of the desert battlefields during the last year – both in defeat and victory. A general is hardly ever seen by his soldiers, or at best briefly. How is it then that a good general's personality can pervade and dominate a battlefield 1,000 miles wide? I can think of no rational answer, except that it assuredly happens. Rommel was the last war's most outstanding example, experienced at first hand by both opposing armies. Our high command, alarmed, deplored needlessly an imaginary ill effect on Eighth Army morale. It was ironic, therefore, that when General Maine was soon taken prisoner, he would find that Rommel had given orders in direct opposition to his own: *Spare prisoners. Don't loot.*

The battle-attack came under Ritchie's command. Our trucks lined up that night widely deployed. We all knew that our battalion's fate was already sealed. The HLI would go into action first, that being the rule for all British units of the Indian Army. Our mission was every whit as suicidal as the previous century's Charge of the Light Brigade at Balaclava. Our general had learned nothing. Infantry cannot attack massed tanks over open ground without close armoured support. We were to get none.

The four-hour barrage from far to our rear sounded awesome. Its continuous thunder, the whoosh of shells overhead, and the unbroken roar of explosion in front, gave some illusion of invisible enemy suffering. In fact, our heavy guns lay four miles back, too far off to disable Mark IV tanks. Rommel simply withdrew them a few hundred yards, so that our shells fell short; then, when the barrage had ended, moved them forward again – but now reinforced with heavy mortars and machine-gunners, and with eighty-eight millimetre guns mixed in, to await our assault. Ritchie's vain artillery barrage had lost us all hope of surprise. It was plain stupid. And we all knew it.

At first light, the barrage ended abruptly. In what now seemed deathly silence, we drove fast across an undulating plain which, rising gently uphill, screened us from enemy sight. After several minutes, the enemy guns found us. Even firing blind they got the range right. My own company's store-truck containing my baggage and eiderdown sleeping bag took a direct hit. I saw the contents go sky high. Another shell struck the quartermaster sergeant's truck full of hens. Shrapnel flew everywhere. We topped the rise. The enemy's armour and guns lay half a mile ahead. We jumped out and took to our feet.

Our companies spread wide in their many platoons and kept a steady advance. The air became loudly alive with the rush of solid shot, the whine of shrapnel and zip of bullets. I felt no fear – the nervous system had either been screwed up not to register or else shocked out of action. I half turned to see how my platoon was faring, and to speak to my runner, who came hard on my heels. His body stood on its legs a yard away – but only the legs, still joined at the smoking waist. The trunk and head had vanished. Yet I'd heard no explosion, felt no blast. Men were falling all around. In that deadly hail of metal I should have accepted that a man's survival was a matter not of fate but of sheer luck, had it not been for another event soon after.

The battalion kept going, despite the heavy toll, until we came on to ground sloping gently toward the panzer division. Col Thorburn had come right forward on a slow moving jeep, on which he stood erect to observe the scene. His open presence gave a powerful steadying effect. The cool efficiency of all these regular officers deeply impressed me. When I'd first met them in their own mess they had seemed empty headed. I had been misled. When they came to action they were quick minded, knew exactly what to do and how best to do it, and with total self-disregard. Their natural quickness and courage set me an example that I could never properly follow. Between the professional soldier and the civilian there is at first a gulf that few can cross – at least in a war's early stages.

Rommel's four-inch mortars now laid a bomb-barrage backed by intense machine-gunning. It pinned us to the ground. One bomb landed just a yard to my right-hand side. It blew out a crater, but all stone and metal lifted close above my prone body. One golden rule in artillery attack is that no shell lands twice in the same spot (wind, powder charge, gun-recoil, all seem to vary). Therefore, get into a crater – the one safe place. I had tensed up my muscles to make the sideways move when I felt inwardly a sudden negative command: 'Stay put!' It came not from my own will or mind, which intended otherwise, yet while soundless, was so authoritative that I chose not to argue. I sank back in position. Just a few seconds later, another bomb came down exactly on that first crater.

The episode hung in my mind unanswered for more than a year. Where had my warning come from? It could not have been instinct, for my strong instinct had been to move; it could not have been intuition, for its field is not in the physical realm. My experience is that on rare occasions a human being may be open to direction from a power higher than his own. The direction is never over-riding of mind or will, but a simple impulse that one is free to ignore. I had chosen not to ignore. For want of another word, men often refer to such beneficent impulse as their guardian angel. Whatever the name given, I have no doubt of its reality.

No such thoughts entered my mind at the Battle of the Cauldron. Our tanks had not come up in support, nor our guns moved forward. We never saw them all that day, and never heard the reason. Something had gone far wrong in our rear. Release came from my company commander. We had orders to withdraw. 'Withdraw' is a military euphemism, suggesting order. Here there was none. We rose and ran. The battlefield was strewn with dead and dying – bloodied bodies everywhere. One man who did not run was our battalion MO. I came on him kneeling by a wounded soldier, and stopped.

'You'll be needed in the rear too,' I said. But he shook his head and stayed. I thought he might be safe enough. The Afrika Korps would honour him. (In fact they did, and allowed him to go back.) We had a long way to walk, the air humming all the while with spent bullets, until a truck driver spotted us, came back all unpanicked, and picked us up. We sped east.

It is notable that while we were on the battlefield, whether advancing or pinned down, everyone stayed self-possessed, no faltering anywhere. But once we had turned back, retreat degenerated to a rout that no commander could have slowed down. The remnants of the HLI – we had lost 600 men – regrouped at a base back in Egypt's Western Desert. The rest of the brigade had taken lighter losses. A big new draft had come to us from Scotland. Within ten days we were back to strength (800 men). I do not say full strength. Our home units had sent once more the men they most wanted to shed. The 2nd HLI was no longer a crack battalion. That had been thrown away. There was no time to retrain. Just before we went back into action our officers were called to meet our new brigadier. His name was Rees. I was impressed. Short, stocky, determined, quiet, he commanded instant respect.

That respect soared when several days later we were back in Cyrenaica, and once again ordered into action against a panzer division. Again without support of tanks or guns. When Rees heard, he refused his orders. He was right. It is an officer's duty to reject an insane command, if its result must be wholesale loss to no gain. We heard that he was bowler-hatted by General Ritchie. It was Rees's act we respected, not Ritchie's.

Rommel's attack had again isolated Tobruk, and was now enveloping Cyrenaica. His armoured divisions had heavier plate than ours, more powerful guns (forty-seven millimetres against British two-pounders), while his bigger eight-eight millimetre guns were mounted on tracks and able to fight in among his tank squadrons; whereas the untracked British twelve-pounders had to lie too far back to our tanks' rear. Despite their manifest disadvantage, the British armoured divisions made long and heroic resistance – brilliantly handled by their crews and commanders. Our forces fell back slowly to Egypt. My brigade fought rearguard skirmishes, trying by distraction to slow down the German advance while escaping annihilation.

The desert battlefield fell into a new and worse state of chaos in which Rommel's tactical genius prevailed. He lured Ritchie's armoured division into an ambush in mid-June with a loss of 230 British tanks out of 300. General Ritchie was dismissed by Auchinleck, who came out of Cairo to take command of our lost battle. A week later, Tobruk fell. An all out assault by Stuka dive-bombers and massed tanks and guns had allowed German infantry to penetrate the streets.

East of Tobruk, such was the swirl to and fro of the different fighting groups, that the units of our brigade lost touch with each other. Finally, the HLI's four rifle companies lost touch both with each other and battalion HQ. We no longer had food and water. It had become impossible to know which group of approaching vehicles belonged to whom. The RAF were baffled by this problem too. Twice my company was bombed by our own aircraft from low level. We dived for the shelter of our own trucks' wheels to escape the more accurate machine guns. By good fortune they scored no direct hits. Our numbers had now been reduced to fifty men and two subalterns.

On our last day (28 June) we found ourselves close to brigade HQ near Mersa Matruh. An Indian battalion was still attached. Our new brigadier had orders to bestride the coast road at El Fuka, forty miles east of Mersa Matruh, and to hold that position at all costs. Here a low escarpment ran east-south-east across the road. My company, or what was left of it, dug into slit-trenches under its southerly flank, while brigade HQ did the same half a mile away on its north or seaward side. Early in the afternoon, our army's gun batteries began to arrive in quick succession from westward, speeding through our positions, bound for eastern safety. We felt positively betrayed. One of these batteries was commanded by Bill Tilman, the Himalayan climber and leader of the last Everest expedition. I had climbed with him in Glen Coe. When I saw his truck race past, I felt a wholly unreasonable sense of abandonment (not knowing Auchinleck's strategy). Brigade had not told us what was happening or why.

Late in the afternoon, I had a summons to brigade HQ. The brigadier told me I was promoted to captain. I would act as his liaison officer. My job was to try to find, bring in, and take orders to his dispersed units. I listened with deep unease. My earlier remark that the battlefield was in chaos had been another euphemism. To get nearer the truth, I should have to add a string of adjectival qualifications, like bewildering; (unidentifiable vehicles racing in all directions); baffling (their missions unknown); frightening (explosive with shot and shell from invisible sources); and gruesome (ground strewn with bloody and burnt-out relics).

My finding the A brigade's lost units seemed not feasible.

The brigadier described our immediate task: to halt (i.e., delay) the advance of the 15th Panzer Division. In short, a last stand. Purpose: to allow all our artillery more time to withdraw to the east and there to fortify the Alamein line. It gave the only hope to save Egypt. Similar commands had gone out to all infantry.

That to my mind was a sane and sensible order. It meant the sacrifice of 100,000 men. But Auchinleck was right. The reason justified him.

Before I could hear more, a scout-car drove in to report that the 15th Panzers had passed through Mersa Matruh. We might expect them in under half an hour. The brigadier turned to me with a grimace: 'Murray, by tonight you'll be either dead meat or a prisoner.'[1]

Our only help in defence was a battery of two-pounder guns, now ranged close behind the brigade's slit-trenches. They could not stop Mark IV tanks, but could destroy lighter armour if that came in first. Beside them stood a number of trucks and carriers.

I wondered why the brigadier thought to keep me here any longer. There was nothing I could possibly do. Whereas by return to the HLI trenches, I could at least let my men know that their now forlorn hopes had this time a real purpose. But fate had different things in store.

---

1 In *Undiscovered Scotland* (1953) these words, to save explanatory space, appeared as spoken by my battalion commander.

The sun was setting and the moon rising with a first faint glimmer of stars, when we heard the rumble of approaching armour. We dropped into our slit-trenches. A first column of enemy tanks, unheralded by light armour, appeared over the top of the low pass to our west-south-west. They kept single file to present a small target. As if wary of some hidden trap, they paused for a few minutes to take a long, cool look. Then, seeing just a thin line of infantry below the escarpment, they spread to open order and came on. At brigade HQ we had now no sight of them. Later we heard that they did not even pause to shoot up the HLI, but passed straight over their top, whereupon the HLI slipped sideways and out to escape on foot.

Dusk had fallen. I went through my pockets and destroyed anything that might be of use to the enemy – prismatic compass, identity card, notes – then found an address book. I glanced through it. Most of the names were of mountaineers. I had a sudden realisation of what they had given me over the years – so much that I'd taken for granted, all that I'd learned from mountains and men, and so little given in return. I do not mean that I took thought in that slit-trench. The ideas came whole, an instant's flash – the mountains too, as an ideal symbol, charged with a beauty not theirs pouring through them.

Suddenly, the tanks were there, dark bulks on top of the escarpment, twenty Mark IVs abreast. At such short range, our two-pounder guns could not miss. The shells struck them on the nose. The armour glowed red in the dusk while the shells glanced off in a shower of sparks. The tanks staggered – but came on. Behind me, a brigade truck packed with Indians suddenly bolted westward while a stream of tracer bullets poured into its open back. An awesome sight. But it got away. The attack became a shambles, quickly ended. Guns blazing, the Mark IVs rolled up to close quarters and machine-gunned the ground for a few minutes. The crews dismounted to deal with survivors, if any. I was so far one of them. I climbed out of my slit-trench. A young tank commander walked unsteadily up to me, waving a machine pistol. His arm shook. He had been rattled about in his tank like a pea in a tin can, not knowing what hit him. Had I been he, with an urgent need to release tension. I could imagine myself just pressing the trigger. I held my breath while he took quick stock. To my surprise, he lowered his gun.

'Are you not feeling the cold?' he asked.

The question was not daft. The desert at night feels exceeding cold if one is still in shirt and shorts and near starving. Perhaps from my recent train of thought I blurted, 'It's cold as a mountain top.'

He looked me straight in the eye 'Good God, do you climb mountains?'

We were both mountaineers and still in our twenties. We relaxed. He stuffed away his pistol and could not do enough for me.

'When did you last eat?'

I told him, 'It's nearly two days.' He led me to his tank and fetched out a British Army greatcoat. He passed it over.

'Loot from Tobruk,' he said, 'and this too' – producing bully-beef and biscuits, a chocolate slab, and a bottle of beer. I quickly put on the greatcoat – I'd begun to shiver. While we ate, we exchanged a few words on the Alps, Scotland, rock-and-ice. We shared the beer and toasted 'Mountains'. Suddenly aware of the brotherhood that implied, he added, 'and mountaineers'.

'Mountains give us some good things,' I suggested. 'Such as friends worth having, battles worth fighting, beauty worth seeing.'

'We call it *Leben*.' He paused, 'It means to be alive. I came here from the Russian front – that was death. Lucky to get away.' He grinned. 'Next stop Cairo.'

To both of us at the time, that looked likely. Neither of us knew the strength of Auchinleck's hold on El Alamein. Despite all the past victories of the Eighth Army, I had seen it only in defeat. I never guessed the truth of its huge resource and resilience. Nor, I think, did Rommel, for all his six months' dominance of the desert battlefields.

The moon was full. We had to part. Italian infantry were now rolling up in trucks.

The British prisoners were herded into a group. One Italian soldier saw my wristwatch, a Rolex Oyster bought in Cairo, and snatched it off me. By good chance my German friend was still within earshot. I gave him a shout. When he came over and heard what had happened, he gave a curt order and the watch was handed back. Rommel had said, 'No looting.'

An hour later the 15th Panzers clanked away, heading for El Alamein. We prisoners slept on the ground. Wrapped in my Tobruk greatcoat, I gave thanks to that German climber – and to General Rommel (raised to Field Marshal a few days later).

Next day we were trucked west to Benghazi, where scores of thousands of prisoners were assembled for evacuation to Italy. During the following week, we were lifted out by sea and air.

My flight of 600 miles went very high to escape the RAF fighters based on Malta. First frozen, then smitten by altitude, we landed at Bari, near the heel of Italy. There we joined 1,500 fellow prisoners, and with them crawled by slow train to the prison – Campo 21 in the province of Chieti.

INCARCERATION

10 Stone Walls: Chieti

Our Barracks, in wooded countryside beyond the town of Chieti, were formed as a cluster of one-storey buildings spread over a grassy compound. We drove in through a gateway flanked by guardhouses. The Italian Army, quite unprepared for this big influx of prisoners, had done a fast and efficient job in throwing up around the compound a high, barbed wire fence, topped every 100 yards with sentry boxes. The walls of the dozen barrack blocks shone cleanly white inside and out. Their dormitories, cool and spacious, were given a warm look by red terrazzo floors. They might have seemed welcoming after desert dust had they not been jammed tight with double-tiered bunks, on which we, as prisoners, were packed like sardines, if happily not in oil, each to his straw-sack mattress.

In the morning we could hardly get outside fast enough. The wide, grassy compound was soon to be reduced to hard-baked earth. Beyond the perimeter fence, which we promptly found to be electrified, our eyes were tantalised by splendid views westward to the Abruzzi mountains, and eastward to a wooded plain sloping far down to the Adriatic – its sea invisible at ten miles' distance. Fortune had favoured us in our campsite. But the Italians had not yet been given time to solve their worst problem – how to feed 1,500 men at Chieti. Their quick answer was the easy one – fruit. The Adriatic coast had fruit in superabundance – tomatoes (factories even made linoleum from the skins), grapes, figs purple and green, and peaches, all as common as spuds in Scotland, and cheaper. The effect on our army stomachs, so long inured to bully-beef and ships' biscuits, need not be detailed. Our lot was this day and night queuing for lavatories. Our plight wreathed our captors' faces in sadistic smiles, until our organised protest, sustained for a month, brought salvation in bread and pasta.

Several months passed before we were allowed to write home and then, it would seem, only because the Red Cross had discovered our whereabouts. Our letters were censored, but I was at least able to let my mother know exactly where I was. Before embarkation, I had told her of a code, whereby the first letter of an agreed word sequence in any note sent her could be extracted to spell a word. Hence she knew of my progress from one country to another. I was worried about her. I already knew that the War Office must have reported me 'missing', believed killed, in action – and necessarily so, because no one in my regiment could have known otherwise (I was in fact right). Having lost her husband in the First World War, she might now be feeling all the greater stress. Nearly six months passed before my first letter from Chieti reached her. Her morale had meantime been fostered by my sister, and by mountaineering friends, who gave assurance that I'd be a survivor, I'd had practice enough.

During those long months at Chieti, we too thirsted for news. Our engineers, aided by latent talents for theft and bribery, had constructed a radio set, hidden below ground. We heard in the autumn from BBC News of our Eighth Army's victory at Alamein – of which the Italian press said nothing – and the push into Cyrenaica. That boosted morale sky-high. We had devised many ways of using our time; our surplus fruit stimulated the crafts of distillation and brewing; and nearly all prisoners were able to lecture on one subject or another; so now we organised classes in the open air while the weather was dry. There was little room indoors. We could study a wide variety of subjects, but at a low level since paper and books were not available, nor had we tables at which to write.

December brought an upgrade to our lives. The first Red Cross parcels arrived. The sight of those great vans in the compound, each packed to the roof with individual food boxes, seemed at first like a desert mirage: could they be real? Our intense pleasure came not just from their fuel value, but still more from their reminder of man's humanity, the latter a point that prisoners tend to forget.

Early in the New Year the food parcels were supplemented by vanloads of books sent out by the YMCA. Their house-to-house collection in Britain had garnered the richest treasure – all the books that no one at home now had time to read – the classics of English literature. From these we started to build up a library that grew through the years to our great profit.

The Geneva Convention of 1939, the last of a long series, forbade cruelty to prisoners of war, and made provision for their living conditions. It was on the whole observed in Italy, and at first in Germany, at least towards British prisoners. Breaches of the rule, like clubbing prisoners with rifle butts on morning roll calls, were occasionally brought on by our own studied insolence, or by involuntary revolt at a parade's prolongation when one or more of our number had made an escape, or when control on either side snapped for some good reason. But control prevailed. The Senior British Officer saw to it, as did the Camp Commandant. We all had cause to be grateful to unknown men who, over the last century, had made these conventions, and to the International Red Cross and its national societies who gave them practical effect.

The British Society was no less efficient. When winter came, and we began to suffer cold in our desert shirts and shorts, the Red Cross and War Office between them contrived a delivery of serge battle dress for all. I had one personal triumph. The Italians had taken our army boots away 'for repair'. They did not come back. I made a brief report by code in a letter home. My mother took the letter straight to the Glasgow branch of the Red Cross. They instantly informed the War Office, who released a cargo of 2,000 boots to the Red Cross – speedily delivered to Chieti. By the close of 1942, the British had shed their peace time lethargy. I began to think that this war might yet be won.

That view had now more support from the BBC. We heard in January that Tobruk and Cyrenaica had been recaptured. Tripoli was about to fall. Thus stirred, our engineers began tunnelling: an experience long planned and prepared, for that electrified fence had been seen as a challenge. Tunnels need roof supports and all had more bed slats under the mattresses than were necessary, material from our empty Red Cross tins joined as pipes. Tools were stolen from the Italians or made from scrap metal. Our cardboard parcel-boxes were used to carry out earth. By February, tunnelling was well under way, preparatory to the spring and summer escape season.

Winter had brought me a benefit of my own. Its onset lightened my life – the first snows on the Gran Sasso. Although nearly thirty miles away, it soared 10,000 feet into blue sky, the highest spire of the Abruzzi mountains. Every time I looked, it symbolised for me a freedom of spirit that now seemed lost. It made me think too of war's lunacy, and of the German tank commander. I wondered how he had fared. Had he survived the battle of Alamein? Maybe he too was a prisoner? Between them, he and the Gran Sasso re-awakened my old urge to write, and the urge to write of mountains. At first a mere spark, it grew over the days to a flame. I took thought. I had a pencil, but no paper. The only paper in Campo 21 was toilet paper, which was, as I explained, in unusual demand. We had none to spare. It was at this point, in February 1943, that I received by post from my mother a most handsome volume of *William Shakespeare's Complete Works*, printed on the finest India paper. When I lovingly handled it, the thought came unbidden to mind that it would make superb toilet paper, compared to the Italians' thick coarse stuff, which would serve better, as writing paper. The idea grew like the first, the flame now a fire. I would write. The means were at hand. I felt sure that Shakespeare would have approved.

The camp had no useable rooms for writing. I would have to make do with my bunk, a top tier. My Red Cross parcel sufficed for a table. When I set to work on my first page, it stayed blank for two days. My neighbours were a bit derisive. 'Why bother?' said they. 'You'll never see it published.' I reckoned they might be right. My pencil would not move on the paper. Where should I begin? Without diaries or reference books, how would I ever remember enough detail to complete a chapter, far less a 70 or 80,000-word manuscript? As to what I should write, there was no doubt. I should write about good climbs. My zest for mountains had been expressed and felt on hard routes on rock, snow and ice, as well as on the high plateaux and long ridges and wide moors. I wanted to share these experiences. The want grew compulsive. At last, in something like despair, I brought to mind one memorable day in Skye and wrote a first sentence: 'It was ten o'clock at night in Glen Brittle ... ' To my astonishment, the pencil kept moving. As if with a will of its own, it kept filling the pages. I began to get involved in a book, and to find that true were the words of Richard Lovelace that 'Stone walls do not a Prison make, Nor Iron bars a Cage'.

I was right in thinking I'd be short on detail – but wrong in believing memories irretrievable. I was to discover, as month succeeded month, that the mind forgets nothing. It holds all experience in minutest detail. It is not memory as such that fails, but ability to extract the detail from its pigeonholes. That ability improves with daily practice: especially the concentrated practice I was in a position to give. In course of time – months in my experience – the detail comes more and more copiously until it grows to full flood and colour. This involved much re-writing of earlier pages to fill in omissions. But time here was no problem. I came in the end to realise that diaries are a trap that I'd been lucky to escape. Too many expedition books, and other exploratory tales, stay dull because their author blindly copies from diaries – a temptation all too easy to fall into when time is short and distractions many. To bring a tale alive, he has to relive it in his own mind, which means to recreate.

I do not mean that diaries are of no use. They are invaluable. In everyday life, as distinct from prison life, the pressure of events is too great, and time too short, to allow a full recall of detail without written notes. At Chieti, we were plagued with every kind of distraction, but in essence they were more physical than mental. The point is that a writer has good cause to refer to diaries: but then, memory refreshed, he should firmly put them aside and never copy.

In thus writing I gained a great benefit. I learned from sheer necessity to live in the mind rather than the body. In the next two years that would become of still greater need and value – even though it did, ironically, earn me a reputation for absent-mindedness.

Others were taking an opposite course and trying for freedom by physical escape. The tunnellers had to learn by trial and error, being still novices. Their beginner's mistake was to start indoors – the very first place that searchers looked, and their search was thorough. The best part of a year's tunnel work was thus lost. Many escapes were made by other means. Some of our men discovered in themselves talents for theft, forgery and tailoring: which, developed as real crafts, produced good Italian identity papers and clothing. One man walked through the main gate unchallenged, dressed as an Italian officer. Escaping blossomed into a summer of liberty-on-the-run, for which they paid on recapture with short periods of solitary confinement. Their reports were all similar. On the Abruzzi and Apennine hill farms, help and shelter were freely given by generous women, but not by their menfolk. Maybe the men felt more protective of family safety – safety less from escapes than from fascist retribution. All reports were consistent on one point – Italians' cruelty to animals other than human.

As our guards' wrath mounted at frequent escapes, so too we were downgraded to animal status. They already dreaded morning roll calls as much as we, and made us pay with long hours on parade in the sun while they searched for tunnels, and in the end found them. Revolts in our standing ranks brought the inevitable clubbings and threats to cut off Red Cross parcels. Such short-term harassment brought us long-term benefit.

The Italians were seriously worried by their nation-wide escape problem. Our nuisance value was high, for the Eighth Army had by May taken the whole of North Africa east to Algeria, bringing Italy itself under threat. Its army and police forces could no longer afford the man-hours spent on countryside searches; they became keen to distract us from escape by provision of all means for our entertainment. We were allowed an abundance of writing paper and musical instruments. We soon had a good orchestra, concerts, music lessons, and classes on Italian language and literature run by their own officers, one of whom gave daily readings of Dante's *Divine Comedy*. The English translation I had once read had left me cold – and Dante stone dead. But read in Italian, of which I knew hardly a word, the beauty of the sound reached even me. I no longer had to be told that this was one of the world's great poets.

The Eighth Army too was winning our respect. With American forces they invaded Sicily in July. Mussolini resigned. Our camp guards suddenly discovered that after all they were our friends. Morning roll calls markedly shortened. I had even more time to write and decided to start transferring my manuscript from toilet paper to exercise books, now suddenly made available. At that point my plan was interrupted. A newly published book arrived from home, *Grey Eminence* by Aldous Huxley. My mother had a genius for picking books. This was one of Huxley's best, and its third chapter of particular interest to me, titled 'The Religious Background'. For the first time in my life I read a good summary of Europe's and Asia's mystical tradition, and the plain common sense of it all appealed to me. Its ideal goal was given practical means of proof. My exploratory instinct sharpened. From another angle if one looked on the world as a desert – and it never looked more like that than in 1943 – and me as a thirsty wanderer, then my finding of mystical theology was like stumbling into an oasis. Its water was pure. I drank.

The next thing we knew, Sicily had fallen, the Allies were into Italy's mainland, and the king in August sued for an armistice. When he surrendered in September, a festive air pervaded Campo 21. It seemed no longer worth escaping or, for me, writing. We had only to wait. We knew nothing of German strength in North Italy. When Naples fell in early October, the German

Command determined that British prisoners must not be allowed to join the invaders. They dropped parachute troops on Chieti and took the camp.

We had time only to seize our most treasured possession, our library. Each prisoner was given a few books to carry – and I, of course, had those thick wads of toilet paper stuffed into my battledress tunic – then we were marched to the railway station at Pescara. Cattle trucks were lined up and waiting. We were loaded on, forty men to each just enough room to lie down, if we arranged ourselves carefully. Air and light came from a tiny window at which we took turns at viewing the countryside. The train headed north, halting every few hours to allow prisoners out. Those who were caught short – and a few had diarrhoea or other illnesses – had our sympathy but were not popular. This journey lasted four days and covered 440 miles. We had no idea where we were going, except north.

I had the good fortune to be at the window when we topped the Brenner Pass to Austria at 4,500 feet, and saw the name. The RAF were bombing the line somewhere ahead. They missed, but stopped the train for an hour. The long descent of the Inn Valley had everyone clamouring to view the mountain scene. We hoped we might stop at or near Innsbruck, but no, on we went by night through Munich. Early in the morning, the long train jolted to its final stop. We tumbled wearily out of the trucks to find ourselves in Bavaria, at Moosburg.

11 To Bavaria and Bohemia

MOOSBURG CONCENTRATION CAMP

In Bavaria we found ourselves in a concentration camp, not a normal prison camp. It held 20,000 Poles, Russians, Italians, French, and others, each nationality to its own compound, divided one from another by high, wire fencing. The euphemism 'ethnic cleansing' had not yet been coined, but its practice well established under Hitler's doctrine of the Herrenvolk (Master race). Clear distinction was made at Moosburg in the treatment accorded each national group. We British, thought to be closest to German Aryan stock, were housed in dirty wooden huts, but the Poles and Russians were given neither shelter nor bedding, but herded like cattle in their open compounds, rain or shine, snow or frost.

We did not feel privileged, or not on our first night. After the relative cleanliness, space, and air of Chieti, we were dismayed. The triple-tiered bunks, jam-packed, held one dirty blanket a piece. We lived like rats in a slum. At night, the bed bugs came out of the woodwork in myriads and crawled all over us, as did fleas from the blankets and lice from the sack mattresses. At first we struck matches to hunt the bed bugs, but they were too many for us. Parasites preyed all over our bodies. After a week or two, we grew accustomed to their endless patter of feet, while envisaging death by a thousand bites.

Each dawn came as a benefaction. Breakfast was black bread and mint tea, dinner, potatoes and turnips. We never saw our Soviet neighbours fed, but they must have been given something. Nearly all were Asiatics of short and stocky build, faces hard and expressionless. They were the first men we had seen who looked subhuman. Was that their natural condition, or induced by long brutal treatment? We had no way of knowing, but suspected the latter. They were starving. Moved to pity, a few of us used to throw bread to them over the wire, while they fought for the scraps like wolves.

Their officers were western Russians of very different quality; they would take no food from us while their men starved. They were certainly no less well educated than we. One or two of us could speak Russian; they spoke good English. We were able to talk through the wire, mainly an exchange of news from the eastern and Italian fronts, but also on political issues. We told them that communism seemed to us impractical, because its goal – holding things in common, and sharing all work and its fruits for the common good – could not be realised short of man's spiritual regeneration. There was no sign of that happening, least of all in their own country where religion had been cast out to bolster materialism. They in turn deplored our system of privately owned capital as leading inevitably to utter selfishness, in rejection of the Christian belief we professed so hypocritically. We showed no more prospect of a spiritual regeneration than they, for we and they had both put the cart before the horse.

We felt on surer ground when we turned to forms of government, and to the freedoms conferred by democracy as against the negativities of dictatorship, citing as one simple example our own people's freedom of travel, which we knew the Russians were denied. But they deplored that too, visualising disorder. To them it seemed a kind of chaos, in which populations could rise up and mill around. They failed to understand how it worked.

We spent over two months at Moosburg. Overcrowding had stopped all further work on my book. In November's snow and cold, night temperatures outside dropped to around –10 °C , and to –15 °C in December. Numbed by cold, we could not understand how the Poles and Russians survived. No Red Cross inspectors were allowed to set foot in Moosburg, nor were Red Cross parcels delivered, nor could letters be sent or received. The camp did not exist; not in terms of the Geneva Convention or international record. For us British, it turned out to be a transit camp. But if it were so for the others too, we saw no sign of new intakes replacing old, unless transfers were made at night.

Our release from that grim cage came in early December 1943. Once again we were suddenly herded into cattle trucks, and in full squalor were trundled eastward for three days. We ended at a station called Mahrisch Trubau in Bohemia in the western province of Czechoslovakia.

MARISCH TRUBEAU: OFLAG VIII F

Our new camp, Oflag VIII F was a former Czech barracks, set in snow-covered, lightly wooded country. Its dozen well-spaced building blocks, each of two storeys with big double-glazed windows that lit the top floor dormitories, were set in a wide compound within the usual perimeter fence with sentry towers and electrified wire.

Formed into columns, we were ushered into a big bare hall, where a dozen Gestapo agents waited behind desks flanked by guards. Each one of us had name and number taken, and then was frisked, photographed and fingerprinted. My personal search at once disclosed those thick wads of toilet paper. The Gestapo were galvanised. This was something new. They hurried me away to a smaller room, on whose bare boards stood a table and chair. Two agents came with me. One sat behind the table, on which he spread my paper; the other stood behind my back. Interrogation began. When I said what this manuscript was, my inquisitor looked down at the toilet wads and believed not a word. The fact that I had 'secreted it on my person' and not carried it openly aroused their worst suspicions. I tried to explain that I carried it under my tunic only for safe transport, and to leave my hands free – all dismissed as claptrap. Interrogation continued, its coldness deepened: were my papers not in fact a coded report of military intelligence picked up in Italy, or Austria, or Bavaria, or news garnered at Moosburg, or events noted en route between all these places? Had I planned to pass information of value to Czech patriots, or to escape with it to England? Or what? The questions came thick and fast without passionate rantings – tone of voice icy, the eyes hard. Whatever I said, they believed not a thing.

These were the first men I'd met able to put a shiver up my spine. Their facial expression was not mean or nasty, which might have implied some element of humanity. Gestapo agents seemed to be men from whom all good had been wrung out, leaving an animated corpse. My flesh crept. I had never before appreciated how much good there is in the common criminal. From this and our Moosburg experience, I began to understand why this war had to be fought. I had hitherto known as enemy only Rommel's Afrika Korps, which had my respect. The tank commander had won more than that from me. My experience with the Gestapo changed my attitude to war.

In the end, they had to let me go. Never again did I see the manuscript. Its loss hit me hard at the time, for the book had been virtually finished.

From the Gestapo we passed to washrooms, where we were given showers and soap to flush out body lice, and our clothes pressure steamed to kill off lice and fleas. Our quarters seemed palatial. The two-tiered bunks were uncrowded, the floors wooden, topped with green linoleum, the compound was spacious, even for 1,500 prisoners. Our library had a whole room to itself and space to grow. Exercise books were plentiful, together with pens and soluble ink tablets. We settled in and organised ourselves. We even had trestle tables and benches, rooms for group study, group debate, worship – Sunday services were packed out – and silence rooms to which we might go and think. I was determined that I would write my book all over again.

Seeing the opportunities offered, we began to plan life as a university. Among our number were several who held chairs at British and Commonwealth universities, and many lecturers. Between them, they managed to organise a curriculum of higher education embracing a great range of subjects: mathematics, engineering, physics, chemistry, biology, anatomy, medicine, psychology, history, literature in all its branches, music, philosophy, theology, comparative religion, and the languages of Europe and Asia, including a score of Indian dialects. Correspondence with universities in the UK was quickly established, so that several subjects could be studied to the standards of first professional examinations. This work had every encouragement from our German hosts. They allowed every facility in vain hope of turning our thoughts from escape.

In trying to cater thoroughly for mind and soul, we did not altogether neglect our bodies. The only feast we were able to plan in Czechoslovakia was that for our first Christmas – on an individual basis, food being insufficient for any communal spread. The German diet allowed us turnip and potatoes, a slice of black bread, acorn coffee and mint tea. Once a week we chewed a tiny square of horsemeat – the carcasses were delivered whole, to be butchered and cooked by our own men in the camp kitchen. These meagre rations were bulked out by the arrival of Red Cross parcels, from which we each kept an empty tin can, converted to use as a cooking stove, and fuelled with husbanded cardboard, or wood-shavings, so that we could brew a hot drink or heat food as occasion arose. After Moosburg, we were permanently hungry, but not yet starving. We could positively enjoy potato peelings, or the cheese rinds thrown out from the German garrison's kitchen: when popped in hot fat the rinds became titbits. Washing up was made easy, for plates and cutlery were first licked clean. We made our Christmas puddings by daily saving up of bread scraps, to which we added, from the food parcels, condensed milk, egg powder, jam and butter. The ingredients blended well when boiled up in a cloth bag. Memories of steamed puddings at home maybe contributed to the Christmas pudding sensation. Bohemia, after all, had been the country of Good King Wenceslas.

Our best-fed prisoner was a tame kestrel with a broken wing. It belonged to a slim, fair haired subaltern named Summers, who had brought it through the desert battles tucked inside his bush shirt, and through Moosburg inside his battledress tunic – kept alive on a share of his own rations, plus camp rodents. The bird survived the Gestapo search, neck unwrung, because birds of prey were approved in this Land of the Eagle – and Goering famously kept a falcon. The Prison Commandant was enchanted. Each day after roll call, he marched with pompous tread through the main gate, holding on a string from his forefinger a tin of dead mice, which he personally delivered to Summers' kestrel. Germans, we found, were as kind to animals as Italians were cruel – a rule not usually observed when they dealt with humans. Summers' kestrel was highly unpopular with his dormitory mates. Its droppings fouled the room; so at Mahrisch Trubau he was given exclusive use of a dead-end corridor, where he and his kestrel could live happily together.

Prisoners' eccentricities were endless, and not only tolerated but given scope. Their development helped to lighten our lives. Thus I soon discovered that our numbers included several mountaineers. Why not, I wondered, set up a mountaineering club? Among them were Tommy Wedderburn, a younger brother of my friend Sandy Wedderburn of the Mountain Commandos; and Alistair Cram, a lawyer well known to me by name as a member of the Scottish Mountaineering Club and the Alpine Club. My first encounter with Cram had come in May 1938 – 500 feet up the *Clachaig Gully* in Glen Coe. He was attempting the first ascent with a strong English party. They were ahead of my own team, which included Dunn and MacAlpine. Defeated after several attempts at the Great Cave pitch – the gully's crux – they allowed me to go through. When I climbed the pitch, they abandoned the gully. The extraordinary character of the man was not discovered by me until now. Like me, he had been captured in the Western Desert and had already spent fourteen months in Italy. He had gained fame (plus a Military Cross at the war's end) by making thirteen escapes – a phenomenal record, which says much for Italian long-sufferance. He owed success to a couple of outstanding qualities. First he had a complete mastery of the German, French and Italian languages – such was his fluency that he could pose as a French worker, speaking German or Italian with a French accent, or vice versa. Secondly he was imbued with the conviction than an officer's duty was to escape, and this conviction became an obsession. Thus toughly resourceful, he had spent more time roaming the Apennines and their coastal strips than in prisons, where he paid due penalty in weeks of solitary confinement.

We pinned a paper to the camp's notice board, announcing the formation of a mountaineering club: qualification, preparedness to deliver a talk on mountains. Soon we had a score of members drawn from Scottish, English, Canadian, South African and New Zealand climbers. They gave good quality performances, since no time could be spent on slides, but much on preparation. At this very time, the British Mountaineering Council was being formed in Britain. We might well have joined had communications been better. But 1,000-bomber raids were destroying land-links, not to mention cutting our food supplies.

Our more serious studies proceeded apace. My own choice was English literature and poetry, psychology, and philosophy, but not more, since I was writing a book. One morning, when I was strolling in the compound, a young English officer came up to me. He looked as if he might be twenty-four. I had never seen him before.

'I've seen you around the last day or two,' he said. 'My name's Herbert Buck. Indian Army. It seems to me you're ready to start on the Mystic Way. Would you let me give you instruction?'

Startled, about to give an abrupt 'No', I took one hard look into his eyes. They were lively and friendly eyes, above all intelligent. With no further hesitation, I heard myself say, 'Yes, I will', amazed at myself.

He smiled. 'Meet me tomorrow morning at the door of B Block. I'll book a room if it's free.'

At that moment, I knew no need to ask more, nor did he say more. He walked off without another word. I returned straight to my own block feeling a little dazed. As I climbed upstairs to the dormitory, I became aware of an extraordinary sense of joy. It suffused mind and body. This was not just because I knew that for once in my life I had taken right action, or turned in the right direction. I had stepped out of time into timelessness. Never afterwards could I say when this exaltation began or how long it lasted, or when it ended (except in an approximate way). I remember seeing through the windows the barbed wire fence with its sentry towers, and the prisoners in the compound, all and each transfigured by a beauty that glowed through them, engulfing all as if from another plane. Its intensity had a new dimension, so that never afterwards could I bring myself to speak of it, or write down the experience until now, when I know that my life is nearing its end. 'Later' that day, I knew myself back in Mahrisch Trubau.

On mountains, I had several times in the past been keyed up by the suspense of a hard climb to a brief relaxation at the top, when I'd suddenly been able to 'live in the present moment', and to have along with it an awareness of a more real world underlying the material. But here in the prison camp, without stimulation of suspense, or unusual beauty of scene, but hearing only a few terse words from a stranger, I seemed to have entered a timeless 'now', of much higher degree than before. My hold on it had not lasted, but this time I came away with a sure knowledge. The eternal world 'is'. Our material world is plainly real too: each inheres in the other; the finite within the infinite. The one embraces both.

When I met Herbert Buck in the morning, he introduced me to a company of half a dozen other men, whom he had unerringly chosen to study the Perennial Philosophy, at first in general terms – its truth inherited by men of all nations through all ages. We went on in following days and months to its practice, through which the teaching is wide open to verification by anyone ready to act, that is to meet its conditions of self-forgetfulness.

The practical approach to that starts with discursive meditation, long continued and accompanied by stripping away of everything that hinders and obscures the soul's vision, or leads away from the goal, which is the unitive knowledge of the Infinite One, to whom mankind has given innumerable names, summarised as God. The union is a paradox, free of pantheism – a union in love, truth, inner vision, and not in identity.

The important point in the lead that Buck gave is this: he made us sit down and think, step by step, until meditation became habitual. This practice is vital. Much reading about it is of little or no value; a waste of time if not followed by the act. Meditation with full use of the reasoning process has to give way at long last to contemplation, an alert stillness of mind that allows its conclusive leap into the spiritual realm beyond time and space. There are no short cuts, no easy ways, no let-offs, but many falls and defeats, therefore a need of over-riding commitment.

Letters from prison, say more of my thinking, during the steadily more austere period of incarceration (see letter at the end of this chapter).

The arrival of books in large quantity gave invaluable help to all our camp's study groups. We eventually had a library of more than 8,000 volumes. As the ground cleared of snow, our classes were held in the open air when weather allowed, which was most of the time. Spreading our blankets on the ground, we sat with our parcel-boxes beside us to hold books and paper. This general practice was seized upon by our engineer escapers, ever alert to assess opportunities. No longer were they novices. Mistakes of the Italian past were not repeated. No tunnels were now started indoors, but instead right out in the open compound. This could be done by using a site not directly overseen from a sentry station. There were several such points. A first tunnel was thus started at a site nearest to the perimeter fence. A study group blanket was spread. A hole was gradually excavated alongside while a scout kept watch. The earth went into empty food boxes. At any German approach, the blanket would be drawn over the hole and the group resume studies. When the day's tunnelling was done, a trap door with an earth top would be placed over the hole and smoothed down to invisibility.

This simple device was much less clumsy than the wooden horse used in another camp, which demanded hours of jumping. Ours drew no attention.

Disposal of the dug earth had been provided for by obtaining German permission for a large kitchen garden, for which they gave us spades and seeds. The tilled soil gave perfect disposal beds for the tunnel soil. That first tunnel was soon dug to end under the perimeter fence. Our radio receiver was there plugged into the German's electric feeder cable. Our engineers had built the radio from parts smuggled in, or purchased by bribe, or made from scraps.

QUESTIONS

Questions
Falling on a sea in storm;
Finding no space for answers.

Questions
Falling on a limpid pool
Finding answers spreading clear.

Questions falling and seeking
Questions falling and finding;
Questions falling and ending ...

For answer is in leaving
And answer is in losing;
And answer is in loving

Questions falling and ending …

For answer is in seeing
And answer is in hearing;
And answer is in being

Questions falling and ending …

As a stream's quiet pausing
As a summer wind's listening;
As a singing sun's rising

Questions falling and ending …

Answers like waves of the sea
Answers surging and breaking;
Answers leaping and lighting …

Questions falling and ending.

We published the BBC News daily thereafter on the camp notice board – avidly read by guards and prisoners alike. The German officers, and two Gestapo agents still on duty, were enraged. Their own people were not allowed to listen to British broadcasts. They searched the barracks daily for weeks, but with no success. Every building had its floors and roofs, basements, walls, ventilation shafts and drains examined inch by inch, all in vain. The news we were getting was not such as Goebels and company could abide us hearing – 1,000-bomber raids over Germany; whole armies defeated at Leningrad; and all ten divisions of their Eighth Army destroyed in the Ukraine.

Encouraged by the proven success of the trapdoor system in the compound, the engineers began full-time work on escape tunnels. While these went ahead, our escapers' group promoted faster means through their Arts Departments: forgery, theft, and bribe. Each Red Cross parcel contained a tin of coffee. The Germans had none. It commanded high prices on their black market. Some of the older German guards had been found willing in exchange to smuggle in a few items of real value, like radio valves, small tools and old identity papers. Our skilled forgers were able to produce copies of the latter, good enough to meet inspection. Our first escapes had already begun through the main gate by stowaway on German trucks. The morning roll calls, when escapes were normally discovered, caused pandemonium, with long hours of punitive standing in the compound regardless of weather, and disruption to our studies. The usual clubbings ensued. While many escapes were made over the next several months, none had final success. All escapers were in due course returned to their camp of origin, alive if caught by the army; dead if caught by Gestapo, who sent ashes back in a box.

I continued work on my book, screwed to a new frame of mind by our worsening condition, quite different from that of Chieti. Those 1,000-bomber raids were taking a heavy toll of Germany's rail and road systems. The feeding of the Reich's own people had priority. Red Cross parcel deliveries dwindled away. Our hunger intensified. I no longer believed that I would climb mountains again, but felt impelled to get the truth of them on to paper. Nor did I want, as before, to write specifically about hard climbs, or to enlighten anyone about techniques and winter severities. I wrote because I must, shedding the twin humbugs of understatement of difficulty and exaggeration of danger and likewise of reticence about feeling for beauty. The whole mountain scene was vivid in mind and in detail. I had learned to ignore distractions of noise and movement, and to shut them out. I now had good paper and could write fast. I had a mind to say what I'd found of beauty and delight, effort and fun. I would try for truth only, and while knowing that it could never be said, still I would try.

The Gestapo's destruction of my original draft became the greatest benefit they had unwittingly bestowed on me. The second draft, which I believed at the time to be final, was finished on my thirtieth birthday in March 1944. It was the day of the war's heaviest air raid. Four thousand bombers had dropped 4,000 tons on Frankfurt in half an hour. The Russian Army in the Ukraine, having cleared the Crimea, were now sweeping west across the river barriers into Romania.

The news of these events, pinned to our notice board, brought more searches by the guards. I no longer carried my manuscript on my body, for random Gestapo interrogations continued. The guards had at last tumbled to the possibility that a tunnel might be starting in the compound (several were under way). They began probing the ground with iron bars, but failed to strike the right spots.

In June we heard that Rome had fallen. A few days later came the greatest moment of all – the Allied invasion of Normandy. We had difficulty in believing it could succeed. Our hopes of deliverance rested more firmly on the Russian Armies, now making such rapid advances into Poland and Romania. The waiting for news and more news seemed interminable. We applied ourselves to study as single-mindedly as we could, I more especially to those practical aspects of mystical theology. I felt astonished at the mental resources of my fellow prisoners. Mealtime talk hit even lower grades than in former battalion mess tents with hardly a noun uttered free of its adjectival prefix. But the study groups were of high quality, the lectures stimulating, the knowledge displayed quite out of the ordinary, far wider than I would have dreamt. These men could and did think vigorously. Only a tiny minority lay on their bunks, stared at the ceiling, and went slowly mad. Small gambling schools, playing for high stakes – sometimes £100 to £1,000 placed on the turn of a card – occupied much of some other men's time. Debts were pledged to be honoured on release. The vast majority applied their energies to giving their knowledge to others, or to receiving from others at all levels. My admiration for my fellow prisoners grew continuously over those years. Two important things I learned were never to judge men by their outward appearance, or by casual talk. Both can be utterly misleading. Nearly all have high qualities or real merits, hidden until educed by circumstance or friendship. They constantly astounded me. Those prison years were the most profitable of my life. They did not seem like it at the time – lack of food, squalor, prolonged physical discomfort, danger to life, all tended to make us identify ourselves with our bodies, and to make us feel hard done by. We derided 'plain living and high thinking' while actually practising it. The level on which we were involuntarily alive and active identified our real selves as spiritual. The body had to be kept going for plain practical reasons, but not even that could be done unless our spiritual-intellectual lives were nourished too. So we set about doing exactly that – while forbearing to express it in such terms. I seemed to be an exception to the general rule: I was most positively thinking of it – although not thinking of time spent on spiritual explorations as 'profitable'. One of T.S. Eliot's lines from the *Four Quartets* always stuck in my mind: 'We shall not cease from exploration.'

The best of all times to start exploring on whatever level is while one is young enough to travel the great distance needed, or to aspire to the great height. All the energies of a lifetime are wanted for that. The age-old symbol of the mountain could not be bettered. Maybe I felt that so keenly being still on the bottom slopes.

Years had been wasted but I had started – albeit late – and, despite the outward circumstances of my prison life, a facet of the present experience was a sense of well-being and peace. Somehow, I was happy.

Coming down late
I race against dark;
Trip over stars
Catch at the moon
Plunge in its beams
My eyes held

While my feet
Set the mountain running …

Breathing and breathing
My heart a drum's beat
I rein in my steps;
Feel the night
Spin still

Hear the silence
Of things

Find its place.

I had thought my book finished in March, but on re-reading found many flaws. It is always very hard to find unpretentious words for simple ideas. I spent some time each day polishing (itself dangerous), blue pencilling, extending. Nearly everyone's main occupation was reading, study, or teaching. Escapes had died away. The Senior British Officer had banned them. Even Cram had his usual activities frustrated. This was not simply because those who did escape and fell into Gestapo hands were beaten to death and incinerated – a rule to which we knew of no exceptions – but overridingly because we had several tunnels excavated under the camp's electrified fence. Their use had to be strictly reserved for chance of a mass escape at the end. The Czech patriots had warned us that the SS were gunning down prisoners in camps further east to forestall release by the advancing Russian armies, which were now threatening Hungary. While speculating thus whether our own release might be forestalled, we suddenly received German orders: pack up. In three days you will be moved to a new camp. Where, they would not say. Our movement order was otherwise unexpectedly civilised – our big library would go with us.

Once again we were packed into cattle trucks. Our journey went westward.

The train was so slow and halts so long that prisoners were thrice allowed out on to the line. One such chance of escape presented an irresistible temptation to Alistair Cram. Before we had crossed the Czech frontier into Germany, he and Tommy Wedderburn contrived to get away unseen. In face of the known Gestapo threat, that was an act of boundless audacity. I never expected to see them again.

At the end of a complicated, three-day journey, we were delivered to a former Luftwaffe barracks in Saxony, outside Brunswick on the great north German plain.

EXTRACTS FROM LETTERS TO FAMILY AND FRIENDS AT HOME

Letters to my family were reassuring:

31 August 1943, Chieti – to my sister Margaret
... You sound most alarmed about me. Pray, lie back, and take it easy – how can I send articles or describe prison camps in face of censorship. My health is no worse than hitherto, indeed vastly better.

12 August 1944, Brunswick – to Margaret
... There seems to be no satisfying you regarding myself. When I say I am happy and thoroughly well, which is the truth, you say you are alarmed! Be sensible. I have not lost my reason, but all worries, anxieties and frustrations. I think you will agree that that is not to be deplored. Best wishes on your birthday.

24 September 1944, Brunswick – to Margaret
The mysticism I follow is that of the Vedanta Sutras, Lao Tse, Christ, Buddha, Plato etc. They are one and the same, but frequently stress different aspects of reality which confuses men of narrow vision. The goal is service of mankind, not withdrawal. The fruits are an undivided mind, inner stillness, self-realisation, and a fullness of life that I never believed possible. The fulfilment of life's purpose will be found in oneness with reality.

But the different 'outward circumstances' of prison life are glimpsed in letters to friends:

September 1942, Chieti – to Archie MacAlpine
Many thanks for sending invalid parcel. Food is as plentiful as on *Garrick's Shelf.*

February 1945, Brunswick – to Ted Zenthon, thanking him for a letter and with hopes of climbing together again:
After this experience I have little hope of climbing severes again. I am literally a skeleton but very well in mind and spirit.

Inner and outer weather

12 Brunswick

Oflag 79 was secluded, screened on all sides from open country by conifer woodland. Its dozen stone buildings lay well spread in a big compound. Their white painted walls, roofed in red tiles, looked immaculately clean, even attractive had they only enjoyed a more open prospect. Instead, the trees shut us in too closely. The compound had the usual perimeter fence topped by sentry boxes.

In July, as soon as we had settled in, our tunnel engineers set to work, aided as before by our open-air study groups. Before they had time to plug the rebuilt radio into the electrified fence, we were receiving the latest war news from an influx of new prisoners, now including Americans, taken on the Western Front. Paris fell in late August. Brunswick had brought us within easy reach of our joint air forces. Their 1,000-bomber raids, long since unleashed, had now become daily features across the Saxony plain. RAF intelligence must have been good. Their pilots quickly knew our whereabouts. In all night-time raids on Brunswick, the leading aircraft ringed the camp with flares, and the main force bombed outside it. The daylight raids by the US Air Force put us at much more serious risk. They kept above 30,000 feet and off-loaded at random. Their waste of Allied bomb production seemed prodigious, and to little purpose, since the Germans appeared to be not intimidated, and the destruction small for the tonnage dropped. The night raids by the RAF were of altogether different quality. Targets were pinpointed, the devastation awesome. The bombing of England, even of London, Coventry, or Clydebank, was by comparison nothing to the fate of Germany's cities. Their people's fortitude seemed to us incredible, until we discovered why.

I now carried my manuscript under my tunic day and night, out of fear of bomb blast. Any risk of loss from Gestapo search had gone. They were off to more congenial tasks – a nation-wide purge following the June attempt to assassinate Hitler. Rommel had been involved. When I heard later of the manner of his death I felt sorry. He alone among German generals had the touch of greatness. His loss of North Africa had been directly due to the diversion of guns and armour to the Russian Front, where all had been lost. We were allowed to read the German newspapers. Each time a general surrendered on that front, public notice appeared of vengeance exacted on his family and friends. The Gestapo's ruthless cruelty in control of their own people alone kept Germany in the war. They were more feared than Allied bombers or the Russian armies.

In the course of our final nine months we rarely glimpsed sun by day or stars by night. The skies were obscured by the pall of dust and smoke arising from the burning cities all around. Brunswick, Magdeburg, Hanover, Bremen, and most others including Berlin, were engulfed. One daylight raid by Flying Fortresses wiped out our German garrison. But we were unaware of it. Crouching in the cellars, almost deafened by the long-drawn scream of hurtling bombs, we had little thought except for our skins. When we emerged, we could see nothing through the wall of flaming trees around the barracks. We might have walked out of Oflag 79 but were stupefied. By the time the smoke had cleared and the dust settled, an emergency guard had been moved in. They were all old men, their hearts not in the war.

Red Cross parcels had long since been cut off. We had black bread, but the potato and turnip rations were cut to a minimum. We were truly starving. The guards no longer dared send their Alsatians into the compound at night. We had commandos in plenty trained to kill. Any dog, and cats too if they strayed into camp, went straight into the pot and their skins would be hung over the wire before morning. The disappearance of dogs helped our tunnel-makers, who worked day and night in relays. The guards, failing as always to find entrance indoors, but suspecting their presence through five years' bitter experience, began as before to probe the compound with iron bars. Our good luck held.

One day a big Red Cross van came through the gates. A great cheer went round the camp. Food! We could hardly contain our joy and streamed out from the building blocks to witness the unloading. That van was stacked from floor to roof with rolls of toilet paper. It held not a crumb of food. The occasion seemed perfect for a good cartoonist, but none rose to it. Real hunger is not funny.

One September morning after roll call, I heard that Alistair Cram and Tommy Wedderburn had arrived back in camp. Astounded, I went at once to see them. Cram's old bold self was no more. He looked, as indeed he was, on the point of nervous breakdown. Wedderburn had a calmer self-control but spoke not at all. His eyes had an uncharacteristic dullness, reminding me of a hurt animal that has lost the gloss from its fur. Cram told me the story.

The pair had succeeded in reaching Prague, where they had tried over many days to make contact with Czech patriot forces. They were betrayed to the Gestapo who, catching them in civilian dress, believed them spies. Their fate should have been sealed, had not Cram been able to claim so strongly in such excellent German that they were escaped British prisoners. Smitten by curiosity, the Gestapo despatched them to Dachau for full and final interrogation. It was one of the worst concentration camps, notorious for its atrocities, 30,000 prisoners died in it. There Cram fiercely maintained his claim. The Gestapo continued in disbelief, judging that no one of Cram's linguistic ability would have been wasted on desert fighting. He, and Wedderburn too, must be Secret Service or SOE agents. Ensnared by their own mix of incredulity and curiosity, they sent their captives' names, alleged army numbers, and fingerprints to Berlin with the query, 'Are these escaped British prisoners of war?'

Meanwhile they were held at Dachau, interrogated day and night under bright lights, forced to watch the torture of Czech women to bring disclosure of their menfolk's whereabouts in the patriot bands, then returned to their cells but denied sleep while Jews, screaming in neighbouring cells, were beaten with rubber truncheons. The truncheon bearers would then visit Cram and Wedderburn and stand around menacingly, before hauling them off again to interrogation rooms. After four weeks of this hell, a written command came from Berlin. It stated that Cram and Wedderburn were indeed escaped British prisoners, ending: 'Return to Oflag 79m, Braunsweig'. In face of the direct order, the Gestapo had to comply. No other of our freedom-bidders had ever come back from the Gestapo alive. That was Alastair Cram's last and most lucky escape.

From first-hand accounts heard at Dachau, they were able to confirm the stories of the gas chambers at Auschwitz and of Poland's other camps, of which we had vaguely heard and tended to dismiss as war propaganda. In our Western Desert days, we could not have reconciled such reports with our respect for the fighting quality of the Africa Korps. Having since met Himmler's Gestapo and SS, we now knew better.

Alistair Cram was one of the toughest of our prison camp characters (and they included men like David Stirling, CO of the Long Range Desert Group). Tommy Wedderburn, on the other hand, did not appear to be tough at all. Why then, I wondered, had both been able to bear a full month or more of torture. They both had the same background, public school and Cambridge, but were of markedly contrasting character. Part of the explanation could be that, while Cram's single minded obsession with duty had given him unusual fortitude, Wedderburn had the more fully relaxed attitude, typical of the Oxbridge undergraduate of his day, in which duty could be shrugged off as humbug, but was in fact done, when it came to the crunch, in almost casual manner. Maybe that gave him a resilience that matched Cram's toughness.

Dachau had left Cram in no condition for further prison life. After a few days, the German Commandant had to send him off into the care of Brunswick's mental hospital. On the night he arrived there, the town suffered yet another 1,000-bomber raid, in which the hospital was hit. I heard nothing of his fate until after the war, and had thought him dead, until his name reappeared on the SMC's membership list, revealing his appointment as a judge in East Africa. Many years later I heard that when his Brunswick hospital had been hit in the air raid, he had made his final escape, and this time reached the Allied lines. He and I never met again. I honour his memory. The man was indomitable.

The demonic evil of the Nazi regime made me jettison my old way of thinking on war's lunacy. When I had seen the carnage of Western Desert battlefields, I resented having part in that lunacy. By the time I arrived in Italy, I had come close to developing conscientious objections. Not until meeting the Gestapo face to face in Czechoslovakia had I begun to understand fully what was happening to Poles, Jews, Czechs, Russians, and to the German people too if 'deviant'. I knew at last that this war was not only right but inevitable.

My second thoughts having quite overridden my first, I tried to look at them in the light of reason. It is an axiom that among our natural instincts the most basic is self-preservation and, while normal for self-defence, it is brought to full power in war. In everyday life, when all operate normally, we know self-preservation as the negative instinct, warding off harm – useful even against the elements, but resisting everything that deprives us of health, happiness, strength, dignity, and all the intangible things of inner vision that we call good, or beautiful, or true: all that constitutes the full life.

Man as an individual has the natural right to resist all deprivation of life as has a nation. The so-called negative instinct therefore has a positive aspect. Our very health as persons or social groups depends on possession of the inherent tension between the negative and positive instincts. They impart to our lives the elasticity of strength that characterises health and best protects us from ills. If that negative, resistant aspect is weak, it points to corruption, whether in a man or society. In short, a spiritual disease. The first signs of it appear in a diminished sensitivity to good, justice, beauty – just as in plants a loss of elasticity in their delicate parts points to some inward robbery: they become flaccid, then collapse. Man's moralities likewise. There is such a thing as a 'right intolerance'. The Nazis had a wrong intolerance. Examples of the right are these: that where there is no intolerance of wrong in ethics, there is no virtue; when there is no intolerance of falsity in religion, there is no conviction; where there is no one-sidedness in holding political ideals, there is no probity, or no loyalty. To all the virtues (inherent strengths) of character, there is need of that elasticity given by the negative instinct under rational control. Lack of control betrays all the prospective good. Positive control subdues negative emotion sufficiently to allow it to power right action. It is the right act to right ends that shows greatness in men or nations. The Nazi intolerance was the perverse kind, to be abhorred.

Man's natural right to violent defence arises only where there is no other way to right intolerable wrongs. That right includes first strike to forestall an enemy's attack. It should never be used while other means lie open. When they don't – when no peaceful way remains open to stop tyranny's injustice, or to establish order in which men can be free to live fulfilling lives, then war becomes the last remedy. Mankind cannot live above a bestial state without ideals: they alone make life worth the living. I had never realised how sure that could be until I had seen and heard with my own eyes and ears the iniquities of Nazi Germany, and what loss of truth, justice, good, honour and beauty can do to degrade men. Without these intangible ideals and the acts they alone can generate, our lives are not worth perpetuating. The war of last resort should never be shirked. This one I now knew had to be fought, regardless of all loss to life and property: far better to be dead than submit to rampant evil, or ever see it prevail in Britain or any other brother nation. Of all the questions ever asked by man, the most ignorant has been Cain's: 'Am I my brother's keeper?' That acme of separate self-love is evil's real root.

I respect the sincerity of those who believe that all kinds of violent defence are wrong in all circumstances. But their ideal is impractical, corrupt in giving inadvertent support to destructive evils. These can be ended only by practical ideals on which action is taken never by compromise with evil itself. A right intolerance is one of man's basic needs.

It is one of the paradoxes of our life on earth that our ideals, our impulses to good, depend for their strength on our impulses to evil, which we all share and even need, to grow strong in our moral responsibilities.

My opinion of right war was tested in October, when I heard by letter that my climbing friend Douglas Laidlaw had been killed piloting a plane over Germany. There was no man alive whom I held in higher regard. I kept in mind that his death was to earthly life and no more. Believing this, I had to regard my dismay, my grief at his loss, as irrational. But still I grieved. His death confirmed my conviction that it was not so much this war in itself that was evil as the Nazi gospel that made it – and which had to be opposed.

October had brought us a big influx of paratroopers from Arnhem in the Netherlands where they'd suffered a crushing defeat. Our hopes turned again to the Eastern Front, where the Russian Army, having taken Bulgaria, were now into East Prussia too. Their victories put all the greater strain on our tunnellers, for we had been getting confirmation from the east of SS massacres.

Greece was liberated that month, and Budapest invaded. But to us all, the invasion forces still seemed a long way off. The Allied Armies were held up at the Siegfried Line. Our tunnelling work had gone fast: we had close to a dozen running out to the perimeter wire. It seemed they might be finished just in time. We had been given too little food for too long. TB was rife. Our potato peelings and turnips were usually frosted. This was especially hard on our American prisoners, who, if they spoke truly, had been accustomed all their lives to substantial meals, inch-thick steaks, and between meals to an endless chewing of sweets. We could see their bodies deflate like punctured balloons. Some had been giving away their food in barter for cigarettes. Many of us knew that temptation of old, and had cut out smoking, revolted when we saw men retrieving thrown away fag ends. We dreamed of food day and night – dreamed not of bloody steaks but of dairy produce and green vegetables, of cheese, and milk, and lettuce. My fingernails were corrugated from vitamin lack, and my hair thinning. I had to conserve energy by cutting down walks in the compound, which made me dizzy, and by climbing slowly upstairs to reduce palpitations of the heart.

Christmas Eve that year was the most memorable of my life for one simple event.

Perhaps because for once there was no air raid, someone went outside into the compound and began to sing 'Silent Night'. A group quickly gathered round him, then more. Before long, all our 1,500 men were out there singing. The Germans too tumbled out of their guardroom and joined in – even the sentries at the perimeter towers. After all, it was their song. Its very volume brought the German staff out of the administration block. The beauty of the music seemed as if heard by us all for the first time. It filled our hearts. Our common folly had never seemed so clear.

During this last year, I had not once thought of myself as imprisoned. I lived on mountains and had the freedom of them. I felt able to wait on the SS machine-gunners, or whatever else fate held in store, without undue apprehension. We nearly all found our own way of doing this for we did prepare ourselves. For my own part, I found of value a lesson I'd learned from mountains in the company of Douglas Laidlaw among others and was to learn again and yet again: that skill, energy, foresight, strenuous planning, are by themselves quite insufficient for success or survival. One has always to make the best efforts one can, but having made them, they have still to be seconded by Providence. Since that was seen by me now as a law of life, I reckoned that efforts should be made hopefully, and the outcome resigned without any more self-concern to God's will. His energies alone bring human actions to their best ends, great or small. These may not be what we first imagined. There is no such thing as luck.

Nearly all of us at Brunswick appeared to recognise that truth, implicitly if not explicitly, in our calm acceptance of events. One of our number, Maxtone Graham, called a general meeting. He proposed that we pledge time and money, if we survived, to founding boys' clubs in the cities of Britain, and so help the nation's young men, so many of whom had lost fathers in war. This proposal was adopted, a signal of faith in our people's future. The Brunswick Boys' Clubs were in fact established after the war had ended.

Events in our last four months moved bewilderingly fast on all fronts. Russian armies swept south across Poland and west through Czechoslovakia. Our own Eighth Army broke through the Gothic Line into North Italy. On the Western Front, the US and British Armies smashed a way through the Siegfried

Line and were now east of the Rhine. Latterly, the Allies' advance came so fast through Saxony that the SS had no time or chance to get to us. Berlin fell to Russia on the last day of April – when shells from the American Ninth Army were whistling over our camp. The German officers fled. Some of the guards stayed, no longer guarding the gates. They had nowhere to go, and openly shed tears of relief that all was over. We seized their office records – our Gestapo photographs and fingerprints were given back to all prisoners. My own photograph, by strange chance, was the best (most flattering) I had seen of myself.

On May Day, the first American trucks cautiously nosed their way through the gates. Having assessed our condition, their commander lost no time in distributing one chocolate bar to each of us. I remember still that swift run of heat through the body as if from neat whisky. More solid food was dispensed gradually not because in short supply, but by good reason of our incapacity to digest richer diet. Our first white bread tasted like cake. It seemed almost too good for daily fare, but right for this celebration.

The Ninth Army was mercifully quick in getting us home.

On the fourth day we were told to pack up and be ready to leave on the morrow by air. We had only small kit bags, but I and many others now had suitcases, taken from the German quarters, to hold our favourite books and a few trophies, like those Gestapo records, and my manuscript of *Mountaineering in Scotland*. Next morning, Dakota troop carriers were lined up on the neighbouring airfield.

We gathered in the compound ready to go when a last order was given: 'Leave all suitcases. They will follow on a separate plane.'

In the hustle of imminent departure I nearly fell for it. But trust the US Air Force? Not on your life! I opened the case and took out my manuscript. I put it where it still belonged, under my tunic. The quick act was to change my life. I need hardly say that we never saw those suitcases again.

The Dakotas had a war weary, battered look. I felt uneasy when we scrambled aboard. Their day was done. Unease persisted through the flight home. My plane landed safely – but not so the one immediately following. It crashed on landing. Among the killed was Herbert Buck. He died only a few miles from his home near Camberley in Surrey. My meeting him in Mahrisch Trubau had been the most important personal experience of the war. And the most far-reaching. Others too might say the same. I felt the pang of loss, yet knew there should be no need. It seemed that the purpose of his life had been fulfilled in the prison camps. When that happens to a man, his time to go has come.

Herbert Buck, when I first met him, had appeared to me an enigma. I had seen at a glance that here was a man in the full flush of exuberant youth. This exuberance was not in speech or act – his voice rarely emotional, or his acts impulsive, meaning hasty as distinct from generous – but instead in the eyes.

Those eyes were alight with intelligence: I have never been able to remember their colour, for the first impression wiped out the superficial. I saw the man.

I gave intuitive trust. But, I had long since learned to be more wary of virtue than vice. Sin is something we know and share and allow for, but virtue – real moral strength – is known to few. Men who imagine they have it do not usually stand long to its testing, least of all if they rise to positions of power, when the seven devils inherit the swept room. I should not be surprised if Hitler in his early days thought he had it, for diabolism on his grand scale does require some high moral virtues – but without love and wisdom the result is evil. This general truth strikes home to the soul in time of war. Its dire results are then to be seen at every hand. Therefore in prison camps I turned a critical eye on Buck, alert for imposture. At the end, I could find no fault. He was all that his words and acts claimed. This man was whole – an occurrence so rare it arrests.

In the course of that afternoon, I exchanged the freedom of prison camps for the chains of civilisation. The war machine delivered us to a reception centre where we stripped, were briefly examined by medical officers, questioned, and given new underclothes and battledress, then issued with ration cards, travel warrants, and a £5 note to see us home. We were granted two months' leave.

My warrant was to Wales. My mother and sister were now sharing an old farmhouse in the Rheidol Valley above Cardigan Bay. I had therefore to spend a night in London, but could find no place in the West End that could take me in. All the hotels were full, and all the Services' clubs. The endless walking, climbing up stairs, knocking at doors, waiting, and getting turned away, sapped all my strength. After some hours, I grew too exhausted to try any more. I began to think of lying down in some doorway.

The MOs at the reception centre had under-estimated the weakening effect on men of three to six years' prison life, much of it on starvation diet. We could still not keep down a full meal, and I for one felt inept at foraging for myself amid the bustle of a big city. I had become out of touch with the ways to get around and do things for myself, or to get them done for me. Close to midnight, I made one last try at a Services' Club in Piccadilly. I had been there earlier and been turned away. The hall porter opened the door. He shook his head.

'I told you. It's no use. We're full. No room here.'

I exploded, 'This is plain crazy! I've been three years in prison camps – freed today and can't get a bed in my own country!'

His eyes widened: 'Come in. You should have said. We do have room.'

I discovered that all Services' Clubs in London, and most hotels, kept bedrooms in reserve for senior officers, who might want them at short notice. They had no real shortage.

THE POST-WAR WORLD

13 Home

When my train ran south down the Cardigan coast, I knew at last I was home – and dry, for the sun shone bright over the great bay, an augury of two months' fine weather to come. Neuadd farmhouse shared by my mother and sister, lay in the Rheidol Valley, near Aberystwyth. It was an astonishing experience to find myself once more in women's company. Having rarely seen a woman for nearly four years, unless at long distance, I had well-nigh forgotten what female kindness was like, its depth of personal warmth, and civilising influence. They in turn were learning how uncivilised men could become without them.

The farm had a big garden: an ideal place to recuperate. The indoor luxuries were overwhelming; carpets on the floors, tables at which to eat, a bed with a spring mattress and linen sheets; in the kitchen, the dairy produce of my dreams. It seemed like paradise; even more so outside in the early morning's air an air of intoxicating purity, free of dust and smoke and the reek of cordite; blue sky overhead, tall hollyhocks by the door, red squirrels scrambling in the trees, and dew sparkling on the morning grass. I rose early for that grass, walked deliberately through it in bare feet to savour its beaded wetness, then to swim in a burn's clear pool nearby.

Shortly after my homecoming Germany capitulated. I shared the Nation's instant explosion of thankfulness – one brief day's delusion. The end of war in Europe and Hitler's sordid death in his bunker had seemed to mark the end of a nightmare, which instead was to be indefinitely prolonged in new revelations of mass genocide: the horrors disclosed at Auschwitz, Belsen, Dachau; the massacres at Warsaw and Dresden; the ongoing war in the Pacific; Japan's atrocities. There seemed no end to human anguish, no end to man's unreadiness for the new power that science bestowed.

I took refuge in the present moment at Neuadd.

My sister Margaret now had three children: two boys named Roderick and Euan, aged six and five, and a daughter, Fiona, still younger. Roderick with jet-black hair and blue eyes was their ringleader. The boys had the boundless energy of young puppies, fun when behaving well, as on the day I arrived, but that peace was short-lived. Next day Euan, egged on no doubt by Roderick, stuffed a cushion down the lavatory bowl and pulled the plug to see what would happen. To my prison disciplined eyes, Margaret was too lenient. Their daily escapades might be just high spirited, but for the good of their souls the pair seemed to me in need of discipline.

On the outbreak of war, Archie MacAlpine had joined the Army Dental Corps. He had taken training in advanced dental surgery to cope with jaw wounds – at East Grinstead Hospital where McIndoe, the great plastic surgeon, repaired the terrible facial injuries to British airmen. Archie had become one of McIndoe's famous team, whose skills were giving new hope to broken up men.

Within a few days, he was back at Neuadd on leave. I rejoiced at seeing him again – and looked forward to his sons' first, wrath-incurring transgression. Nor did I have to wait long. I was in the garden next morning, sunning myself behind bushes that screened me from the two boys. We all saw Archie come out of the house and walk into the wooden garage. A bright idea struck the boys – what a good joke to lock Archie in! They ran to the garage, stealthily closed the doors, turned the key in the lock – and ran. Euan in high glee threw the key away into long grass. No one had seen me. I chose to lie low and watch. If I let Archie out, my mischievous nephews would too easily lose the wages of sin. We all waited. After some ten to fifteen minutes, there were still no ructions from the garage, no irate shouts or bangings on its door. The puzzled boys drew near, listening with a growing unease. Dead silence. Another ten minutes passed. Now anxious, the boys crept to the door and put their ears to it. Not a sound! They grew scared and called, 'Dad, Dad!' but in vain. What could have happened?

Roderick racked his brains, and came up with the answer, 'The garage has run out of air! Dad has passed out!' At that they panicked.

'Could he be dead?' cried Euan. The key! Where was it? Off they ran to the long grass, where after long and desperate search the key was found. Back they raced, unlocked the door, and flung it wide. Archie walked out, bestowing on them not a glance or a word. He sauntered back to the house and in. The boys, utterly abashed, were now so contrite that they stayed quiet for the rest of the day.

That was typical of Archie's style. And a splendid style it was. He had not only won the round without effort expended, but taught us all the needed lesson. Non action can be far more effective than reaction, if well chosen: it is longer remembered. The choosing needs wisdom.

14 The Right Holds

Thus far I had been unable to think of getting on to the hills. At first, fifteen minutes' walk on the flat still made me feel faint. Mercifully with impaired mobility went lack of desire for bodily action. Before the month's end I could feel new vigour flowing back into me. My weight had risen to nine stone (normally ten stone four pounds) and new energy called for employment. My last climb had been on the Buachaille Etive Mor in Scotland and my first must be the same; that is, if I could get up the easy way from Glen Etive. At this point Bill Mackenzie wrote to me that he was in Glasgow, on leave from the Lovat Scouts. Was I able to climb? Uncertain though I felt, I took the plunge on 2 June and headed north.

The only climbing boots I possessed were my army boots which by good chance had narrow welts. My first act on reaching Glasgow was to get them nailed with tricounis and clinkers. My second was to find out if my old car, a Morris Eight, had survived the war. Five years ago I had laid it up in a garage at Kelvinbridge. To my great surprise the proprietor was still there – and my car too. He had maintained it free of charge for five years and now filled it up free with rationed petrol. It fired at first turn of the handle. I had bought that old car in 1939 for £80. Now it was worth £240. I drove joyfully to meet Bill Mackenzie.

He was still the same, lean and brusque and keen to get back to Glen Coe after six years. He'd had a much better war than I, climbing with the Commandos in the Cairngorms and then skiing in Canada and the Lebanon and finally fighting through Italy. Not once, he told me, had he enjoyed a really good rock climb, but now –

'Bill,' I said gently, 'you won't get one now if you go with me. I'll be lucky to get to a top by the easiest route.' I could see an almost quizzical alarm in his eye, but I had meant what I said.

We left town very early next morning for the weather was still perfect. I had written much in the prisons about the hill scene for memories had been bright indeed but not even these matched the reality of Loch Lomondside. The woodlands crowding close to the road speckled the surface with yellow-green light: on open stretches the cottage gardens were fiery with red and yellow azaleas, with rhododendron and roses; but most enthralling of all were the spilling bluebell woods north of Luss. Every year I had looked forward to that blue haze and here it was, still lifting the spirits.

It was the same over Rannoch Moor. The genuine, golden air of the good old days which I had begun to think were the spun fantasies of imagination were here in reality, spread again across mile after mile of moorland. The liveliness of all spring mornings entered into us both, 'Bill', I said, 'half measures won't do, I must get on to a top after all, or drop dead trying.'

I felt as I remembered Mackenzie when the first snow of October came on the hills – wild with enthusiasm. Those days when MacAlpine drove us north, usually under clouds that boded ill, until we had first sight of snow-capped hills which evoked Mackenzie's war cry, 'Bound along, Archie, or the snow will be away before we get there!'

We rounded that last great bend beyond the Black Mount and saw the Buachaille. On the instant I was back ten years to the day I first saw the pointed cliffs spring from the moor, black and frightening. I felt the same fright now. We went straight to Coupall Bridge in Glen Etive. This long approach over the moor is lightened by the shapeliness of the mountain, its every line of ridge and crag pointing to the summit cone. As we drew close I recognised every detail of the rocks, now dove grey or pale pink. Only from a distance is the Buachaille black. Its every wrinkle and scar gave delight to the eye.

Any avoidance of the steeper cliffs, such as we had first thought best, suddenly seemed wholly wrong. 'Maybe we could manage an easy rock climb? Say *Curved Ridge*, if we roped?' I made the suggestion hesitantly. Mackenzie grinned and agreed. The moor was dry underfoot. Our boots took a polish from the swish of dry heather. I drew deep draughts of the moorland air so enlivening after the dead air of prison compounds. I was free! I could turn around and go home if I wanted but I had learned in prisons that to go to the mountains is to go home. I stopped. 'Bill,' I said, 'maybe we could manage Central Buttress?'

'Ha, now you're talking!' We could try the direct line but keep to a Very Difficult. We changed direction to the buttress. We roped. I hesitated over the bowline knot but to my relief tied it first time. Mackenzie started up the face and ran out about sixty feet of rope. He turned, ready for me. Now came the test. I looked at the rock, light grey and crystalline, but so very steep. What would my fate be? The old skill gone, rock climbing a thing of the past? I had to take a firm grip of myself, force a foot up and climb.

At the instant my hands and feet came on to the rock, six years rolled away in a flash. Rock was not strange but familiar. At each move I was taking the right holds at the right time. I did not have to take them – of their own accord they came to me. Hand, foot and eye, nerve and muscle – all were co-ordinating, the climbing effortless. I reached the top trusting rock and, what was still more wonderful, trusting myself.

Central Buttress is divided halfway up by Heather Ledge at around 3,000 feet. Close below it the rock is split by a crack at high angle. This for me was my next test; the body is forced out of balance over a long drop. The exposure scared me for a moment but I got up under control. The real test was not 'Did you get up?' but 'Did you enjoy it?' if not while making the move then immediately after? I could say 'Yes' to that which meant that all would be well on the harder and steeper upper buttress.

Central Buttress is the sunniest cliff on the mountain, for it faces south-east and Heather Ledge is a balcony made for rest and reflection. We lay back at ease. Our eyes were led across Rannoch Moor to its furthest rim, pricked by the distant point of Schiehallion. Our inner eye roved further still to a momentary contemplation of our world: the pitiful masses of humanity still crowding the rusted barbed wire fences of mud compounds in Europe and Japan; government folly; multipartite man's infinite capacity for evil; and here, wide and boundless skies, symbols of our freedom and of spirit, stretching too far to be identified, fresh and clean like their purifying wind.

We rose. The upper buttress offered a choice of several routes. Mackenzie chose *Slanting Ledge*, one of his own first ascents of pre-war days. Its middle parts were little less than vertical, as exposed as anything on Rannoch Wall. I watched him carefully, noted how he resisted temptation to hug the rock, forced his body away from it, to avoid the wasteful technique of the unpractised climber so that he could move in perfect unhindered balance. His rope hung quite clear of the face, swaying eighty feet down to me in a white and rippled curve, beautiful in the sun – a much bleached rope on which wartime moths had probably hatched. But I reckoned it would hold a second man, if not the leader. Mackenzie vanished upwards.

When my turn came to follow I felt weak in advance and frightened in action – the drop, the angle, the lack of good holds – but now the fear was a healthy one not like entering a bare room to face the Gestapo, nor lying flat in a midnight cellar listening to the big bombs whistle. Here I was free to act on warm rock and to follow Mackenzie's example and rely on my own skills. The moment I committed myself, all went well. I could tread precisely, although at high tension with set jaw. I could not have led that climb, but what joy when I made the top! I gave inner thanks for it all: the bite of boot nails on rough rock, the fingertip's touch, the elation of self-mastery, the infusion of energy in my limbs in a practised craft – fighting, winning, and sharing with a friend.

'What did you think of that?' asked Mackenzie.

'Not bad. Best climb for years.'

'Now,' said he, 'do you tell me? Who would have thought!'

Moments later he added, 'Best climb I've had too.'

We went over the Crowberry Tower to the summit. When I clapped my hand on the cairn I suddenly remembered my blank despair when I last stood here and made the same movement and found I could laugh at my folly. For this day had been for me another rebirth.

Bill had now to rejoin the Lovat Scouts while I, appetite whetted, sped back to Wales intent on more rock climbing. I wrote from Neuadd to an old climbing friend, Dick Morsley, a bacteriologist at Bangor who kept a guesthouse at Capel Curig in Snowdonia. He could give me a bed there at the end of the month. Meantime, I fetched out my dog-eared manuscript to work on.

Although the war in Europe was barely a month ended there was already much talk of a General Election. Churchill was the war hero, held in respect by all. But the Conservative Party was not. On it was blamed the nation's unprepared entry into war. The coalition of Labour and Conservative Parties could no longer hold. Churchill alone had held them together. His leadership had virtually won the war. The man towered above all others of the time. But already I could guess how a General Election must end. In the Army and prison camps alike I had heard Britain's government endlessly discussed and the verdict was unanimous: the Conservative Party of the 1930s had paid no heed to the Nazi menace or to Churchill's dire warning; its pre-war leaders had betrayed their nation's trust. The Tories were out – out the moment the war ended. Churchill, the people honoured; his party they damned. In mid-June Churchill resigned Parliament and the die was cast.

I went off to North Wales, settled in at Capel Curig and quickly heard that a Mountain Commando Unit happened to be stationed down the road in Llanberis. Their Commander asked me to climb with them. He was looking for someone to teach his men and to lead them on to Severe rock. Their present climbing limit was Very Difficult. I had to tell him that after three years in the camps I would need some practice first. We teamed up. After some thirty climbs mixed in with long hill walks we were all on to Severe and Very Severe routes. It has to be remembered that in those days protection was not used on climbs, rope run-outs were around 150 feet and all of us were using army boots nailed with tricounis and clinkers. If the rocks were dry we might use plimsolls. On of the young Commandos was Chris Preston who won fame after I left for his first ascent of *Suicide Wall*, in Cwm Idwal – for long, the hardest climb in Wales. He was a short, dark-haired youth, not particularly good on rock at the time I climbed with him, but keen. He had newly discovered the rocks and was content to be led up routes like *Holly Tree Wall* and *Balcony Cracks* on Idwal or the *Pinnacle Wall* of Craig yr Ysfa until he found his own feet. Then he took off. His enthusiasm was infectious.

By now I felt completely rehabilitated, at least as a mountaineer and was climbing as well as I ever had.

I returned to Neuadd in time for the General Election.

Just as I had forecast, Attlee's Labour Party won handsomely. We all felt sorry for Churchill who at first wrongly took his party's defeat as personal. To him we owed victory and knew it. We honoured him in our hearts.

Less than five weeks later we were startled yet again by the dropping of atomic bombs on Hiroshima and Nagasaki. We heard the news with undisguised relief, quite unaware of the long-term implications like nuclear fall-out, the threat to the health of whole populations from radiation – the threat to life on our planet. We were aware only that the war had already cost the lives of nearly fifty million human beings worldwide. We rejoiced briefly that mass slaughter had come to an end, that Japan's infamous prison camps could be thrown open and prisoners released at long last. Perhaps the world would be at peace, having learned at such high cost. But I wondered …

I had been hoping that in the turmoil of such great national events the War Office would have forgotten me, but no such luck. They recalled me from leave in mid-August but gave me a sinecure – adjutant to a Royal Engineers' unit at Vale of Leven in Dunbartonshire. The posting seemed heaven sent: midway between the mountains and Glasgow. Apart from my daytime job, which took a morning's easy work and maybe an hour in the afternoon (my office staff took the brunt of paperwork), I had most afternoons and evenings free and weekends too. Thus I was able to keep myself busy typing my manuscript of *Mountaineering in Scotland*, meeting with friends in Glasgow and hard climbing at weekends.

That latter activity had taken on a new purpose. Dr J.H.B. Bell had asked me to write the first rock climbing guide to Glen Coe and Ardgour for the Scottish Mountaineering Club. No payment could be made. They, like me, were short of money. My army pay was negligible but for that very reason the bank had continued to pay my salary right through the war. Hence I felt able to agree. I chose to write as a service to the mountaineering fraternity to whom I felt indebted. Our casualties in the Second World War had been two-thirds less than the first, low enough to ensure no loss of records. My guidebook would help to keep up standards and to set example for a fast take-off by the young of the 1940s. But not until I started planning the work did I realise what I'd taken on. A fresh rock guide as distinct from its sequels, involves an immense amount of preparatory work, digging into old records checking them out in the field and repeating all the climbs – 160 in Glen Coe. The next two years gave me the most intensive climbing of my life, summer and winter, not to mention long evenings in Glasgow's Mitchell Library.

I had served only one month with the Royal Engineers when I was given a week's leave. Bill Mackenzie was free too and Gordon Donaldson came up from Cambridge where he had been reading medicine all through the war and was now in his final term. His climbing skills which had so impressed me before the war were his still but, like everyone's, too long unexercised. We knocked off several climbs that I had wanted assessed in Glen Coe, then Gordon and I sped onwards to Skye. He and I had done the traverse of both the Cuillin main ridges in a fine twenty-four hours in the hot and glorious August of 1939 just as war was about to break. The memory of our wonderful day aloft had stayed vivid in our minds. In this year's repetition of that long, hot summer might we mark the war's end by a repetition of the traverse? We arrived in Glen Brittle to find that we had the whole Cuillin range to ourselves – a phenomenal experience – but even as we looked up to those alluring ridges black spiked against the sky, we saw to the west a mass of dark Atlantic clouds moving in fast. Our dream here ended. In torrential rain we managed to climb over Sgurr Sgumain to Skye's highest peak, Sgurr Alasdair, then fled back to the mainland, each to his own sheltered work.

My army days were now clearly numbered. Sometime within the coming year I would be free, and fortunately freedom came by degrees. Release from prison camps had given me one level; release from the Army would be another, more radical. My relaxed life at Vale of Leven was good preparation, easing me out of the discipline of a fighting regiment, allowing more time to myself – time and chance to develop other work and to reflect on future prospects. Already I was thinking that if I were successful in selling my book to a publisher I might drop banking. I hastened on my laborious typing chore.

The Army too had become very conscious of the demobilisation problem. Hundreds of thousands of men, so long accustomed to having everything done for them, feeding, housing and clothing all laid on – a daily routine with its personal responsibilities imposed – would suddenly be cast out, freed of discipline, left to make personal choice for themselves. How many would be up to it? How many could find jobs on their own? Aware now of this urgent problem, the three fighting services did their best. At Vale of Leven I was appointed Educational Officer and given the task of first finding out what employment the firms and companies of Glasgow, Clydebank and Dumbarton had available, what qualifications they wanted, what training they offered, and second, what educational establishments were planning useful courses. I then had to pass all this to the men of my unit.

Towards the end, my own affairs began moving ever more quickly. In March, I finished typing my manuscript and sent it to J.M. Dent & Sons, of London. I chose Dent because I'd heard that their literary director was a member of the Alpine Club and might therefore be disposed to at least read a book on mountains. While I waited for his verdict my demob papers arrived in mid-April. I was out and free. But not free as the wind.

15 Freedom – Decisions to Make

Release from the prison camps had given me one level of freedom. Now I walked out of uniform into another – and into problems. I felt befogged by uncertainties. I had changes to make, too many of them. 'A 1,000-mile journey begins with the first step,' said one of the world's sages. But what step should I take, what way should I go?

I came out of prison camps with one clear idea in mind: I wished to enter monastic life. I did not want that for refuge but to find spiritual fulfilment. A monastery would allow single-mindedness. I came out of the Army with two other clear ideas: to earn my living as an author and to make a return to the mountains. Mountains enthralled me still. None of the ideas was wholly incompatible with the others. But what course should I set?

Before I could firmly decide I had duties to fulfil. First I had to find a house for my mother in Glasgow and second I had to report to my bank. Its managers had paid my salary through all the years of war. For that I owed them respect. I could not now walk out on them without appearing in person and offering service by way of trial. Therefore I told the bank of my demob and was immediately appointed to the Charing Cross office starting in one month's time. That left the housing problem. My mother's old house in Jordanhill had long since been sold and her wartime house, shared with my sister in Wales, had been given up for Archie MacAlpine had been demobbed last year. He had returned briefly to Glasgow only to find that his Ibrox practice had vanished into thin air. Having a wife and three children to support he had promptly moved back to England and bought a practice at Tunbridge Wells. He had been immediately welcomed back at East Grinstead Hospital with appointment as dental consultant.

I had already been searching for a Glasgow house and found the market expensive and in turmoil. I was offered respite by my good mountain friend, Douglas Scott. He had been demobbed from the Royal Corps of Signals. Hearing of my trouble he offered me and my mother rooms in his house at Jordanhill while I continued the search. That gave me breathing space. Now the real decisions loomed. Not yet committed, I wavered, feeling in my newfound freedom less free than I had felt in prisons. To try to get some perspective I turned instinctively to the mountains. I would take a full fortnight's break. Glen Affric sprang to mind. I had never been there, although the glen by repute was Scotland's best. The lure of the unknown drew me as always, so I headed north in mid-April.

On reaching Fort William by happy chance I met Donald McIntyre. Donald was a young geologist at Edinburgh University. I had climbed with him several times around Glen Coe during the last four months when we had enjoyed an extraordinary spell of weather – every weekend good without fail. Until I met him I had thought geology one of the duller subjects, especially petrology. One day on the rocks banished that error. He could communicate. His voice, his face with alert eyes, his whole manner, came alive when he spoke of rock, his enthusiasm infecting all who heard him. Even I was converted. The man who could do that had to be a teaching genius and in fact as soon as Donald graduated his professor engaged him as a lecturer. His love of rock was fully matched by his skill in climbing it. I felt lucky to have him on a rope. I still remember how on our climbs in Glen Coe and Ben Nevis he used to pause on a steep pitch to lick the rock to bring out its texture and colour.

Spotting his tall lean figure this April morning on the Fort's main street I found that he was on vacation with no companion. 'So you know Glen Affric?' I asked.

'All I know,' said he, 'is that Gladstone was once taken to the foot of Loch Beinn a' Mheadhoin and was so affected by the view he'd raised his top hat.'

'Donald, how long have you got?'

'About ten days.'

'Then let's go. Do you have a tent?'

He had no tent but knew the Reverend Bob Clark of St Andrew's Church across the road. Bob was a member of the SMC and he might lend us one. Not only did he lend a tent but, finding us short of ration tickets for petrol, gave us enough for the return journey. We did at least have ration tickets for food and were able to lug a week's supply of oatmeal, kippers and sausages (but not bread). Thus armed, we sped up the side of Loch Ness, until we could strike west through Glen Urquhart to the foot of Glen Affric. We camped overnight at its junction with the River Glass. Early morning frost and a cloudless sky had us moving by sunrise. There was no tarmac road in lower Glen Affric only a track flanked by woodland not yet in leaf. Every trunk and branch was awash in the sun's flood. An hour's walk took us to where the Affric hurtled through the throat of a gorge – one short column as white as a column of ice but vibrant in power. A short way beyond, the river widened and opened out to the shores of Loch Beinn a' Mheadhoin. Its wide flat banks bore well grown Caledonian pines all in bottle green clusters well spaced with plenty of room to walk between the trunks. Through the clearings the glow of sunstruck hills was reflected in calm water to rich colour glowing like an ancient stained-glass window. The scene was the finest of all the Scottish glens or indeed of any I have since seen in the Alps or Himalaya – I make this brief mention because it was soon to be destroyed by a dam built by the North of Scotland Hydro Electric Board which flooded the old shores and their trees. The deepened loch has lost its natural shape and been shorn of the woodland beauty.

On the green, grassy sill of our magic window I stripped and swam while Donald sunbathed on the shore. Warm in the sun, we moved on over a low ridge to where the track ended at a stalker's white-washed cottage. It stood alone on a green field. The stalker was out but his sister, eager for news of the outside world, welcomed us with tea and hot scones – hardly, we felt, a fair exchange for her.

A short way beyond the cottage we came at last to the northern shore of Loch Affric. We continued four miles to beyond its head where the scene changed. We were now in the glen's mountainous heart. Close above rose Mam Sodhail, Sgurr na Lapaich and Carn Eighe, the loch at their feet a perfect blend of mountain, wood and water. Our track became only a rough path through stone and heather. A more abrupt change at the head of Loch Affric brought us into treeless deer forest, moorland threaded by a river flowing west to Kintail. Here we camped fifteen miles out from our start.

We spent the next week roaming the hills and their long ridges. We made an excursion down into Kintail to explore the hidden Falls of Glomach before crossing the range north to Glen Cannich and on to the shores of Loch Mullardoch. This loch, also then undamned, had splendid woodland all down its grassy banks (today destroyed). We camped down beside a shingly beach. The woods yielded unlimited dry fuel for our campfires. The days stayed hot and cloudless, the loch dazzling blue except where the snow peaks shone clear in every reflected details. We swam in the cool water, basked in hot sun, alive and alert in our mountain paradise. When we at last had to strike camp because our food had run out, we knew that the mountain gods had given a reward beyond all our deserving. We came out readier to face the battles ahead.

I returned to Glasgow with a much firmer resolve to take a grip of my life. First I brought my mother to Douglas's house in Glasgow. Then I made arrangements with the Prior of Buckfast Abbey in Devon. I would go there for a trial run during the summer months. Meantime, I resumed my bank duties but all my spare time went on writing the Glen Coe guidebook.

Before the end of May I heard from Dent, the publisher. They wanted *Mountaineering in Scotland*. My heart leapt. Their reader however had a criticism. In certain passages, for example in the chapter 'The Evidence of Things Not Seen' I had expressed my feelings too freely. Would I accept editorial cuts? My reaction was instantaneous. I would not accept. Their reader was known to me, R.L.G. Irving, then a housemaster at Winchester and Vice-President of the Alpine Club so I thought again. I could see his point but again refused. The book had to be as it was – written from the heart of a holocaust and not as if written on home ground. Mutinous at proposed restraints, I argued that writers who are too guarded turn out dead books. Dent accepted that by return of post and sent me a contract.

It was then that I took the decision to change my life's course. I would resign my job at the bank and henceforth either earn my living by writing or enter a monastery or do both. I took the decision on no tide of euphoria. The good news from Dent did give me a big lift but I stayed aware of the risks. Seven years of war's wholesale slaughter had taught me that loss of money and property are unimportant in the balance of real living, provided that one is still young, unattached and in good health, as I was. The German tank commander had summed it up in a word – 'Leben'. I could, I knew, be a competent banker but my heart and interest did not in truth lie there. I had to be myself – and follow a way right for me and develop what talents I had. Writing met all my criteria: it was creative, for me enjoyable and, once I was committed, might bring food and shelter. I had no illusion of riches.

I chose as a matter of simple prudence to stay with the bank for a few more months while I cleared the way ahead. I stayed active on the hills. In June Douglas Scott and I were drawn to Garbh Bheinn in Ardgour whose great eastern buttress (rough gneiss and quartzite) is split down its full 1,200 feet by the *Great Gully*. This gully bore a magic halo, now flashing like a lure – it had recently been dubbed 'impossible'. A climber had been stopped halfway up by a cave pitch bristling with overhangs. While entertaining no foolish hopes, we hastened to the scene. Such was our good fortune that after a day crammed with difficulty, initial defeat, renewed effort, suspense, success was finally ours. We returned to Glasgow full of the joys and I more confident than hitherto that if I faced up to life's problems they might be dissipated.

I sat down to write the Glen Coe guide. I wanted to make a good job of that and to have the main body of work done before I left the bank. I signed my contract with Dent and trusted that my first book might be out within the year. The next step was the most urgent of all – to reach a final decision on monastic life. I had strong inclination to it, yet felt uncertain whether my purpose might not be better achieved by life in the world under right rule. I had chosen the Benedictine Abbey at Buckfast simply because I knew of several RAF pilots who had gone there. I arranged to stay for a full week to see what I thought.

The monks had built the abbey themselves over a period of thirty years starting in 1907. They had no money. Placing full trust in Providence, a few monks appeared on the chosen site and began to clear the ground by hand. The simple act aroused public interest. Local authority officers, surveyors, an architect and masons offered free service. Help and money began to flow in from every needed source. Imaginations had been fired. The completed abbey is magnificent, inside and out.

When I arrived, the Guest Master gave me a small room to myself and made himself available to answer questions. The monks were each and all encouraged to follow their own talents, whether in the arts and sciences, or whatever. Some ran a most efficient and profitable farm, made medicinal wine, kept bees, or taught in school. They worked hard and took recreation, filling every hour of the day; but whatever the pressure, never missing the Divine Office (the seven rites of day and night) or the time needed for meditation and contemplative prayer.

I attended the Divine Office, had the use of a splendid library, and ate in the refectory with the whole company. Meals were eaten in silence, except for readings from scripture. I was forbidden to speak, unless to the Guest Master in my own room. The organ music of the Divine Office, itself sung with flawless skill, had an extraordinary beauty that intensified the rites' inner intent. The latter's sound sense, together with the music's powerful, emotional appeal, might have moved me to seek conversion to the Roman Church had not two things stopped me. The Church of the time required that I accept their own way to fulfilment as the only way, and the infallibility of the Pope's ex cathedra pronouncements. I believed neither to be true. In whatever way I followed, I had to be free of conscious fallacy. Therefore I decided in the end, somewhat reluctantly, to reject monastic life, which in some ways would have suited me well.

Such at least were the reasons I put to myself at the time. They left me perplexed with myself for even to my own ears they sounded thin. I had thought myself a good candidate, devoted to monastic aims, for which prison camps had laid a foundation. On the other hand, I could not gainsay my joy in the natural world, especially its wild land and life. I saw no sure benefit in shutting myself away from it when already it had given me so much good. The monastic life, as proposed to myself in the prison camps, had been meant to speed up the inner approach to spiritual summits by allowing me a way more free of distractions. More free? This was what I was now questioning.

The outer world was a good teacher too if one paid heed to its strong mix of good and bad, of beauty and ugliness and learned how to discern. Time, much time, would have to go in earning a living, or fighting to survive. But I had this strong feeling that the fight need not be time lost, that much could be learned from it – and more gain made than the needful money, food and shelter. I had an inkling that the advantages of monastic life over the more worldly would carry their own load of ills. Given that doubt, my natural enthusiasm for mountains, for the company they gave me, and for writing and explaining life in both worlds instead of one exclusively, turned me off Buckfast. But I turned with reluctance, far from sure if I were right. Before the year was out I found the guidance I needed through a teaching order. Many such are suspect. This one was free of humbug.

On leaving Buckfast I went to visit my sister and Archie MacAlpine in Sussex where they had bought a house. I found them in good form. I commiserated with them on their exile from old friends in Scotland. The grass must now seem to them greener on the other side of Hadrian's Wall. Archie's eye twinkled.

'You remind me of an old story,' said he, 'about the lost passage of Holy Scripture, the one censored from Genesis.'

> 'And God said, "Let there be a British Isles," and it was so. Thus Scotland became the last of all the lands he made. Then he said to his angel Gabriel, "Gabe, go down and see that all is well."
>
> And Gabriel, knowing that the last shall be first, started in Scotland. He flew back in haste to report.
>
> And God said unto him, "Gabe, you look troubled."
>
> And Gabriel answered, "Lord, Lord, you have been far too kind to the Scots – given too much for their own good – mountains high as the firmament, pure air, wooded glens, lochs full of light and colour, showers to keep the grass green – the Scots live as if already in Heaven – no grim trials, no pestilences, no dire afflictions ..."
>
> But the Lord God cut him short "Trust me, Gabe – just wait till you see the neighbours I've given them south of the Border."'

The story's last point was brought home to me forcibly next morning, when I took the chance to enjoy a day's rock climbing at Harrison's Rocks, a sandstone outcrop nearby. There I met a slim black-haired youth of twenty, who offered to show me some of the easier climbs first. I should have taken note of his bright, sardonic eye. He instead put me on the hardest, and stood back grinning when I failed to get off the ground. He was Michael Ward, then reading medicine at Cambridge. We became friends.

The friendship grew and in the following years we were destined to reap a rich harvest of good mountain days, climbing in Scotland, the Alps and the Himalaya.

16 First Steps

> 'Come forth, the sky is wide and it is a far cry to the world's end ... There is a road which leads to the moon and the Great Waters ... and it has no end: but it is a fine road, a braw-road – who will follow it?'[1]

I read those words from John Buchan's version of the 'Rhyme of True Thomas' on my train journey north to Scotland. For me, they seemed most apt. I had set my course, and mind and heart and will were at last as one. Strangely I had no sense of foreboding that things might go wrong. I felt light-hearted.

Where to live? It would no longer have to be Glasgow. After the barrack room life of prison camps I determined to be free of the stone-brick-concrete-tarmac environment and to live among living and growing things. I wanted out of town into countryside. So, on getting back to base in Glasgow. I tried the lowland's fringe near the Campsie Hills, Killin in Perthshire, Glen Coe in Argyll – but defeat was mine at the auctions and I could not raise a loan being about to give up the bank and 'gainful employment'.

I had better fortune on the mountains. The winter of 1946–47 was the iciest of my lifetime, giving splendid days in Glen Coe when most needed. A peculiar occasion was a first ascent of *Twisting Gully* on Stob Coire nan Lochan, for I went there with Douglas Scott and Jim Simpson under protest, since I had a bad cold, on the strict understanding that we went only to look at it to assess it for some more auspicious day. Having looked we could see that the crux was the first pitch of high-angle ice. We tried in turn, myself last. I pushed the effort to a point of no return. The result was that we made the climb but with such an expenditure of nervous energy on my part that the bad cold disappeared – simply thrown off. Maybe this had something to do with dire necessity and the integration of all nervous and mental powers. It was for me a unique experience. I did not, however, having got away with it once, feel tempted to try a hard climb as a cure for bodily ills.

I enjoyed some even better days and nights with Donald McIntyre. One was a double traverse of the Scottish mainland's thinnest ridge, the Aonach Eagach

---

1 John Buchan *The Moon Endureth*

in Glen Coe, by moonlight. Winter was indeed on the hills and even down in the glen the frost was so hard that we had to drain the car's radiator. Up on the ridge we wore RAF flying suits to keep out the bitter wind. On the mountain tops a full moon with a clear sky will usually allow twenty-five miles visibility – tonight it was forty. Across the great gulf of the Leven Valley which divided Glen Coe from the Mamores there suddenly rolled a long wave of light which broke over the sharp crest of our ridge and surged across Glen Coe, veiling it behind a wide and shimmering curtain. It was quickly followed by others which continued to sweep over us out of the northern horizon all night long. It was the *aurora borealis*. Never before or since have I seen a display of such pulsing power. The mountains around seemed to be burning in white light rather than clothed in frozen snow. Towards dawn the fireworks diminished and the sun came up as a thin gold rim, quickly radiating over the earth's prickly surface until all the hills and the moors stood clear.

Donald and I had another good night on the tops when we pitched our tent below the summit of Bidean nam Bian – not this time in moonlight but under a black sky packed with electric-blue stars. The Northern Lights again flickered from time to time, skimming the stars but not lighting the mountains as before.

Throughout February and into March Glen Coe had unfailing sun and frost which fetched Bill Tilman north from Wales. He was planning his first return to the Himalaya since Everest 1938 so wanted to pack in training climbs. I invited him to climb with Donald and me in Glen Coe. Donald took him along the Aonach Eagach and next day we all three went to *South Centre (SC) Gully* of Stob Coire nan Lochan. Donald and I had made a January reconnaissance and been startled to find that the gully which is 500 feet high began with an unbroken ice-fall of 250 feet. The three lower pitches had merged into one sweep of hard, clear ice. Only five ascents had ever been made of *SC Gully* and none in such ice conditions. In January and February we twice tried to climb it but were defeated first by making too late a start and second by lack of training for the prolonged one handed cutting of hand and footholds at high angles, imposing continuous strain on arm and shoulder muscles. We ran out of time. Now in March we had come prepared. We were fit and made an early morning start from the SMC's hut – Lagangarbh. After a night of clear sky and brilliant moonlight the weather was perfect.

It was freezing hard when we stepped out of the hut but the cold was still more intense 2,700 feet, up on Bidean as we viewed the gully. It was in its former condition pure ice, with any projecting ribs plated in snow-ice. Where its bulges overhung they would have to be cut away. This was Tilman's first Scottish ice climb and we could see the doubt in his eyes. Were we up to it? It would have been dishonest to try to reassure him. It was now a question of time. In four hours of unremitting and intricate cutting, often above the head, balanced on boot nails with long run-outs of the rope, that 250-foot pitch was behind me. When Tilman's head appeared over the top he paused and looked up at me from below his bristly brows.

'Murray,' said he, 'I find this climb an eye-opener.' Tilman was not a talker. Later, after he'd cut the last 250 feet to the cornice – which we left for Donald – he added, 'I was terrified.' Such words from Tilman are not to be taken literally. He was a top-class climber, able to move on a hard climb with quick precision. He could not have led the ice pitch himself that day but, given practice, would have revelled in the skills of high grade cutting and line-planning. His own skills were those of a higher and wider field which made demands on varied qualities of character and judgement. In this Tilman was my superior. My climbing with him fired in me a wish to explore the greater ranges. I could not realise the ambition just yet but the final push to that end came at Easter.

Michael Ward and John Barford joined me on Ben Nevis at Easter below the great north cliffs. Barford had newly written the instruction book, *Climbing in Britain* and was secretary of the British Mountaineering Council, founded in 1944 when I was incarcerated in Czechoslovakia. He had the restless drive of the born organiser and could, if necessary, be ruthless. I believe that given time he could have organised even the UK's mountaineers into military efficiency and on this score felt wary.

Considering the date, we thought it only right to try *Good Friday Climb*, especially since Graham Macphee's first ascent had been at Easter 1939. This climb lies on the Ben's highest rocks and goes up the right-hand edge of *Indicator Wall*, close beside Gardyloo Buttress. We arrived in deep snow under its base to find that it was far more heavily iced than described in 1939. The weather had turned not just bad but vicious. A gale was raging across the summit plateau 500 feet overhead and, while the cliff gave us shelter, the wind was driving a heavy stream of powder snow over the corrie which fell on us like a blizzard. We forced a way up the first steep ice-pitch climbing right and left for seventy feet, cutting hand and footholds, then up a series of steep snow chutes down which the drift snow now poured in a continuous torrent allowing nowhere sure footing. On struggling through the cornice Michael echoed Tilman's, 'Terrifying'. The climb was nowhere as hard as *SC Gully* but certainly dicier. Back down at the hut John Barford wanted me to join Michael and himself in the Dauphiné in July. I agreed.

The agreement brought my decisive break with the bank. I had no holiday coming up in July. As soon as I returned to Glasgow I gave notice of resignation.

I had to find a house at once and the finding could not have been quicker or more haphazard. I walked into a Glasgow estate agent's office one morning, said what I wanted and named my price-limit. The clerk shook his head but fetched out a heavy ledger listing addresses. 'I don't think,' he started unpromisingly – and at that moment a telephone rang in the back office, to which he was called away. The ledger lay on the counter unopened. I pulled it to me, opened it up at random and read.

'Cottage at Loch Goil, Argyll' … Here was a house by the sea with three acres of ground at less than my right price. I had never been there and knew it only as a branch of Scotland's heavily indented coastline. The clerk was still engaged, so I closed the ledger, went out to my car, and looked up a road map. Loch Goil I saw was a branch of the Firth of Clyde lying thirty miles inland from the open sea; by road, fifty four miles north of Glasgow. I drove straight there.

At Lochgoilhead Post Office I was told that Lochwood lay three miles along the west shore where the final approach went 300 yards down a wooded drive to the loch.

I first saw the house on a sunny April day when the cherry blossom was in full bloom. The house stood on a rock by the sea's edge. Its garden lay on ground gently sloping down to a private beach with a boathouse and jetty. The more level part had been planted with azaleas and rhododendron and had a small orchard of well grown apple and plum trees. The steeper upper part was wooded in Scots pine, oak, holly, birch, rowan and sycamore. The beach was separated from the garden by a stone wall four feet high which circled around a grassy headland, this in turn bounded by a burn which fell via a rocky gorge from the hill above.

Close behind the cottage an outcrop of mica-schist crags divided the lower grounds from the upper and offered two or three vertical rock climbs; in front, the beach was favoured by herons that fished from the jetty on which seals hauled out to bask. The cottage stood on its rock so close to the loch that at full spring tides the walls rose almost vertically out of the water. The front windows looked out to the blue water of the loch cruised by a pair of paddling swans and a flock of *oo-ooing* eider ducks. The bay was busy with diving mergansers and up-ending mallards and its shingle beach with piping oyster-catchers. The scene looked to me like a slice out of paradise – a far cry from prison camps. I bought the house forthwith: four rooms upstairs and three down, two of them small, plus kitchen and bathroom. I did notice that I would have to do some work on the house but, this being my first experience of house buying, I fell into all the traps set by a house of the previous century with all the defects of its Highland site and age. I arranged to move into it in mid-May.

Before moving from Glasgow I had to dispose of that growing bugbear, the Glen Coe guide. I had not been working on it for some time. No sooner had rock climbers heard that a guide was on the way than they hastened to climb all the new lines they'd long noted but not yet tried. I was thus afflicted by a spate of first ascents, especially from members of the Creagh Dhu

Mountaineering Club. They were beginning to gain fame by raising the standards too – but I did feel exasperated by the pressure put on me, enjoyable though the new climbs were. Early in May with Donald McIntyre I had one last triumph – not just a new climb but a whole new cliff on the west face of Aonach Dubh, one of Glen Coe's Three Sisters. We had discovered this cliff in March when passing under it with Bill Tilman. It was 600 feet high and 400 yards long in the lower part of Coire nan Lochan. Like innumerable climbers before us we had often passed through this corrie so intent on our climb higher up that we hadn't seen the obvious. Not one route had ever been made there – an almost incredible neglect in Glen Coe as late as 1947. We put up seven routes, none more than Very Difficult but good lines that are not too hard are valuable because all could enjoy them.

I finished the Glen Coe guide at last and sent the manuscript off to the printer and began to clear the decks for earning a living. On the last day of April I left the bank and in mid-May moved house to Loch Goil. My mother joined me and the renovating tradesmen. Two months later I was off to the Alps with Barford and Ward.

17 The Alps: Highs and Lows

I had last climbed in Switzerland in 1938 at Arolla. My return to the Alps nine years later began at La Bérarde in the Dauphiné. Our plan was to acclimatise on the rocks of several lower peaks then move on to more testing routes on higher mountains. After this we would move to Chamonix where we should try for a south face route on Mont Blanc and the *Walker Spur* of the Grandes Jorasses (the latter still awaiting a first British ascent). All went well at first. We enjoyed a few good rock climbs, including a memorable descent from the summit of La Meije in a snowstorm when we had no little difficulty in finding the route down the Promontoire Ridge to the south.

We ended our stay at La Bérarde by making the second ascent of the Ailefroide by its severe *Coste Rouge Arête*. We started up at dawn after a bivouac below the snout of the Coste Rouge Glacier. The main obstacle on this hard climb was not, as I expected, a snow ridge but its most exposed red wall which overhung the Glacier Noir far below to our north. Always our footing was insecure first on loose steep rock then on verglas on which crampons skited, and finally on very unstable snow at high angle. We had to climb at constant nervous tension. Up on the summit ridge the rocks were sound and clean. Here I found that Barford and Ward had advantages over me by wearing Vibrams – corrugated rubber soles which had newly come on the market. They could move faster than I in my nailed soles which I hereafter abandoned. We picked our way down a gully on the mountain's south flank to its wide glacier where we spent the night at the Refuge Sélé.

Two days later, on return to our old bivouac under the Coste Rouge, since the weather had turned good after a thunderstorm we planned to have one last climb on the Barre des Écrins before moving to Chamonix. To reach the Écrins we had to cross the Col de Coste Rouge from west to east. We arrived on the next morning to find the snow iron-hard, and a couloir dropping several hundred feet at an angle of 45° to a bergschrund. We strapped on crampons and roped up. I went first, Barford last. A hundred feet down, I ran into soft snow lying on hard. Its surface layer tended to ball on the crampons, so I stopped and warned the others to go slow and take care.

'Nonsense,' cried Barford, and stepped down. Next moment he was flat on his back and hurtling down the slope – the snow had balled on his crampons. By good fortune, Ward was standing on a patch of firm snow frozen to the underlying ice. Quick as a flash he drove in his axe and whipped the rope round it. When the jerk came the shaft snapped. The pair swept past me. I was torn off. But Ward had hung on to his broken axe-head and we all three braked hard. In a few seconds we stopped ourselves. While resuming our old order on the rope, Ward dropped his balaclava, which I fielded and clapped on to my bare head – for me a most fortunate incident. We had no sooner begun to move down again than a shower of stones fell from the wall of the Ailefroide. They came straight at us. We were all struck on the head and fell together.

I alone did not lose consciousness, for Ward's thick balaclava had saved me. This was my first experience, on mountains, of the total detachment of mind from body. As if standing apart, I could observe alertly the fast slide of my own body, Barford and Ward shooting past it to one side, head first. Directing my body to brake – not to stop, for that was impossible – but to keep my body upright and so let the feet take the impact with the bergschrund's lower edge. This detachment being complete, I felt no pain or fear, or any sense of alarm. I had control of a body, not me, an instrument to be used therefore valued, even if expendable. We all ended up in the bergschrund. My detachment there ended.

I felt myself stopped by a wrench on the shoulders, legs swinging in space. My heavy Bergan rucksack had jammed in the mouth of the 'schrund. I was blinded by blood running into my eyes, and could do nothing at first. After a few minutes I managed to force my arms over the top edge and to spike the snow with my axe. I dragged myself out, wiped blood off the eyes and looked back in. Barford lay dead on a ledge ten feet down. Ward was still lower, jammed by his shoulders at a narrowing of the walls. A deep chasm opened below him into blue-black depths, but he was alive and kicking. His head was more badly gashed than mine. We both had fractured skulls – not then knowing it. I climbed down to Barford's ledge, and using all my strength tried to pull on Ward's rope. After long and desperate efforts he managed to pull himself up, using his broken axe-head and crampons. He was concussed, his memory had gone. He did not know my name, or Barford's, what mountain he was on, or where he was going. As quickly as I told him, he repeated the questions. However, after he had taken stock of me, he agreed to go with me down the hill. He had sense enough to leave his heavy rucksack at the edge of the 'schrund but I was determined to carry mine down – it had clothes and food that we might yet need, for the Glacier Noir dropped seven kilometres to the Ailefroide Valley. We climbed slowly and unsteadily down to the upper glacier basin where the heat was enervating and the steepening glacier looked heavily crevassed. We surveyed it with something near despair. Just then I saw a figure on the far side of the basin – a lone climber heading for the Col de la Temple. I fetched out my whistle and sounded the mountain distress signal – six blasts a minute. He halted and came over to us.

He was French, perhaps forty, a man of confident bearing. I judged from his vigour of eye and movement and his good equipment that he would be a competent mountaineer, so I told him what had happened – Barford dead, Ward and I doubtful of our strength and wondering if we could get down to the valley unaided. Would he go down with us just to make sure we arrived? He made no answer at first – just looked us over carefully. We made a bloody and ugly sight. Then he smiled, and explained that he was making his way to La Bérarde over the Col de la Temple. He had an engagement for the morrow, and if he were to go down with us through the Glacier Noir that would take him in the opposite direction. Therefore he must continue on his way but wished us well, we should be able to find our own way down. Meantime, was there anything more he could do? A mouthful of wine, perhaps? His manner was studiedly courteous. He had no care what befell us.

I waved him away. I felt too dismayed with the man to plead or argue. Promoters of outdoor education were to say much in later years commending the so-called character-building effects of mountaineering. Effects there certainly are but whether good or bad depends not on mountains but on what personal attributes the individual is able to bring to the mountains (or to any other field of action). Hence, a not uncommon side effect of climbing is to sharpen self-conceit, harden arrogance and whet egotism. It can also foster quite opposite effects. The choice is ours. Mountains are not the arbiters.

Ward and I descended on to the glacier which fell away in a maze of crevasses, mercifully all narrow, of a kind we could jump. But they caused long delays while we hovered trying to summon the energy and resolution to make the jumps. I was badly handicapped by the weight of my heavy rucksack. Michael following behind offered to carry it for me. He had lost much blood, still did not know who I was, and had been unable to lift his own rucksack from the ground. Yet, seeing me in trouble here he was offering help beyond all common sense. The contrast with the Frenchman was so marked that it gave me the energy I needed both to shoulder my own burden and to find the best route.

We stumbled down to the valley in seven hours. As soon as we met other humans on the track our sustaining energies vanished. We collapsed. I had time to tell the tale then passed out. The next I knew we were propped up on chairs in a hut waiting for an ambulance while a gendarme searched my rucksack for a passport. Guides were gathering to bring down John Barford at daylight.

I woke up next day in a hospital at Gap, thirty-five miles south in Les Hautes Alpes. Ward lay in the bed next to me still unconscious. There were no other beds. The ward was spacious and well lit with a highly polished hardwood floor. The nursing staff were nuns and treated us gently, as did the visiting doctor. We spent ten days at Gap. The remarkable feature of our treatment was the lack of it. At first I could not see very well for encrusted blood had closed my eyelids. The nurses were devoted to cleanliness; they polished the floors, dusted the furniture, changed our sheets – the ward gleamed, the room was spotless – but they drew the line at washing their patients. Michael's face too stayed bloody. I wondered, was it because we were male, therefore not touchable? I came to the more reasonable conclusion that the nurses thought that unwashed, undisturbed blood gave good cover for our wounds which might heal better without interference even from clean water and antiseptics. When Michael woke up I told him what had happened. This time he was able to retain the principal events, if not all of them. He at least now knew who I was and where he was. As the days slipped by we washed our faces, leaving the scabs on our heads untouched. All seemed free of infection. We were somewhat astonished that our heads were not X-rayed for fractures of the skull nor our eyes examined for tell-tale signs of the same. After a few days we received visits from a pair of teenage girls who brought gifts of fruit and flowers. The *Daily Express* sent a reporter from London. His return journey would be well over 1,200 miles so I knew that if I did not give him the story he would invent one. I told him exactly what had happened, which Michael confirmed.

His report was printed a day or two later under a blaring headline:

> 'A party of 70 mountaineers were overwhelmed by an avalanche near Argentière in the French lower Alps and most of them were killed. The first to be extracted was William Hutchison Murray. He said that he was with two Scots friends ... One had been killed. He did not know what had happened to the other ... all 70 were holding on to one rope.'

– and more of the same absurdities. The *Express* had taken the trouble to send their man 1,200 miles. The true story perhaps was not enough to cover expenses. My advice? Never give the press a story except under commission to write it yourself.

We had a much more welcome and unexpected visit from Donald McIntyre. I knew that he had won a Carnegie Scholarship to the University of Neuchatel in Switzerland where his work was research into granite but could never have thought he would take the time to come such a long way to see us. He had entered the ward with a wide grin as befitted one come to bring cheer to the injured. But his grin dissolved when he saw us. Any curiosity we might have had about our own appearance faded in the mirror of his new expression. We were a mess. He had been caught unawares but rallied and soon had us laughing. He, a doctor of geology, speeded our recovery more than Gap's doctor of medicine.

Granite was just one of Donald's preoccupations at Neuchatel. There were others – like high Alpine skiing in which he took a demanding guides' course. Likewise, the Swiss professor under whose general direction Donald worked was expert in more than geology. He was a connoisseur of fine wines. Clarets and the lore thereof fired in him a missionary zeal to educate the mind and palate of this young Scot. Donald, always an apt pupil, responded and rapidly acquired taste and a 'nose'.

His professor had been visited by a colleague from the USA. Americans, like the Scots, were believed to have no proper appreciation of good wine and to dwell, as it were, in outer darkness. The professor hoped to bring his visitor enlightenment. Donald knew only too well what this might mean. Humiliating embarrassment awaited the American guest. Having suffered much himself on his path to knowledge Donald resolved to rescue him and to turn the tables on the worthy professor. He took the American discreetly aside, gave warning of the plan and schooled him on the way to play the game with full advance knowledge of the bottles that he already knew to be chosen for the table. The American was no sluggard in learning – he had been left in no doubt of his fate if he failed. He brightened as Donald expounded and began to look forward to dinner. So did Donald.

When they sat down to dinner and the first decanter of white wine came with the fish, the Swiss professor steered the conversation to the topic of Bordelais wines, gave a brief dissertation on the vineyards of Gironde. Then, in magisterial tones, he invited his guest to give his opinion on three wines to be served and to name the district of origin and identify each chateau if he could. He was startled to find his challenge swiftly accepted. He had come to expect either stunned silence from foreign guests or humble excuses.

The American took up his first glass and sniffed, then he sipped and looked thoughtful. 'A product of that gravelly soil of Graves,' he announced, 'There can be no mistaking the flavour – more alcohol than the usual run of Bordeaux, yet light and medium dry ... and the chateaux? I judge its home to be Haut Brion ... but not one of the great years, so I can't specify.'

And of course he was right. The Swiss professor could hardly believe his ears. Had this just been a lucky guess? And yet the man spoke as if familiar with his subject. The real test followed with the meat. As the claret was poured the Swiss professor turned a sharpened eye on his guest. 'Now,' said he, and he spoke slowly, 'I would very much like to hear what you have to say of this Bordeaux.' He uttered the word reverently.

The American inhaled the bouquet. He sipped and rolled the wine round his tongue. He sniffed again. He made a show of consideration ... 'A Médoc,' he pronounced. 'Without doubt a Médoc ... another sip ... and a splendid breed it is, of complex individual character. It can only be a Chateaux Margaux and of *Grand Cru* class – right proportion of sugar to acid.' He sipped and sniffed. 'I would place it somewhere in the last decade – m'm – carries just a faint hint of oak from the cask – what you call *Barrique Formulation,* I think. How interesting too that the aroma from the grapes' quality should have such important side effects on taste! The vintage year I'd say must be 1939.'

His host was dumbfounded. He managed a weak nod of assent. Where in the world, let alone in the Benighted States of America, could this man have so trained and refined his palate?

Then came dessert, when a second white wine appeared. The American held up his glass to the light. 'Pale gold' – he applied his nose – 'my first guess would be a Sauternes.' He sipped 'A Sauternes it is! Flavour delicate – a perfectly proportioned palate – equal balance of fruit with the tannin. It has to be Chateau d' Yqem … and the year – most likely 1936.'

The Swiss professor, now quite crestfallen, felt like hiding his diminished head. Thereafter he looked upon his guest with a respect amounting to wonder. His table had been graced by *un connoisseur de plein Goût* – and as such he was to be honoured henceforth by all at Neuchatel.

Relishing his triumph the American felt much indebtedness to Donald. He took close interest in his research work and spoke so highly of it on return to the States that Donald, a few years later, was offered the Chair of Geology at a university in California. He accepted. Years later his work in geology won him fame throughout America.

But this happy dénouement was hidden from us all at Gap. Donald's story told with a mimicry and élan that cannot be conveyed in print, gave us the first laugh we had enjoyed at the hospital. It helped our recovery.

We were discharged after ten days. On the morning we left to catch a train north our clothes were handed back to us. To our consternation they were unwashed – still covered in dried blood – shirts, trousers encrusted. We could do nothing about the situation for the train was soon due. We could hardly believe what we saw. These nuns had taken care of us, given us clean beds and good food, kept a spotless ward and, although they had not once dressed our wounds but left them to Mother Nature, we guessed that might be due to France's dire shortage of surgical dressings at the war's close. The inaction on fouled-up clothes seemed quite another matter – the nuns had not even blanched on handing them over. It remains a mystery.

I at least had a spare shirt in my rucksack but Michael had nothing, only his bloodied rugby-jersey. If the nuns showed no recoil, the public did. In the train's compartment the seats to either side of us were left unoccupied. On the cross-channel ferry when we sat down to our meal passengers took one startled look and sought other tables.

After reaching London the first journey I made was to visit Geoffrey Winthrop Young at Cambo in Northumberland. Britain's greatest alpinist, he had foreseen in the midst of war, when President of the Alpine Club, the urgent need that must arise at its end for a British Mountaineering Council and he alone possessed the force of personality required to persuade British climbers, an unruly breed because individualistic, that they must become able to speak with one voice in an international society changed greatly by two world wars. He had chosen John Barford as the man best equipped to carry his idea into effect. His choice had been right. Barford had the quick perception, drive and energy needed to set it up and keep it going. Now he was dead. I wanted to tell Geoffrey Young how that had happened and to be sure that his ideal would not die too. I liked Geoffrey Young when I met him. He had presence. Now in his early seventies silvery hair capped a white bushy moustache. He had the bearing and penetrating eye of a natural leader, instantly recognisable; yet his style was informal and friendly. He could move himself only with the aid of a stout stick for he had lost a leg in the First World War. Such was his dominant character that this did not seem to matter any more – a man who rose above anything that the fates might throw at him. Since my mission was to tell him of John's loss, I sensed all this with great relief.

Above everything, I liked Geoffrey Young's attitude to mountains and mountaineering, for these attitudes were mine too, probably strengthened, at least in part, by my early reading of his books, both prose and poetry. The principles are simple: that the true joys of mountaineering are spiritual and only to be had when the climber, however high or low his skills, goes to the mountains because he loves and respects them and not just for display of his own skills, or to compete for records or first ascents, or the collection of summits. These latter rewards are froth, none of them worth a man's life – or even his time. If the approach is right – for love, not gain – mountains enrich life and are worth all the risks entailed.

It was only after getting home that Ward and I at last found our skulls to be fractured. Michael discovered at once – as a medical student he'd had the good sense to go straight to an X-ray unit. I more carelessly waited till I felt strong enough to take on a mountain and then went to Glen Coe alone and climbed the *Crowberry Direct.* At the very exposed, severe crux of this climb, with all the space of Rannoch spread out below me, I was disturbed to find myself going dizzy for a moment as I raised my head upwards looking for holds. On the next good ledge I overtook a small SMC party one of whom was Martin Nicholls a neurosurgeon at Killearn Hospital. So I told him of the Dauphiné accident and the moment's dizziness below. 'Come in to Killearn tomorrow morning,' he said, 'and I'll X-ray the skull.' This I did and sure enough the skull had a two-inch fracture at the temple. Nothing could be done except (as with Michael too) keep off mountains for a month.

While somewhat dismayed at my sentence – the rebound of relief that there was no worse damage – I realised its sense. I realised also the foolhardiness of my climb when in truth I had suspected that my skull was fractured – the blow to it had not been light. That day on the Buachaille I had been lucky just as we had been lucky on the Col de Coste Rouge – managing to stop a first fall and two of us surviving a second.

Another time in the Alps traversing the Grand Charmoz I heard a sound like a gun and high above glimpsed white smoke. An ice cliff had broken off. Hypnotised by the speeding avalanche I stood in its tracks – then as the first ice block whined past, terror unrooted me and I jumped blindly a few feet into a crevasse. The avalanche thundered over the top. I hadn't known when I jumped that the crevasse was only eight feet deep.

Again, I was lucky on two counts – but it could rightly be said that I shouldn't have been there, for the Nantillons Glacier is notoriously prone to avalanche and the summer of 1949 had been too long dry.

Certainly 'luck' is useful, but good or ill, it is often self-earned.

A mountaineer may imagine his prime need is just to be born lucky but the truth is not so simple. His prime need is self-possession: to be alert and to stay that way day-long, aware of what he is doing, and of the environment, from the loose hold at his nose to the thawing snow at his feet, to the dark cloud on the horizon. Alertness must be developed until it is a sixth sense. It will do much to eliminate loss of life. Yet this essential alertness can be dimmed by the overbrimming optimism of ignorance, inexperience, youth, resulting in a comfortable immunity to the warning signs a mountaineer must always recognise if he is interested in surviving to climb another day.

On the mountains, nothing better discourages luck from running out than alertness.

Narrow escapes come to us all in a lifetime. A good mountaineer will endeavour to control their number and balance risk with survival. On mountains, fearlessness is a good companion – provided fear is there too as the watchdog.

FIRST EXPEDITIONS TO THE HIMALAYA

18 Introduction to the Garhwal

My dreams of the Himalaya came a step nearer to realisation in 1950 when my friend Douglas Scott asked me to join him, Tom MacKinnon and Tom Weir in an expedition to the mountains of the Garhwal in northern India. Would I come? Yes, I would – this decision was effortless. I need curb my dreams no longer. Even Scott's request that I take the lead could not dim my joy – I simply delegated work to my companions. Preparation proceeded apace. We were to go in April.

No one in the 1950s, planning a first exploration of the central Himalaya, could afford to lose a chance of discussing his plans with Tom Longstaff. He lived at Achiltibuie on the Coigach peninsula of Wester Ross. We proposed to travel light and to live on the country after the manner set by Longstaff in the century's first decade.

I called to see him at Bardentarbet, an old shooting lodge set on the moorland high above Outer Loch Broom. He was then in his seventy-fifth year, small in stature and spare of frame, almost frail until I looked him in the eye. Instantly I knew the presence of a strong personality, possessed of the energies that can make for greatness. The cheekbone was high, the nose thin, the eyes cool and deep-penetrating when he chose, the mouth firm as a fighter's – it might have been the face of a desert Arab, but more particularly the face of a man born to explore the unknown, on whatever plane.

In his dealings with me, and all other persons, he was at once upright and downright. The moment he started to talk, pouring out generously his vast store of Himalayan knowledge, a dynamo seemed to switch on inside, the current to speed through his body, and electric sparks, one would swear, to shoot out from the point of his red beard. Fifty years before, he had been indeed a prodigy in power and performance, and had never aged since in spirit. 'Whom the gods love die young,' said Byron: true words when understood that men who live true to their life's purpose stay young in heart. Tom Longstaff was such a man. He did with his life the one thing he most wanted to do – travel far. In his autobiography, *This My Voyage* (1950), he declared that his boyhood's ambition was to become a mountain traveller. He explained what he meant:

> 'Mountaineering is but an expression of the basic instinct to explore the unknown ... Since happiness is most often found by

> those who have learned to live in every moment of the present, none has such prodigal opportunities of attaining that as the traveller ... attainment of a set objective is but a secondary matter, the traveller should not anticipate the journey's end. So long as he loses consciousness of self, and is aware in all his senses of the present scene, almost any part of the world is as good as another. Mountain or desert it is all one.'

His words were those that I held in my own heart.

Douglas Scott worked out our plans for Kumaon. This was the great angle of India between Tibet and Nepal. It comprised the districts of Garhwal and Almora. In Garhwal three famous mountains already climbed were Trisul, Kamet, and Nanda Devi. In Almora, little mountaineering had ever been attempted. The unclimbed peaks of Kumaon were numbered by the score. Semitropical valleys and profound gorges wound in among a maze of snow peaks rising above 20,000 feet, packed close in clusters – several of which had never before been explored by mountaineers. Our prospect could not have been more alluring. Scott's plan was to start in Garhwal from the hill-station of Ranikhet, and work first north then east in six moves: in May, cross the foothills 100 miles north to the Rishiganga Gorge of Nanda Devi, and there try to climb Bethartoli Himal – a mountain of nearly 21,000 feet. In June, move north up the Dhauli river-gorge to explore the Lampak range from its south; then, when the monsoon broke in late June, do the same from the north by crossing the main Himalayan axis to its Tibetan side, where rain and snow-falls would be lower. In mid-July force an eastward traverse from the upper Dhauli twenty-two miles through the gorge of the Girthi River to the headwaters of the Gori in Almora district. If this were not too difficult, we should link two of the great trade-routes of central Asia, and that could be of greater value to travellers than the ascent of mountains. Finally, in August, we hoped to cross the remote Ralam Pass (18,439 feet), again eastward through a range of twenty mountains, which would lead us to the great valley of the Darmaganga, close to the triple frontiers of Tibet, Nepal, and India. There we should reconnoitre and try to climb the Panch Chuli – the 'Five Fires' – a group of five shapely peaks, the highest summit of which was at 22,650 feet, though all were unclimbed and famed in Hindu mythology.

We reached Ranikhet with all our stores and equipment in the second week of May. Here we hired eighteen Dotial porters and on the morning of 11 May set out eighteen loads under a big tree. Most porters had two packages to carry: a crate and a kit bag. These loads had been carefully weighed. None exceeded sixty pounds.[1] But we were soon to find that the Dotials had a system

1 Approximately 2.25 pounds (lb.) imperial weight equals one kilogram.

of their own, in which spring balances played no part. Their own food was carried by one man, not eighteen; Kuar Singh, as head porter, and with the acquiescence of the others, took no load at all. The loads had thus to be completely rearranged, and Kuar Singh did this with exceeding swiftness by eye and by feel. He thus dealt out the loads to each man, not necessarily on the basis of an equal load to each, but in some measure according to capacity. Thus, Shivlal, our youngest porter, was never given more than fifty pounds, while Perimal, Kuar Singh's second-in-command, had a full eighty pounds, although he and Kuar Singh were as thick as thieves. The main points were that no man had more than a maund (eighty pounds) and that all accepted Kuar Singh's verdict without question. He had a very real authority over the other porters. He reminded me more and more of an old Alpine guide – exceedingly brisk, tough and confident, and wise in the ways of men, but always ready to put his employers' interests before his own, and truly to serve. We were very lucky with Kuar Singh. The porters squatted against their loads, settled the headbands across their foreheads, then one by one gave a heave and lurched upright. We were off!

By the second day the Dotials might be said to have 'discovered' us. They haunted the rest house veranda and seized any good excuse for coming inside to look us over. It was Scott's camera tripod with the telescopic legs, our lilos and binoculars that most fascinated them. One of the brightest was a young lad of seventeen called Ram Badur. He was small, and was always smiling. He was quick in discovering how the binoculars worked – a problem that mystified most of the others until he showed them. From that night onwards he appointed himself one of our orderlies, his specially chosen task being to blow up the lilos, which he did with excessive gusto, leaving them tight as drums and with corks driven too hard to be drawn without employment of blasphemy.

Our third day's march, Gwaldam to Bagargad, was a full day's work. At 6.30 a.m. we descended 2,000 feet to the Pindar River. MacKinnon and I went ahead here and travelled a mile upstream to an old suspension bridge. As rock climbers we were accustomed to the idea of exposure on a cliff face, but this tottering contraption of broken beams, fifty feet above the white race of the Pindar, made our stomachs turn over. We turned hastily away and looked 100 yards downstream for the ford, which turned out to be one half ford and one half log bridge. The bridge over the deepest sweep of the river had to be reached by a thigh-deep wade to an island of boulders. We crossed. On looking upstream to the old bridge, we were horrified to see an old woman and young girl already halfway over. That they could not have crossed where we did, without being carried, was certain; that they should choose to risk the old bridge testified to strong nerve. This was but the first of many enlightening proofs that we were to receive that young and old in the Himalaya show that their attitude to the chances of daily life is braver than ours.

The Pindar Valley was the richest we had yet seen. Its broad wheat fields glowed in the sunshine. We turned north up the Kaliganga, which flows south from the Wan Pass. On either side the hills rose to 10,000 feet, heavily wooded, but never giving us a shut in feeling, for the eye was at once drawn to a little promontory by the river and caught there by the brilliant white of a temple spire. It gave a lift to the mind and heart, causing head and eyes to lift in sympathy, until – how unexpectedly! – they beheld the snow spire of Trisul shining bright and sudden through the right-hand branch of the Kali. Nowhere else have I seen a temple sited with such inspiring effect.

Not until our meal was finished and the plates washed did Kuar Singh limp up for medical treatment that night in the Dak bungalow. He was wearing a pair of good brown shoes, one size too small, and now he had a bunion. We had already seen that these shoes were worn to dignify his post as head porter. There was one obvious cure. Tom Weir picked up the shoes and went through the motion of throwing them away. A look of incredulous horror crept into Kuar Singh's eyes. He would die in his shoes rather than cast them. So MacKinnon opened up his medicine chest for the first time and dabbed some iodine on Kuar Singh's toes, then on Prem Singh's swollen knee muscles. This humble unveiling of the medicine chest was in reality a great occasion, although we knew it not, and should have been marked with rounds of musketry and airs on the pipes. The gradual unfolding of its mysteries was to fascinate Dotials, Kumaonis and Bhotias daily for months hereafter, and to give MacKinnon many a metaphorical headache in diagnosis. Within a quarter of an hour the local headman had arrived for treatment. Everywhere we went henceforth, in every village near which we halted overnight, our expedition was to be valued chiefly on account of its medical stores and MacKinnon's service – the more so the farther we went.

The very next day three shepherds asked treatment for an inflamed eye, a swollen hand and asthma. Rather than disappoint the asthmatic shepherd MacKinnon gave him a Gelucil tablet for stomach trouble. This was the first of many times when we regretted not taking Dr Longstaff's advice to bring fizzy drinks, which give comfort where cure is impossible. When MacKinnon's dispensary next opened the shepherd with asthma had returned, not to upbraid us, but joyfully to declare himself cured. We could only stare in silent wonder.

We had to wait a day for new supplies of flour for the Dotials so Weir, Scott and MacKinnon took the opportunity to climb Jatropani (13,300 feet) which was close at hand near the Wan Pass. They set out at six o'clock on a perfect morning. I went off alone shortly after them and returned at midday to find the Dotials waiting for me with a goat. Would I buy? – just twelve rupees. I said no. Later I was to find this a modest price for Himalayan goat. But the beast was scraggy and we had not yet developed a craving for meat. To my utter astonishment, the Dotials then bought a rather fatter goat for themselves, still at twelve rupees. They led it over the lawns to the shade of the great cypresses, where the scene assumed the likeness of some immemorial rite of sacrifice. The officiating priest was Zungia, with a kukri, or long curved knife. He stood beside the trunk of the biggest tree. In front of him Perimal held the end of the halter, stretching it tight while the goat dug in its hoofs and bent its neck forward. The Dotials formed a wide semicircle round the tree, intent on the execution. Far across the glen the forested slopes were baking in white light, but over the lawn in the foreground only wide shafts streamed through the branches of the cypresses.

Kuar Singh stepped up and parted the wool at the back of the goat's neck. He stepped back quickly. Perimal gave a quick pull on the halter. Zungia rose on the balls of his feet. The knife flashed – thud – and the head rolled away.

There could be no quicker death for a goat. The rest of the afternoon was spent carving. Himalayan goat is tough and needs mincing; this the Dotials did with our two hatchets, pounding and chopping the meat on blocks of stone or wood. Kuar Singh at length went round all the men, apparently getting their opinion on some matter of moment, at the end of which he came to me with the heart, liver, and one hind-quarter – a gift from the Dotials.

That porters should on rare occasion get a goat from their *sahibs* was an old custom, which we intended to honour. But that *sahibs* should get the best part of a goat from their porters was something I had not conceived possible. One goat does not go far among eighteen porters, so I reckoned the gift too generous and accepted only the liver.

This we enjoyed when MacKinnon, Scott and Weir came back at 4.30 p.m. They had spent ten hours on Jatropani all finding altitude trouble near the summit. The route was easy and the view not outstandingly good. On the whole, they had enjoyed themselves, and Weir, who had had a high temperature on setting out in the morning, was at last thoroughly fit.

Rain that night brought a fresh morning. We reached the Wan Pass at eight o'clock. Through the branches of the trees we could see Nilkanta, like a blunt Matterhorn, glittering in the sun and flanked by the long Badrinath range. I at once decided to climb Jatropani, just to be alone on a hill in the sun, with the Himalaya spread out northwards. The party would meanwhile continue to Kanol, above the Nandakini River.

A lammergeyer, or bearded vulture, with a wingspan of nine feet, was soaring overhead. I climbed by the east ridge from the col. My route along the crest led me into a broad green avenue between pines and giant rhododendron trees in full bloom – pale purple, scarlet, and pink – not in a tangle of crowded bushes, but each a tall tree standing well spaced and apart from its fellow; each a blossoming of individual glory, encompassed by sunlit air. At the top of the avenue, where the trees began to thin out on the steepening hill, I sat down and watched them for a while.

I tried to let their beauty soak in, and when I did so a new beauty, something additional to all I had yet seen, seemed to shine out of them; out of the grass an added richness of green, out of the pines more fragrance of resin, from the blossom of the rhododendrons a glow of colour still brighter; unfathomable deeps and gentleness bloomed in the sky's blue. This newness taken on by the world was like that of something freshly created. Its loveliness had youth and vigour and an immortality so obviously not of its manifested self, but of that ever new and ancient beauty, wherein all individual things have being and life, and which they serve. Five thousand feet under me, from the dark greens of the Nandakini Gorge up to the brown tip of the lammergeyer's wing, turned to the sky where it wheeled in thin pure air, and in all that lay between, there was displayed the overwhelming harmony of things sharply strange and separate, that fully and from their beginning were entered into one another and oned. How clearly this integrating principle of the universe disposed and flung forth His power that morning. His name men called God, or the Infinite One, Beauty or Truth, according to the context in which His works happen to be seen.

I spent an hour at the head of my avenue on Jatropani. There were clouds gathering when I rose to go, still high and not threatening. But the summit of Jatropani was capped; nothing would be seen if I went there. Farther ascent loomed as an anti-climax. After a step or two I halted and turned down. A pair of lammergeyer were now circling the pass below me. They are one of the greater birds of the Himalaya. They seem to be particularly fond of bones, breaking them up just as a herring-gull opens mussels – by dropping them from a height.

From the pass I sped downhill to Kanol. It began to seem that my quick return was providential, for the expedition had not stopped at Kanol. MacKinnon was wearing moulded rubber soles (Italian Vibrams), and I could follow his spoor in the dust, going on and on, passing the village by detour and descending along the flank of the Mani Gad. The Mani was the deepest gorge I had yet seen. From the distant bottom of that immense V came the roar of a torrent and sometimes glimpse a white flash where the water shot down to the Nandakini.

The track, descending now into the Nandakini Gorge, was extremely steep and stony. At last, on the final and most abrupt descent of all to the Nandakini River, I saw on the floor of the gorge a flat meadow, and standing on it our green base camp tent.

The march carried on in this manner over passes and down to valleys until, having crossed the Kauri Pass (12,140 feet), we dropped down to Tapoban on the Dhauli at 6,000 feet, close to the outflow of the Rishi Gorge. No entry can be made into the gorge at this point, for the river route runs through a box canyon that is said to be impassable.

The heart of the Rishiganga is protected by an inner and outer screen of mountain ridges, which we had now to cross by two passes of 14,000 and 15,000 feet. The first of these was on the ridge to the left of Lata Peak and situated 8,000 feet above the Dhauli. On its right-hand, Rishi side, Lata Peak fell in sheer precipices; but the left-hand, Dhauli side was an immense, thickly wooded slope. Somewhere under the slope lay the village of Lata, whence we should depart for the Rishi country and Bethartoli Himal.

This seemed to be a good place to let Kuar Singh know about our plan of action. So I took him aside and pointed out the Rishiganga, Lata Peak and the pass. He recognised them all instantly. He had never been into the Rishi, but had come thus far once with Tilman. I told him then (after some laborious searching through my vocabulary) that we should probably spend seven days travelling through the Rishi, ten days in the Trisul Nala to climb Bethartoli, and six days withdrawing – a total of twenty-three days. After this had sunk in, and an understanding light had appeared in his eye, I went on to say that all eighteen porters would go as far as the Trisul Nala, then twelve would be sent back and only six would stay. Did he think that six men would stay with us for mountain work? We wanted six men to stay with us for five months. Would we get them?

I was anxious about this last point. Friends in both London and Bombay had warned us that Dotials would not stay so long. Yet I felt certain that these men were as devoted to us as they very well could be: that wherever we chose to go, they would come too – and few questions ever be asked. To my consternation, however, I saw dismay written all over Kuar Singh's face. He waved his hands in expression of sheer incredulity. He said that he did not understand me, meaning that he could follow my words but refused to believe their implication. Some misunderstanding had arisen and my Hindustani was inadequate to get to the bottom of it. Nor could I explain more clearly what we wanted of the Dotials. However, I tried again. I was satisfied then that Kuar Singh followed my words, but the worried and pained expression on his face was more marked than ever. I broke off the conversation.

On reaching Lata we wound our way through the village to reach the main Dhauli track. There was no camping ground here, nor wood for our campfires, but a bungalow rest house (wood-fuel supplied) stood at the eastern outskirts, beside the track and overlooking the river. There we stopped to make our preparations for the great trek to the Rishi Gorge.

19 To the Rishi Gorge

To reach the Rishi Gorge we had to climb to the grassy saddle of the Lata Kharak, from where we were able to make an initial study of the problems of Bethartoli Himal. The peak lay on the rim of the outer curtain of the Nanda Devi Sanctuary, a circling mountain ridge that we must first cross [by the Dharansi Pass] before we could descend to the Rishi and its tributary the Trisul Nala, our intended line of approach to the peak.

The outer curtain was only 2,000 feet above and only one and a half miles to our left, as judged by the map. I could see it to be true mountain ground, but not difficult in a technical sense, apart from the matter of route selection. I remembered that Shipton and Tilman had experienced trouble in finding the route sixteen years before and been bogged down by deep snow. They had been forced to spend two days in crossing the pass from here. Accordingly, I resolved to make an immediate reconnaissance.

We pitched the tent. There was wood in plenty around but no water. However, an old snow wreath lingered several feet down the north slope, and Kuar Singh was soon boiling it down by the potful. I waited only long enough for a mug of tea, then snatched a few biscuits and set off alone. There was a rounded hill 2,600 feet above the camp, and my half-inch map marked the pass immediately to its left. I took no spare food or clothing, for I intended to be back for afternoon tea. The ground looked easy for a mountaineer. The scale had deceived me.

I climbed 1,800 feet on a leftward slant, then began contouring 800 feet under the summit. This was in fact the correct line of the summer route, but in May it carried far too much snow for laden porters. Repeatedly I found myself crossing broad, shallow gullies, brimming with old, well packed snow. A porter who slipped there would slide several hundred feet and might easily strike one of the projecting boulders and so break bones or kill himself. Dotials, of course, are as surefooted as goats, but I had still to see them at work on mountains. Tomorrow, I decided they must go by a lower route. We could not afford time to rope them over so long a traverse.

Other and no less cogent reasons for preferring a low route appeared when at last I had contoured round the hill to the slopes under its long north-easterly ridge, which embarrassed me by offering not one col but four. From each hung shallow gullies filled with soft snow. Between them were long, gently inclined rock ribs. This whole flank, having a north-easterly aspect, bore far more snow than the westerly aspect above the kharak.

I had no choice but to try each of the four cols in turn and the true pass was the fourth. Up each I toiled several hundred feet in knee deep snow, only to find myself on sharp rock edges, from which cliffs dropped 6,000 feet to the Rishiganga. Then back I had to go, scramble over the rock rib lower down, then try the next gully. The drain on energy was immense. Driving myself hard, I spent five hours reaching the pass. The 7,000-foot ascent from Lata had been too much without a meal, and now I proceeded to pay the penalty.

I took my descent direct by a snow gully, dropping 1,000 feet or more and then contouring below the snow line. I had hoped that this route might be easier, but the only advantage it gave was freedom from snow. It traversed in and out of the same gullies, which had now cut deeper into the hill. My pace grew slower and slower. I had made too high an expenditure of energy for too low a fuel intake. Darkness fell when I was little more than halfway to the kharak. Halts became necessary every five minutes, yet if I did halt, fits of shivering came over me, for at 13,000 feet the cold after sundown is around freezing point. In short, I was exhausted. I cannot recall ever having felt so exhausted on a mountainside before. To feel an urgent need to rest, in order to summon up energy for each 100-yard move, and yet to be scared of halting because of the penetration of cold into the body, is a punishment to fit the crime of bad mountaineering tactics. But I had not thought to find myself mountaineering at all.

The situation was partially saved by the discovery, in the pocket of my bushshirt, of a handful of sugar, in the form of sweets, which had been a parting gift to the expedition from Miss Jenny McNeil, of the old Tricouni Club of Glasgow. These got me back to the slopes above the kharak after a fourteen-hour day. I was still several hundred feet above camp, creeping down foot by foot in the dark, when suddenly I came on Kuar Singh and Ram Badur. They were wrapped in blankets and coming up the hill in the faint hope of meeting me. I have never heard such salaams as I heard then. It did me as much good as a noggin of rum.

Scott, Weir and MacKinnon, knowing me better than Kuar Singh, had bedded down, but had kept a potful of hoosh simmering beside the fire for me. I could take no more than a spoonful or two. I had a high temperature and felt flat out and shivery. Just before falling asleep I heard Scott saying that Kuar Singh had brought us bad news: some of the Dotials had insufficient ata (flour) for the double journey. (Truly, I thought, this is one of my bad days.) He had sent Gulab Singh and Gopi back to Lata to fetch up more. But I knew that we should never see them again. Tomorrow we should be over the outer curtain.

THE OUTER CURTAIN

We had barely lain down, I felt, before we were up again. At half past six we were moving up the hillside, climbing 600 feet to clear the scrub on our left, then contouring well below the snow line. My regrets about yesterday's reconnaissance vanished as we contoured, for the Dotials were inclined to grouse at this low route; they wanted to go high as I had done. From below the snow higher up looked ever so much less than it was. It is an optical illusion common to all mountains that expose crag. But for the good fortune of my unfortunate reconnaissance, we should certainly have gone high and quite as certainly been benighted.

So, the Dotials toiled among rough heath and broken ground and called on Shiva to preserve them on their next birth from route-selecting *sahibs.*

At the halfway mark they set fire to the heath behind them, which I assumed to be a route-marker for the benefit of Gulab and Gopi. An acre of the hillside was burning well, and the smoke might well persist until the afternoon.

After four hours we entered the 1,000-foot gully below the pass. We were now at 13,000 feet, the approximate height of Jatropani, and the altitude began to tell on the Dotials. MacKinnon went ahead and kicked the steps. He was the heaviest man we had (about 200 pounds). Where MacKinnon treads no snow will again subside. Accordingly, the first ten Dotials enjoyed a staircase, but wear and tear left unpleasantly outward-sloping steps for the last half dozen, who by natural process were the very men who needed good ones. For the men who were most ill at ease had modestly dropped to the rear. From a good strategic position on top I watched everyone coming up. Like myself, Scott and Weir were impressed by the strength of Zungia. We could see now that he was a man of immense energy and could use it unsparingly. He was thoroughly happy on steep snow with a fifty-pound load. He arrived well ahead of the others, grinning widely. And we knew why. We had nearly turned him down at Ranikhet because we had thought him too old. He had then claimed to be thirty-six and we hadn't believed him. This he knew well. Now and henceforth, until the end of the expedition, he proved himself the best porter we had for mountain work.

A close second was Goria, aged twenty-two, who climbed fast and confidently despite a high-altitude headache. The men who did least well were the very young. They had heavy loads to contend with, were unfamiliar with snow, and not confident of their own capacities. It was obvious that Shivlal and Ram Badur could not be asked to go on high mountain work. The latter was so excellent that we regretted ruling him out.

We rested on the sunlit col for half an hour and gazed across the chasm of the Rishi to the jagged miles of rock slabs rising 6,000 feet on its far side. We pressed on. The goat track went well round several wings of the cliff face, largely free from snow by grace of its south aspect, until at last we came on snow steeply banked on a long ledge. The crags below and above were almost vertical.

The snow being hard-packed, MacKinnon went ahead and cut a line of steps and we rigged a rope across for the Dotials to use as a handrail. There was no need to rope them. If any man slipped, he need just throw back his head and away the load would go, leaving him free. But Dotials, we could see, do not slip. They may go slow, and hesitate, but they stay on their feet. They all used the handrail. Matbir revealed himself as a first-class man on snow. He had confidence and made several journeys at speed to carry loads for his weaker brethren. Four of our permanent men were now fixed – Perimal, Goria, Zungia and Matbir.

The line of ledges led downwards into the bed of a gully. Around here Munmir's headband slipped off. His load went sailing over the cliff, never to be seen again. At one stroke he lost us five days' ata. His own bedding and jacket were lost also. I felt exceedingly sorry for Munmir. He was the only Dotial we ever saw drop a load, and he clearly felt the moment's carelessness to be a professional disgrace. He had dismay in his eyes from then onwards. Our first reaction was profound thankfulness that we had lost a load and not Munmir. But the blow to our plans in the Trisul Nala was severe.

Shortly afterwards the ledges became much easier. When we had travelled half a mile from the pass we emerged on a broad, grassy gully, down which we dropped 1,500 feet, collecting juniper firewood as we moved, to the deserted kharak of Durashi [now known as Dharansi]. It lay in the fold between the outer and inner curtains. Several grey stone huts marked its entrance, doubtless to shelter the shepherds from monsoon rains which are exceptionally heavy in the Rishi country. We passed on across boulders to a meadow of wild blue irises and garlic, watered by a rivulet from an old snow-bed. There we camped. The alp was a sun trap. We sat back and relaxed, looking far across the Rishiganga to the gleaming ranges of Badrinath.

Everyone was exhausted. The Dotials had done nobly but we had never seen them look so weary. All had felt the altitude. To give them a hand, I fetched out the kettle and a canvas water-bucket and made the first of the fifty paces to the snow bed. At once Kuar Singh, Ring Badr and Ram Badur leapt to their feet, exploding with concern at the very thought of my doing camp chores in the presence of sixteen porters. Ring Badr ran up to me and pleaded in a horrified tone of voice for the kettle and bucket. I handed them over. Off he went to fetch water, while Kuar Singh got a fire going and the others helped to pitch the tent.

We gave them an issue of tea leaves that evening, which pleased them mightily, and more cigarettes, for there was going to be frost at night and the firewood ration was too small to keep the cold at bay. They had only one blanket each.

They pitched the high-altitude tents, and these must have been warm enough in all conscience, with three men in each. The remainder used caves and a tent made from the spare groundsheet. For my own part, my high temperature was still with me, so for the first time I took refuge in both of my duck-down sleeping bags.

As might well be imagined we made a late start in the morning. At 8 a.m. Kuar Singh and Goria left us to return towards Dharansi Pass in hope of salvaging Munmir's load, and to see if they could link up with Gulab and Gopi. A forlorn hope. We gave them nylon rope and said that they must be back and across the second pass and down to Dibrugheta before dark. This they promised. Our day's work was indeed easier, in terms of physical strain, than yesterday's. Eastwards lay a gentle slope of 2,000 feet to the pass on the inner curtain. We arrived there early.

As our heads rose above the rim we were suddenly confronted by Nanda Devi (25,645 feet). It filled the whole world, a vast projectile bursting arrow-like from the bent bow of the Rishi Gorge. Essentially it was a rock mountain, and the greatest that we had ever seen or imagined. Circling round its foot within the blue depths of gorge and chasm were the great peaks of the Sanctuary Basin, raising at their iced centre the broad dark plinth from which the peak fairly hurled itself through thin air, tapering to a flame tip, white upon blue space.

The main body of peaks due south of us were much closer and more awesome in their detail of ice and rock. Bethartoli Himal was now only seven miles away (as against Nanda Devi's thirteen). We looked straight on to its 8,000-foot north wall, heavy with ice both from hanging glaciers and the cornice cliffs of its ice cap. The north ridge seemed feasible but the glacier basin under the north col looked certain to be swept by ice avalanches. I accordingly favoured trying the east ridge, which ran left from the summit. We should thus avoid entering the basin, but would need an additional camp and take a day longer to make the summit.

The Dibrugheta alp was 3,000 feet below us, a bright green hollow tucked away in a fold of the opposite mountain, which was called Hanuman (the Monkey God). Between us and it a deep ravine cut southwards from the Hanuman Glacier to the Rishi. High rock walls edging the glacier stream delayed us. On the near wall the Dotials gave a splendid display of rock climbing. They showed ease of movement even when climbing at high angles. They climbed 'on their feet' in the best English style, using the hands only for balance. We have still to see a rock climber in Britain capable of climbing with a fifty-pound load plus a Dotial's grace.

The alp was a great bowl of grass and flowers. Across the Rishiganga the black and white spires of the Nanda Ghunti group stared down at us, starkly hostile. And that made the alp itself all the more a heavenly spot. Carpets of irises and white garlic and forget-me-nots were spread across its wide lawn. We offered up praises to Dr Longstaff, who made this alp famous after his entry to it in 1907, in which year he climbed Trisul.

We were now truly within the anteroom of the Rishi Gorge. Next day was the great day. We had to force a way along the left flank of the gorge to approach the Trisul Nala – a distance of only three and a half miles, but which, judging from the records of our predecessors, would take us two days. We had no idea where the best route went from Dibrugheta, save that we had to turn the wooded shoulder between the Dibrugheta stream and the Rishi.

At 7 a.m. we took a steep slant uphill towards this shoulder, climbing 1,000 feet through a pine forest on softly carpeted ground. That move brought us on to the south flank of Hanuman, 1,400 feet up on the wall of the Rishiganga. At this average level we contoured for the rest of the day, rising and falling in and out of shallow ravines, scrambling up or down to turn crags. Underfoot was a fearsome tangle of dwarf cotoneasters, rose bushes, berberis, brier, laburnum, dwarf rhododendron, flowering currant and plain thorn, which, literally, ripped the pants off the porters. Our climbing boots were scored and the backs of our hands scratched all over; I still cannot understand how the Dotials, wearing only flat rubber sandals, were able to cover the ground without tearing their feet.

At the end of eight hours' hard work we had travelled three miles. The easiest ground for travel lay high, well above the tree line, but there was no ground here flat enough to give rest for the night. The only patch of flat ground that we could see in the gorge lay far below at the edge of the river, and was named Duti [Deodi on modern maps] on the quarter-inch map. It was half a mile short of the Trisul Nala. We descended and pitched camp.

The hard going continued, we took four hours to cover the half-mile, climbing 1,000 feet up a spur, then forcing a way through dense scrub and thorn down to the Rishiganga. We were still below the Trisul Nala, though very close to it, and had now to find a bridging point. The river was here a bellowing flood. We made reconnaissance along the beach, scrambling on a jumble of stone, and chose the narrowest place where enormous boulders on either side could be spanned by saplings. We wanted three of these and fetched out our hatchets. They were seized by Goria and Matbir, who selected and cut the trees. They had a birch and a pine down in half an hour. We tied ropes to the top of the birch, four men poised it on one end and four men on the ropes let it slowly fall. But the final drop was too sudden. The far end bounced on its block and the whole birch fell into the river. While we dragged it ashore the water tossed it about like a straw. Two more attempts failed in the same way. We were new to bridge-building in the Himalaya.

The art of bridge-making is to get a light birch across first to act as a guide rail for the heavier logs. The Dotials were first in realising what was wanted.

They cut a third, more slender birch, which was forced across by MacKinnon and three porters, who sat down and pushed the butt with their feet, while Perimal and I pulled on a rope tied to its top. The heavier birch, its tip resting on the lighter one at a slight angle, was then forced over in the same way. The structure was most unsafe, because the face of the opposite block sloped like a roof and was much higher than that on our own side. Scott tied on a rope, took to his bare feet, and crossed gingerly. Matbir sped after him and together they adjusted the ends of the two trunks. Matbir was in tremendous form, romping like a monkey. He wanted to manage everything himself and to show off a little; for he had real powers of initiative and was young enough to be still freshly aware of them. The heavier pine was now pushed over the other two. All were straightened out and lashed at each end. Goria, Zungia and Matbir were the dominating trio, and remained so always.

We now used 200 feet of rope to form a double handrail and began crossing. The Dotials crossed on their feet carrying eighty-pound loads. Only with difficulty could they be persuaded to tie on to a climbing rope, where one slip on the two uppermost logs, which were wet, would otherwise have cost loss of life.

We pitched camp on ground as flat as a tennis court, raised thirty feet above the river, and were no sooner in shelter than rain was hissing on the rocks and drilling on the roofs. Grey and dismal veils choked the Rishi.

20 Attempts on Bethartoli Himal and Hanuman

From our provisional camp by the Rishi we had two miles to go to reach the snout of the Bethartoli Glacier, which we hoped might take not more than six hours. At 1 p.m. we stopped in a grassy hollow, a far better camp site, a quarter of a mile short of the glacier.

I went on alone along a sharp-crested moraine, which swept in a great curve up the right-hand side of the glacier and eventually was able to look straight on to the north-east face of Bethartoli, which was completely clad in snow and ice. From the east ridge on its left and from the north col on its right plunged two glaciers, which eventually joined at 16,000 feet on the face, then flowed down to the Trisul Nala at 12,500 feet. As a route the glacier was quite impossible. It looked like the Géant ice-fall at Chamonix, multiplied by two. At that moment I was certain that our best line of approach was up the east ridge.

When I returned the tents had been pitched at the new site. Apart from being better placed as a base it also had more firewood.

BETHARTOLI HIMAL

Weir estimated and extracted five days' food for the assault on Bethartoli. It was agreed that tomorrow all four of us should go high into the north-east corrie, satisfy ourselves that no good route led to the north col, then study the east ridge from selected vantage points. Assuming that our choice did fall on the east ridge, we should return by noon to move Camp 2 up to the Trisuli Glacier, close under the ridge.

We now issued the climbing clothes to Zungia, Goria and Matbir, the three who would accompany us on the climb. The boots, all size six on Dr Longstaff's recommendation, fitted them well. We could never quite understand this, for their feet looked of different shapes and sizes. The windproof suits and helmets gave them a lot of fun. On a first fitting they were all self-conscious, and at sight of each other had fits of laughter. The boots were the greatest prize, then the helmets, which had an almost Tibetan appearance.

At eight o'clock the next morning, leaving all porters below, we started up the moraine and in two and a half hours we had climbed to 14,000 feet. From this situation the character of the basin was seen to be quite different from what we had dared to imagine. Running down its centre was a ridge of snow-dusted rock, rising 1,000 feet above the glacier – a perfect and fool-proof screen against ice avalanches falling off the north-east face. By its crest we ought to be able to approach the north col. The entire length of the ridge was in view and displayed no wall or tower capable of stopping us. Thus we scrapped my alternative plan for the east ridge and reverted to the original, myself concurring. And that was a most unfortunate decision.

For the Dotials our situation was a completely new experience. Directly opposite our camp was the great ice-fall of the glacier, discharging its occasional avalanche in a puffing cascade. Goria exclaimed 'Pani!' (water) when he first saw one, and had to be corrected, to his wonderment. The Dotials had never before seen a big mountain close up with its hair down.

Neither here nor at any other time of our journeyings did we see colourful sunsets and dawns such as we can even begin to compare with the vivid beauty of those common to west Scotland in hard and frosty weather. The sky instead had a magic clarity peculiar to rarefied air, a dazzling darkness of outer space, a gargantuan emptiness like that under the dome of some long-deserted palace, where sound echoes hollow. From across the Rishiganga came a shining of peaks that flashed like sharks' teeth – Changabang, Rishi Kot, Dunagiri – their names wound a soundless thunder-note across the empty Himalayan skies.

The night promised to be bitter. We all retired then, but came out again at half past eight – despite the cold. Moonlight bathed the peaks of the northern watershed. The Plough stood directly over the tent and the sky glittered frostily, a dark but distinct blue. The nearest of the great peaks, Rishi Kot, turned to us an edge like a cutlass but black as gun-metal, whereas Changabang, its neighbour, by day the most like a vast eye-tooth fang, both in shape and colour – for its rock was a milk-white granite – Changabang in the moonlight shone tenderly as though veiled in bridal lace; at ten miles' distance seemingly as fragile as an icicle; a product of earth and sky rare and fantastic, and of liveliness unparalleled, so that unawares one's pulse leapt and the heart gave thanks that this mountain should be as it is.

The Bethartoli attempt began well enough. Zungia, Goria and Matbir had helped us with loads to a high camp but at two o'clock thunder clouds began blowing up the Rishiganga and over Dunagiri. At the same time the ridge was growing difficult. I roped the Dotials down a short wall to the continuing snow edge. At that point we halted. It had become necessary to send them back. We could not take them farther and expect them to get back alone. They had natural talent, but not enough experience of snow-bound rock; nor dared we hold them longer in face of the weather's threat. Accordingly, I waited with the rope at the mauvais pas, while the Dotials went only to the top of the next tower and returned unladen. I saw them safely up the wall and told them to be back in two days' time. We parted with many salaams, Goria at the last turning to Bethartoli Himal and raising his clasped hands to his forehead in a special salaam to the summit. They were glad to go.

I joined the others at the top of the tower. The situation there was unexpectedly bad. A short way ahead was a great gendarme, neither high nor steep on our side, but on the other dropping in a chasm. Beyond it the ridge led easily to the north top and so to the north col; but the chasm looked ugly. On the near side of the tower was a snow-saddle. On this Weir and MacKinnon began to hack out two platforms for the tents. Meanwhile, Scott and I roped up and went forward to try the descent of the tower.

We found it to be 200 feet high. Scott belayed. I climbed down a wafer-like edge, where thin cornices of rock and snow overhung space on my right. A hold cut too vigorously on the left flank was apt to puncture the ridge and grant sudden, alarming vistas through the peephole. I dropped down a series of vertical steps and landed on a big block. I lay flat on my stomach and looked over the brink. Under my chin was a vertical wall of twenty-five feet, then, leaning out like a tilted pencil, a huge finger of rock with a clear drop of 100 feet below. We might be able to go down on a doubled rope. But if we did, we could never climb up again. Nor was there any way of descending the left flank to the upper glacier, the angle of which was now easing off as it drew near to the col. I went back to Scott and reported: we were defeated. A ridge otherwise perfect to our purpose was marred by this one gap, which had been invisible from Camp 2. Scott now climbed over the edge to look for himself and soon came back to confirm my verdict. We could do nothing more – save camp.

An ascent of Bethartoli Himal was thus no longer possible. My own wish was to complete the reconnaissance of the mountain by climbing Peak 18,110 feet and examining the east approach at close quarters. We should then know definitely if an eastern route existed and thus contribute something of value to help a future expedition. Weir preferred collecting the northern top, for the route to it was assured. Scott, on the other hand, wanted to cut our losses on Bethartoli Himal and go to Hanuman, which rose above the junction of the Rishi and Rhamani Gorges.

HANUMAN BY THE EAST RIDGE

Hanuman (19,930 feet) was unclimbed, and displayed before us its east ridge that looked positively easy – easy at seven miles range. Its ascent should need no more than our remaining three days.

After returning to the Rishi Camp and recrossing the river we climbed 5,000 feet, first by a boulder-filled gully and then up open hillside, and established a camp in a small corrie on the south-east face at around 16,000 feet. From the rim of the corrie we had good views of the Upper Rhamani Glacier.

The following day we gained Hanuman's east ridge at 18,000 feet by kicking a ladder of steps up a long snow couloir.

The ridge provided an excellent route. The crest was rocky and narrow but allowing us good and steady progress. Sometimes an abrupt wall would force us off the crest but no rope was necessary – until we had climbed another thousand feet. There we came on a square-faced tower of fifty feet, which completely blocked the ridge. It had of course not been seen by us from Bethartoli.

Wide, outward-sloping ledges allowed us to traverse rightwards, but we could find no way there and came back. We roped up. Scott attacked the cliff on its right flank by the line of a broken inset corner. The angle was close to vertical. At the very top an overhang had to be turned leftwards by an awkward contortion. It was a good lead. We emerged on an arching snowfield in mist. We must be close to the summit, perhaps 900 feet below it at most? The rest of the ridge should be a straightforward snow ridge. One hour would take us up.

We climbed optimistically into the mist until a sudden gulf opened at our feet. It was the brink of a vertical chasm, a complete break in the ridge – there was no way round. Peering into the mist we could just distinguish a col perhaps 300 feet below. Across the gap we could see the rock ridge continuing, broken and stony and swiftly soaring. A most tantalising ridge, for it was climbable. As for the chasm – that was impassable.

Our attempts on Bethartoli Himal and Hanuman had given us valuable experience in diverse ways.[1] They had given information of routes that could be useful to other parties; helped us to acclimatise; shown us that even the one chance in 1,000 of dropping a load must be guarded against while traversing cliff faces, by spreading as big a variety of food and gear among as many men as possible, and so never having, say, all sleeping bags in one load. We had been most fortunate in losing only one load of food. Had we lost anything else – tents, sleeping bags, climbing gear, or stoves – the result would have been catastrophic. We had been alerted also to the Himalayan scale, and to the rashness of placing trust on the evidence of inexperienced eyes. Snow conditions had been revealed as alarming.

1 Bethartoli Himal was attempted in 1956 from the north-east by a German team, and in 1970 by the south face by an Indian team that had four fatalities. An American expedition also attempted the south face in 1977 and in the same year an Italian group led by Renato Moro made the first ascent by the north ridge. The summit was gained on 17 September by Cesare Cesa Bianchi, Maurizio Maggi, Renato Moro, Marco Tadeschi and Gian Luigi Landreani (*AAJ* 1978, p.604). The south summit (6,318 metres) was first reached by the 1956 German group led by F. Hieber and has since been climbed twice, both ascents in 1977, by Australian and American groups. The fist ascent of Hanuman was made in 1966 by seven members of an Indian Expedition led by A.R. Chaudekar by a route up the eastern flank of the mountain.

These last two matters, of scale and snow, are worth noting. We had learned not to estimate the difficulties of any Himalayan ridge by its average angle. On Hanuman especially our chosen ridge did look easy as seen through binoculars from seven miles' distance. But the tiniest nicks and steps, rock or ice, which look trifling from the foot of the mountain and may be invisible at long distance, can turn out to be chasms and walls 200–300 feet high or deep. The swift effect of the fierce Himalayan sun on snow had taken us all by surprise. We had thought that the effects would be less around 18,000 feet than in the Alps. The reverse was the truth. In the Alps a mountaineer reckons that snow will not go bad on him before midday. In Kumaon it was getting dangerous at 8 a.m. and was bad by nine – in pre-monsoon days. Our lesson had thus been learned rapidly and early on, to our profit.

The double defeat in the Rishi country we felt to be no failure. On first crossing the threshold we had felt well assured that come what may we should see great and curious things, work hard, meet beauty, encounter trouble, learn much and that of value. We came out of the Rishi well satisfied in soul if not in belly. Our apparent misfortunes had no sting.

21 Mountaineering and Medicine in Dunagiri

By mid-June we had moved to the village of Dunagiri, set at 11,800 feet, high above Ruing in the Dhauli Valley. From here we hoped to explore the Lampak range. It lies eighteen miles due north of Nanda Devi, bounded north and south by the Girthiganga and Dunagiri Gad. They were completely untouched mountains. No one had explored them before or made attempt on so much as one peak, of which there were ten. Five were over 20,000 feet. With our base at Dunagiri village, we should also have access to half a dozen unclimbed peaks to our south, outliers of Dunagiri (23,184 feet) which had seen several attempts before its ascent by the Swiss in 1939 by an approach from the Rishi side.

Trevor Braham of the Himalayan Club had seen the whole group in 1947 when descending the Banke Glacier on the west side of the Dhauli; he had described them to me as unusually beautiful. The first man to advise us to go there was Dr Longstaff; only he had recommended a first approach from the north via Malari. He had seen their south aspect when crossing the Bagini Pass in 1907 and had not been tempted. They had looked hopelessly difficult.

When MacKinnon and I walked by tilled fields close under Dunagiri, we could tell that this was going to be the most prosperous village of our journey. These fields were well cared for and the goats big and healthy, with long glossy coats.

The village was set in steps on the north slope of the glen, looking high over green terraces. It comprised some sixty houses, one near the centre having a large courtyard, which we singled out as the meeting place. No more than one or two men were to be seen but within a few minutes that courtyard was crammed to capacity. Rugs were spread for us on the wall and the schoolmaster came forward as host. He was a man of sixty.

I wasted no time. I gave a quick summary of our plans. Could we have twelve porters in a week or ten days to carry loads to Malari? 'Yes.' Such quick agreement nonplussed me. I suspected that my schoolmaster was a Scottish West Highland type, courteous to the death and, as a matter of high principle, would never say no, however much he may mean no. When I looked round, however, all suspicions vanished. In men, women and children we had not seen elsewhere faces more friendly or good looking. They were free from all trace of trouble, whether of body or soul.

Having heard our tale and taken stock of us, the people called forward the children, perhaps twenty. Each child came towards us in turn, without either haste or bashful hesitation, clasped both hands and salaamed, bowed, then stood back and sat down. Their ages varied between six and twelve; such excellent manners and bearing are not to my knowledge found in the western world in children of like age. The people are Bhotias and migrate south in winter to Pursari, at 4,000 feet. Their principal occupation in summer is the trade with Tibet, when sixty families occupy the village.

I asked a few more questions. We could have all the ata we needed and all the potatoes. Then everyone dispersed, leaving us with one or two young men of fifteen years. When I laid out the half-inch maps on the wall I found that they could read them. Moreover, they could read names in Roman script, whether Hindi or English. This they did with some difficulty but without error.

Scott and Weir arrived, followed closely by the Dotials. A great bout of photography ensued. The school had resumed work in a nearby yard, the children sitting on individual mats before a blackboard. They had slates on their knees, and over their faces that charmingly worried look with which the human learns something new. Outside many of the houses the women had returned to their weaving on looms. Scott and Weir were in their element.

MacKinnon and I left them to it and went in search of a campsite. We found an excellent place a quarter of a mile away on the opposite side of the glen. The ground was steep pasture, save for this tiny level hollow beside a birch wood. A rivulet ran through it. Thus we had firewood within a stone's throw and pure water within three yards.

Thus far we had been unable to see the mountains we hoped to explore because of the cloudy conditions, but there seemed to be every promise of a big-scale clearance. We were now able to see the long hill-ridge that walled the north side of the Dunagiri Gad and the snout of the Bagini Glacier. This ridge comprised half a dozen peaks, which screened from us the still higher mountains of the Lampak group. Our course of action was clear. We must climb one of the mountains of the screen, and from it reconnoitre the big game behind. None of these mountains had ever been named or attempted. We chose the nearest, Point 17,830 feet, on which we could see a route slanting from left to right up the south flank. We should then strike the crest a mile west of the summit. What obstacles the crest might provide we could not see. We should have a climb of 6,000 feet, for which Weir and I resolved to rise at 4 a.m. MacKinnon and Scott wanted a rest day.

We gained the crest relatively easily but the visibility was poor, preventing any useful assessment of the Lampak range. The peak we were on remained desirable however, being unclimbed, so we followed the narrow and shattered ridge eastwards and reached the summit at 1.30 p.m. after a somewhat trying ascent. To keep fatigue at bay on the last 800 feet, an exhausting slope of shale, we had to breathe deeply, once to each step. Nevertheless our performance was greatly improved from the Rishi days.

Our descent we shall long remember as one of the most exasperating of our lives. The various gendarmes on the ridge were tricky but stimulating, whereas the shale slopes and boulders were unstable and dangerous. On the low-angle boulders, even with care, we had narrow escapes from crushing a foot or leg between toppling blocks. We became short-tempered and peppery.

However, we came into camp in the evening feeling cheerful again, feeling that we had had a good climb. For Weir and me tomorrow must be a rest day, but we earnestly hoped that Scott and MacKinnon would rectify our reconnaissance failure. For their first ascent they selected Point 16,690 feet, two miles to the south-south-east of Dunagiri. This would give them a view of the south-west aspect of the Lampak peaks, clustering around the head of the Bagini Glacier some six miles from their viewpoint. In particular, if the sky were clear, they would look for the approach to the peak at 20,560 feet. As clear conditions were unlikely after 9 a.m. they planned to be away by 3 a.m. Perimal was warned to have a fire ready for breakfast at 2 a.m.

We then heard that MacKinnon had spent one of the most useful days of his life. His remaining behind had been a stroke of good fortune. After a brisk morning's business at the dispensary he had been called into the village with Scott to attend to a girl's foot. She was only two years old and her hideously septic foot was puffed out like a football with old pus: encased by dead and blackened skin, which the mother had kept carefully wrapped around the putrefaction. It stank sickeningly. Even the toes had lost their separateness and were joined in a mass of infected flesh. At first sight it had looked like a case for amputation. MacKinnon had cut all the skin and stripped the foot down to its tissues, then washed with antiseptics until the blood had begun to flow. After that he had burst one of our few phials of penicillin. We were glad of that. It sounded a desperate case, but one of the very kind that would be most likely to yield to penicillin treatment. The question was whether we should be long enough at Dunagiri to see results.

Perimal excelled himself. Without having to be roused, and having no watch, he rose at 1.20 a.m. to get the fire going. Zungia and Goria were up also. We had sometimes cursed Perimal on account of his uncertain handling of his men and lack of decision compared with Kuar Singh, but in truth we had little to complain about. Kuar Singh had set high standards. Tonight and forever Perimal won my respect.

At half past one MacKinnon and Scott returned. They had had the climb of their lives on a long ridge of granite, narrow and spectacular, like the west ridge of Sgurr nan Gillean in Skye prolonged to 2,000 feet. They had reached their summit and come down by a gully, which had given them the father and mother of all glissades – 3,000 feet, they said, with never a stop. Weir and I listened agape, and cursed our ill fortune in missing this wonder. For a mountain that can really be enjoyed in the Himalaya – enjoyed while one is actually climbing it – is a wonder indeed. Not even the descent was tiring, but instead a climax to the day's exhilarating thrills.

The sad fact remained that no reconnaissance had been made of the Lampak group. Not a hill had they seen all day; nothing but the everlasting cloud, getting daily worse. The date was 16 June with probably ten days before the monsoon broke. We decided to spend no further time on reconnoitre efforts, but at once to establish a camp on the Bagini Glacier stock it with seven days' food, then try to put in another camp on the peak's southern glacier at 18,000 feet, where the maps showed wide spaced contour lines. I accordingly told Perimal to get twenty seer of ata. He came back to report that ata would be ground tomorrow and delivered at 5 p.m. This left us with one clear day: a gift to Weir and me. We promptly agreed to repeat the ascent of Point 16,690 feet.

That same afternoon I accompanied MacKinnon into the village to dress the girl's foot. To me it looked a horrifying mess, but MacKinnon swore that it was so greatly improved that he could hardly recognise it as the same foot. He now managed to separate the toes. He washed, and applied more penicillin. I had fetched the schoolmaster along to watch MacKinnon dress the foot, for it was necessary, while we were away, that someone should know how to deal with it. We left him with a good supply of bandages and acriflavine tablets and told him to wash the foot every two days. He saw the performance; I think he understood. From the look in his eye my opinion was that he would not act. We could have no conversation with the mother, for she had no Hindi. But she might get the schoolmaster to tell her what to do.

That night I slept alone in the high-altitude tent. Such peace I never knew. I read by candlelight until 11 p.m. – an intellectual debauch. I read most nights, but rarely for long. One always felt that other people were being kept awake by the light. My own reading matter was a notebook of highly condensed philosophy. Weir had Homer's *Odyssey*. Scott had the four Gospels, and MacKinnon had forgotten to bring anything. We did not find our reading heavy. At this stage we had no desire of light reading. My own feeling was that my mind was getting no tough or weighty employment during the day and accordingly welcomed a stretching at night. At home, in the climbing huts, mountaineers read *Men Only* and *Lilliput*. I never see them read anything else for more than two minutes together. But that is short-term holiday fare, and for such soporifics we had no taste at all. We wanted meat, concentrated – but not in bulk, for that would be too expensive in candles.

DUNAGIRI PEAK

Weir and I set off at 3.30. It was a dark night with no moon. Thick mist was pouring up the Dunagiri Gad and sheet lightning flickered incessantly among the clouds on the Bagini Glacier. The little stream flowing through our campsite issued from the northern corrie of our mountain which we followed by torchlight until a quarter past four.

Our peak sent north to the Dunagiri Gad two long ridges enclosing the corrie. The route taken by Scott and MacKinnon went up the right hand of these ridges which we gained by contouring. After a few hundred feet we came on to solid granite, milky white, like the rock of Changabang. There was never a loose hold anywhere. The ridge became a true arête thrusting cleanly through the air. Many small towers had to be taken direct and long sharp edges traversed, sometimes on the crest but more often by lower ledges. This fine ridge gave us over a 1,000 feet of airy rock climbing. Near its top the edge became horizontal but sharp, riven into innumerable teeth, each encircled most emphatically by thin air, and all brightened by occasional rents in the cloud letting in the sun on to our ridge. Its level edge gradually broadened to give us easy walking where it swung round a corner then narrowed in a series of spikes and dropped to a col 1,500 feet under the summit.

Above were two buttresses, one above the other, their pale grey faces imposing another 1,000 feet of rock climbing. At ten o'clock we laid hands on two rock points, which turned out to be twin summits.

On one of the points we built a little cairn, then settled down to see if the clouds might lift. After several minutes there had been no sign of change. Thus our third reconnaissance was doomed, we thought, to failure as before. There seemed no alternative to going blind up the Bagini Glacier tomorrow, hoping for a close but foreshortened view of Peak 20,560 feet.

We were just about to descend when a whole mass of cloud at the head of the Bagini Glacier swirled aside. One after another the Lampak mountains emerged shining from head to foot, the sky above them a stainless blue; such a sky, one might have sworn, no cloud had ever sullied, or ever would sully. All this in a trice. At the back of the Bagini Glacier stood the unnamed summit of the range at 21,770 feet. Its top was an icecap, shaped as a right-pointing triangle like the turned-back cowl of a Cistercian monk. Slightly below and to the left Point 20,560 feet appeared as a shoulder of the main summit. And from head and shoulder, as though from the erect back of the Cistercian standing at his altar, there dropped 6,000 feet to the Bagini Glacier a mantle of white. This wide, snow-draped precipice was higher and more terrible by far than the Matterhorn north face.

The south-west glacier, by which we had hoped to make our ascent was revealed as a hanging glacier, steeper, if anything, than the northerly ice-fall of Bethartoli Himal. The well-spaced contour lines on the map bore little relation to the reality. Mountaineers accustomed only to Swiss and French Alpine maps should take warning. In face of the vastness and complexity of the Himalaya, the Indian maps represent a human triumph over great natural obstacles, and are amazingly accurate. The Indian Survey won our whole-hearted admiration. The map contours are sound guides to the shapes of the mountains, but their spacing is not reliable. Often they are right; often, as now, we found them wrong.

We determined to go down at once and cancel the Bagini Glacier trip. As the cloud returned we descended north by another ridge that actually formed the other arm, with our ridge of ascent, of a great horseshoe. After an 800-foot descent we came to a col, from which a broad snow gully fell to the north corrie. This could be none other than the glissade. Down we sailed, 1,000 feet into the mist – 1,000 feet out of it – non-stop to the floor of the corrie. In two hours from the summit we covered the 5,000 feet back to camp.

We had now set our hearts upon climbing a virgin mountain of over 20,000 feet. But it was now evident that that was no simple matter in eastern Garhwal. We had thus far not set eyes on a peak of such height that did not offer a high degree of difficulty. What prospects would there be further to the north? The map contours showed more inviting lines of approach – but we no longer trusted contour lines. However, to the north lay our only hope.

A CHANGE OF PLAN

We had been prepared to operate from Dunagiri until the breaking of the monsoon. Now we resolved to put into execution, without delay, the third part of our plan. Our strategic move to the Tibetan side of the main axis should give us the relatively clear skies here denied us. But there would be more likelihood of this theory working out true if we could get there just before the monsoon and climb during its earlier stages, rather than wait until the heavier weather, delayed by the Nanda Devi massif, had had any chance to move north. We hoped that such heavy weather would never reach us, but hope is not knowledge.

It was decided. Tomorrow we go north. I told Perimal. He replied enthusiastically saying that instead of taking porters from Dunagiri we should be able to hire *jhopa*. We had no idea what *jhopa* might be. A hurried search through a dictionary and two grammars made us no wiser.

I tried other means. How many *jhopas* were at Dunagiri? 'Six,' said Perimal. What weight could each one carry? 'Two maunds (160 pounds).' How much did they cost? 'Rupees ten per day.' The only conclusion we could come to was that they must be horses. We had seen no other pack animals save goats. They would be no dearer than porters – indeed, a little cheaper. So I went into the village to find the *jhopawala*. But he and his *jhopas* were all 'ooper'. It was arranged that tomorrow morning he would visit the camp to make a bandobast.

Thus we were graced by another 'rest-day' – one of these exceedingly busy rest-days, which are the only kind that the Himalaya grant.

Our plan was simple enough, as it might appear on paper, but not so simple to carry out. We proposed to move just nine miles as the crow flies – from Dunagiri to the Lampak grazing ground on the north-east side of the group – an alp like Durashi, utterly deserted except when goats were driven over the Surans ka Dhura Pass. It looked a very lonely place on the map, situated beside the snout of the Uja Tirche Glacier. To reach it we should have to travel two days north to Malari, either by the Dhauli track or by a high-level route over two passes of 13,620 feet and 14,790 feet, and then go eastwards two days over the Surans ka Dhura at 15,000 feet. The move thus involved 9,000 feet of ascent and four days' travel over sixteen miles. Two days more would have to be spent at Malari to buy in thirty days' food, and get porters for the eastward move.

Two *jhopawalas* appeared prompt at 8 a.m. I told them our needs: five *jhopas* for a two-day journey to Malari. For once no long bargaining was required. They asked Rupees ten daily per *jhopa*. I agreed. And each *jhopa* would carry two maunds? They agreed. They were young shepherds with frank faces and friendly eyes, with hearts no more set on hard bargaining than our own. In our innocence we thought how pleasant and easy it was to deal with the men of Dunagiri, not yet realising that behind the shepherds lay their master, a dragon with whom we had not reckoned. I asked them what route they would recommend. To our joy they chose the high route. The Dhauli they said, was *kharab* (we heartily agreed – its dust and traffic seemed unattractive after the freshness of the 12,000-foot level), whereas 'ooper' was a *thik rasta*, which means a good route. This surprised us. On the map it looked a bad one from the standpoint of a *jhopa* – not that we knew what *jhopas* were – for the passes were exceedingly steep and the second had crags around the top. The men, however, were mountaineers to the bone; their *jhopas* would be trained accordingly.

They departed to fetch the *jhopas* down from 'ooper'.

In the afternoon I accompanied MacKinnon into the village to attend to the girl's foot. The bandage as usual was covered with mud and dust, but when MacKinnon unwrapped it the foot was disclosed as clean and healing. I can only assume that the penicillin must have worked this miracle. He had been dressing it for only four days. No less a word than hideous can describe its original condition; now it looked healthily raw. Cure was certain – if the mother kept it clean. We tried again to impress upon the schoolmaster the need for washing it in acriflavine every two days, and today we had the mother wash it herself. We both felt much concerned lest all the good work should now be undone. At the back of our minds lurked the notion that MacKinnon's work on that foot was of consequence greater than the expedition's mountain plans.

Our last evening at Dunagiri was celebrated in a manner befitting the ripening genius of Weir. He honoured us with a four-course banquet, nine-tenths of which (estimated by weight – not bulk) consisted of a steamed pudding made out of ata, suet and raisins, wrapped in a bit of old pyjama and boiled one hour in a pot. This was a great and resounding triumph. We wanted to stay on at Dunagiri, surrounded by our dozen unclimbed mountains, and eat Weir's puddings forever. This night we can claim as one night of our lives when the desire of mountains did not afflict us, and when our books lay unopened and unheeded. There are things more weighty than philosophy and epic.

THE HIGH-LEVEL ROUTE TO MALARI

Early in the morning of 19 June the long-expected *jhopas* plodded like a squadron of tanks into camp. They were like yaks – beautiful, long-horned animals with black and grey coats of deep pile, a cross between the yak and the cow. They were true beasts of burden, enormously strong, short in the leg, and broad in the hoof. I heaved a happy sigh, for there was no doubt that these *jhopas* would be able to carry two maunds. And their eyes, we had noted, were mild.

This morning, alas, the real *jhopawala* had turned out himself. He was a stern-mouthed man with a roman nose, long grey hair, and a lean and leathery cheek. His eye was fierce. He sucked fiercely at a hubble-bubble pipe. He gave quick, short orders to his shepherds, who then ignored the loads we had weighed out and just seized the boxes at random, lashed one on each side of each *jhopa*, and with a calculated lack of ceremony heaved a lighter kit bag in between. The resultant load was barely one and a half maunds. I protested. A great mound of baggage was left over – very heavy loads for the Dotials. The *jhopawala* declared that one and a half maunds was the maximum (later I discovered that this was the normal load), but I reminded him of yesterday's bandobast – two maunds at ten rupees. He refused to listen.

There followed a protracted argument over what was to be carried. The price was eventually settled at five *jhopas* each to carry two maunds for ten rupees. It was the original agreement. Everyone was happy and smiling; one would have thought that no breath of dispute had ever ruffled these serene and amiable faces. Nothing said in heat seems ever to be held against a man; neither defeat nor victory is ever gloated over; no doubt that explains why Indian hillmen are free to wrangle so vehemently.

The *jhopas* were loaded and away we went, heading north for the pass of the Kanari Khal (13,620 feet). The descent into the Kalla Gad went easily. This glen runs westwards from a cirque of four 20,000-foot mountains. It was adorned by two widely distant alps, each an emerald oasis in that ice-worn ravine. The upper one lay directly under the south wall of our next day's pass, the Kalla Khal (14,790 feet) a very tough-looking proposition.

The following morning we set off for the pass. Suddenly the clouds parted to reveal a clear view of the western flank of Lampak (20,280 feet), and it was clear that no ascent from this side was likely. There seemed to be no way of gaining access to the north or south ridges.

I followed on behind the labouring *jhopas*. The animals were (I admit) too heavy-laden. They were not unduly distressed. They simply went dead slow; one step at a time, responding reluctantly to whacks, whistles and prods.

Near the top the route became a ledge winding among rock. This was more than the *jhopas* would face, so the Dotials returned from the pass and carried the loads.

The Kalla Khal was cold and cloudy. As soon as we had descended out of the cloud, we saw the first clear evidence of our having crossed the main axis of the Himalayan chain; we were entering an entirely different kind of country. It was a more barren land. Over a wide moor and a lower grassland the soil was dry and the vegetation sparse. On all the northern slopes of the mountains the rock was crumbly and rotten, usually reddish brown in colour.

After descending 2,000 feet we could again see the Dhauli, still a mighty canyon, and still twisting, more sharply now, among mountains. Malari was invisible, but we passed through its highest cultivated zone of bare, grey and stony fields. The track narrowed on the side of an escarpment and then the path straightened along the top of a broad ridge. From its utmost tip we saw Malari.

It lay several hundred feet below. A hundred or more houses clustered above a huge, flat table of pale grey soil, elevated some 500 feet above the Dhauliganga. The land seemed smooth as a billiard table, prepared with a lavish care and now crying to all the heavens for rain-rain-rain. I have rarely seen any work of man more appealing. This monsoon of which we were so scared was to Malari the one and needful friend, without which all life here must come to an end. The village was built in tiers with roofs set so close that we could hardly see any gaps between the houses. The formation was typically Tibetan, set upon the very brink of a precipice. The whole great cluster hung together like a bee-swarm on a bough.

In all this grey land stood one tree, startlingly green, at the centre of the great grey table.

We came down to the rest house, which faced Malari across the westward plunging river. The *jhopas* were unloaded and the Dunagiri men paid off for they had to get the animals back to pasture before nightfall. We visited the village that evening and found fresh eggs in good supply. The narrow and twisting streets and the house verandas gave deep, dramatic vistas into the gorges.

The long-awaited rain fell all that night and continued into the following morning. Scott and MacKinnon set out on a seven-mile trip up the Dhauli to Bampa, attracted there by a post office and two Canadian nurses from whom we hoped of replenish our supplies of iodine. This was for Perimal, who had goitre, which had caused him shortness of breath ever since Bethartoli Himal.

NEGOTIATIONS IN MALARI

I had to spend the afternoon bargaining with Bala Singh, the head Malari porter. He refused to allow his men to carry more than forty pounds for four rupees. I agreed at once but demanded that they travel to Lampak in one march instead of two. He refused so I said they must carry sixty pounds. At intervals I retired, to eat one of Weir's steamed puddings or to write letters and diaries, while Bala Singh and his men argued among themselves, since they could not argue with me. But they always supported Bala Singh when I came out. The Malari men, it seemed, had never heard of Scotsmen and were slow to learn. Towards evening I cut all further discussion and they had to go home.

This meant still another full day at Malari while our own Dotials sat on their behinds doing nothing. We determined not to be held to ransom in this way. Tomorrow morning we would put on an act and stage a departure: Scott and MacKinnon would go down river to Kosa, Weir and I up river to Bampa, in pretence of seeking porters. That would bring the issue to a head.

At this juncture Scott and MacKinnon returned. Most of the Bampa men, they said, had already left for Tibet. We might get one or two porters there, not more. Otherwise they had had a most helpful day. The Canadian nurses had known of our progress through the Dhauli from Tapoban to Dunagiri and the time of our arrival at Malari. Being innocent of such an efficient bush telegraph, we were astonished. Scott and MacKinnon reaped its benefits in arriving at Bampa to find tea just ready for them.

The nurses had given MacKinnon iodine, with which he now began dosing Perimal, and given Scott the recipe for making biscuits and pancakes out of ata, which he now passed on to Weir.

Early on our second morning Bala Singh and his men were again waiting for us in the yard. They were keen to come, but as unrelenting as ever in their wage demands. We therefore made preparations to leave – packing rucksacks, making sandwiches, consulting maps.

Perimal came in haste and asked where we were going. In a voice loud enough for the Malari men to hear I said:

'Two *sahibs* go to Kosa and two to Bampa. There are plenty porters at Bampa.'

We could hear quick, agitated, argument in the background. Bala Singh's men were in revolt against him. All that we needed now was an excuse for a few minutes' delay. But our rucksacks were on our backs and we must not appear to linger. Just then an old woman came to MacKinnon bearing a sick child – a naked baby, perhaps eighteen months old. He looked sadly underweight and bloodless; his head hung to one side and his stare was vacant. There was nothing we could do.

When the boy had been taken away Bala Singh stepped forward. His men closed round. They would carry sixty pounds at four rupees, plus two rupees for the return – our original offer – but now Bala Singh proposed that instead of twelve men I should take seven. He would provide eighteen goats to carry the bulk of our 500 pounds of ata, these goats to be reckoned as the equivalent of five men for purposes of pay. I looked at his men's faces. They were in agreement. The smaller number of men would share more money.

Everything was now settled. Weir and I spent the rest of the morning juggling with stores and supervising the packing of ata, while Scott and MacKinnon visited the village where they were lucky to witness a series of exotic ritual dances in honour of the monsoon.

The sky that night was heavy with cloud.

22 The Ascent of Uja Tirche and an attempt on Lampak South

Eighteen goats arrived at 6 a.m., accompanied by two young shepherds, who attached the saddle-bags and set off. We and the thirteen porters followed an hour later. The spine of the Lampak group runs south to north from the Bagini Glacier to the Girthiganga. The last big peak at the north end is Kunti Bhannar (19,340 feet), from which the ridge slopes down to the Girthi (pronounced *Geertee*) at 10,000 feet. To reach Lampak we had to cross this northern spur by the Surans ka Dhura Pass (15,000 feet). This was crossed two days later, after which the track wound down among shattered crags. Then we slanted down and rightwards across hillsides everywhere covered in wild flowers. They scented the air all the way down to Lampak.

We had descended just half a mile from the Surans ka Dhura Pass when the crossing of a rib gave us our first and urgently desired view into the Girthiganga. Next month's opening move for part four of our plan was revealed. We looked down into a monstrous gorge where it branched. The left branch, the Kio Gad, looked terrific – walled by rock peaks like the Dolomites. Ramba Kot (17,150 feet), separated the two branches, its innumerable buttresses plunging straight into both rivers. The right-hand branch was the true Girthi, but we could not see into it. Access to it went from Lampak, low down across the northerly spur of a mountain called Uja Tirche, which faced us now for the first time. The route into the Girthi Gorge was clear but all our thoughts of that future adventure were forgotten when we turned our eyes to Uja Tirche (pronounced *Ooja Teerchay*).

The day was sunny. As always clouds had spread over the Lampak group, which formed one side of a vast horseshoe of ten 20,000-foot mountains. They fed the Uja Tirche Glacier, which had its origin in the north wall of Tirsuli at the back of the horseshoe, and which flowed seven miles north to Lampak grazing ground, thence sending a stream three or four miles down the Siruanch Ghat to the Girthi.

Uja Tirche dominated Lampak from across the glacier with a 7,000-foot wall of cliff and hanging glacier, culminating in a peak of 20,350 feet. Towards Tibet and the pass of the Kungribingri La to India, it presented a sheer north-east face rising 8,000 feet out of the Girthiganga. To ourselves it presented a sharp north ridge of 10,000 feet, which we saw in profile. The entire mountain was clear of clouds.

As we looked at that north ridge a flicker of hope began to stir in every one of us – at last we might be able to climb a 20,000-foot peak. From Lampak a good route slanted right to left up the west flank, aiming towards the saddle by which we hoped one day to enter the Girthi Gorge. Well before the saddle we should have to turn rightwards, then strike straight up for the crest. There the ridge ran level for a half a mile, bearing on its edge nine gigantic pinnacles. The centre three were at least 200 feet high. If these were possible – and we could indulge no fond hopes after our Rishi experiences – access would be had to a twisting snow ridge of 2,000 feet, twice interrupted by high steps of ice.

We determined to try this route at once. The first essential was to get our Base Camp established. As we dropped down towards the snout of the Uja Tirche Glacier the clouds lifted from the north wall of Tirsuli. Probably we were the first mountaineers ever to see that stupendous face – a precipice of snow and ice three miles long and 7,000 feet high. Tirsuli had only once been attempted, by the ill-fated Polish expedition of 1939,[1] and that from the Milam Glacier on its far side. Not one of the other mountains surrounding us had ever been attempted or reconnoitred, or indeed ever been seen from the north except by officers of the Indian Survey. Let the mountains be climbable or unclimbable – in all Kumaon we could not have chosen a more inspiring base for exploration than Lampak.

On the morning of 25 June we set off with all six porters to put Camp 2 as close to the nine pinnacles as possible.

On the north ridge of Uja Tirche, falling to the Girthi, rose a minor peak of 17,280 feet. Between it and the main peak lay a corrie, which we entered. We took to its right-hand ridge. It became snowy and ran a 1,000 feet up to a great scree-field, 600 feet under the pinnacles. Here, at 17,400 feet, we pitched Camp 2.

MacKinnon had gone ahead to examine the pinnacles, which were clouded, but continually revealing themselves in whole or in part. We could see that the first four were detached, then came three huge ones all linked together, then two smaller ones, and finally a buttress lying against the start of the snow ridge. The latter's edge looked remarkably thin from Camp 2. It twisted up to the summit, twice interrupted by high walls of ice. We were thus confronted with four points of doubt. Firstly, the pinnacles. They could certainly not be climbed direct; could they then be turned? Secondly, where the rock abutted against the start of the snow ridge – might there not be a great gap? Of this we were much afraid after Hanuman. Thirdly, 1,000 feet up the snow ridge came the first ice wall, shaped like a triangle and 200 feet from base to apex. The true ridge ran up the left-hand (easterly) edge. We had difficulty in estimating the

1 The Polish climbers tackled Tirsuli from the south. Dr Adam Karpinski and Stefan Bernadzikiewicz were lost when a windslab avalanche inundated their camp during the night. Earlier two other members of the same expedition had made the first ascent of Nanda Devi East.

angle near the apex; might if not be too steep to climb? Fourthly, 400 feet under the summit came the second ice step, 100 feet high, of the same shape and character and posing the same question. Each of these ice walls was the apex of a hanging glacier falling 4,000 feet down cliffs into the north-west corrie, which harboured a bright blue lake.

Despite all this doubt, each one of us felt curiously optimistic, and our feelings were soon heightened by MacKinnon, who came romping down out of the shifting mists. He had passed the first four pinnacles, had been unable to deal with the central three alone but, having seen a possible route up their left flank, was full of hope for the morrow.

That we should need daylight to deal with the pinnacles we took for granted. Rock climbing would be necessary and not of a kind that we could deal with by torchlight. We were away shortly after 5 a.m. A dull grey haze pervaded the long scree slopes leading to the pinnacles, but there was no mist to embarrass the route selection. We roped up at the pinnacles in two pairs, Weir with MacKinnon and myself with Scott. The first pair led off. We had never seen pinnacles so fantastic. They stuck madly askew out of the ridge. Fortunately, the whole of the mountain's west flank (to our right-hand side) was bounded by horizontal strata, yellow, brown and purple; these provided seams by which we turned four pinnacles.

Then came the central trio, sheer on the west and overhung in front. The first tower was 150 feet high, but ledges allowed us to traverse the east flank into the gap behind. Thence by a short scramble we gained the long narrow crest of the second, and by its airy edge the gap under the third. It was the biggest and propounded a riddle, so that ever after we called it the Sphinx. We had to turn again from the sheer west to the broken east and climb down a short snow slope on to a ledge. The face of the pinnacle there exposed to us was furrowed by a groove, snow-filled in its upper part. If we could climb that groove, the crest of the pinnacle was ours. What we should be faced with on its far side, no man could tell.

MacKinnon led the first rope. His ascent forty feet up to the tongue of snow looked sensational in the dim grey light. When Scott and I came to follow we found this rock gave straightforward climbing; but the fifty feet of frozen snow above was banked almost vertically against the right hand wall of the pinnacle. Rock handholds taken to one side greatly helped us there; then came fifteen feet of easier snow and rock to the crest of the pinnacle. We looked quickly over the far edge and the descent was a mere nothing.

There were still two smaller pinnacles in front, but we passed these by long thin ledges on the west. Rotten rock troubled us. Our next fear was the last buttress. Could we get up to it and, if so, could we get off it? The front of the buttress had not looked too bad from Camp 2, but as we drew near we could see plainly that no ascent was possible. It was, quite simply, too steep and smooth. We continued to traverse its western seams, on rock that continued rotten, along a face that continued impregnable. We now drew close to the edge of the first hanging glacier. Here we saw a chimney splitting the buttress directly overhead. We turned straight up. The chimney went well for eighty feet, leading us on to easy rocks, and so to the top. We looked hastily for the gap beyond. And there was none. The rock abutted against the snow ridge. The bogey of the Rishi was laid.

The time was 8.30 a.m. Two thousand feet of snow and ice ridge swept to the summit. Our greatest concern was the urgent need of getting high before the sun got to work on the snow. I felt not at all concerned about the ice walls; either they would go or they would not – it was a technical matter; but if the snow deteriorated at the same speed as it had on Bethartoli Himal, then lack of time would defeat us. A great mercy was vouchsafed in the cloud that now wrapped the whole upper ridge. It would act as a protecting screen. We strapped ten-point crampons on to our boots and hastened into action.

The ridge opened mildly with a great dome, over which we passed swiftly to a col, where the pulling away of the western glacier had opened small crevasses. These were snow-covered and, not expecting them on the crest of the ridge itself, we twice broke through knee deep. The ridge narrowed, swinging upwards this way and that in majestic curves. On our left hand side cornices overhung the north-eastern wall, which dropped 8,000 feet to the Girthi. These cornices were discontinuous and so required all the greater attention. The true edge, when uncorniced, naturally gave the best route; it was appallingly easy to continue on the edge unwittingly after a cornice had developed. Scott and I were spared this risk by the good work of Weir and MacKinnon ahead. On that first 1,000 feet not a step had to be cut or kicked. We proceeded speedily to the first ice wall.

The angle there rose from 40° to 50° throughout two thirds of its 200-foot length, then gradually steepened over the last sixty feet. The edge was that of an ice pyramid; ice formed the flanking walls, but the edge bore snow. This snow was good near the foot, thin towards the middle; there the sun had begun its deadly work. We could find no support for our crampon-spikes without cutting steps in the underlying ice. Towards the top the excessive angle prohibited a direct ascent. In Scotland we should have thought of it as an excellent ice pitch, and rejoiced, but here we had no time to spend on it. MacKinnon, therefore, began a rightward traverse across the face of the upper wall to gain its west edge, which seemed to lie at a lesser angle. He made this move thirty feet under the apex. It imposed much axe-work, for the face was clear ice and gave us all very hard climbing near the west edge, which was corniced. There were some tricky moves here. On an alpine cliff I should have made them relatively gaily, but again I was impressed by the greater nervous strain of making them at the top of a hanging glacier, on the face of a

4,000-foot cliff, at an elevation of 19,000 feet on an unclimbed mountain. Technical difficulties in the Himalaya are not enjoyed.

However, we pulled ourselves over the vertical wall of the cornice and found good firm snow-ice on the west face. The angle proved to be higher than we had imagined; slashed steps were still required to take the edge spikes of crampons. We gained the apex. The ridge levelled.

I confess that I reached the top of that wall feeling a certain sense of dismay. The forenoon sun was already loosening the snow-skin; this we had taken for granted before ever starting. But our return route in the afternoon could not go back over the cornice, nor use the steps in the middle section of the true edge, which would become too dangerous. This meant that we must make our descent much lower down on the west edge, thus involving ourselves in hours of downhill and transverse step-cutting in ice.

Meantime, we were fully halfway up the ridge, and for that were thankful. In front of us the edge twisted up in huge, swinging zigzags, raw edged and corniced, falling abruptly on the right into cloud. We balanced up, drawing two full breaths to each step. The work became most exhausting. None of us was able to refuel properly. We did manage to eat two biscuits and honey, but quite without relish. Chocolate we loathed above 17,000 feet and at 19,000 could not persuade our throats to accept any. We enjoyed barley sugar.

At half-past twelve, after seven hours' climbing, we reached the second triangle of 100 feet. We took it by the left edge and were again forced off the ascent of the apex and compelled into a traverse towards the right edge. This on exposed ice. MacKinnon cut the steps big, despite which the rounding of the cornice was again technically difficult, even for myself, who came last. The west edge, as before, was too steep to take in crampons alone, bearing as it did a loosening snow-skin. Sixty feet of quick cutting brought us back on to the true ridge. We were now above 20,000 feet. Ahead, the edge ran straight as a die for 300 feet, and beyond any shadow of doubt the way to the top was clear.

At 2 p.m. we gained the summit.[2] Its sickle of snow gave just enough room for four men. Clouds encircled us. The ascent had taken eight and a half hours

2 Shortly before publication it was found that the Scottish climbers did not make the first ascent of the mountain. The article 'An Initiation to the Survey of India' by Maj. General R.C.A. Edge (*HJ* 45, 1988, p.1–16) reports an ascent in 1937 by the west-south-west ridge by Edge, Ang Chuk, Gyalgen and two other Sherpas. This ascent was not noted in *Exploring Hidden Himalaya* by Harish Kapadia and Soli Mehta (Hodder and Stoughton, 1990) and was only recently noted in the AC's 'Himalayan Index'. Messrs Murray, Scott, MacKinnon and Weir were also unaware of the ascent. The late reporting (fifty-one years later) stems from the fact that Edge, an army surveyor, seems to have had no links to the Himalayan Club at the time of his ascent. The WSW ridge (which is mainly rock and scree) was repeated in 1975 by three Indian climbers and two Sherpas, and again in 1984 by two Indian climbers. There is thus a clear option to traverse the mountain using the north ridge for ascent and the WSW ridge for descent.

and we reckoned that four or five hours should see us back to the pinnacles. But we feared the deterioration of snow. So at 2.10 p.m. we started down, going all on one rope for greater security. I went first to do the cutting and MacKinnon went to the rear as anchor. We cramponed down to the second ice wall. We noticed that the moment we turned down we felt delightfully reinvigorated. We were acclimatised. This did not mean that at altitude the effort of ascent gave us pleasure. But the descent did, because then we had energy to spare, were thus more alive, and were even capable of appreciating beauty when it appeared.

On coming to the brink of the ice wall I had to recut all the steps down the west face slope. Most of them on that fifty-foot traverse had been sun-wrecked. I had to recut until near the far edge the steps looked sound, so I used one without reshaping. At once the step broke off and I fell, braking with the axe until the rope tightened. The rope checked me at ten feet. I took a short rest then cut back to the line of steps, made the main ridge, and the rest came cautiously on.

Below, the snow greatly worsened. It balled on the crampons. I stopped and suggested removing them, but the general opinion seemed to be that we could still save time by retaining them, if we cleared them at each step. We went on, but despite all precautions were finding it impossible to prevent slips and slithers. The descent of rotten snow in exposed situations is, in my opinion, the most unpleasant and unnerving experience one may have in mountaineering. The retention of crampons only makes it worse, and the truth of that fact was borne in on the party when Weir shot off, to be stopped by the rope. We called a halt, removed our crampons, regained control of our feet and edged slowly down.

It was half past four when we reached the top of the first ice wall. We did not even take a look at our original route over the cornice and under the apex. The very thought of it was bad for morale. Instead, I began cutting steps down the ice slope of the west flank, reflecting how much pleasanter it was to cut down than to cut up, if only the angle be not excessive.

After a sixty-foot descent we came on to some broken rock, mixed with snow and ice on which the greater speed of climbing movement was offset by the need of moving singly from belays, so that we took one hour to reach the crag. The rock there was exceedingly rotten, but we climbed easily enough to its foot. We untied and joined both our ropes together. The full 200 feet would be needed to get the first man across the ice wall. The time was then six o'clock. A thin mist hovered round us. I calculated that we still had nearly two hours of daylight on hand, which seemed adequate to see us down to the pinnacles.

I began cutting. At once came the first disappointment. I had been hoping that so far below the apex we might be blessed with snow ice, which would cut easily. The white and granular surface encouraged such a hope. But a few whacks with my pick soon proved the ice to be pure: neither clear nor grey nor blue nor green, but a dark neutral colour compounded of all others. Although hard, the ice was thoroughly wet and inclined to be brittle. Steps had accordingly to be large and time consuming. About fifteen blows were required for each. After cutting one quarter of the way, I returned to rest and MacKinnon went out to cut the second quarter. He wore crampons. As he too came back the edge-spikes of his crampons split off the base of a step. He flashed down the slope, braking with his pick as hard as he could – with a nil effect. The rope twanged tight. Scott stopped him. Since the ice sheet fell 1,000 feet to a precipice of 500 feet, followed by a second hanging glacier of 1,000 feet, then more ice cliffs to the corrie of the blue lake, it was a situation to test the nerve of anyone with thought of falling. MacKinnon showed no discomposure. He still had his axe and so cut steps back to the crag. On Alpine ice in the afternoon his use of crampons would have been fully justified. On Bethartoli Himal the speed of the sun's effect on snow had taken us all by surprise. On Uja Tirche its effect on ice caused less surprise than shock.

Scott now went on the traverse, cut a third of the second half, and returned. Then Weir went out, cut, and returned. I took his end of the rope and again tied on. As I did so I saw that the sun was setting. The sky had entirely cleared. To the north-west there was the most wonderful and fiery glow behind Kamet. I exclaimed and drew the others' attention. It was the first truly spectacular sunset that we had seen in the Himalaya.

I started off. Weir had returned from a big bulge on the slope. I cut vertically down below it and in ten minutes more, with 200 feet of rope dragging heavily at my waist, reached the main ridge. That was a glorious moment when I stepped on to its steep but comforting edge. There was no cornice on the far side, so that I could descend there a couple of steps and thus ensure the party's safety. The sky was frostily clear. A first prickle of starlight was just beginning to creep into it. North-westwards the spikes of Kamet and Mana Peak stood black upon the afterglow; eastwards, the risen moon swung to the top like a thrown orange.

The question now before us was how to bring across the party. Our whole 200 feet of rope was stretched across the ice sheet, MacKinnon at one end, I at the other. And we had no more. We had earlier dismissed the idea of crossing on two ropes of two men, because no one man could have held the other. We now also dismissed the idea of three men crossing at once; such a notion gave me the horrors. Instead, Scott tied a spare loop round his waist, then clipped the loop on to the 200-foot rope with a karabiner. He came slowly over the line of steps, sliding the ring along the rope. The only weakness in this method was the need of giving him a good deal of slack rope, so as not to pull him away from the face, which was concave. He arrived safely. Weir followed. And at last came MacKinnon – just in time; only a last pallor lingered on the snow.

In one hour we reached the pinnacles. The moon had most obligingly moved over to the west side of the ridge, where we had greatest need of it. MacKinnon went first, for he knew the way better than anyone. His route selection was tonight unerring. One after another he hit off the turning points that led rightly through the maze of spires. We walked into Camp 2 at 11.15 p.m. Hot sweet tea was all that we desired. Eighteen hours on a Himalayan ridge had left us too tired for food.

As we turned in Uja Tirche still thrust its silver wedge to the moon, and the great north ridge rose jagged against the stars.

THE LAMPAK PEAKS

The fine weather was continuing. Despite the Malari dancing rite, no sign of the monsoon could be seen. And the Lampak hills were clear. For the first time we saw their north-east faces. Across the Uja Tirche Glacier stood a six-mile row of six peaks. At the north end Kunti Bhannar and Lampak could at once be ruled out as inaccessible; likewise the three most southerly mountains (21,770 feet, 20,560 feet, and 21,340 feet). But in the centre rose an unnamed mountain, which we called South Lampak (20,750 feet). It threw eastwards, 5,000 feet down to the Uja Tirche Glacier, a parallel row of three rock ridges. The farthest of these looked climbable. Indeed, the upper 1,700 feet of that ridge was low angle snow; its lower 4,000 foot rock, neither gashed nor pinnacled. Around 18,000 feet, however, the rock ridge was interrupted by a buttress of 800 feet, about which we could form no firm opinion, save that it looked formidable in front but more inviting on its south wall. Our resolve was made. We should try South Lampak.

Our immediate need was more rest so we descended to Base Camp. There we relaxed. I cannot remember ever having had so much enjoyment out of consciously doing nothing. This seemed a plain indication that we ought to lie low for two days, and deal with South Lampak thereafter. On the other hand, the settled weather called for action.

We agreed to put Camp 2 some three miles up the Uja Tirche Glacier, Camp 3 on the ridge below the doubtful buttress, Camp 4 above it if need be and so to the top. To this end Scott and I would get away next morning to reconnoitre the campsites, while Weir prepared stores. On 1 July the whole party would begin moving up the glacier.

This point settled, I had occasion to wash Matbir's feet with acriflavine. He had cut them on Uja Tirche. A little later I saw him take the hatchet and go out for firewood. I watched him admiringly as he made a swift round up of juniper on the less accessible parts of a cliff. He brought back his load and went off again. But this time he took no hatchet. After zigzagging with pace and precision over the cliffs he came back with a bunch of alpine flowers.

I had noticed before that Matbir loved flowers and he had gone back for them now from a need to give them to someone. Accordingly, he came to the tent door and gave them to me. No doubt he knew that I would not laugh. I accepted them thankfully – blue primulas and rock geraniums, anemones (both the small blue ones and the large white with five big petals and a yellow centre), forget-me-nots and red potentillas; they were indeed most beautiful and I did not hide my admiration. Matbir hovered round the door for a minute to enjoy our enjoyment, then went off to join the porters. I placed the flowers in a can of water in the centre of our table – a stone slab on crates – where Matbir and we would see them. Before long he whisked off again and presented a second bunch.

A Scottish or English youth of eighteen would not have dared such an act; he is too self-conscious. The charm of a Matbir is that no thought of self enters into the act. It is such freedom that alone makes it good and possible. Altogether, it was a revelation to me of what a man can be like when he is unspoiled: at once firm of eye and bearing, yet unhesitating in his love of the world and men and unembarrassed in showing it. I tried to think of men whom I had met outside the Himalaya, who in unaffected grace of manhood could stand comparison with Matbir. I was unable to think of any.

In our experience of the high Himalaya there occurred nothing to make a more lasting impression on my mind than this trivial incident. Again and again it recurs, accompanied by one or other of its witnessed opposites: Italian sentries at Tobruk staving in a prisoner's face with rifle butts; one pundit of British mountaineering disparaging another; the corpse-like face of a Gestapo agent interrogating me at Mährisch Trubau. From these I can turn to Matbir at Lampak and feel a respect for man.

At ten o'clock Scott and I set off to reconnoitre the route up the glacier. By the time we came level with the far east ridge of South Lampak, we had travelled three miles and risen only 1,500 feet. And there, for the first time, the flanking cliffs yielded an easy climb to an alp on its crest. It was ablaze with wild flowers, flat and fed with water from old snow beds: a perfect campsite.

The alp commanded an extraordinary, close-up view of the north wall of Tirsuli: 7,000 feet high, three miles long, laden with hanging glaciers and immense sheets of ice, topped by fluted snows. Avalanches growled down its precipices at long intervals. It gave us the sharp, vivid sense of unbounded power and awfulness; it seemed appropriate that out from its upper cauldrons should issue the superlative ugliness of that stone hidden glacier. This was mountain nature in the raw seen close; a fascinating comparison with the Himalaya seen from Ranikhet, so loftily elegant from there, as delicate as a painting on Japanese pottery. But here was the crude reality. So does a man look back momentarily from a bloody day on a battlefield to the memory of a drawing-room, where he once sipped China tea with ageing ladies.

In one matter we were disappointed: South Lampak was in cloud and no reconnaissance could be made of the east ridge. Thereupon we returned to Base and arranged that tomorrow two men should get away early to reconnoitre the ridge while the main body moved up in the forenoon.

Scott and MacKinnon set off early on the second reconnaissance. Weir and I followed with the porters three hours later and established Camp 2 on the alp. Scott and MacKinnon came in at four o'clock. Cloud was thick by then, but they had crossed and climbed the upper glacier in time to look back on to the east ridge. They gave a gloomy report, describing it as steep and doubtful with only one campsite visible, 1,500 feet up.

A further examination along the actual crest proved more promising – the appearance of difficulty had been an optical illusion. After climbing 2,000 feet we had seen enough. The whole of the Uja Tirche Glacier stretched sinuously below, no longer ugly but unmistakably a living glacier clad in a bronzed and glowing skin. Five peaks were ranged on its far side. Two routes attracted my attention as seeming feasible. The most southerly peak (20,200 feet), looked climbable by its south-south-west ridge, and Tirsuli by its north-north-east ridge – if access could be gained to the col below.

At noon we returned to camp and basked in the sunshine among wide beds of buttercups and other ranunculi, primulas, white and yellow anemones, and a host of alpines. The gentian and edelweiss were still noticeably absent. The alp was frequented, too, by a great variety of birds, which Weir named glandara, a thrush-like bird of cobalt blue and black, and plain backed mountain thrushes, and white-browed rosefinches. Scott was most delighted by the sight of a wallcreeper, flying in a flash of grey and crimson over the ridge. Its fluttering flight made it look like some large butterfly or hummingbird. Weir's happiest moment was listening to the song of meadow-pipits while they made their love flights. My own less observant eye and ear caught only the big and obvious things, like the lammergeyer, yellow of head and white of body, which flew over us like a Flying Fortress. I count that day at Camp 2 as the most carefree we had had in the Himalaya. Our use of it for reconnaissance had been quite unnecessary; one might have said a waste of time, had it not been for us all a day of unadulterated enjoyment. Few indeed were the days of which we could say the same without some qualification.

The morning of 3 July we began climbing with four porters. Beyond the initial shattered ridge and the central scree slopes, we came on to a 1,000 feet of mixed snow, scree, and ice, where step-cutting was required, and so to rock towers below the 800-foot buttress. The porters were exhausted and would not go past the first tower. We were in mist, and the weather was breaking into a drizzle of sleet. But they had done well; carried to 18,000 feet. We said *Shabash*! and told them to return in two days.

We shouldered the loads and carried them 250 feet past the towers, using shattered ledges on the left flank. Below the buttress we found a big blade of snow. On this we spent an hour excavating platforms, then pitched the tents.

The weather was now foul and after waiting two days for suitable conditions we were forced to descend. There could be no doubt now that the monsoon had broken in real earnest, and for those two days it gave us hell. I do not exaggerate. The word 'hell' denotes a very real mental state. Our tents were sited on a narrow arête on either side of which drops yawned 1,000 feet to glaciers. In their grey gloom avalanches roared day and night, like stags bellowing at our ear drums; sleet hissed angrily on the canvas; and we, in the moist interior, were like Queen Victoria – not amused. We just lay and occasionally wished we were dead. My diary records that MacKinnon and I discussed atheism, literature as a profession, the interpretation of history, and sulpha drugs. This sounds well but should not obscure the truth.

Base Camp, after our miserable sojourn in the high camp, seemed extra ordinarily warm, roomy, and comfortable. We could not imagine why we should ever have thought it bleak. Perimal was waiting for us with a haunch of goat, which inspired Weir to make a dumpling to match it and pancakes to precede it. To the Dotials the pancakes were a revelation of the higher life; they called them henceforth 'Bampa memsahib's chapatties'. Goria learned to make them, but the dough had always to be mixed by Weir, for a Dotial's hand was far too thrifty in dispensing the rich ingredients.

That night I had my best sleep since coming to India. I suppose that we had well nigh 100 camps in the Himalaya, and I slept well in no more than one or two. Provided that the body is at rest, sound sleep seems unimportant on mountains. It certainly means nothing to my own health. At home I sleep soundly, on mountains never, and most men say the same. But always one feels refreshed.

We were also well fed. The old luxury expeditions, disdaining native food, were harassed by piles; but on this expedition none of us had ever before eaten so much roughage. It came in the ata, rice and lentils, and now also in tsampa. This ground and roasted barley made a perfect substitute for porridge. Chapatties made a satisfying bread substitute, although some kind of British spread seemed essential. Thick, they were tolerable; but thin, as made by the hand of Goria they were delicious. He started them as little balls of dough, would flip-flap them from palm to palm, then from fingers to fingers and finally from fingertips to finger-tips, until he had them as thin as wafers, maintaining them unpunctured only by some miraculous sleight of hand – as made by such a craftsman we would normally eat between the four of us sixteen to a meal.

Living on the native diet, then, was proving to be a great success, but for one matter. For three months on end we were destined to move above 10,000 feet, and the reduced boiling point of water made for slow cooking – a full hour for potatoes. Lentils defied us; their adamantine hearts never softened, however long Weir might woo them with fires fierce or languorous. In consequence, they had consistently given us indigestion, until now, when we learned to eat them in small quantity.

We had seen little opportunity of shooting for the pot and were thankful to be unburdened with a rifle and ammunition. The stalking of the swift and high climbing bharhal would have consumed more time and energy than we had to spare, whereas domestic goat or sheep could be bought. But in camp next day we did have pangs of regret. In the afternoon three bharhal appeared at the brink of the cliff just 400 feet above and began descending the ledges of the face. Their bodies were clearly outlined against the dark crag; we could not have missed. They would have fallen to our feet. It was the first time that bharhal had ever come so close. Phakir rushed off to make a detour to the top of the cliff, for he could almost certainly have cut off their escape had he got there. He was two thirds of the way up – when they saw him. They turned, leapt up again from crag to crag, and vanished for ever.

The cliffs were busy that day. A lammergeyer kept sailing in and out among the corners, and we could see an immature shahin falcon perching there in the evening – and snow-pigeons roosting under the overhangs.

The weather had improved. We allotted the next four days to a second attempt on South Lampak. On 7 July we all went up the glacier again and pitched Camp 2 as before and, next day, established Camp 3 at 18,000 feet shortly after eleven o'clock.

On the main Lampak ridge, and seemingly close above to our left, was a spear-like peak of 21,340 feet, from which unusually wild ice ridges fell to the col connecting with our own peak. This col was nearly at our own level. In the evening mist kept forming and dispersing around the two summits. When South Lampak cleared the ice cliffs of its summit were seen to tumble down a short way like a stubby glacier and overhang the east face. Our east ridge just turned them with a southward sweep. We could see our ridge to be corniced but easy. As we looked now our ascent seemed assured if only the weather would hold.

During the night the weather deteriorated but at 6 a.m. it was good enough to make a try. We climbed the upper curve of the snow saddle to the foot of the buttress. Its east face was good rock, but smooth as a concrete dam. We traversed leftwards. The south flank revealed itself to be a series of bright brown and shattered ridges, divided by still more shattered scoops and gullies. The first ridge was so unsafely rotten that we pressed on across a chute fined with clear ice, moving as fast as we could to escape stonefall, three minutes sufficed for the step-cutting. Beyond, we edged round the awkward ledges of the second ridge to its broad back.

This too proved unstable and we could find no safe way of proceeding. The angle was not high, but the rock was peculiarly hard, yet none of it sound; holds were small and all of them sloping, and the whole broad back of the ridge was littered deep in sharp edged debris, delicately poised.

Accordingly we retired. Scott proposed climbing the gully on its left wall, but desisted after trial. Similarly, I tried the first ridge. One brief experience of its slaty crest brought me to my senses. We then gave up and returned to camp.

Despite the obvious dangers, the decision had been a hard one to make. The snow ridge above joined the top of the buttress without a gap between, and the final ridge went easily to the summit. It is just possible that a party disposed to disregard all danger might have forced the buttress and gained the summit. In my own judgement the rock gave no reasonable hope of such a party's survival.

We packed up and descended and were down at Base Camp by two.

23 Through the Girthi Gorge to Milam

The brightest idea that Scott gave to the expedition was, to my mind, the eastward traverse from Malari to Milam by way of the Girthi River. If we could make it we would link two great trade routes of Central Asia, a way which, if not too difficult, might ultimately prove of value to travellers. From the broader viewpoint, this passage of about thirty-eight miles would be of greater importance than the ascent of any mountain, and for that reason we had been puzzled by the lack of records.

We should have to follow the full length of the Girthiganga to its source, the lake of Gangpani at 16,570 feet, under the Unta Dhura Pass. The pass, 1,000 feet higher, is a double watershed between the Dhauli and Gori rivers and between Tibet and India. The trade route from India goes over it, turning sharply north-east to cross the frontier at the Kungribingri La. So that once we gained the pass we were 'made'; there would follow a descent over glaciated country to reach the Goriganga. Our estimate was seven days from Malari to Milam.

Our Lampak base was already seven miles along the Girthi track which had been worn by Malari goatherds moving to the eastern grazing grounds. Six days, we thought, should therefore be sufficient time allowance, and ten days' ata sufficient food supply. The ata had been stored these twenty days in the goats' saddlebags. At first I was unhappy about the goats. They are magnificent rock climbers, but the difficulty that we most feared in the Girthi Gorge was the fording of swollen glacier streams rushing in from the south. In this gorge we should have no trees to fell and the monsoon was upon us. Rain had so far not been excessive, but the glaciers were bound to be melting faster. *Jhopas* in glacier streams are magnificently tank-like, but goats – surely they would be swept off their feet? Bala Singh swore that all would be well. At streams the goats would swim unloaded. They were his goats, worth five pounds apiece, so that I knew that he must be right.

As usual the goats were away early and the rest of us delayed by a fuss about loads. The Malari men had found one or two overweight. Much readjustment was required, and in the end we were delighted to see that Perimal was driven to exercise authority. He at last entered into his head-portership, made the changes himself, distributed the loads, silenced the querulous, damned the grousers, and ordered all with a brisk, commanding air. All

Perimal had been needing was practice and experience, and now development followed.

THE GIRTHI GORGE

To get into the Girthi Gorge we aimed to strike over the north ridge of Uja Tirche by a grassy saddle called the Mukhtiar kharak, at a little over 14,000 feet. In brilliant sunshine we slanted up across the flank of Uja Tirche, its broad acres now covered thickly in alpine flowers, especially above the lower juniper. They grew densely in fields sweeping 1,000 feet down and across the hillside – a manifestation of pure colour seen through a sun-drenched mountain air, incomparable thus with anything to be seen at low elevations. Everywhere, were delicious and heady scents.

At the saddle we rested and looked back for the last time to Lampak. Banks of cumulus had formed low down on the far side of the Uja Tirche Glacier, lending splendour of height to a fortress wall of six white mountains; buttressed by ranked ridges, armoured with serried glaciers between, hollowed above in a row of corries, and on top fined by sparkling towers. Against the snow-white background of the cumulus the very grass beneath our feet took an emerald burnish in the low slant of the sun. All space had become unusually translucent, as though hitherto we had looked through windows of thick glass, which now on the Mukhtiar kharak had opened to the light of the world.

Then we crossed the saddle and began contouring into the Girthi – and what a change of scene confronted us! The naked rock of Ramba Kot sprang straight up in a chaos of jumbled towers and spires. It walled the opposite side of the gorge for six miles and, though colourful, to us looked stark and fearsome after those flower-thick alps on the Lampak side.

We were contouring round the foot of Uja Tirche's north-east face. Thus the walls of the gorge were 8,000 feet high on our side, 7,000 feet on the other. So stark and arid a scene might have been imagined of another planet, although at no time was it ugly. The colour in the rock redeemed all.

Our goat track contoured a full 1,000 feet above the river, passing from Garhwal District into Almora. We picked our way along rock walls lying at angles gentle in relation to the lower precipice, and bedecked with countless flowering shrubs and plants.

Far ahead, perhaps three miles away, we could see that our flank of the gorge was buttressed by a projecting cliff, which hung like a curtain across the route. It was impossible, from this distance to see any feasible way of getting round its outer edge, but beyond it the bed of the river rose and the gorge seemed to open out encouragingly. We could not hope to go so far today. Already we had been travelling five hours from Lampak.

Occasional silver birches thrust out of the rock, their bark shining, and often a dwarf pine stood among them; always the scent rose rich, warm, and fragrant to the path. Each turn of the many bluffs brought us new scents and new colours, until the route reached its climax by running in among red rosebushes: a Hanging Garden of Himachal.

And far aloft clouds flitted among the wild pinnacles of Uja Tirche.

Towards one o'clock, when we had covered a total distance of four miles, we came on a sudden, steep descent, first on scree then across bare slabs. It was an exposed situation, but our goats seemed to have no nerves. Humans had to use handholds. The final traverse went across a waterfall – the first of the day, although ten streams had been marked on the map and down to a shelf where a cave yawned a welcome to the porters. In front of it was a patch of flat ground, just big enough to take the floor space of one tent; elsewhere the slope was precipitous. We pitched camp.

That cave was most fortunately sited – a good day's march from Lampak, the only bit of flat ground we had seen, and beside the only water. Our host was less fortunate – a black scorpion, whom we had to kill. This was ideal scorpion country: dry, bare, and stony. On the other hand, this very dryness had nearly removed our fears about trouble at river crossings – unless when they drained glaciers. Dryness in the Girthi Gorge was not, we soon discovered, to be matched by prohibition in camp. As soon as the campfires were burning briskly in the caves – for still another cave had been found and occupied by the Bhotias, beyond and above the first – the bar opened. In sign of which Bala Singh presented us with a full bottle of chang. This was generous, but not kind. For appearance's sake we had a sip all round, sharing with the Dotials, then set the rest aside as scorpion medicine. Bite for bite, no scorpion would beat chang.

On our second day we had hope of passing through the toughest part of the gorge to the Girthi kharak. Eight great ravines had to be crossed, one of which drained a glacier. We got away early in fine weather. As Perimal had promised, we slept warmer on the rocks of the Girthi than beside the ice of the Uja Tirche Glacier.

We crossed the first ravine shortly after leaving camp, and then began a most astonishing day's journey. From the first craggy corner the track plunged like a belfry staircase, arched by red roses, down into the second ravine. I paused there to watch the porters and goats traverse across the face of the opposing cliff to its outer edge, which overlooked the river. It looked a sensational move, yet when I followed proved to be quite simple.

I arrived at the edge to find the sun shining straight down the gorge. The huge face of Ramba Kot was now lit from one side, and along its cliffs a thin mist floated; sun and mist together picked out and revealed for the first time the incredible number of towers, pinnacles and crazy spires into which that seemingly flat face had in reality been weathered. It had suddenly become a dream world of spires, like the land of the *Wizard of Oz*.

The track doubled back into the third and greatest ravine of all, its bed filled with old hard snow. Weir cut a line of big steps across this for the porters. On the far side was the great projecting cliff, which we had seen yesterday as a hanging curtain. Gradually the entire party emerged on to its face, twenty-seven dots winding across invisible seams, the goats nose to tail like a beaded string. Not even in the Rishiganga had I seen anything so spectacular.

As before I followed without difficulty, but rarely have I trod more cautiously, for a stumble meant loss of life. It is safe enough on that same account, for at such places no man does stumble – instead he becomes alert. At the curtain's outer edge the rocks above the seam overhung unpleasantly, so that I had to crouch under them, placing the feet slowly, with that 1,200-foot drop an inch from the boot's welt – a track so dramatic that all it lacked was a black bear coming round the next corner.

Beyond this edge I could see the Girthi Gorge open out and become sunny far ahead. The height of the path was 12,000 feet, the riverbed around 11,000 and rising to 12,300 feet at the Girthi kharak. Pinnacles taller by far than the Dolomites of Italy pricked through the circling mists – Uja Tirche.

We made camp a mile short of Girthi.

A REMOTE CULTIVATION

This was the farthest point to which Malari colonisers had penetrated. On the far side of the river was a flat plateau where two Malari men had adventured to grow potatoes. They had made a house, and had their wives there and some children. A hundred yards upstream was a bridge, which Perimal had already crossed to buy potatoes. We had these now for lunch. They were good. Everyone visited the plateau that afternoon, but I delayed my own visit until the morrow.

The cultivated area was oval shaped, 200 yards long, and 150 yards at the widest part. Above it lay an almost equal area of uncultivated ground, mostly covered with dwarf broom. On either side the plateau was demarcated by deep gullies, cut by two streams flowing from the hills behind. The entire area was diamond-shaped. The fields had been carefully prepared in terrace formation and irrigated from the stream on the right. No aqueduct was necessary, other than a long trench cut along the flank of the upper plateau for a quarter of a mile, then led over on to the lower surface. The irrigation channels were all carefully thought out and thoroughly devised.

At the centre of the lower part were two semi-detached houses. They had been solidly built of the local stone. The floors were of hard mud and the roofs thatched. I thought the thatching poor, but in the upper Himalayan valleys no great store is set by good thatching. The houses are occupied for a brief period only in the summer, evacuated and snowed up in winter. A house without a roof signifies neither ruin nor desertion, but only that a family is away for the season.

We came down to the houses after inspecting the fields and found there two young women. They had three children. Their husbands had gone to Malari. In all India there could be no more isolated a family than this, nor any with a more enterprising courage. As one might well imagine, the women looked cheerful and of noticeably good health. The crops they grew were phaphar, pul, barley, and potatoes. The phaphar is buckwheat, producing a grain that is ground into flour (inferior to ata). The leaf is ivy-shaped and the flour either red or yellow. Here it was yellow. The pul grows on a long stalk and produces a grain for goats and *jhopas*. Potatoes were the most valuable product, for the quality was excellent. They stored them in a deep, stone-lined pit.

The more I looked round the more stirred I felt at thought of the energy and hard work that must have been directed into the cultivation of these fields. The clearing out by hand of the broom and roots and stones was in itself a triumph of determined effort, quite apart from the construction of irrigation channels. The soil was fourteen inches deep on top of hard glacial mud, the top three inches looking very good indeed. We could see these heights distinctly where the left-hand gully sheered the wall of the plateau.

A hundred yards behind the houses, at the fringe of the rough upper ground, we could see votive flags: strips of cloth fluttering from the tops of tall poles. I walked over to them and found two stone-built shrines, semi-detached like the houses below, each family presumably having its own. The roofs were ridged and slated with stone slabs.

The siting of the shrines had been well judged; they stood in front of a great rosebush, now in full flower and bending over them in dense white sprays as though in sign of their God's blessing. And the doorways faced to the snows of Tirsuli and Uja Tirche (at present in cloud), where the gods dwell. Within each shrine a broad platform at the back had been raised one inch high, its left-hand half being screened by a flat stone. Behind each screen lay a tray containing the ashes of juniper. On the unscreened half a rough stone stood on end, marked with a daub of red pigment. On one platform there also stood a small hand bell, painted gold, with a handle carved into the bust of a winged god; on the other platform lay a large seashell. In the foreground of each shrine a metal incense tray and stand still contained cinders and burnt twigs of juniper. At the outside wall of each doorway the shoot of a plant was plastered to the stone with dung.

The Hindu religion is a pure and most practical mystical religion, its practice therefore drawing out of a man all the good works that attend the growing union of a human soul with God. As we turned to leave the Girthi settlement I was full of a most enthusiastic admiration for the Hindu hillmen. I felt that they brought honour to the race of man.

Scott and I returned to the Girthiganga, which we crossed and followed for more than a mile to the Girthi kharak, where a wide valley broke in on the right. A dazzle of tumbled snow and ice at its head showed where the Girthi Glacier flowed down from the unclimbed peaks of Chalab and Kholi. A route over that col would have led straight down to Milam. We were not tempted to try this icy short cut, for which the Bhotias were not equipped. Our immediate purpose was to try to follow the Girthiganga.

The alp was a wide one, at first sight better and more open than the lower settlement, but a closer examination showed the soil to be hard, stony, and dry, and the grass of thin, poor quality.

I descended alone to the glacier stream. This was the first of the big ones and would have been unfordable later in the day. After careful selection of a fording line, the Malari men had formed themselves into a chain across the river and driven over the goats upstream. My delay at the shrine brought me to the riverbank after they were well up the opposite hillside. The result was that I landed in trouble. I stripped off my trousers but took the wrong crossing point, and found myself up to my waist in an icy channel near the centre. After several narrow escapes from being swept away I withdrew, found a lower thigh-deep passage, but failed to get safe footing – the boulders were moving on the bed of the stream. The force of the current prevented me planting my feet by choice – always the current swept the leg lower than aimed, imperilling balance. Again I withdrew. Perimal and Goria then came up behind me and gave me a demonstration of how to deal with a fast glacier stream. I had been groping with my feet too tentatively. One should lift the feet high and plunge them down hard and boldly and go fast. I did this at last, porters escorting, and crossed without capsizing. It would seem important always to cross this stream in the morning; never in the afternoon.

We climbed 1,800 feet up a grassy hill, then made a long traverse across treeless and now flowerless slopes to another alp called Talla Khanda where we camped. Our height was 14,000 feet, a rise of 2,000 feet since morning. The Malari men had made a tent from our spare groundsheet, but despite a grey drizzly mist they sat out late into the night round a huge bonfire of juniper. It was 100 yards away, yet lit the entire alp and made of it a weird oasis amid the outer blackness and the barren gorge. When we dropped off to sleep in the big tent we could still see their lighted figures crouching round the blaze and hear the soft patter of rain on the fly-sheet.

Our fourth days march brought us into new country. From the moment we left camp our feet were rarely off grass. Travelling high above the river in gradually strengthening sunshine, we crossed a series of hollowed alps where we discovered our first edelweiss, forded a third glacier stream, and then scrambled 500 feet up to the col of a barrier ridge. The porters were there before me. As they breasted the saddle a great shout of joy burst from them. I was startled. They had never done that before. They had thrown off their burdens and were now on the crest gazing east, like pilgrims at sight of the Celestial City.

I joined them. Ahead of us the gorge broadened into a strath, and long, rich pasture fringing the Girthiganga stretched a mile to the alp of Matoli. The alp was occupied by flocks from Milam. Shepherds had pitched three tents. We were through the gorge. Beyond Matoli gleamed the ribbon of a fourth glacier stream; beyond that again, at higher elevation, the greater alp of Topidunga awaited our campfires. Far to the back of Topidunga circled great and clouded peaks, somewhere in the midst of which must lie the Unta Dhura Pass.

The Malari men were already pleading for a sheep as *baksheesh* and since they had carried exceedingly well we were not disposed to refuse if prices were reasonable. They gave a performance, then, reminiscent of the Lata greyhounds. Dashing helter-skelter down the slope they left us far behind and made straight for the three tents. They had been squatting in a circle there, explaining our presence to the astonished shepherds, for several minutes before we arrived. Some 200 sheep were gathered to one side.

As I approached two big Tibetan mastiffs came trotting out, tails in air, apparently bent on giving a friendly welcome. Suddenly, at a few yards' distance, their attitude changed. The foremost dog went down on its haunches and took one spring at my throat. Luckily I had my ice axe. I jabbed the dog in the chest and whacked its flank. It turned and circled, getting ready with its mate for a joint attack. At once the outraged shepherds ran up with stones and beat the dogs into abject, trembling submission. They stood over them, hurling stones down on top. The wretched animals lay flat, making no show of resistance, utterly inert in face of the severest punishment that I have ever seen a dog receive. I was sorry but the scene ended quickly. The dogs were carried away by their scruffs and thrown into one of the tents.

That was my first lesson in the care required when approaching a Tibetan or Bhotia flock. I was lucky. Two of these dogs can bring down a black bear. The golden rule is never to approach a Bhotia flock without first attracting the shepherd's attention, and never to move at night in a Bhotia village.

The Girthi passage had been the most wonderful journey we had ever had.

At Milam we were welcomed by Len Moules, the medical missionary. He and his wife invited us to 'lunch' which was nothing less than a banquet fit for Himalayan appetites. A member of the Himalayan Club, Moules knew all about climbers' appetites and he did not underestimate. The feast ended with sweetmeats, originally destined for certain governors of Tibet, followed by coffee.

Len Moules's work at Milam made full use of his medical training. Though not a doctor, he served the people in that remote area with abounding vigour, disciplined by a keen sense of humour – working twelve hours a day dispensing medicine, setting bones, extracting teeth, amputating limbs and once operated for cataract. He was held in high esteem by all.[1]

MacKinnon's three months' leave had ended and he had to head for home. For the rest of us the way lay eastward by the Ralam Pass to Darmaganga and Panch Chuli.

1 Leonard C.J. Moules (b.1912, London) went to the Tibetan border in 1939. At the outbreak of war he was commissioned, serving in Iraq, Persia, Syria, the Western Desert, Cyprus and Italy. He and his driver (he was then a Major) were the sole survivors of his unit in the escape from Mersa Matruh. After the war he returned to medical missionary service in India until 1957 when he was appointed the British Leader of the World Evangelisation Crusade. He died from a heart attack in 1978.

24 The Ralam Pass and Panch Chuli

Ralam is a tiny village in a mountain cul-de-sac set high above the Milam Valley. There were some twenty stone houses situated at the side of a green glen that was the most fertile we had yet seen. Many cows were grazing the lower pastures and the fields just under the village shone golden yellow with flowering buckwheat.

I was much taken with the idea of Ralam as a climbing centre, especially for those making their first visit to the Himalaya. On the other side of the glen were numerous 16–17,000-foot peaks, notably Shivu and Tihutia. Beyond them to the north and east were a host of glaciated mountains of 20,000 feet and upwards. Chaudhara (21,360 feet), which overlooked the Ralam Pass might well be climbed from Ralam by its west ridge. Northwards the unexplored Chiring We (21,520 feet) had an obvious glacial approach. There was no end to what might be done, or at least attempted, in this great and complex range between Gori and Darma.[1]

THE RALAM PASS

Our way lay over Yankchar Pass to the great corrie below Chaudhara and from where we could gain the higher Ralam Pass (18,500 feet) by following a glacier flowing down into the corrie. The route lay below the imposing north face of Chaudhara. A moraine allowed us to bypass an initial ice-fall but we were eventually forced on to the bare ice higher up, cutting many steps for our local Bhotia porters who we had hired in Ralam.

Before this glacier passage we had felt some concern at the likelihood of the porters getting snow-blindness in crossing the pass. We had snow goggles for our own Dotials, but for the Bhotias nothing except an advance warning. But

1 Chiring We (6,559 metres) was climbed in 1979 by the north-west ridge by an Indian expedition led by Harish Kapadia. The summit was reached on 10 June by Zerksis Boga and Nayankumar Katira with the Sherpas Lakhpa Tsering and Kami Tsering. Chaudhara (6,510 metres) was climbed in 1973 by the west face by an Indian expedition led by Prof A.R. Chandekar. The summit was reached on 2 June by Nayankumar Katira and Subhash Desai with the Sherpas Ajeeba (aged sixty) and Kami. (*HJs* Vol. 36, p.68; Vol.33, p.115.) Ralam is now spelt Rhalam on maps, guides and reference sources.

we need not have troubled ourselves. The Bhotias know snow. They produced a hank of goat's fleece and laid the strands over their eyes, ends tucked behind their ears or held by a hat. The protection proved adequate. It had not occurred to us that anywhere in the world men do, literally and for practical ends, pull the wool over the eyes.

After gaining the upper basin of the glacier, a shattered gully led up the final slopes to the pass which we reached at noon. Clouds had been forming around the base of Nanda Devi and we feared we were going to lose the view but we gained the pass just in time. Facing us north-east, across the valley of the Lassar Yanti, were rows and groups of unnamed mountains, snow and ice-plastered. Clouds surged round them and spun 10,000 feet above.

Chaudhara, to the south of the pass, had a 2,000-foot ridge leading [via a small intermediary top] to its summit but it was too steep and pinnacled to be seriously contemplated.

The descent down the glacier and ice-falls on the other side was at times dangerous and sometimes not obvious. The local knowledge of our porters proved invaluable and at 5 p.m. we camped in a meadow on the far side of the Nipchukang Glacier after a long and tiring day. The porters were extremely tired, we gave them some aspirins for their headaches and treated one with castor oil for his inflamed eyes. During the following days we moved down the Darmaganga Valley for our attempt on Panch Chuli.

THE PANCH CHULI

The Panch Chuli, the Five Fires, symbolises the home fires of five famous brothers of Hindu mythology, saints and heroes who all married an Indian princess called Draupadi.

At the close of long and adventurous lives, the five brothers and Draupadi travel into the Himalaya, climb up to the Abode of the Gods, and are there symbolised by these five peaks, called the Panch Chuli.

On a first reconnaissance in the monsoon the ascent of even one of the five was more than we could expect; for they are difficult even by Himalayan standards. But we did hope, by trial and error, to discover a route that might take some future party to the top. Our task was to explore and help distinguish bad ways from good. If lucky, we might gain the summit.

In the morning of 4 August the Panch Chuli were clear. A semicircle of four sharp snow peaks thrust out of thinning cloud. They were craggy and ice-clad, grouped around the head of the vast Meola Glacier. At one glance we could say that the three southward peaks were inaccessible. We had no later cause to revise that opinion. The summit was the right-hand peak at 22,650 feet. It soared far above all the others, none of which was under 20,000 feet. The fifth and northerly top was invisible.[2] The north and south ridges of that summit peak, by one of which any ascent would have to go, were thin, steep and icy. From seven miles distance we could not decide whether either were possible, only that they were worth trying, if they could be reached. That east wall of the Panch Chuli was 10,000 feet high.

We settled on a north-eastern approach by the snow-covered Sona Glacier. During the first week of August we established three approach camps and on the morning of 7 August reached the upper level of the glacier. Although we had risen above the ice-fall, the slope remained steep. I cut a long line of steps through the marginal crevasses, which were set very close together, so that our passage had to cross a narrow bridge between two of them. Weir followed, but when Scott tried to coach Goria and Zungia across, they dithered at the edge, unwilling to come. The use of the rope always seemed to rob the Dotials of their natural confidence. I unroped and traversed back 300 feet to assist. I think that the sight of me walking easily across the steps, despite the long ice-slope below, gave them the necessary reassurance. Goria at once went across on the rope with Scott, while Zungia, waving the rope aside, followed on his heels.

Our way went a mile and a half up the easier-angled glacier. Behind the clouds the sun burned intensely. Its heat became overpowering and Goria and Zungia were enervated by glacier lassitude. We ourselves had too much to think about to be enervated. The glacier being snow covered, we had to keep wide awake to spot the hidden crevasses. It was flanked too by great mountain walls, from which avalanches poured at five-minute intervals. In such thick mist we had to advance with caution lest we stray too far leftwards into the danger area.

When we came under the central corridor of the upper ice-fall, Goria stopped and said that he could go no farther. We rested for five minutes, after which Zungia said that he was willing to go on, whereupon Goria followed. We rose slowly up the corridor. Towards the top we had to thread a way among the crevasses, which were much bigger than we had expected, and cross snow-bridges, surprisingly sound for such a time of day. At the top of the ice-fall Zungia and Goria stopped of one accord. Their limit had been reached. In such oppressive, windless heat they had done marvellously well. They had carried to 19,000 feet. We sent them back alone to our approach camp, warning them to keep strictly to the steps made on the ascent. We could trust them, for they were men of resolution and good judgement, no less intelligent than us.

2 The peaks are numbered from north to south as one to five. Chris Bonington's article 'The Indian British Panch Chuli Expedition 1992' (*AJ* 98, p.98–103) gives a full topographical briefing with Panch Chuli Two (6,904 metres/22,650 feet) confirmed as the highest peak.

Scott, Weir and I now carried the loads by a tortuous route in among long, transverse crevasses. We came to a patch of flat snow, spread like a magic carpet at the very brink of the biggest crevasse, which gaped blue and hazily profound, as though it were a hole in the surrounding clouds. This would be the ideal camp site – if safe. We hung around undecidedly, until the mist lifted for a few seconds. We were just out of range of the debris falling from a great ice cliff on the flank of the east ridge.

After the tent was pitched the clouds lifted. Since our work for the next day was to carry Camp 5 up to the north col, Scott and I set out in the late afternoon to reconnoitre. Level snowfields led easily into the glacier basin. The col came into view.

And great was our dismay. It was buttressed by cliffs. A few minutes' very silent study showed them to be 800 feet high and close to the vertical. We would be incapable of carrying loads up them. On the left, under the north ridge of the summit peak [Panch Chuli Two], were bare and hopeless ice slopes, crowned by enormous cornices. Towards the right, under Point 20,850 feet, the wall was lower and less terrifying, perhaps 600 feet. But all these cliffs were ringed below by a bergschrund, above which 300 feet of polished ice swept up to the rocks, and that ice was raked by stonefall. We were beaten.

However, we were given no cause to regret our ascent thus far. The entire basin was of undulating snow, ringed by satellite peaks, whose long skirts were splayed out fan-like and fell silkily to the basin's floor. At the outer rim perched our tiny tent, a pinpoint on the brink of the first great fall, where the Sona Glacier plunged to the Darmaganga, now 10,000 feet below among the clouds. Beyond its bottomless gorge the ranked snow ranges of an unknown mountain land, all topped by towering cumuli, receded into the everlasting blue that roofs Tibet. Truly that was the Abode of the Gods and the Five Brothers, worth much sacrifice of the flesh.

Despite this reverse, our expedition plan had been carried through in all essentials, with all the mingled triumphs and defeats inevitable to such a long and varied journey – 450 miles, rising and falling across gorges and mountains from 6,000 feet to 21,000 feet.

Since one of the aims of life is its enjoyment, and a feature of exploratory mountaineering its daily uncertainty as unforeseen events set one back or help forward, the best way to shed anxieties is to understand from the start that with every move our own part is limited. We have to plan as best we know, organise efficiently, and then push on, freely accepting the end vouchsafed us. If that is success or defeat, in either event and day by day, we should enjoy what comes so far as we can. The Himalayan traveller who cannot acquire such a philosophy and apply it will find that however long his life it will not be a happy one.

On the morning after arrival at Ranikhet, we eagerly anticipated our first sight of the Himalaya. It was a glorious morning of soft fresh airs, but a great cloud-screen rose tall above the curve of the world. I was about to turn away disappointed when a wild thought made me raise my head higher. They were there. An arctic continent of the heavens, far above earth and its girdling clouds, wholly divorced from this planet. The idea of climbing over such distant and delicate tops, the very desire of it, could not enter my head or heart. Had I been born among them, I might have been led to worship this Abode of the Gods, but not to set boot on their crests. They seemed out of this world. The wonder of it all has never left me.

A month later, I wrote to Tom Longstaff from the heart of the Rishiganga. His reply reached us within three months by way of the Kaliganga at Nepal's frontier.

> 'I was entranced to get your letter from the Dibrugheta Alp ... There is no more lovely place in all Himachal. You have seen the best – and now understand what I mean by "living in the present" just forget all before and after and soak the moment in you so that it will never come out. Just travel is the thing. Number your red-letter days by camps, not by summits (no time there) ... Enjoy and for always, as you can through concentration.
>
> Yours, Tom Longstaff'

The red-letter days (or hours, or moments) have on the whole not been those of intense climbing action or incident, but those of the relaxation that immediately follows them. Perception is keenest then, the mind and heart most open. I had already found that in Scotland as an occasional reward of hard climbs, and in the Himalaya after the hard effort of finding ways and means to make progress. Always it is unlooked-for, a gift of the gods; if looked for, it never happens. Having said this, I can think of exceptions, few enough to prove the rule. Longstaff's advice to learn to live in the present moment is the best possible advice to the Himalayan explorer. It can be taken at different levels.

Exploratory mountain travel demands the resignation of outcomes to Providence. The relaxation that comes of it assuredly helps to let the scene soak in. It is much harder for this experience of 'the present moment' to come to members of big expeditions, other than to their leaders. My belief is that the bigger an expedition the more wasteful of its members' opportunities, and the smaller their hope of having the reward.

Our small expedition, the first British expedition since the war, was admirable for this purpose. Our experience was a happy one that has stayed with me. I can still see the milk white granite spire of Changabang soaring in moonlight, seemingly as fragile as an icicle. I can delight in the wild Himalayan rhododendrons in full bloom in sunlit air, tall trees bearing a glory of pale purple, scarlet and pink against the gleam of distant snow-covered mountains. I would try to let their beauty soak in and a new beauty would shine out of them, 'Beauty, so ancient and so new'.[3] I can see the peaks beyond the green gorge of the Rishiganga flashing like sharks' teeth against blue Himalayan skies and our Dotials gazing in silent reverence while flipping dough from hand to hand to make chapattis. We shared these moments with them. There were days spent moving in the high Himalayan world of space and frost. A world sufficient unto itself, not made for man's purposes; on our eighteen-hour day on Uja Tirche – the difficulties, the effort, then the return to camp, food, fire and rest – and as we turned in, the sight of Uja Tirche thrusting its silver wedge to the moon, its great north ridge jagged against the stars.

I remember Matbir bringing me that beautiful bunch of wild flowers after our Uja Tirche climb. That incident made a lasting impression on me. It was a simple act of human fineness, an action that contrasted so reassuringly from others I had seen just a few years earlier.

Humankind had manifold diversity and a potential for good too rarely realised. I deeply respected these hill people of Nepal and India.

Completely under the spell of the mountains, I was grateful for the four months spent exploring and travelling among them. We had climbed virgin peaks in Kumaon and Garhwal and, despite difficulties, succeeded in reaching the summits of five out of nine of those attempted. We had made a reconnaissance of Panch Chuli, its upper edges so thin that over a stretch of 1,000 feet we could see the sun shining through it. Our route proved unclimbable but I spotted another route which I believed possible but which we lacked the time to try.

This route was successfully climbed by Chris Bonington and Graham Little in 1992. They were able to enjoy that 'chisel blade of ice' I remember so well and they succeeded in reaching the summit.

3 St Augustine

25 The Untrodden Ranges: Around Menlungste and Gaurisankar

I was fortunate to be in the Himalaya again in 1951 as deputy leader of the Mount Everest Reconnaissance Expedition. We were a small party – Michael Ward, Tom Bourdillon, Eric Shipton and the New Zealanders Ed Hillary and Earle Riddiford. After time spent in the Western Cwm finding the route up Mount Everest by its difficult, dangerous and reputedly impossible ice-fall, of which more anon, we turned to the exploration of the untrodden ranges westwards around Cho Oyu. Still further west a big Tibetan salient of 240 square miles thrust south into Nepal, marked unsurveyed on the maps. Tibet was now in Chinese hands. Dared we go in? We resolved to take a closer look.

Early in November we made our approach from the village of Namche Bazar (12,000 feet), by way of the valley of the Bhote Kosi. It takes source from a glacier falling from the Nangpa La, the world's highest trading pass on the Tibetan frontier. Six miles up the valley we came to the tiny village of Thami, the birthplace of Tenzing Norgay, who was to climb Everest two years later. Here the party split. Ed Hillary and Riddiford set off home by turning west across the Tesi Lapcha into the Rolwaling Gorge, and so to Kathmandu. The rest of us went another nine miles to Chhule, a drovers' stone hut. From here we could see the unsurveyed area to the west. It looked so packed with high and spiky mountains that we felt convinced it must be uninhabited, probably congested with glaciers allowing us safely to penetrate to its interior without encountering Tibetans or their Chinese conquerors. Again we split, Shipton and Ward struck west up the Pangbuk Valley to seek a pass across the high frontier ridge. Tom Bourdillon and I planned to join them later, meantime we chose to continue up the Bhote Kosi to the Nangpa La at nearly 6,000 metres (close on 20,000 feet). We had found no record of any European ascent from Nepal, and felt too that the chance to reconnoitre Cho Oyu (26,750 feet) was too good to be missed. It had not yet been climbed. We should rejoin Shipton and Ward within a week, supposing we could find them, or they us.

One mile up, we came to the glacier's snout, where we took to its west moraine. We thought we could see the Nangpa La exactly as marked on the map – when suddenly our track swung right (north) into what turned out to be the true continuation of the main glacier. The map had clearly marked the westerly branch, but not the greater northern. We had travelled nine miles in nine hours when we dropped from moraine to glacier and camped in a stony hollow. We were now two miles short of the pass.

In the morning we followed a trail of yak dung through a mile-long mass of stone covering the glacier's surface till we came to bare ice, in which the yaks had trodden deep channels. No snow had fallen for many days; daily sun and nightly frost had transformed its surface into clear ice, in which the Sherpa drovers were cutting hoof-steps for their yaks. They used short-shafted axes with a pick but no adze. Had they been cutting holds in ice before the founding of the Alpine Club? It does seem likely, for the need was there.

In four hours we arrived on the pass. A wide and spacious snowfield stretched far northward to the warm brown hills of Tibet. The pass was full of sun and the stir of air, and set around with splendid snow peaks, many of which looked climbable. At the centre of the pass, a thick mass of tattered prayer-flags hung from a short pole. We sat by it and sunned ourselves. The snowfield fell away before us at a gentle angle for half a mile, then continued as the Kyetrak Glacier, curving eastward, still at a mild angle, out of sight toward the Sherpa trading depot of Kyetrak, ten miles distant.

A long caravan of yaks and Sherpas passed us on the Nangpa La. The maps marked the pass 'Open May to August' but in fact it can be used freely throughout the autumn, and is crossed often in winter, although not without loss of life in blizzards. From one of the drovers we bought a bag of apricots and two dozen oranges – a memory brighter than our main object of reconnoitring Cho Oyu. The mountain lay farther inside the Tibet frontier than we had expected. We walked half a mile on until we had a good view of the north-west face, and were able to pick out two good routes. My report was later read by Herbert Tichy of Austria, who used one of our routes to make the first ascent.

We withdrew to Chhule, and next day struck west between the rock spurs of the Pangbuk Valley, hoping to find a pass into Tibet's salient. A few miles up, we spotted a huge boulder with prayer-flags on top. To our pleasant surprise, we there discovered our Sherpa porter. He delivered a note from Shipton. He and Ward with one Sherpa and seven days' food had crossed the pass. He urged us to come on fast, for there was truly wonderful country on the other side. He had left Ang Tharkay behind with the baggage, ten days' food, and a sheep. We lay and sunbathed in our shirt sleeves – this at 16,000 feet in November – while the sheep was killed and cooked. An eagle with a rich, red-gold breast, soared close overhead, vainly hoping for scraps. We lunched on fried liver and fresh peas. Bourdillon unhappily topped up his feast with apricots, an unfortunate error as he ate them unskinned and unwashed.

Luckily for Tom, our 4,000-foot climb to the pass next morning went up easy rock until near the top. He was ill, and had to lie down every ten minutes; he could move only twenty-five steps at a time. I cut big steps at the final snow slopes and we all arrived on a broad col. Huge snowfields, which covered a hanging glacier, fell westward down to a glaciated valley. It ran far to our south to an unseen end. Its opposite side was flanked by a tall rock ridge ending many miles south at an icy spire, now named Menlungtse (23,560 feet). Its splendid isolation reminded me of Nanda Devi. In the opposite direction, we looked north across the valley's head to a jungle of rock ranges in Tibet, all foothills to the distant snows of the Lapche Kang range. Our prospects were enchanting. Would we find a way down? Where would the glacier lead? What new valleys would we find? For us, this was unknown country, far more rewarding and exciting than the siege of a big peak. Mountain travel held me in thrall.

Beneath our feet, the hanging glacier fell away 2,000 feet, covered at first in six inches of snow, but unplagued by crevasses. Then it plunged. We had to make a semicircular sweep of nearly a mile to avoid cliffs, bearing rightward on to easy ground, and so down to the main glacier. We camped on its far side. We had only two small tents for nine Sherpas, but they all packed in. The night cold was intense. Bourdillon and I had two down bags each, yet even with our clothes on did not feel warm. The day had been a hard one for him. We did not move off until 10 a.m.

Almost at once we found the tracks made three days earlier by Shipton's party of three. All these were distinct. We had followed them only a few hundred yards when I was surprised to see a fourth line of footprints descending from the base of a rock buttress close above to our right (west) and joining the three others on the glacier. Sun had obliterated all but the broad imprints. I was puzzled. Ang Tharkay had told me that Shipton had taken only one porter, Sen Tensing. Shipton's note likewise. It now seemed that he must have taken two. But how could Ang Tharkay not have known? He was far behind us – clearing up the campsite – so I pointed out the fourth set of tracks to Bourdillon, who on impulse snapped them with our colour camera.

We followed the tracks for the better part of two miles, for they had taken the best route through the crevasse system until the ice became excessively riven, when they diverged on to the stony moraine, where we lost them. We continued another few miles to rough grazing grounds and camped in a hollow under Menlungtse's wall at the great south-west bend of the valley.

Shortly afterwards, we spotted Shipton's camp just a quarter of a mile lower down. He and Ward came up to join us. They told us of their several ascents to passes on the valley's flanks, as a result of which they now knew where we were close under the great north ridge of Gaurisankar; and to avoid its pinnacled walls, our own valley turned south-west into the Rongshar Gorge – the principal trade route between Tibet and Nepal. No European had yet travelled through it. Then came their most astonishing news – the discovery of clear yeti tracks two days earlier.

They had crossed the Menlung La early in the afternoon. On reaching the glacier, they had started down valley when Eric (like me) had seen a line of tracks converging on his own from the right-hand flank. He felt utterly baffled. Who could have made such prints? In the deep snow of this upper basin they were shapeless holes, no bigger than a human foot. Sen Tensing had no doubt. They were the tracks of the Yeti, or Abominable Snowman. He and many other Sherpas had seen the creature two years earlier at Thyangboche Monastery, at a distance of twenty-five yards. Its height was that of an average Sherpa with reddish brown hair and a slightly pointed head. As Shipton's party continued down, the snow-cover on the ice grew shallower and the footprints clearer, more regularly shaped to the size of a booted foot. Where they came to open crevasses, the snow became crisp and only half an inch thick. There the prints were sharply defined, probably made that same morning, and not by one animal but two. They measured twelve inches by six inches. At least half a dozen were so clear that the pad marks could be seen distinct within the prints. The big toe was rounded and widely separated from its neighbour; three small toes were closely grouped. None showed claws. Where the animals had jumped crevasses, the toes had clearly been dug into the snow on the far side to check backward slip. Shipton had photographed them.

I repeat this old story because in recent years it has been questioned and Shipton not alive to defend. In a *Sunday Times* article, it was suggested that Shipton might have been a practical joker. I can refute that. Michael Ward and Sen Tensing were there too. Eric Shipton, like us all, had a sense of humour, but we are not practical jokers or party to public deceit. When Bourdillon and I met Shipton, Ward and Sen Tensing, we found all three in a state of subdued excitement, recognisably genuine as they described the detail. Moreover, when they told us of the yeti tracks converging on their own, we knew it to be true. We had not only seen the convergence ourselves, but Tom had photographed it (he later sent me the colour transparency), and I had recorded the incident in my diary, which I still have. Our substantiation escaped Shipton's attention when he came later to report the story, for I had not interrupted the flow of his talk at the time, and when Sen Tensing and Ward then took up the tale, I again had to wait. When I did mention our confirmation of their track sighting, it had seemed unimportant, for their minds, like mine and Bourdillon's too, were racing on to our real dilemma – how to escape from Chinese-held Tibet unseen and find a safe way back to Nepal.

We debated that problem again next morning. Michael wanted to cross a glacier col at the south rim of the Menlung Basin and descend 7,000 feet to the Rolwaling Khola on its far side. They had reconnoitred that route the day before. Shipton doubted whether its lower plunge down big cliffs into the gorge would prove feasible. Both he and I were inclined to favour the Rongshar Gorge, were it not that it was inhabited. Our presence might be reported to the Chinese before we could cross the frontier. When these fears were put to Ang Tharkay, he bristled, and angrily declared that we talked nonsense.

Chinese power did not extend to such remote areas. Many Sherpas used the Rongshar, and our own presence would draw no attention if we passed straight through. Let us go, said he, through the great gorge by night. The moon was full; the distance to the frontier under twenty miles. We could cover the first eight down the uninhabited Menlung Chu before dark.

Shipton was not entirely convinced. Sherpas were always light-hearted about frontier observance, for they traditionally enjoyed free passage. In the end, we were all persuaded. Eric longed to be one of the first westerners through the Rongshar.

We packed up and set off down to the Menlung Chu. We were moving on a high and open valley floor that curved first west then north. Along the opposite side of the great bend, still seven miles away, rose the many-spired wall of Gaurisankar (23,440 feet), once thought to be the world's highest mountain. Close behind us, the pale granite face of Menlungtse soared to a sky of shining blue, one of the most finely shaped mountains any of us had ever seen. Among its gravel flats we saw the spoor of several wolves. The valley narrowed, steepened, then plunged to its northern bend. We came in among pines and rhododendrons and rich red scrub. A mile or two from the Rongshar we met our first Tibetans. Ang Tharkay spoke a few words, pretending that he thought this to be the Rolwaling Khola. We hastened on. At the final drop to the Rongshar, we found a big monastery called Chupar at the river junction. There was not a soul about. We passed close under its clean white walls, which ringed a pink domed temple.

The Rongshar Valley was still wide open to the afternoon's sun, its track heavily fringed with bamboo and wild roses, the latter exactly like the white rose of Scotland. At 6 p.m. we took cover in a wooded clearing above the river and ate a quick meal, waiting there until dark fell and the moon rose. Then we sped south-west, and passed unseen under the high walls of a fort at Topte, which guarded the entrance to the true gorge. Its walls narrowed, rising sheer and far. I had seen nothing like them since last year's travel through the Dhauli Gorge of Garhwal, but here they were set much closer. We viewed them through a lacery of moonlit pines, amazed to see the cliffs tower another 4,000 feet above, lined at the last by a silver edge of snow.

The gorge twisted, screening us from the moon. We had to go very slowly, feeling with our feet for the narrow track. We crossed the river by a cantilever bridge and passed occasional clearings, one bearing the village of Shoktra. No lights showed, but one dog barked. A canine chorus followed. We hoped the Tibetans would as usual ascribe that to the passage of bear or wolf. The gorge was now widening, but the light still black. All went well until 2 a.m., when we began to feel exhausted after nearly sixteen hours on the move. Shoktra, said the Sherpas, had been the Rongshar's last village, the frontier could not be far off, therefore it seemed safe enough to bivouac until dawn. We bedded down at the first clearing. Shipton had been most uneasy at our yielding so easily to temptation. He was right. We fell asleep and failed to bestir ourselves until broad daylight, around six o'clock.

No sooner were we on the move than we heard shouts. Startled to a halt, we were surrounded by a band of seven Tibetan militia, brandishing swords and pistols. They had seen our Vibram-soled tracks, and now wanted to see our chiti from the *Dzongpen* (Governor) of Topte – failing which, we should have to go back with them to Tingri for interrogation. Tingri lay sixty miles back, garrisoned by the Chinese. We asked Ang Tharkay to try bribery. We had only 1,000 rupees left in the expedition's kitty (£75), and feared that this would not be nearly enough to buy our freedom. Ang Tharkay took firm charge. To our near-dismay, he opened the bidding at five rupees. The Tibetans' leader could not contain his anger ... he shouted imprecations. The veins swelled on his forehead. But Ang Tharkay was never to be outdone in a shouting match.

The battle seemed long-continued; at the end Ang Tharkay turned to us: 'They want ten rupees.'

He would not pay them ten rupees. The shouting was renewed; the heat turned full on. They looked like coming to blows, when Ang Tharkay spoke a few words – I never heard exactly what he said – and sudden silence fell. Suddenly, smiles all round! They had split the difference. Ang Tharkay paid over seven rupees. We were free. Our lives had not been highly priced, however much we prized them. Two chickens and four eggs would cost three rupees, a sheep twelve – we knew our worth now!

Just one mile farther we slipped across a frontier bridge into Nepal.

Behind us lay three months of exploratory travel through mountain ranges either little known or hitherto quite unknown. They had been packed with incident, new discoveries, varied peoples, and constant surprise. We seemed for a while to have lived enchanted lives. Now we lay at ease in warm sunshine beside a juniper fire and breakfasted. The present moment was ours.

Eight days later, we walked into Kathmandu.

EXPLORING THE API MASSIF

26 Approach to Api: The Kali Gorge

The expeditions to Garhwal, Almora and Everest had convinced me that the richest Himalayan experience comes in exploratory travel and climbing, not in the siege of a big peak. For me, there was no hard choice. A plain siege was the quickest way to raise money and make a name for oneself in the press; but the true rewards – enjoyment, interest and discovery on all the varied planes – did not lie there. Mountain travel had whetted my appetite. A new exploratory goal was already in mind. In 1953 I wrote of my plans to Tom Longstaff who replied:

> 'I was shattered when I learned that you were not going with the Everest party. Now I am very pleased. You will have a far better time in Dotial. You'll enjoy it immensely. Make a map.'

On the Panch Chuli in 1950, from a height of nearly 20,000 feet, Scott, Weir and I had seen thirty-odd miles to our south-east, an array of high mountains. One was outstanding. We identified it on our maps as Api (23,399 feet) in Nepal's west corner. Its outliers formed a chain of wild ice ridges and splintered peaks, zigzagging nearly thirty miles along Tibet's frontier. They looked mysteriously remote. I felt the urge to go and explore as soon as I could. Nothing could be done in 1951 when I was on Everest, and in 1952 I was too busy writing, to earn money both for myself and the Royal Geographical Society. Scott and Weir were then climbing in east Nepal. However, I did apply to the Nepalese government for permission to explore Api. They refused access, but I felt sure that it would be only a matter of time until they relented. Sure enough, they told me the way was open early in 1953.

I asked John Tyson to join me, and he agreed. He lived in Edinburgh, but I had met him the year before at Magdalen College, Oxford, where I was giving a talk, and he was an undergraduate reading geography in his final year. He had newly returned from an expedition to Tehri Garhwal, where he had made first ascents of two Gangotri peaks. Ginger-haired, with all the energies of his early twenties, he was keen to carry out work on the nature and distribution of Asian food crops and seeds at high altitude, and to collect plants and insects for the British Museum. These aims were secondary to our main purpose of exploratory mountain travel. I was lucky to get Tyson, for I knew no one else free at that time or at such short notice. Aspirants to the Himalaya were few in the early fifties, its land unspoiled. The only slight reservation I had to our plan was due to the activity of the Chinese in Tibet. Westerners tended to be imprisoned as spies if found in the wrong places and, as I well knew, innocence can be difficult to prove.

THE KALI GORGE

We drew up a simple plan. The Indian Survey maps were then of low quality. We rightly guessed that glaciers and spurs of the massif would be incorrectly marked. The range stretched thirty-two miles east from the Indian frontier, which was defined by the great gorge of the Kali River flowing south from the Tibetan plateau. We hoped to make a complete, close-quarter circuit of the range, and if possible climb Api or whatever other peak proved feasible. Our approach would go up the Indian side of the Kali River, which had a good track north to Tibet. Our return would strike east of the range, if we could find a pass, and thus allow us to reconnoitre Nepal's Saipal group in the state of Bajhang. Our supply policy was to live on the country. By cutting tinned foods and packaged food to a bare minimum, we should buy locally, help local trades and eliminate litter. Simple as our plans were, they suffered a couple of blows destined to complicate our lives in the field. The first came before we ever booked our passage from P&O. The Indian Government refused access up the Kali River beyond Darchula, a village twenty-five miles short of Tibet. The presence of Chinese troops across the frontier bothered them. This meant that we should have to find a way up the Nepalese side, where no route was known. Its crux would be the last ten miles, where the Kali had cut a huge rock gorge, into which the spurs and ridges of Api dropped 15,000 feet from their crests. No European had ever attempted that passage. I went again to see Tom Longstaff, whom I knew had once viewed it from the Indian side. He was doubtful if a way could be forced. Supposing we did find a way through to Api's Tibetan side, he knew of no pass by which we might break south again over its main range. If we did find a pass, we should then descend into the vast, unexplored basin of the Seti River, with need of yet another unknown pass to reach Api's south flank. My view of these problems was, as always in exploratory work, to put trust in Providence and go ahead. Only thus can plans be made; otherwise we should all have to sit at home.

The second blow came soon after. We had planned to be into the foothills by early May. But Kathmandu delayed the grant of our pass, and so lost us a full month of good, pre-monsoon weather. This delay allowed us to invite Bentley Beetham to join us. His outstanding alpine record, which had taken him on to the 1924 Everest Expedition, seemed likely to strengthen our joint skills.

Travelling out to India by sea – an experience far more rewarding than air travel – we docked at Bombay in mid-May, and steamed into our Tanakpur railhead on the 19th. Three Darjeeling Sherpas were waiting for us there. On the station platform, we discovered that our ten hundredweight of baggage had been off-loaded at Bareilly, about seventy miles down the line. Leaving the others to retrieve the gear, I went on alone by bus to Pithoragarh, ninety-five miles into the foothills at 5,000 feet. This was our roadhead. I hoped to save time by recruiting Dotial porters, and buying in food for our first ten days' march. The road, an amazing feat of Indian engineering, dispensed all the expected scares along its cliff-edges, including land-slips – its lucky travellers not reaching Pithoragarh until well after dark on a wet night.

Ensconced somewhat traumatised in the Dak bungalow, I was handed first thing in the morning a note from two medical missionaries, Laurie Baker and his wife, inviting me to breakfast with them next morning at their hilltop house on Chandaq. This hill of 7,000 feet rose close above the village, and would give me a view of Api at sunrise. I had to be there at 4.30 a.m., because cloud or haze would later obscure the hills. This prompt kindness was typical of the many missionaries I had already met in the Himalaya. Also typical was their advance intelligence of our coming – usually known hours or even days before we arrived. I was never clear how this worked, but work it did, and most effectively, even to detail of our numbers, origins and aims. The Bakers already knew that we were bound for Api, had three Sherpas and, even more remarkably, that I had arrived late last night alone in the dark.

I went in search of the porter contractor and hired eighteen Dotials, three of whom I hoped would stay with us for the full three months or more.

When Tyson and Beetham arrived late that night, complete with Sherpas and baggage, I had gone early to bed, and rose at 3 a.m., as did Tyson (while Beetham slept), to climb 2,000 feet for my breakfast. The Bakers were young and positively emanated goodwill. They ran a leper colony nearby with more than a score of patients. Yet, like all other missionaries in India at that time, they had to live under a cloud of suspicion as 'spies for the west.' Even their letters were censored.

The sun rose behind Api, sixty miles away to our north-east. The mountain was very lightly hazed, burnished in pale gold light, but the mountain's pyramid rose clear above the sea of mist covering all the intervening valleys and ridges. Hence it looked extraordinarily close, more like twenty miles than sixty. Just a stone's throw (it seemed) to its west rose the ivory horns of Panch Chuli, from which I had first seen Api two years ago. Chandaq's splendid viewpoint included so many great peaks of Kumaon that I could not thank the Bakers enough for this heaven-sent chance to enjoy the near and unexpected presence of Nanda Devi, Nanda Kot, Trisul (which Longstaff had first climbed), and many others well known to me. I felt back among old friends.

Back at Pithoragarh, I met John and Bentley and our three Sherpas. I could see that Nima, our sirdar, was a top-class Sherpa. His eyes looked alertly intelligent, alternating between thoughtful reflection and quick mirth. They were not mischievous eyes, but certainly quizzical. Above all, they conveyed to me an honesty as bracing as hill wind. His companion, Da Norbu, was a relative of Tenzing, the present Everest sirdar. His sense of humour tended to overflow, but his eyes quickly hardened when anything or anyone came really to trouble us. He was the most competent climber of all three. The third, Sen Thendup, was a youngster of seventeen, good-natured to a fault, if not too bright. (I once saw him turn a jam-pot upside down to shake out the flies, forgetting that the jam would come out too.) He was always willing to take on the more uncongenial tasks. They made a good team. And that was to prove our salvation in later emergency. The eighteen Dotials came up from the bazaar to look us over. They turned out to be good men too. We gave them an advance of pay to let them buy in a week's food, and they in turn slept on the ground outside and around the Dak bungalow to let us get away at five in the morning.

The weather stayed fine. Bound for Darchula, forty-two miles north, we covered more than half that distance in three days' easy walking along airy hill ridges. The forest tracks gave occasional glimpses through the treetops to the snows of Nanda Devi and Trisul East. The third day began with a long descent to the confluence of the Gori and Kali Rivers; therefore we had thought it safe to make a late start at 6 a.m. That was a bad mistake. At the confluence, the views north up the Gori Gorge were awe-inspiring, their blue heights filmed with haze and striped with wisps of cloud, but the riverbed lay here at merely 2,000 feet. A relentless sun blazed down upon our laden porters, and the valley's walls concentrated its heat. By 11 a.m. we were all immobilised. Even the Dotials were caught out: they were now running from one patch of shade to another to try to avoid burning the soles of their feet. I had never known such a situation before, nor have I seen it since. We could no longer move without damage, so found an empty teashop, where we all lay in the shade for four hours or more. We did well to travel ten miles that day in twelve hours, ending at the jungly village of Balwakot.

In one more march we reached our farthest point in India, Darchula, a thriving village where a three-log bridge spanned the Kali to Nepal. Having learned our lesson, we arrived at 10 a.m. The Indian police hastened to investigate us, and to examine our pass from the Nepalese government, the first of its kind they had seen. We had now to cross the growling Kali – stones were grinding along its bed under the surge – and continue if we could up that no-road gorge. When we asked the men of the local panchayat (village committee) if a route were possible, they laughed openly and shook their heads.

In the afternoon, I crossed the bridge to visit the tiny village of Bagar in Nepal, and asked to see the headman. I was led to a big, stone-floored room, where he was sitting with village elders smoking a communal hubble-bubble pipe. I showed him my pass, which they all studied in turn while the headman sent for the *munshi* or schoolmaster, who spoke English. John now arrived, and we explained our plans. They at once offered all help. On the vital question, 'Can we find a way through the Kali Gorge to its top end, where the Tinkar Valley branches to Tibet, and so to Api's north side?' their eyes clouded. When they gave thought, they tried to suppress smiles: 'You will find tracks for twenty miles to the last village, Dumling; beyond that, the gorge is walled for ten miles by thousands of feet of rock. There is no way for sahibs, only for goats.'

John and I pricked up our ears. If goats could manage it, so could we. Between goats and mountaineers there is kinship. I said we would try, then told the headman that five of our Dotials wanted to go back to Pithoragarh. Could he replace them? He at once said that he could. His people were Dotials.

We had much trouble crossing the Kali at sunrise. The Darchula-third of the bridge was missing. Dry as the weather was here, the Kali had swollen overnight to a powerful flood. We had to rig long ropes and spend two hours getting the porters across. The path north dwindled; now thin as a goat track, it climbed steeply uphill for 2,000 feet, then after a long traverse above the river, climbed another 2,000 feet to a terrace at 6,000 feet, where we camped beside a spring. We had risen out of the heat of the Kali. The night was cool, the sky starry; the moon lit distant snow peaks across the river.

I should never have believed, looking at the quarter-inch map, that travel up this east side of the Kali could be so varied. On the map it looked constricted, like a deep trench. In fact, it was openly pleasant with several prosperous villages and friendly people linked by this narrow track. We passed through one named Higla on our second day, built on wide terraces where bulls, goats and sheep grazed on the hillsides, bells tinkling at their necks. Mingled with the tinkling, we heard the music of a shepherd's flute, hauntingly beautiful always in short bursts of melody never completed, abruptly interrupted by pauses long or short, followed by a new outburst. It reminded me of a nightingale's song. Beyond Higla, we passed through a wooded glade where cuckoos called. A clear stream flowed down its middle, so we stopped for lunch. Nima showed me a wild fern like young bracken, which the Dotials cooked as a vegetable. The leaves had a brown streak down their outside centre-lines. The flavour was not unlike cabbage.

In the afternoon, we crossed a broad pass at 9,000 feet between one side glen and the next, wooded in oak and covered in wild strawberries. Dropping our loads, we all lay in the shade of the oaks on top of the strawberry beds and picked the fruit in handfuls. They had the full strawberry flavour – the first we'd found in the Himalaya. Cuckoos and a host of other birds were still calling among the trees. The ravines were alive with birds and loud with their calling, though none were warblers with song to compare with Scottish glens. But they called, and the echoes lingered long across the Kali, the sound in harmony with its gulf and great space. An occasional monal pheasant, with cry crudely startling, might rarely rocket away from us like a grouse, a pale purple bird with an orange splash on its back and white on the tail. More elegant was the Himalayan tree-pie, gliding through the branches with a long slender body trailing a blue tail. Beyond the branches, we had our first distant glimpse of the snows of Api. Thereafter we dropped down to a clachan named Sina, passing under rock overhangs from which three dark brown beehives hung well out of man's reach.

We stopped at Sina overnight, and climbed in the morning 1,500 feet up an airy path to Rapla, where a few houses had been built up on shelves. All had their door and window-frames adorned with elaborate wood-carvings, coloured red, white and blue.

Barley and wheat grew in the fields and cows grazed. The men, as usual when they heard of our planned passage through the gorge, looked amused, and would say only *Bahut kharab* (very bad). For that reason, John and I began to worry about Bentley Beetham.

Over the last week, he had suffered so badly from diarrhoea, and lost so much strength, that his continuing the journey seemed no longer possible. He had, we found, been drinking from wayside streams without having the water boiled. This was folly. We had thought him knowledgeable on the Himalaya. I dosed him with sulphadiazine. His trouble was compounded by an inability to eat the food of the country – rice, dal, and flour – and his dislike even of our own ships' biscuits. He could take dried soup and eggs, but now we had no eggs, and so he had lost too much energy and become weak and dispirited compared with his astonishing vitality on the voyage out.

He managed to cover the six miles to Dumling next morning because the passage was unusually slow, the track congested with goats, driven south by Bhotias, who inhabited the upper Kali. Bhotia means 'Men of Bhot', or Tibet, who carry the trade between Tibet and India. Near Dumling, we surprised and were startled by one large langur monkey, a most handsome beast with a black face lit by a huge white frill, which circled its head like a halo. The village was built in three clusters, each with stone walls and thatched roofs. The women wore silver necklaces, strings of red beads and gold nose rings. The men wore gold earrings. To our great relief, they heard our plans without that amused surprise of villagers of the lower Kali. They affirmed that we could make a way through the great gorge ahead, but certainly not with sixty-pound loads. The rock walls, they declared, were far too difficult. We should have to cut loads to forty pounds. Nima had meanwhile been making his own enquiries. He reported that neither Dotials nor Dumling Bhotias would come unless loads were cut, but all were prepared to carry forty pounds. We, therefore, declared the morrow a rest day for break up of the baggage. I engaged seven Dumling porters.

Bentley Beetham told us next morning that he would have to go back. The sulpha drug had worked; his temperature had dropped to normal. But his food problem remained. He could not eat the country diet. After discussion, we agreed that he ought to return. We gave him two porters and food enough to see him and them safely back to the railhead at Tanakpur. We parted sadly. He promised to report how he fared by sending a note up the Kali to Garbyang, the Indian trading post near the Tibetan frontier.

Before us now lay a long traverse of several days across the lower flanks of Api, where its spurs fell away in wide cliffs to the Kali. The next two miles took us three days. On the first, a way was always discernible, although with long drops below. To our astonishment, we were afflicted by midges at night, the first we'd met in the Himalaya. Our outraged feelings were assuaged by a Dumling Bhotia, who had brought his bamboo flute. His interrupted airs, exactly like those near Higla, soothed us each night round the campfires. The second day gave the crux of the traverse. We left camp at 5 a.m. to climb on to the day's first rock spur, then around it to its Kali face. Before us stretched a vast precipice, high above the distant river. When we looked closely, we could see that exposed ledges crossed the face on a falling line to the river below Api's next spur. We could see too why the loads had been cut: the rocks required the use of both hands for balance-moves; for the porters, a slip would be fatal. At one cliff, where the angle suddenly eased, we saw a deer bound like a chamois across the ledges, an acrobatic feat beyond emulation. On reaching the banks of the Kali itself, we entered a side glen filled by a tributary draining the snows of Api. Above us, it plunged in a series of high waterfalls until close to its Kali junction, where a three-log bridge gave first proof of Bhotia use. On its far side, we climbed 1,000 feet up the second spur's flank to an airy site on its crest marked Thin on the map, named from its spring water. We camped there on a wide ledge.

One of our Dotials had taken a bad chill. We fed him aspirins and put him into a red sleeping bag within a tent. This mollycoddling evoked gusts of laughter from the other porters – but the patient was cured by morning.

The day's work, again a short mile, was long in time, first up the crest of our spur, which fell from Api's west ridge, then abruptly down the face of its more northerly cliff, the longest and most tiring descent of the gorge. It led us into a steep, bamboo jungle peppered with chestnut and holly trees, amongst which scampered many huge langur monkeys, all with black faces frilled in white. Their bodies, both grey-haired and dark brown, sported long tails.

The Bhotias said that there were bears too, but we saw none. On rounding the spur's base, we climbed on to a low hilltop and camped on grass where a stir of air repelled the midges. The worst of the journey was now over, said the

Bhotias: we should have a good track for the next two days. The Bhotias in camp kept very much to themselves. Three of our Dotials, of whom I'd already taken note at Pithoragarh, were such excellent men that we resolved to keep them on to the end if they would stay. They were all in their mid-twenties. Their leader Gujbir, tall, tough and cheerful, had been quietly observing our ways and been helping the Sherpas more and more of his own accord, clearing ground for tents, fetching water or gathering firewood. A blue cap topped his mop of black hair. His friends Salwan and Ranzing were of different temperament, more reserved, and a bit diffident, as though not yet sure that we wanted their help for more than load carrying, unless we made it obvious. Salwan was the more inward-looking, Ranzing the more outgoing with a ready smile and relaxed nature. All three bearing us goodwill, they had only to see that we really did want their help to give a quick response. At this early stage of our journey we had made few calls on them, apart from porterage, but their time would come.

To encourage the trio, John showed them our maps and tried to explain what we hoped to do. They were interested, and quick on the uptake, soon able to understand our plan of action. They were quite naturally bright lads, ready to be enthused. They told us now that they wanted to stay on. We said yes to that. As night fell, we heard a mutter of thunder – followed by a quick and fearful scatter of porters seeking shelter. The Sherpas, as always thinking of John and me first, set up our tent just in time. A blinding flash and repeated thunder rolls filled the gorge. Rain sheeted down. We fetched the Sherpas in with us. One of the great sounds of this world is Himalayan thunder. Its deep boom, resonating between the vast mountain walls, has a quality of power heard nowhere else on earth by human ear – as if belonging more to our spiritual depths than to earthly shallows. The gods speak in it.

The morning dawned fine. We were able to cover six miles along the bank of the Kali in five hours. The path twisted narrowly through woods, where whistling thrushes sang among chestnut and walnut trees above an undergrowth of flowering currant, berberis and cotoneaster. The Kali alongside us twisted too, eastward into open, sunlit ground. On its Indian bank appeared the village of Budhi – which meant that we must be just four miles from Garbyang, and the Tinkar Valley of Api's north side. We had won through.

Although the Nepalese bank bore no village, it did have well tilled fields, apparently cultivated from Budhi; for the Kali – here foaming white and awful in power – was bridged by logs spanning two gigantic boulders within the river. The bridge would certainly hold in the monsoon, for the logs were poised fifty feet above the water. We camped on a sunny terrace under the twin peaks of Api's western ridge. The snows at last looked close, streaking the gullies and flanks. We were now within a mile of the Api Khola, whose valley ran up to Api's summit between two mighty ridges. Since the monsoon would break soon – and last night was a warning – it seemed wise not to continue to the Tinkar Valley farther north, but instead to speed up the Api Khola and reconnoitre Api's north-west face. Then, when the monsoon broke, we could transfer to the north, Tibetan side, where I felt sure that after the weather's first onslaught, the huge mass of the Api ridges might dam the monsoon, holding the worst of the weather to the south of the main chain. The guess was to prove correct.

Six of our Bhotias and five Dotials now wanted to go back. So we sent Nima across the bridge to Budhi to recruit more men and to buy eggs. Meanwhile, I and the two Sherpas re-packed the baggage as sixty-pound loads. John collected insects (butterflies and beetles). In a few hours Nima returned triumphant. He had found five men to replace the Dotials. Then his face puckered in deep sorrow. Budhi had no eggs. We had no sooner registered sympathetic distress than his face creased in a white and delighted grin. From behind his back came a bag of twelve eggs – typical of Nima's humour.

That night I made the mistake of pitching only my tent's flysheet. In the early hours it became a cold wind tunnel. I was too lethargic to rise and change its position, for which I was later to pay penalty. In the morning the Budhi men arrived at 5 a.m. and we set off soon after. The track had vanished. It began to look as if I had been over-hasty in raising the loads to sixty pounds. Rough and deeply overgrown ground, clearly long unused, led us steeply up, over and down the butt end of a high spur. The side valley of the Api Khola opened out on our right-hand side. Down it rushed a deep glacial river, spanned by a single log. We crossed – and the great Kali Gorge lay at last behind us.

The Api Khola fell straight down to us between two parallel ridges from near the base of Api itself. The summit stood clear, seven miles up and bearing a huge icecap, which sloped toward the head of our valley. Another top, like a great dog-tooth, stood to its left on its north-west ridge. The icecap between the two looked like a broad and promising route, but we could not yet see how to gain access. Lowering our eyes to the ground, we found ourselves standing on a terrace covered in strawberries. Of one accord, we laid down our loads and feasted.

27 Api and Nampa

The lunch break was long, to celebrate our arrival. Then we climbed 3,000 feet in two miles to a wide and grassy shelf or maidan. Here at 12,000 feet we camped beside a crag near its middle. All around us the ground's green bed lay hidden under a spread quilt of bright-coloured flowers: gold, red and white potentillas, yellow anemones and ranunculas and a multitude of blue primulas, some of them dark purple. Among that dense cover, many had stalks so short that they seemed to have none. We felt it worth coming to the Himalaya for this sight alone.

Our first act after pitching the tents was to issue our three Sherpas and three Dotials with windproof clothing, boots, socks, balaclavas and sleeping bags. There was much embarrassed joking by the Dotials as they tried on the clothes. They did not, like the Sherpas, appreciate as yet the need for this fancy dress. But they liked having it as a trophy.

We had carried four tents. Two were now allocated to the Sherpa-Dotial groups, leaving John and me one each, which turned out that night to be a real blessing. I had a high temperature chill – the result of that wind-tunnel at Budhi – and John was in bad shape after five days of diarrhoea. At 6 a.m. I rose to pay off redundant porters, despatch six others under Da Norbu to establish base camp 2,000 feet higher in the great corrie below Api, and to send Nima with our three Dotials to Garbyang to buy in food. Duty done, I took to my sleeping bag, sweating and shivering by turns.

John turned our rest day to profit by starting his flower collection, pressing the plants, roots and all, in the presses supplied by the British Museum. He had dozens of species before nightfall. When Da Norbu and Sen Thendup arrived back from base, where they had set up camp beside a green lake, John put them to work netting butterflies. But this was no work to them. They took the game as a joyful frolic, and were adept. John soon had a score of specimens for his cyanide bottle.

Just before nightfall, Nima and the Dotials returned with ample food for the next ten days. They had been closely questioned about us by the Indian police at Garbyang, but now all were happy around the campfire. I lay in my bag enjoying the smell and crackle of burning juniper and listening to the men's laughter.

Dawn came with a promise of sun at our level, but far below we could see cloud rolling up the Kali and spreading over the hills of Kumaon to our west.

We moved up to base camp at 14,000 feet beside the green lake, where it began to snow around 9 a.m. The flowered ground was quickly covered. I girded my loins and climbed up to the moraine of the Api Glacier. I could see then that the approach to the great icecap must be made by a huge ice-fall, no less impressive than that of the Khumbu on Everest. And here the set-up looked not dissimilar: 10,000 feet of ice climbing with the main obstacle low down. A closer approach was today not possible, neither John nor I being well and the wind rising.

The Dotials looked as miserable as John and I, as they tried, in the cold and falling snow, to coax a flame from the wet firewood. The Sherpas fared better, being well accustomed to snow and altitude. They were laughing and joking as always. But the wind began to whine through our tents' guy ropes and we all fled inside. The Sherpas occupied the largest tent, from which they cooked and served tea and hot meals from our Primus stove. During a lull Nima pushed into my tent a cake of Lux soap from Garbyang. Its wrapper bore the blurb:

'BEAUTY CARE OF THE STARS
The world's most beautiful women, the lovely stars of stage and screen,
use this to guard complexion beauty. Gently pat creamy
Lux Toilet Soap into your skin with warm water, then with cold.
Use this fragrant soap for a beauty bath too.'

For the first time I realised that Nima could read English, and must have translated for the other pair – I could hear their whinneys of laughter as they imagined my reading the words on the wrapper.

John still felt ill next morning, but I much better. When sun struck the tents, I set off alone to reconnoitre the great glacier basin. I followed a narrow moraine ridge past two more green lakes until I came under the icefall. I had seen nothing of its kind more impressive in Sola Khumbu. The basin itself was fully a mile wide, its walls higher than those of Everest's Western Cwm, and its ice-fall taller and steeper and narrower. I had hoped that its left-hand retaining ridge might offer a route free of avalanche, but in fact the ice-fall filled it to the brim with cliffs and séracs. The whole was dominated by the icecap, whose snout overhung its top. This started to avalanche from 9.45 a.m. onwards. The falls came from the cap's edge in blocks as big as houses. One fell over the flank of the retaining rock ridge. Twice I had to run to get out of the line of fire. I had never seen a more dangerous mountain flank. There was no route on this ice-fall.[1]

---

1 The mountain was attempted in 1954 by an Italian Expedition led by Pierre Ghiglione (aged seventy-one) with Giorgio Rosenkrantz, Roberto Bignami and Giuseppe Barenghi with Gyaltsen Norbu and two other Sherpas. After attempting the Chamlia (south) face, Bignami fell into a river and was drowned. The rest of

I returned to camp to find John living off the medicine chest rather than the kitchen: codeine, gelusil, chlorodyne, and finally castor oil. The latter worked wonders, for next morning he and Da Norbu went up to the basin and confirmed my negative report, except that he thought a possible way might be found up a difficult rock ridge second to the left of the ice-fall. I could see yet another alternative. Api's north-west ridge, which sloped to the Kali and bore on its crest the dog-tooth top (19,920 feet Pt. 6,070 metres), might be reached from our camp by its north-west flank. But the tooth would then obstruct the route to Api: the truth was we had seen nothing to free us of siege tactics, which we were in no condition to try, and so would be better employed on a new reconnaissance from Api's opposite side. We therefore sent Nima back to Garbyang to recruit nine porters for shifting all our gear to the north side of the range, where a long, parallel valley, called the Tinkar Khola, fell from the Tibetan frontier down to the Kali River, joining it below Garbyang. While waiting for the new porters, we spent two busy days on a thorough reconnaissance of the glacier basin.

On 12 June, nine Tibetans arrived from Garbyang. Two were women, who although smaller than the men and of lighter build, carried the same loads with the same ease. The men wore big earrings inset with large green or red stones. Some had pigtails tasselled in red cloth and wound round the head. A few wore amulets round the neck, holding, said Nima, sacred scripts, probably mantras. We all moved down, then traversed around the butt end of Api's north-west spur along a pinewood terrace carpeted with primulas: this in marked contrast to the Indian scene across the Kali, which was bare and bleak. A high southerly wind blew clouds of dust around Garbyang.

We contoured farther, screened by the pines, until we came into the Tinkar Valley. On its far side we could see the village of Changru, on a shelf 300 feet up from the Tinkar River. On our own side, the Nampa valley opened out rightwards. Here we found a meadow ringed with pines and fed with clear spring water. Big boulders dotted the surface. We camped there in the early

---

the party then tried the north face to the north-west ridge via the Api Glacier approach reconnoitred by Murray. Avoiding the dangerous icefall by the left-flanking rocky spur Rosenkrantz, Barenghi, Ghiglione and Gyaltsen mounted a summit bid on 15 June from Camp 3 at 20,180 feet. Ghiglione soon returned to the camp. Higher up Rosenkrantz became ill and accompanied by Gyaltsen was forced to bivouac to wait for Barenghi who continued alone. He never returned (he may have reached one of the summits). Lacking crucial bivouac equipment and food (which was with Barenghi) Rosenkrantz died during a second bivouac and Gyaltsen, rejoined the others on 18 June (*Mountain World* 1955, p.124–128). Gyaltsen Norbu returned to the mountain in 1960 with a Japanese expedition and reached the summit with K. Hirabayashi by the north-west ridge. The climb was repeated the following day by M. Teraska and Y. Tsuda. The mountain was climbed from the Chamlia side by the south face to the east ridge on 16 October 1978 by the Italians Cesare Cesa Bianchi, Maurizio Magghi Angelo Rocca and Vittorio Tamangi (*AAJ* 1979).

afternoon. Nima went off to Garbyang (as the Tibetans did too) to post our letters home and collect mail. He brought back a letter from Bentley Beetham, reassuring us that he was safely out of the Kali and back into India. With Nima came the chauki (frontier watchman) from Changru to inspect our pass. He offered help. In his company was Padam Singh, a Bhotia trader of local renown. I fetched out maps and asked Nima to explain our need of a pass south across the Api range, because return by the Kali route would be impossible when the monsoon broke.

Padam grasped our need immediately, and said that our best way was to turn the whole range by a journey of several days along the Tibetan frontier plateau, when we could cross the high pass of Urai Lagna, close on 20,000 feet, and so into Nepal's Seti valley. This was the very solution that John and I had hoped for, but hardly dared to expect. We promptly engaged him as a guide to come with us after we had finished exploring the Api-Nampa range. He and the chauki went off as twilight fell, for the midges were again becoming bad. The whole Kali-Tinkar area is infested with midges at around 9–10,000 feet.

On 13 June, the first unmistakable monsoon clouds began to billow up the Tinkar Valley and roll over its high ridges. No rain fell as yet. At 6 a.m., Padam Singh came across from Changru with a gift of sixteen eggs – Nima had yesterday been told at Garbyang that no eggs could be had. Although freely offered, we did pay for them. We knew well how scarce eggs were at this height. The nine Tibetans arrived close on his heels at the time promised. All these frontiersmen kept their given word. They were raised from youth to its scrupulous observance, all their own trade having to be done without paper contract. Their word of mouth was their bond.

We all moved up a beautifully wooded track in the open valley. To either flank rose high mountain ridges, and down its middle thundered a big glacier stream. Moving with us were thirty or forty Bhotias, many with guns – for 'protection', they said, against snow leopards (skins were valuable). All carried carpets and bedding, and one a wooden plough. Among them were women and small boys. At one o'clock we reached a maidan two miles long, dotted with grazing sheep, goats, cows, bulls, ponies and jhopas – the latter a cross between cow and yak. At least a dozen of the herdsmen's coarse canvas tents lay scattered over the green pastures, which grew alpine plants more than grass. Nearly a mile ahead, the valley became a main junction for a series of side valleys running right and left into the heart of the Api/Nampa range. Down these flowed a succession of glaciers, each of the upper overriding the lower. Close to our right rose the dog-tooth of Api's north-west ridge, from which a glacier hung. We pitched camp below its snout on flat green ground. Our nine Tibetans sold us their tsampa (roasted barley flour), after which I paid them off.

John and I now wanted to buy a sheep, but Nima had Buddhist scruples and disapproved. He would not act. We felt respect for his ethical code: the very first vow of a lay Buddhist is not to kill or injure any living being. But John and I did not feel bound by its application in all circumstances. So we walked half a mile to the nearest Bhotia tent, and with Da Norbu's help haggled for a sheep, which we bought for twelve rupees. The Sherpas would not kill it, so the job was done by the Dotials. Nima scowled, but was ready enough to cook and to serve the tenderly fried liver with chip potatoes. Both Sherpas and Dotials ate the mutton. We moved camp in the morning to a still higher maidan at 14,000 feet, close below the main Api Glacier. Heralded by a rainbow spanning the valley, the monsoon broke over the main chain. Rain sheeted down and cloud rolled to our tents' doors; but when the sky cleared after twelve hours' deluge, we found the hillsides transformed – covered so thickly in the blossom of alpine plants, much of it red potentilla, that we might have thought ourselves transported to paradise overnight on a magic carpet. When we climbed to 16,000 feet on the north flank to get a good reconnaissance point, we met there a herd of twenty horses. So intent were they on cropping the alpines that we could move right in among them without drawing more than a sideways glance. They enjoyed rich feeding: I reckoned each mouthful worth several pounds in any British garden catalogue.

We had good views of the glaciers flowing down from Api between the tops to its either side. We could see possible routes on to the upper ice slopes, but at angles hopelessly long and steep without the ice climbing tools to be developed twenty years later.

I climbed next day high into the main Api Glacier to verify my opinions. Its lower end flowed into the Nampa Khola, where it was overridden, as noted earlier, by three other glaciers from peaks farther east, each flowing over the top of its lower neighbour until all four overrode into the Nampa Valley, which thus made a chaotic spectacle, their stony moraines intermingling until no trace of the underlying ice showed through. I had not before seen such glacial desolation over so long a distance, nor in such contrast to a valley's flowering flanks.

John and Da Norbu, with two days' food, had meantime set off to explore the upper Nampa Valley by a route 1,000 feet above its tangled floor. Late in the day they tried to descend to its glacier and became benighted on a ledge above a great cliff. The wind rose and rain fell. In his record (*AJ*, Vol 59, p.421–427), John modestly remarked:

'Benighted here in a storm high among the cliffs of a remote Nepalese valley, I think this was as lonely a night as I have ever spent.' At dawn, they found a way down to the glacier and back to camp.

It was now clear to us that in present weather we could not hope to go high on Api or its neighbour Nampa, which we had not yet seen, and should try instead to look for that pass from Tibet across the range southward. On 20 June we descended to the junction of the Nampa and Tinkar Valleys and re-occupied our old campsite at 10,500 feet.

In the afternoon, while the Dotials were still ferrying down our baggage, I crossed the Tinkar Khola and climbed alone to Changru on its far side. The houses were Bhotia, like those of Rapla, all having splendidly carved doors and window-frames. I had hoped to meet Padam Singh to make a bandobast for crossing the Urai Lagna, but he was off north on business. Instead I met the police chauki, who was again helpful. He assured me that the route over the Tinkar Lipu into Tibet would be safe – and here came the sting – because the Chinese guards were not stationed on the pass itself, but four miles beyond toward the Tibetan village of Taklakot. At this first news of such a close Chinese watch on the pass, I took alarm. I felt wary of his reassurances, coming from a man who would not be one of the party. Apparently flying off at a tangent, he pointed out to me 'The Cave of the Dead' about 1,500 feet up the rocky hillside above Changru. Last century, said he, the men of Marma on the south side of Api had found a pass across the range to the Tinkar Khola and taken as wives the women of Changru. The settlement was then ravaged by smallpox. Thinking a curse had been put upon them, the people fled for refuge to this hillside cave. They took all their treasures with them, but were too late. All died in the cave. I knew this story to be true. Gansser, in *The Throne of the Gods,*[2] had reported visiting the cave in 1936, when he found the skeletons of men, women and children still there, bones and skulls covered still in parchment-like skin. All around lay their ornaments, coins and weapons, and several wooden chests partially covered with rock debris after an earthquake recorded around 1920. I had no desire to inspect the grisly relics. My real interest now was in that alleged pass across the range. Maybe that part of the tale was legendary, but legends can sometimes have a basis in truth, though the glacier-valley had disclosed no likelihoods.

Leaving our dilemma unresolved, we sent Nima to Garbyang next morning to get porters for a move up-valley to Tinkar, and to collect mail. He came back with a two-pound pot of honey, a gift sent up the Kali by Narsang, a swami whom we had met at Pithoragarh. His gesture seemed most kind, but I wondered why – until I opened the old newspaper in which the pot was wrapped. It bore the big headline – EVEREST CLIMBED – and news of the first ascent on 29 May by Hillary and Tenzing.

When we told the Sherpas, Da Norbu shook his head in wonder, and exclaimed, 'There will be no living with him now!'

2 *The Throne of the Gods* by Arnold Heim and August Gansser (Morgarten, Zurich, 1938; Macmillan, London, 1939).

When I met Tenzing later, I found his modesty undiminished. My own reaction was mixed: natural exhilaration that the way we had found two years ago had been proven good; followed by dismay that the world's summit was no longer inviolate. Its old, inspirational value had, I felt, been diminished. The thought had seemed to me at the time a bit irrational. In the long term, it has proved right.

That 'success' was the most damaging to mountains and to real mountaineering that there has ever been.

28 Yokapahar Himal – Warnings

The porters arrived by early morning and carried our loads in five hours up the very narrow gorge to Tinkar. The small village stood on sunlit terraces at 12,000 feet, the highest settlement of west Nepal. Its summer population was 200. Only a few families wintered here. The fields had all been tilled, with wooden ploughs drawn by yaks, and sown with grain crops and potatoes, so that we had no choice but to camp in the village itself. This comprised about forty stone-built houses set close, all with stone-flagged roofs, through the cracks in which rose smoke from the hearth-fires within. The village centre had a big, stone-flagged square on two levels, on which we were allowed to set our tents. The flags, like the whole village, were perfectly clean and kept swept. The Bhotia people were immediately friendly, and thrust out their tongues in greeting, the Tibetan fashion. Officially they were Hindu, and tall stone lingams stood at the edges of both squares. Many of the men wore long tufts of hair at the crown of the head, by which the dead Hindu might be pulled up to Heaven. Others wore the Tibetan pigtail curled into a topknot. Buddhist prayer-flags, nailed to tall poles, fluttered at the courtyards' edges. The truth is that living at the frontiers of three different nations, they accepted the ideas and customs of all, turning each to their own use. Originally nomadic, the Bhotias had taken root in the upper valleys, pastured sheep, goats, yaks and jhopas on the hills, and traded, by barter, all kinds of goods between Tibet, Nepal and India. Their dress was likewise varied, some in Tibetan boots and head-dress, others in hide shoes and white pork pie caps, and all wearing jackets and trousers made of home-woven cloth spun from the wool of their own flocks.

The headman, Lef Singh, received us warmly. He told us that we were the first white men to enter Tinkar since the two Swiss geologists of seventeen years earlier. He and his fellows sat cross-legged on the flags and watched us carefully, their faces impassive but thoughtful, their bright, brown eyes full of curiosity. They silently took note of our gear, and our actions. Out of politeness they remained grave of face, and did not laugh at a camp scene which to them, must have seemed like a travelling circus – especially when Tyson and the Sherpas were netting butterflies. Each time I looked a man in the eye, he responded with a smile that for breadth and spiky whiteness reminded me of the Api range. Their principal curiosity was to find ways to help us. They placed at our disposal an abundance of goodwill and detailed knowledge of their own mountain territory. We fetched our maps and explained our campaign with its difficulties (this in bad Hindustani but with many helpful words from Nima). Their ready intelligence grasped our problem. Lef Singh took the lead in dealing with us and helping our next move. He said that there was certainly no pass across the barrier range, despite the Changru legend, but confirmed that we could turn the range (which he called the Yokapahar) by climbing east up the Tinkar Valley to cross the high pass into Tibet. If we went down into Tibet, the Chinese would arrest us. Our imprisonment might then be reckoned in years. But there was no need to do that. From the pass of Tinkar Lipu, 5,000 feet above our heads, we could travel several days south, below the general level of the high frontier ridge, in a virtual no man's land between the two countries. After thus bypassing the whole range of Api, we should find the pass of Urai Lagna at nearly 20,000 feet, which would allow us to get south into Nepal.

This was excellent news; that is, if the route were truly as safe as he said. Lef Singh agreed to get porters, and promised a sheep for the pot. This meant delaying here for a day or two, which we were not loath to do – the village was a happy one, and the weather threatening.

Rain poured down by morning. The Bhotias sold us a sheep for seventeen rupees, plus a ten days' supply of rice, flour, and ghee. Nima advised that to ensure fast movement we should cut loads to fifty pounds, but keep porters' pay at three rupees a day. In the afternoon, Lef Singh asked me to give his wife medical help: she appeared to have rheumatism in her legs. I gave all that I had available for brief pain relief – chlorodyne. At night, Nima discussed porter pay with the men of Tinkar. They wanted double pay, plus half for the days of return. Nima refused, but still they would not budge. Nima was incensed that we should be held to ransom, as it were. Such was his wrath that at 9 p.m. he and Da Norbu thrust their heads into my tent, the rain drumming on its canvas, to announce that they were going at once to Garbyang to recruit porters, for they would have to catch the men before seven in the morning, when they usually dispersed, tending herds, or crops, or setting out on trade travel. This resolute decision on such a black and dirty night took me by surprise. Before I could think the subject over, they were away, down a valley choked with mist and rain, and before them eight miles' travel on bad and narrow tracks.

Nima was an excellent sirdar, but in the grey morning I knew that I ought to have over-ruled him, and not been pressed into hasty assent: we needed Lef Singh's guidance to escape Chinese eyes. At Tinkar, all was bustle. The weather had dried and the people held a fertility ceremony with much beating of drums, scattering of grain around the lingams, and offerings of food before a candle-lit altar on the courtyard. Late in the afternoon, Nima arrived back with twelve Garbyang porters, engaged at three rupees a day. John and I at once saw Lef Singh. As amiable as ever, he agreed to come with us at six rupees a day. He advised that we must travel by night in Tibet, because the Chinese had 200 troops at Taklakot, with a chauki post three miles out toward the pass, where they used field-glasses to observe movement below the Tinkar Lipu. He thought that with our lightened loads we might be able to reach the Urai Lagna in three or four days.

We felt much relieved, not realising that our friend Lef Singh was playing a poker game of his own, much more skilfully than we were. That same evening, we noted a marked change in the attitude of the Bhotias. Their eyes had grown unfriendly. Then we found that our Garbyang porters were also of changed mind and refusing to cross the Tinkar Lipu. They had suddenly become afraid of arrest by the Chinese, who might open fire on our party. In short, travel with us had become dangerous, even by night. The reason was not hard to find. The men of Tinkar, resenting our use of porters from Garbyang when their own men were idle, had spread disinformation. Nima's triumph had been short-lived.

Morning dawned with sun and blue skies. By happy chance, a Bhotia had remarked to John that he felt sure there was another route across the barrier range to the Seti basin of Nepal. We should find it up the valley running south-east from Tinkar, which valley he named the Yokanadi Khola. The pass would be difficult but possible. With twelve porters on our hands, plus six of our own, we had to make a quick decision. Nima and Gujbir urged us to return down the Kali with double marches on the Indian side to Rapla, cross to Nepal, then follow passes eastward over to the most southern spurs of Api to Chaubisho in Marma. We had to reject that. It would end our expedition. The Indian police would expel us – a fact that Nima and Gujbir found hard to believe. We knew that the Nepali route down the Kali would be closed by flooded tributaries. On this Tibetan side of the range we should at least have clear skies on occasion, and be able to see. This decided, we moved forthwith into the Yokanadi Valley. Its floor and both hillsides were charged with colour, brilliant even beyond our previous experience. The greens were emerald. The massed flowers sparkled along the flanks like belts of fire. The path we followed kept level through wide, sun-flooded meadows, giving us leisure to let it all soak in. After five miles, our way was blocked by a great wall of snow and ice, formed by a chain of three peaks at the valley's head. We camped at the edge of its tangled moraine debris. If there were any pass, it must lie hidden around the corner to our left-hand or east side.

The night being fine, we agreed to start at 3 a.m. But the mountains clouded over, so we delayed until after seven. Some two hours later, we glimpsed a probable pass up the side valley, its upper half being filled by a glacier snout. We climbed a few hundred feet up to a good campsite, intending only a brief halt. The Sherpas and Dotials joined us. The Garbyang men had chosen to go slow. When they arrived, they struck. The very prospect of a pass ahead demoralised them. The Tinkar Bhotias had done their nefarious work only too well. The Garbyang men, now disorientated, thought that any pass ahead must lead into Tibet. To protect themselves, they threatened to send a child to the Tibetan chaukis, warning them of our impending arrival, unaware that our pass, if found, would lead instead to the Seti Valley of Nepal. Nothing would convince them otherwise. The weather was worsening, so we paid them off. We made camp, and chose to reconnoitre our pass from here when the skies cleared.

Excruciating toothache kept me awake all night. The wisdom tooth affected had been filled just before leaving home. The apparently wise precaution had become my undoing. The inhalation of cold air, and maybe the chewing of tough Tibetan mutton, had played havoc with the nerve. I accompanied John and porters in the morning for an hour or more until we had turned the glacier's snout, and by a long traverse come on to its top. There I had to turn back. The cold air lit all the facial nerves into fiery agony. Back in camp, I doped myself with veganin. John returned in the afternoon. He had climbed a mile up the glacier into its basin, from which snow-and-ice slopes rose another 1,500 feet to a col, the nearest of three others between a curtain of peaks. He proposed to camp in the basin and explore.

In the morning, John set off early with Da Norbu and two Dotials. I was running a high temperature and began a full course of sulphadiazine, for the swollen gum was suppurating and had to be washed repeatedly with antiseptic. I have spoken of living in the present moment – a highly desirable state of mind – but in practical terms it does presuppose good health of body. Instead, I was now living in purgatory, conscious only of pain.

The Dotials were back in camp by late afternoon. They had placed a tent for John and Da Norbu at 17,500 feet, and now brought a note from John with a sketch of the mountain scene above, drawn during breaks in the clouds. It showed a cirque of four peaks with three cols between. In my twilight world I had difficulty giving it full attention.

After another and still worse night, I awoke feeling so hot that I reached hurriedly for the thermometer. I took my temperature – 110! A hundred and eight was supposed to be fatal. In near panic I stripped off my sleeping bag, shook down the mercury, and tried again – 101. The relief made me laugh for the first time in days. Sun had been striking the tent. Maybe the thermometer had been catching it. Pain was still acute, but now I could use my eyes appreciatively for a few minutes and rejoice that all around our three tents were clumps of dark purple stonecrop, freshly vigorous. In the background, the more southerly of the three spires barring the head of the Yokanadi Khola pierced a sea of cloud like the fin of a killer-whale.

In worsening weather, Sen Thendup and Salwan went uphill with supplies for John and Da Norbu. I could hear avalanches roaring down the great wall of the Yokapahar Himal, and should have been concerned for John's safety, but was again comatose from the morning's intake of drugs. On my third morning, I at last awoke feeling much better, although still with a temperature. At least half-alive, I fetched out John's diagram and reread his note of alternative propositions, and his final determination to try to climb the nearest of the three cols. Salwan had yesterday brought down a second note: '6.30 a.m. Setting off to try pass.'

Only now, on re-reading these notes and diagrams, did I realise the real danger they were in if they did try for that col. The route involved a long traverse where snow lay in bulk at high angles on ice. One cannot safely judge monsoon snow, and a 6.30 a.m. start was far too late, especially for the descent, supposing the col had been reached. The traverse, reversed, would then be ripe for avalanche. I sent two porters up to give warning and to bring back a report. In short, I felt most uneasy.

They returned at 5 p.m. with John's third note. He and Da Norbu had avoided that dangerous traverse by attempting a centre line up the ice fall – and been defeated after an hour by difficult work above a monstrous crevasse, which they had crossed. They had tried another line and were two-fifths of the way up, with the worst below, when foul weather had forced withdrawal. Today, 30 June, they hoped to climb a peak of 20,000 feet or more that rose close above their tent. A long snow arête seemed to give a safe route. It appeared from his report that no pass over to the Seti Valley would be feasible for Bhotia porters; and if we used only our own six men, that would mean repeated ferrying across a difficult pass in unsettled weather – too long and dicey.

Two days later, John and Da Norbu walked into camp at eight in the morning, both in rude health. I too was well again, pain gone, nerve dead. Just as I surmised, their climbing had been nasty on foul snow. Their central snow slope route toward the col had been grooved down to its underlying ice by deep avalanche scores. But they had succeeded in climbing the snow ridge above camp to a minor top. The snow had not felt safe, crackling and sizzling as if about to peel. They had been able to look into the Seti Valley of Nepal, but mist filled its vast basin. In five days they had made four attempts to gain the crest of the range, and everywhere found bad snow on steep ice – far too risky for laden porters. During these climbs, they had clear and splendid views of the Api/Nampa group. Api had looked climbable from its north-west ridge, if that could be reached from the Nampa Valley. (I had looked into that same approach from the valley itself, and judged its lower part feasible.) John had been able to identify the elusive Nampa, which Gansser had aptly named Chisel Peak, but which we had failed to find from the upper Nampa Valley, perhaps because the first rush of the monsoon had cast a veil. The sketch John had sent me had covered most of the hidden peaks of the Yokapahar, or north-eastern half of the range, hitherto unknown. A pass might still be found there, another year. They had found the snow and ice of the upper slopes covered in dead locusts. Down on the Indian plains, it had often been wondered what became of the swarms that plagued them, for they afterwards vanished, no one knew where. The answer was here: the crests of the Himalaya.

We could now agree on one thing – the die was cast. We had to turn the range by the Tinkar Lipu and the Urai Lagna frontier passes. We consulted the six porters. They alone could make the plan work. The Tinkar Bhotias had to be won over. Our first move must be back to camp in the lower part of the Yokanadi near Tinkar. That evening clouds forming and drifting, and rising up and across the faces of the snow peaks at the head of the Yokanadi, made a most lovely sight. As the clouds slowly rose up the flanks, the peaks above seemed to rise ever higher, until they reached heights apparently incredible, so far above us that we felt mere specks at their base. The porters, just as entranced as we, stared long in wonder. Their jobs might be more laborious, but they were not less sensitive to beauty than John and I.

29 Tibet – Into Chinese Held Territory

Like a mark of fortune's favour to our plan, a perfect morning came on a cold, northeast wind, chasing every cloud from a blue sky. It stayed with us for one vital week. By noon, all loads save three had been moved by willing porters back to that idyllic meadow-land about a mile short of Tinkar. A few goats were grazing on its emerald 'grass'. Sprouting everywhere on its floor were orange or white potentillas, blue rock-geraniums and, most eye-catching of all, tall clumps of rose root bearing purple flowers broadly edged in white.

After feasting our eyes, we had to get down to business. Our loads totalled 684 pounds. We could not travel through Tibet thus laden. Fast movement meant light loads. We agreed to split the party. Nima and Salwan must take six porters and more than half our baggage, plus half our money, fifteen miles back down the Kali on its Indian side, cross into Nepal at Rapla, as they had earlier proposed, and meet us at the village of Chaubisho below Api's south face in about sixteen days. Salwan knew this district of Marma – as we now discovered. John and I, with the two Sherpas and two Dotials, would engage a few Tinkar Bhotias to carry forty-pound loads eastward through Tibet to the Urai Lagna, then south into Nepal and west to Chaubisho. We had no hesitation in trusting our money and gear to Nima and Salwan. Mutual trust was complete. Nima and Gujbir went off that night to sleep at Tinkar, and there to reach an agreement with Lef Singh – whom we all knew to be basically friendly to us. He had said he would help us, so we knew he would.

Another perfect morning made us wonder if the monsoon could be drawing to an early end. Before noon, Nima and Gujbir returned in high spirits. They had made an excellent bandobast. Tomorrow, five Tinkar men would come with us over the Tinkar Lipu into Tibet, guide us unseen past the Chinese chauki post, and in five days, at six rupees a day, carry for us over the Urai Lagna to the village of Dhuli at 11,000 feet below the pass.

Meantime, Nima and Salwan would be given yaks to carry the other half of our baggage to Garbyang, where they would get porters for the rest of the journey to Rapla, thence by high mountain tracks south-east over Api's long spurs into Marma. We asked them to meet us there in twenty days – which would allow more time for John and me, based on the Seti River, to climb on the Saipal group.

Now keyed up for the move, we were all up early on 5 July, packed and ready to leave by 6 a.m. There was no such sense of urgency up at Tinkar. An hour later, Lef Singh strolled in with a herdsman driving three yaks for Nima, and with assurance that the five men would be here 'soon' – an ominous word, like the Italian's *domani*, preparing us for a three hour wait. He could not come himself, but he would give us for guide and sirdar his trusted lieutenant Dep Singh.

Nima and Salwan loaded their beasts and set off for the Kali. We walked with them a mile to the parting of the ways and shook hands, blithely promising each other to meet in twenty days. Inwardly, we were wondering if we should ever meet again. We had to trust not just each other, but the Fates too.

Leaving Da Norbu and Gujbir to wait for the Tinkar Bhotias, John and I carried on up the Tinkar Valley, which although steep-walled was grassy and sunlit, gradually opening to wider alps. We climbed in a leisurely way until early afternoon, allowing the Bhotias to catch up with us at a little promontory, where we camped. Their day had been absurdly short (from an employer's point of view), but next day would be for us all-crucial. We were now in a position to ensure its early start. We rose at 4 a.m. to a misty morning and were all on the move by six. We had already agreed with Dep Singh that this day we should cross the Tinkar Lipu and descend 2,000 feet or more into Tibet under the lee of cliffs that would at first screen us from the chauki post. Any farther move before dark would depend on what we discovered. The nervous tension that John and I had felt on first rising relaxed on our sensing the Tinkar men's confidence, which they positively exuded – and by the rising sun, which dispersed the mist and revealed the now usual blue skies. The track ahead lay at no great angle over the grassed hill-slope, revealing ever more splendid views of Api's forty-mile range, now seen as a truly formidable wall of ice peaks, of which only one – and that a minor top – had been climbed, by Tyson and Da Norbu. Seen from here, Api itself looked climbable from our old campsite in the lower Nampa Valley, by way of the glacier flowing down the flanks from its north-west dogtooth (19,920 feet). This was a most important discovery. Three weeks earlier in the Nampa Khola we had rejected the idea of climbing the glacier from there, because that north-west top appeared to block the way to the summit. Now we could see that it had shrunk back towards the opposite flank of the ridge, leaving the way to the summit unobstructed. Consequently, if the glacier is climbable, and I thought it was, Api could be climbed from the Nampa Khola. Our first reconnaissance had given a too foreshortened view. This route has still to be climbed.

That most elusive peak, Nampa, whose name had hitherto been wrongly given by Gansser and Heim to its bigger sister Api (and whose very existence they had therefore doubted), projected high above the range five miles to Api's east. It took the form of a chisel, as noted by Heim, its summit the short, horizontal blade. The elegant form made it look higher than its 22,000 feet. Its north wall lay at such a high angle that we thought the best hope of ascent must lie to its south side (a guess that has since proved true). The remainder of the east running range, the Yokapahar Himal, looked spectacular, affording no visible passes. The score of peaks between, looking near to inaccessible in 1953, might be climbable now with the new ice tools.

Our grassy track changed to bare screes, which continued thus for two or three miles to the Tinkar Lipu at 17,000 feet. Behind us, the cloud was welling up from India, isolating the high peaks until they seemed to float in the skies, just like the visionary continent we had seen from Ranikhet three years ago. The view to Tibet stayed clear. This was my first proper view of Tibet, and a memorable one it was – colourful, wide and enticing – superior to anything I had seen from the passes of the Everest region. On the Tinkar Lipu there was no snow, apart from a few old beds streaking its Tibetan flanks. Straight ahead, nearly twenty miles to our north, Gurla Mandata filled the scene across the Karnali River. At over 25,000 feet, its huge bulk screened from our eyes the sacred mountain of Kailas and its twin lakes of Manasarovar. As we continued down the Tibetan side, the view opened to the vast plateau, on which snowy peaks near and far ran in all directions to its farthest horizons. Our flanking cliffs, which screened us from the chaukis near Taklakot, and all the screes for miles around, were yellow or pale red. Beyond the Karnali, the land was all pale browns, reds and yellows, merging into the lower slopes and white crests of Gurla Mandata. Tibet seemed to us entrancing, sun-bathed and open compared to the enclosed Himalaya. Never flat, its rolling hills spread indefinitely, enlivened by the nearby white crests.

At 2 p.m. we stopped at a grassy patch amidst the scree and cooked a meal on yak dung. Dep Singh gave us all great handfuls of roasted whole wheat, nutty and delicious. As evening fell, we moved in the cliffs' shadow down half a mile to another hollow called Tharedunga, meaning 'the straight stone', used to mark a frontier. A reconnaissance was made below: no sign of any troop movement at Taklakot, or from the chauki post three miles nearer. Dep Singh waited another hour, then at 6 p.m. judged that twilight had deepened enough to allow us an open move rightward into the Jungjung Khola. This was a longrunning nulla, whose north escarpment again screened us from Taklakot. We walked two miles up the old riverbed, delightfully cool at this evening hour, and easy going under foot. We halted in a wide hollow at 15,000 feet. Our plan was to sleep here and hide all tomorrow until sunset, when we should climb the escarpment to our left on to the open maidan. Movement thereafter must be by night to evade capture by the Chinese. We pitched the tent's fly-sheet to screen us from heavy dew, which soon turned to frost. We shared this cover with our Sherpas. The Bhotias and Dotials lay under the stars.

Morning dawned no less brilliant. The Jungjung Khola might be a stony desert, but most stones sheltered alpine plants, some with creeping blue bellflowers, others were covered abundantly with yellow stonecrop. They attracted butterflies, and John opened his day in triumph by capture of a dwarf Apollo. The Tinkar men were enthralled by his activities: he kept busy all day, pressing plants, netting butterflies, and collecting other insects. The Bhotias spent the hours brewing tea in big brass bowls, in which they cooked their tsampa-porridge. Being off the beaten track, they lacked yak-dung as fuel, but nature had provided an alternative – clumps of dry moss that grew plentifully between the stones in hard round cushions, which burned well. Danger seemed worlds away.

As usual in Tibet, the wind began rising about 10 a.m., and by noon blew clouds of dust around us. The Bhotias, I noticed, wore no additional clothing by windy day or frosty night. At night they used one blanket apiece. In every kind of weather they wore by day only their home-spun tweed jackets, much-patched, cotton or else wool-woven trousers, shoes of coarse yellow leather nailed with metal studs, and round white caps. Nearly all had moustaches.

At 2 p.m. the Bhotias held a group conference, when they decided to make the big move. I was much surprised at such early action – until I realised the true reasons. First, tension had been mounting; the men wanted release. Second, as soon as we breasted that escarpment a couple of hundred feet above our heads, we should be in sight of Kailas, the holy mountain from which the Indus and Brahmaputra both took source. And that would mean prayer with long rituals of abasement and elevation. All our men now began to gather clumps of bellflowers. Each carried his own while we moved slowly up to near the crest of the ridge. There we lay on our stomachs and looked carefully over the edge toward Taklakot, calculating when and how we could move without being seen. The sun was behind us. This northern slope of the Himalaya would be in shadow long before the Karnali Valley. We should be able to move in less than three hours. This decided, we turned our eyes to Kailas.

At 22,000 feet, the mountain stood out as a clear white point, sixty miles distant. The Bhotias, Dotials, and Sherpas, all of us still lying flat on our faces, offered up prayers aloud, each group in its own tongue. This was no merely formal rite. There could be no mistaking the men's reverence. They were awe struck. Europeans have lost the humility needed for wisdom.

At 5 p.m., we rose to our feet and passed over the top. The slopes below and around were now in deep shadow, but the Karnali still in full sunshine. The houses at Taklakot and neighbouring villages looked neat and sparkling white, their flat green fields all most distinct.

Kailas, the Abode of Shiva, again drew all eyes. The men built a small cairn, to which each contributed stones. The Bhotias each tied a piece of cloth, or wool-fleece, to his own bunch of flowers and placed the whole at the foot of the cairn, at the same time casting grain in the air and offering a spoken prayer. Each prayed for a few minutes with raised hands placed palm to palm. Sherpas and Dotials who had no cloth or wool to offer each plucked his own flower and placed with it a few rupees beside the cairn, which to all was their altar.

We descended some 300 feet and traversed for a mile or more eastward on the gentle slopes of the maidan. The men continued in prayer, turning often to Kailas and briefly stopping. At 6.30 p.m., when it began to get dark, we crossed a low pass into a deep bowl of the hillside with high, serrated flanks. The ground became stony. There was no moon, but we had no trouble finding our way. The Milky Way spread overhead like a sunlit cumulus cloud. So dry and clear was the atmosphere that nearer planets were distinguishable from farther. They hung in space with three-dimensional solidity, like lamps. Away to the soundless south, lightning flickered incessantly.

At eight o'clock we called a halt to give the porters a rest. As we talked, we suddenly heard a great tinkling of harness-bells, a clattering of horses' hooves, and someone shouting aloud as though calling on us to stand and reveal ourselves. Immediately our men scattered. We all seized our loads and dived behind some tall gorse that luckily flanked the route. The noise and clatter increased. I felt certain that this must be Chinese guards, that our days of freedom were ended, that even though they might fail to catch us tonight in the dark, most certainly they would find us tomorrow. The horses came right past within a few yards, the riders still shouting 'Whoa whoa', not as if to their mounts but to persons on the ground. I lay low, fearing the worst. Having known imprisonment I wanted no more. The reputation of the Chinese in Tibet gave little hope of mercy if we were captured. The shouting continued, but dying gradually away into the distance.

Everyone around stayed dead quiet for nearly ten minutes. Meantime, it dawned on me that no chaukis searching for intruders would make loud, warning noises – enough to scare off the track anyone they might be hoping to arrest. Or was this just wishful thinking? Were the enemy so conscious of omnipotence that they revelled in the belief that none could elude them? Still we waited, doubting, tense, eyes straining into the darkness. Then cautiously we emerged and conferred. I had seen neither horses nor riders. But Da Norbu had seen. He reported only one rider with two horses. He thought the rider may only have been shouting because he was drunk on arak. The Bhotias thought this story possible but we were still unsure. We lay low for another hour, senses alert. The Chinese were unhealthily close. Hearing no more, we shouldered our loads and moved slowly on. No talking or smoking were allowed. We had no desire to view the inside of a Chinese jail. Suddenly as we passed through the bowl, we could hear a dog barking far away up the slope to the south. We stiffened, ears pricked for any warning sounds. Something had disturbed these dogs. The Bhotias said there was a summer shieling for yak-herdsmen in the area. Far more than the Bhotias, we were aware of our presence in enemy-held territory. That we were not in fact spies would be difficult for the Chinese to believe. In their position I wouldn't have believed our story either and we couldn't prove it. After many short halts to decide on the best route, which we had now lost, we had to take a longer one while Dep Singh reconnoitred the ground ahead. At length he found a good track with a bridge over a river in the valley bottom. Here we turned upward 1,500 feet to the Kathan Pass, which led into a higher corrie on the mountainside. I was ahead at this point, when I heard more tinkling of bells. Might this be our mysterious horseman returning with more troops? I waited and let the Tinkar men go ahead. We edged slowly forward – only to discover that the bells hung around the heads of a dozen yaks, all resting beside the track at a cairned upper pass. Relief overcame all sense of foolishness. We had been lucky. The danger in this area was real. Suddenly everyone felt tired, the nervous strain telling. We bivouacked at 1 a.m. Gorse clumps gave us good cover and we were glad of it.

Two hours later, we packed up and moved on. The track rose and fell into another valley, again called Jungjung Khola. We climbed up it three miles to a river, which we crossed as dawn was breaking, to a stone ruin also named Tharedunga – the Urai Lagna lay just eight miles and 4,000 feet above. Now in broad daylight, we camped on flat grass beside the track. Having eaten little in the last twenty-four hours, we all felt exhausted through lack of fuel. We cooked up a meal on piles of dried sheep-dung. The porters then slept the day away while John collected flowers and insects and I wrote up my diary. By evening, the first heavy clouds were billowing over Tibet. Thunder boomed. Lightning flashed and crackled. Rain poured down, soaking the shelterless porters – who did not seem much troubled. John and I envied their stoicism, which we felt far from sharing.

We were up at 5 a.m. and away at six on a dull morning. Three miles up under clearing skies, we came on a big grassy hollow holding three lakes. The two lower held red water, filled by a red river, while a mile beyond, at 18,500 feet, the third and smaller held blue water amid the feeding glacier's terminal moraine. Whistling marmots abounded among the fringing gorse and scree. They were yellow, like the stone, as big as rabbits but agile as monkeys. The ground was honeycombed with their burrows. Beside the lake, flat grass would have given an excellent campsite with wild rhubarb alongside. Below, long vistas down the crags of the canyon led the eye down to Tibet, roofed once more in blue sky and fleecy clouds. Our track entered a huge basin, apparently a cul-de-sac, until a sharp rightward turn disclosed a narrow defile – and there, at long last, stood the Urai Lagna. We traversed snow under its summit crag on to a small rocky bridge, which led to the crest at 19,500 feet. It bore a gigantic cairn with a pole for votive offerings. Our Bhotias again tied on bits of wool or cloth, threw grain in the air, and prayed. Our Sherpas and Dotials uttered thanks more briefly. Kailas was no longer in sight. We had escaped.

Today, with knowledge of the genocide and horror perpetrated by the Chinese in Tibet, I am forced to wonder if our courage would have been up to this journey had we been granted prescience. Yet, being young and imbued with belief in our ability to combat vicissitudes, and desiring to explore wild, unknown country, we would probably still have gone. Optimism has long been an attribute of youth, giving a decent disregard for trouble and putting springs on its feet:

> 'Youth must be learning the ancient story
> Let the wearied oldsters bide.'[1]

It is the things we don't do that we usually regret – not the chance taken, the thistle grasped.

1 Neil Munro

30 The Seti Gorge

We returned to Nepal. Our map showed that this great face of the Himalayan chain dropped 14,000 feet to the village of Talkot at its base. The immense plunge was cut by the Seti River, mostly in waterfalls of mighty power. We now had to follow them down from the pass in days made memorable for their natural and human drama. At first the ground fell gently for 2,000 feet on mixed scree and grass, flowered everywhere with violets, golden potentillas, blue rock-geraniums and a host of other alpines. Among and beyond them, miles of the visible hillside were stained red by a great multitude of dying locusts, which fluttered feebly from one spot to another. Brought here by wind-currents, they were now too weak to live out the day. Our track swung sharply rightward into the head of the Seti Valley. We stopped to take in the scene below.

Dep Singh gave us each a big handful of roasted whole barley, which had the same nutty flavour as the wheat given at the Tinkar Lipu. It made a tasty and sustaining hill food – I wished we had it at home in Britain. The Bhotias roast it on a pan full of hot sand, which can then be sieved.

The skies to the south were heavily clouded. We were coming into monsoon country. In the deepening valley, the Seti, as yet only a stream, dropped past a flat meadow on which we could see a cluster of low stone walls, a few of them roofed in canvas. This, said the Bhotias, was Saipal, Nepal's highest outpost for Tibetan trade, and the farthest point south to which local Tibetans travelled. The Nepalese in turn traded north-west no farther than Taklakot, using a much lower track into Tibet than the one we had followed from Tinkar. The Chinese encouraged this mutual trade. Tibet needed Nepalese and Indian grain in exchange for its own salt, wool and borax. All such trade was by barter. Money rarely changed hands.

We were astonished to receive a visit from a Nepalese chauki, who examined our pass. He was the first of a chain of chaukis maintained by the Rajah of Bajhang, in whose state we now were since crossing the Urai Lagna. The chaukis patrolled between the village of Dhuli at 9,500 feet and Saipal at 16,000 feet, continually moving back and forth on the twenty-mile beat – much more efficient than their Chinese counterparts.

The rain began that night, and continued incessantly for nearly a week. Yet such was the interest of the Seti that we hardly noticed our discomforts. Each morning we set off early. The first day we moved down 1,000 feet through huge banks of rock-geraniums, the area again alive with whistling marmots – one of them a giant as big as a terrier. The Seti, rapidly gaining tributaries, had deepened into a thunderous gorge. We had to traverse across the face of its cliffs by narrow ledges above sheer and overhanging drops. Where the track at last broadened, tall blue poppies grew alongside, all with big yellow centres, and one with a jet black eye as well. So beautiful was this specimen (we never saw its like again) that I felt thankful when John missed it out of his plant collection. It was a rarity better left to reproduce if it could. One or two northbound traders passed us, driving goats laden with grain in saddlebags. The Seti is much too difficult for yaks, for some of the ledges are too narrow and steep for the animals' bulk.

The river plunged in a thousand-foot waterfall down a rock-gut, while the track alongside rose and fell among pines and oaks. About 7,000 feet below the Urai Lagna, we came on a series of big caves called Nayarodyar, which offered good shelter for a wet night. The floors were dry under a carpet of goat dung. The porters soon had big fires going, before which John sat drying blotting papers for his flower press, while the porters cooked. Such was the roar of the Seti waterfall that we could hardly hear ourselves speak. To be free of the dung, we pitched our tent outside, preferring the penalty of wet clothes and sleeping bags. That was not a restful night, but we were now halfway to the village of Dhuli, just ten miles and 3,000 feet below. We were, we hoped, about to receive the benefits of human civilisation.

We were off at dawn. In less than a mile, we came to a second set of caves. Here a wayside shrine had been created on top of a stone wall. Our porters one and all held it in a reverential awe hardly less than that shown to Kailas itself. On top of the wall stood two vertical tree trunks, one at either end, bridged by a horizontal beam, from the middle of which hung a huge bell, with scores of smaller ones alongside. All three beams were heavily covered in small metal coins, and one with rupee coins hammered into the woods. Behind the shrine lay a round, walled pit, above which hung numerous offerings, including a pair of yak horns and a leather umbrella. No Buddhist mantras were carved on stone or wood, yet our two Sherpas prostrated themselves before the shrine three times. Every one of our porters offered up one rupee, either throwing it into the pit or wedging it into the wood. I gave our Sherpas a few rupees, for they had run out of coins after the Kailas obeisance. The Bhotias offered up grain as well, and the Dotials flowers.

All raised their hands and prayed. I never discovered why this particular shrine (there were others) won such marked devotion. One thing clearly evident was that Hindus, Buddhists, and Christians too, here revered the one God, and that those who down on the plains might try to set them at odds are badly mistaken. All our porters, I noted, had been more refreshed by this brief ritual than by their breakfast of tea and chapattis or tsampa.

The scene changed. The track went up and down stone-built stairways, always among woods of oak, walnut, chestnut, holly, or pine, with much bamboo and rhododendron mixed in. Rose bushes and flowering currants flanked our way until we came to the Seti's greatest tributary, the Niuno Khola. It swept in to our left-hand side, spanned by one enormous tree trunk whose whole top side had been cut level. Given no handrail, each step needed attention. Just a few miles farther, we climbed to the top of a spur, where we suddenly found the track closely walled over its next half-mile to Dhuli. The village houses were a very model of good maintenance, and its street clean, even though chickens were everywhere and fields of potatoes grew alongside.

John and I had gone ahead first, eager to meet the villagers. Our arrival caused consternation. It was a dry morning at last, and the women were out in the street. They took one startled look at us and fled indoors. We had been so long unconscious of our outward appearance that we failed at first to realise our scarecrow reality. We had not shaved for two months, our clothes were soiled, and Tyson sported a long red beard. To the women of Dhuli he looked like a yeti. Alarmed by the women, the men hastened out to look us over. At the same time, Dep Singh arrived and all was well. The women emerged. A friendly hospitality was then lavished on us all.

The men were all short and strong of body, dressed in woollen, homespun plaids, striped in dark and light greys. None wore shoes or trousers. The plaids, kilted at the waist, were draped to knee-length like a Scottish Highlander's, and secured at the throat by a silver brooch. Each wore a bangle at his wrist; most had small gold earrings and black or white caps on their heads. Feet and legs were bare, as were those of women and children.

The women, by contrast, wore black dresses down to their ankles, and loose grey hoods over their heads to the shoulders. Around their necks hung ropes of red and yellow beads, and a longer string of big silver rupees. Each had a silver throat brooch, several finger-rings, and a wide but slender gold ring piercing one nostril. Their prevailing spotlessness was in marked contrast to ourselves. Perhaps we were excused as long-distance travellers, for the people showed us nothing but kindness, friendly smiles, and generous provision of food and shelter – the shelter free and the food at low price. (Two chickens and four eggs, for example, cost three rupees.) The people were not much concerned with money, for their trade was by barter. We tried to take no advantage and to give what goods we could spare. Paper rupees were accepted only in small denominations, and the larger refused.

Dhuli was built in two parts, well separated: the main village, in which we stood, with forty-five houses, and twenty more a quarter of a mile down river. All were strongly built in stone cemented with light brown mud, some whitewashed, others terracotta, and all thatched. Several were stacked with big bags of grain and other merchandise bound for Tibet. In one week's time the Dhuli men planned to move up to Saipal, then over the frontier to Taklakot. The Bhotias of Nepal and India all make this same move into Tibet during July and August, returning in late September and October bearing bartered goods south.

John and I were shown to an empty, two-room house of the main village. The floor was dry, hardened mud, swept clean. The walls, smoothly rendered in mud, were only five feet high, but the roof rose to a full ten feet at the apex. The main room was ten feet square; at the south end, its five-foot wall gave access to a second room extending a further ten feet like a low roofed loft. Without being asked, we were brought firewood, potatoes, flour, eggs and a couple of chickens. There was no sugar, but we were promised honey. Outside, the gorge had filled with mist and relentless rain. We felt wrapped in luxury before a bright fire set in one corner. The other corners were filled with ten fascinated onlookers. We did not grudge them this. Now warm, we dried our damp sleeping bags by sleeping in them.

I rose early to pay off the five Bhotias, who planned to leave at 5 a.m. They had served us well for six days. We had learned so many good things in their company that we doubled their pay. They were very well pleased, but delayed their departure – the Seti being still shrouded in mist with torrential rain – until next day's dawn. I spent my own day dispensing medicines to the villagers, mainly women. As in Kumaon in 1950, I felt frustrated by my lack of medical training. The best I could do was treat symptoms, or briefly eliminate pain. The headman's young daughter was seriously ill, and spitting foam. I had no idea what might be the cause or cure.

While I vainly gave first-aid to the few infirm people of Dhuli, John pressed still more plants, dried his blotters, and popped insects into bottles. Among them, although we knew it not at the time, were several new species and even one new genus, to which the British Museum later gave his name. Finding his now long hair becoming a nuisance while he bent over his work, John asked Da Norbu to trim it. The gleeful alacrity with which he accepted the job on a wet morning, when the Sherpas were plainly eager for some distracting fun, should have given warning. Da Norbu gave him a convict cut. The Sherpas' eyes shone with a wicked joy, soon to be shared by the ladies of Dhuli. John looked to them more like a yeti than ever.

We waited in vain for the weather to clear. After four nights at Dhuli, we abandoned plans for the Saipal mountains. On 15 July, the headman gave us five porters to help carry our loads down to Talkot at the foot of the gorge. They would not go farther, being needed above for their now imminent move to Tibet. They disliked the heat down at 5,000 feet. When I went to the headman to give thanks and to say goodbye, he gave me, and his son too who was going with us, a ritual blessing. He took grain and grass, threw the grain in the air and prayed, then placed wisps of grass behind our ears, wet a few grains of rice which he placed on our foreheads and then on his own, and finally blessed us both.

Our twenty-mile descent to the base of the Himalayan range took four days, because daily the track would climb and fall several thousand feet between the rocky spurs that divided the Seti's incoming tributaries. The first day gave the most impressive display of the deep plunging river, even more so than that of the gorge of the Rishiganga below Nanda Devi, and more heavily forested. At one clearing we took shelter in an empty stone hut so heavily infested with fleas that they spread out like a doormat on to open ground in heavy rain. We brushed them in scores off our legs, and still had many dozens more. Their numbers far surpassed those of Moosburg's concentration camp. Here at least we had the remedy to hand, for we had brought a packet of DDT. After a dusting of our whole party in camp that night, we had no more trouble.

When we camped next night, on a knoll close to the village of Dhalaun at 9,000 feet, I heard the unmistakable purr-purr of a powerful motorbike. Astounded, I hastened to investigate. It came from a swamp full of huge, olive-coloured frogs, croaking in chorus. They shared the pool with two water buffaloes: all at an unusual height for their species (normally nearer 5,000 feet). Lower down, the track became excellent, padded underfoot with pine needles, and emerging on our fourth day on to open hillsides dotted with villages. Talkot was perched on a small hilltop, its few dozen houses packed closely in tiers, with others more widely scattered over the slopes below. We camped a quarter of a mile short of the village, on a meadow behind a screen of trees. The Sherpas were erecting our tents when a chauki arrived with followers. They were on their way up to Dhuli and Saipal. After reading our pass, the chauki was friendly. He sent one of his two servants back to the headman of Talkot, who promptly came with twenty men to make us welcome. They gathered firewood, sold us all the food we wanted, and promised four porters to replace the men of Dhuli, who now went off up hill with the chauki.

31 A Meeting with the Rajah of Bajhang

Our descent to 5,000 feet had brought an abrupt change of climate. In the hills, the monsoon had been the worst in ten years. Now we had clearer skies and great heat by day. In the paddy fields down by the river, the rice grew two feet high, light green, rippling like waves of gold where the wind rushed through. By night, fireflies danced over the bushes at the fringe of our meadow, and the song of cicadas replaced the croak of frogs.

Our morning's destination was Chainpur, the summer capital of Bajhang, where the Rajah was now in residence. The path wound eleven miles down the Seti, at first between the paddies at the river's edge, bordered by flowering cacti, then among pines as tall as those of the Scottish Highlands, and mercifully shading the track until replaced by broad-leaved banana trees.

We arrived at Chainpur early in the afternoon and camped by the river. It was a big village, and bore three unmistakable signs of a civilised society: cultivated flower gardens; a long line of shops selling hardware, clothing and wide varieties of food; and shop-keepers with spectacles on their noses – the first we had seen in Bajhang. They used paper to keep accounts, but their scales were of true Himalayan type – just two small pans balanced on a horizontal rod, with a string at centre held vertical by hand.

We paid off our Talkot men and explored the shops. They sold exotica like soap and baseball boots, electric torches and batteries, ink and coconuts. Absorbed in window-shopping, John and I soon lost touch with each other. His explorations were luckier than mine. He turned up for dinner that night reporting a chance meeting with the Rajah who had invited us both to lunch next day at noon. We felt greatly pleased, for our diet over the last month had been spartan. We were hungry, and hoped that Bajhang's prince might guess we were.

A hot morning helped us in our first duty to our host – total immersion in the glacial Seti: our first thorough wash since Pithoragarh. After thawing out, we moved a mile upstream to the palace. Close beside it stood Chainpur's school. It had been opened by the Rajah in March last year, yet already had 250 day boys and girls, seventy boarders, and eight masters. They were expecting us. We were quickly surrounded by teenagers. They spoke good English, and were eager to test out their accents, still more to hear ours: we were the first Englishmen they had met. Their teaching must have been first-class, for they spoke well and fluently and with ease of manner after just fourteen months. Having told us the story of the school's founding by the Rajah, who paid 3,000 rupees a year in support, they added that he had newly established Chainpur's first medical service. The doctor appointed had arrived just last night from Kathmandu. This I was thankful to hear, having already spent two hours of the morning dispensing first-aid and medicines to the usual queue of patients. The boys told us too that the Rajah had this year opened the first postal service to India and abroad, via Jhulaghat on the Kali. He was clearly their hero; they spoke of him with pride. I felt all the more eager to meet him.

One of his servants led us into the school to an airy, upstairs room. A receptionist showed us to European-style chairs, which ordinary houses do not have. As soon as we were seated, the Rajah was announced. Ram Jung Bahadur Singh, Prince of Bajhang, looked about fifty, of broad build and benign face. His dress was a long jacket of dark fawny grey, smartly cut and buttoned to his throat. White trousers fitted closely to the legs, with grey socks and black shoes. His bearing was informal and friendly. We shook hands and were seated.

He at once produced maps. We showed him where we had been exploring Api, and how we had found our way from Tibet into Bajhang. It seemed that our unheralded arrival had caused him consternation. We should not have been able to cross the Urai Lagna, far less come fifty miles south, without his hearing of our presence long since. The Chinese were his potential enemies. They had already made claim to Bajhang. Therefore he maintained a chain of chaukis to give warning of all who approached from the north, and had spies at Taklakot and its neighbouring villages, and so ought to have heard of us before we ever got near Chainpur. We too, knowing from past experience how efficient is the bush telegraph in unguarded Himalayan valleys, were surprised that we had managed to slip through the net. I thought it likely that on this particular week of July nearly all movement on the Seti had been northbound to Tibet on the seasonal trade, and virtually none south. I could recall no one passing us southward. Obviously Talkot's headman or chauki should have sent word back. I imagine they would soon be hearing their Rajah's wrath.

We now learned that China's troops at Taklakot were building barracks, laying an airstrip, and opening a road link to Lhasa. The Rajah did not as yet take too seriously their threat to Bajhang, for any action to extend their territory south would mean war with Nepal or India. Meantime, they had put no obstacle in the way of trade, which was valuable to both peoples. The people of Bajhang were in fact more closely related in trade to Tibet than to either Nepal or India. If the Chinese were ever to invade, he reckoned that while their infantry could descend in a few days from the Urai Lagna, they would be quite unable to get horses, guns or heavy stores down the Seti Gorge. He reminded us, however, that his state comprised several districts extending east to Humla on the Karnali River, which cut through the frontier range from Kojarnath in Tibet. It gave a good track all the way. For the present, the Chinese recognised his frontier at Tharedunga, close below the Urai Lagna. The best of all deterrents was a strong, independent government at Kathmandu, where he wished that the Rana family – the former hereditary maharajahs – would cease their plotting to oust the king and his new government. A disunited Nepal would play into the hands of both the Peoples' Republic and Nehru's India, neither of which exerted as yet undue influence at Kathmandu: a situation that could change rapidly given unstable government.

The Rajah appeared to enjoy a great measure of independence from Kathmandu, but took care to give diplomatic respect to central government, on whom his own safety and that of his subjects depended. He added that his people, who were all known as Dotials, were spread over many thousands of square miles.

Lunch was served on the outside verandah, which faced the Seti. The river last year had changed course and taken a big bite out of the palace-garden. All the flat ground had been swept away to a breadth of 300 yards. It looked as if more would follow. One big chunk remained as an island in mid-stream. The Rajah sat beside us at the head of a low table, but did not eat with us, excusing himself as a vegetarian. In truth, his Brahmin caste forbade. The meal was served in a variety of glass bowls, from which we transferred the food to our china plates. Forks and spoons were provided, and knives later when he saw our need. The main dishes were a huge bowl of curried rice, two roast chickens, chip potatoes, and four large fresh fish, grilled; green cooked vegetables, and large, juicy fruits like mangoes, but much bigger, and wild berries. There were numerous accompaniments, like chutney and gold-coloured popadams. Drink was water. In short, we were served the banquet we had so much needed, and were grateful.

The Rajah gave us much more information about his country and people, and Chinese neighbours. He feared Chinese fascism in its communist disguise, and its possible spread to the unthinking younger generation of Nepal. Their religious-mindedness had formerly been a strong barrier to Communist propaganda, but that might now change if political unrest grew through the ungenerous policies of central government.

After lunch, he introduced us to his son and two younger daughters. Their mother, the Rani, was living twenty miles south at the village of Mini. The boy, who looked about twenty, was hoping soon to get his BA degree from Lucknow before going to a British university to read either law or economics. The two princesses, like all other girls in their teens, were much more brightly dressed than the boys we had seen – robed in blue and yellow to the feet. At least this was our impression until we went outside to the palace gardens for yet another surprise – a troop of Boy Scouts drawn up on parade, awaiting our inspection.

Their uniforms, gaily appropriate to Nepal's sunny climate, were blue shirts, yellow neckerchiefs, green or blue shorts, and white pork pie caps. Each carried a long ash pole. The boys looked clean, fresh and intelligent. John and I were impressed.

The Rajah took us to his own house, but not inside. We strolled and talked among tall eucalyptus trees. When we parted, the Rajah presented us with a ball of musk and an ivory-handled kukri. He seemed to John and me to be an astute and alert ruler, and a wise one. His recent reforms may have been a response to threat on his frontier, but they were reforms that came naturally to the man, he being vigorously thoughtful. We had liked him, and also his Dotials.

On return to camp, we were visited by the headmaster bearing his school's Visitors' Book. He told us that his school was annually inspected from Kathmandu. Taking the hint, we wrote in a tribute to him and his staff and to the Rajah.

Our urgent need now was to find our way to Chaubisho in Marma, which lay fifteen miles south of Api, and thirty-five to our north as the crow flew. Nima, we trusted, would be waiting for us there. First we had to cross a deep tributary of the Seti called the Bauli. It was bridged by four stout grass ropes held together by wooden struts at three-foot intervals – the first of its kind we had seen. At 6 a.m., the Rajah sent six of his men to help us get our loads across, and a bearer with a big tray full of mangoes and pears to refresh us on the march. We thus had a quick and easy river-crossing, struck up hill on a long slant of several miles, and so by good fate met some Dotials, who told us they had come from Chaubisho that same day. I queried, 'Surely not today?' How could that be? But they even assured us that we would arrive there today ourselves. Chaubisho in Marma was, we knew, a full week's march away by the Chamlia River, which took its source from Api itself. So there must be two Chaubishos. Our concern mounted to a full alarm. Between the two lay a wild tangle of foothills, criss-crossed by a maze of alternative tracks. To which village would Nima go? I had briefed him well. Surely he would not come south to the Seti – unless Salwan, the Dotial, knowing the farther Chaubisho to be the bigger, would persuade him south.

We consulted Gujbir. He decided that Salwan would wait in Marma, but that, if he did come south, he would use the track we were presently on, for it was the best of all the alternatives. John and I felt our dilemma more keenly than the Dotials. Refusing Gujbir's advice to go on, we resolved to camp where we stood, although we had covered only four miles, while we cultivated second thoughts. John was in favour of using the good foothill weather to head west for India, which might take two weeks, while despatching a messenger to look for Nima, while I favoured moving north into the monsoon cloud that still shrouded Api's south face, in order to keep faith with Nima, whom a messenger might all too easily miss.

Our dilemma was still unresolved by morning, but our decision to camp had found favour with Providence. We had barely begun to move off when a local man told us that just a few minutes earlier he had passed our Sherpa sirdar, Nima, on the track to Chaubisho. Gujbir and Ranzing dropped their loads and sped off on his trail. Five minutes later they came back with Nima, Salwan and six Marma porters. We could hardly believe our good fortune. The pair were in excellent health and spirits. Their Marma Dotials looked good and likeable men.

On leaving Garbyang, Nima had yet again been closely interrogated at the police post, but allowed to cross back to Nepal at Rapla, and thence had followed the high mountain route to Chaubisho in Marma. Salwan had there persuaded him to go on to the principal Chaubisho, assuring him that they could not miss us on the track. They had indeed missed us, but so closely that we picked no bones. Nima had kept detailed accounts of all his expenses. I had no cause to question any of them. I could not have done so well myself.

The date was now 22 July. The weather had broken this very morning. Marma would have given us a most rewarding approach to Api in fine weather; in this thick monsoon cloud, little could be seen or done. Therefore we resolved to head west for India – a journey, we thought, that might take us two weeks or more to the Jhulaghat bridge across the Kali. We continued in heavy rain to the town of Bajhang. Its big, stone-built squares bore tall trees. A principal building was the town jail. Grimly tall, its thick, windowless walls were pierced only with breathing holes for its prisoners. Built in earlier, unhappy times, its heavy wooden door now lay open, the jail empty. I felt glad for all Dotials.

We continued moving westward for ten days, virtually lost after leaving Bajhang, in the sense that we could not tell where we were except at one or two of the bigger rivers. Since Chainpur, the narrow tracks we followed grew narrower still, unmarked on the map. They branched every half-mile or less to tiny villages, likewise unmarked, and climbed or fell sometimes several thousand feet through a maze of foothill ridges, along their forested flanks, or over and along their crests; then down to unidentifiable valleys growing tall crops. The confusion and constant wonder of it all made for fascinating travel. In the last resort, we knew that if we kept steering west we should be bound to hit India. But that was the only sense in which we knew where we were going. Without our Dotials' guidance, we should have been much delayed by our daily mistakes.

The lower ground by the rivers grew a huge range of crops. Apart from the usual maize, rice and flour grains, there was much ginger, purple amaranth (said to have healing properties), lime, banana, peach, walnut, cucumber and an eggplant called rinzel (excellent fried). We saw much bhang or hemp. The Dotials made rope from the stalk, flour from the grain, but did not smoke hashish. Our own porters did not even smoke tobacco, in contrast to those we recruited along the way.

Two of our six Marma porters had been kept on to carry John's crated plant specimens. Their remote hill country had given them skills now rare in the use of flints. In camp, they lit their fires at night using flint to strike a fire stone – a kind of iron pyrites – and the spark lit a shred of moss, which all carried under their shirts. They were so quick in its use that they habitually struck flints to light their cigarettes and pipe tobacco, for the moss smouldered long when the spark fell, and no hurry was needed to blow up a flame.

Our third day took us over a succession of 7,000-foot hill ridges, ending with descent to a map-marked river, the Kali Gad. The village of Mini, where the Rani of Bajhang was living, stood on its bank. This bridgeless river, fast flowing and fierce, presented a major obstacle forty yards wide. We could hear boulders churning along its bed. Spanning its gulf we saw one thick grass rope, each end tied to a tree trunk stake set on its high banks. That rope earned a daily revenue for its two keepers from Mini. They were expert in its use, and could make the traverse look easy. Most others, even our Sherpas and I were, like John, intimidated. Our three Dotials luckily knew this river – and several others like it that lay ahead – and so could boost our other porters' morale, which otherwise would have vanished away.

We camped by the river's edge. The local men gave a demonstration. They placed a bow-shaped wooden bar over the rope. This bar had thick, upturned stubs at either end.

They showed us first the way to cross without any aids: the simplest way, hand over fist, bare feet curled round the fixed rope, pulling with their arms and pushing with their feet by pressure on the rope's top sides. Then, to make this process safe for the unskilled traveller, they passed a rope loop under the small of the back, and attached its ends to the stubs of the bow-shaped bar, which slid along the fixed rope while supporting the body's weight to conserve arm and leg strength.

When I watched this effortless demonstration, I still wondered how they would deal with our sixty-pound loads. Salwan told me not to worry, and next morning went across himself with one end of our 220-foot nylon climbing rope tied to his waist. Disdaining the wooden bow and the river's roar, he went over 'the simple way'. The Mini men then hauled back their end of the nylon rope to its halfway mark, and replaced their wooden bow with a much stronger one, more acutely angled, with a crossbar inserted to make it an A shape. To this cross bar the loads were tied and one by one hauled across by Salwan. We and the porters followed. Everything went well and easily. The Mini men asked only two rupees for their gear and time.

The next day we came into our own Dotials' home district. We had climbed 4,000 feet up one side of a hill ridge and down the other, when Gujbir came to me and said that his house was just three miles up the valley. Could he have permission to go there for a day with Salwan and Ranzing? John and I readily agreed. They promised to be back tomorrow morning. Their three loads were spread along the other nine porters. We went on for just one mile more in torrential rain, crossed a small river, and camped. In two minutes flat, those Marma men had lit a campfire and cigarettes, all on their flint sparks. They could not be bothered with time-wasting matches in such a downpour. Even the Sherpas found their wet weather act prodigious.

When the Dotials had returned, still heavier rain became our daily lot, with ever muddier tracks and repeated crossing of bridgeless rivers, with and without ropes. Leather boots would have been impossible footwear. We envied our porters their bare feet, and were thankful that our baseball boots, in their now holey condition, allowed water immediate escape.

Seven days out of Chainpur, we discovered that rarity of the wildlands, a wayside shop. It sold sugar. Nima, somewhat nervously I thought, warned me that I ought to buy more. I looked at him in open astonishment. I had bought fourteen pounds of sugar at Chainpur – strictly for John and me, as Nima well knew – but two pounds a day! The Sherpas must have been feeding on it, and probably dishing it out to the Dotials too. On the point of erupting, I took sudden thought of their labours in rain – and of that much flouted commandment, 'Thou shalt not muzzle the ox when he treadeth out the corn.' I swallowed my wrath and bought another fourteen pounds. With comical abruptness, Nima's brown eyes switched from wary concern to open joy.

One dry evening, just before dusk, I was enjoying a swim in a small river to clean off the day's mud, when I heard much shouting and saw a tiger on the far side. The slopes there were sparsely covered with pine and berberis, so that we all had a clear view. Its tawny colour showed up well against the green hill flank. A short way upstream stood a small homestead, where the young tiger (we heard later) had been prowling with an eye to dining off the livestock. So two or three boys had turned out to chase it downstream. This they did by traversing the hillside above, shouting, and trundling boulders down to its rear. The tiger was reluctant to go, yet not unduly angry. Each time a boulder came down, it would bound on a few paces, then slowly draw to a halt to recover poise and dignity, and to wave its tail. Then down would come another boulder and on it would go. The boys seemed not at all scared, nor the tiger threatening. Soon they all vanished down valley. When I questioned the Dotials, they thought the incident not unusual, if infrequent. Tigers seem not worried at man's proximity, and go about their daily business without thought of attacking him, provided he keeps the critical distance, which here seems to be fifteen to twenty-five yards, inside which the tiger feels threatened.

At this point, John and I still did not know our precise whereabouts, except that we must be nearing Baitabi and, some three days short of the Indian frontier, the Kaliganga. In our last valley of Nepal, where green parakeets flew around, we enjoyed the sight of two civet cats gambolling on a paddy field beside our track. They played with each other like kids – most beautiful beasts, dark glossy brown on the back and Siamese fawn below. The tail was very long and thick, the nose long too. They chased each other in high bounds over the tall, green rice, occasionally dashing up a tree. We watched within twenty yards, yet they paid no attention.

John closed his contribution to the British Museum by collecting his 150th plant specimen, and several prize centipedes, striped brown, six inches long, and as thick as one's little finger.

The sky cleared, the track rose and, now excellent, ran west for miles on the dry crest of a ridge to the village of Baitabi, which spread over its low hilltops. The views north to the high Himalaya were made splendid in piled up cumulus cloud; the vistas westward, spacious over the foothills of India, alternately dark and sunlit. Their huge gorge lines were marked by shadowed gulfs, their upper ridges bright green where the sun fell. The rain areas across this vast field were marked by grey curtains, always shifting position. We could see that across the entire regions of Kumaon and west Nepal the weather was really fine, yet in some unlucky areas, like our own a few days back, the inhabitants must have thought the whole world engulfed in monsoon rain.

Teashops strung along our ridge were selling roasted corn-on-the-cob, and that most delicious of all thirst-quenching fruits, green mango. We felt like Homer's Lotus Eaters, who lost all desire to return to their native land, and dawdled, feasting.

We camped on a hilltop. We made leisurely descent in the morning to the brink of the Kaliganga. It loomed deep below. Its mighty river, swollen by the monsoon, made a boundary worthy of Himachal. But we went down into it with mounting reluctance. Below, at the white guard-posts of Aulaghat, the chaukis of two nations subjected us to scrutiny as close as Peter's at the Pearly Gates. Barely passing muster, we crossed the first and last good suspension bridge of our three months' travel. At noon on 31 July, we were back in Pithoragarh.

We paid off our twelve porters, wishing all the while it were not so. They had each and all won our hearts and become friends. The Sherpas and Dotials, between themselves, had developed their own comrade-ships and learned a lot from each other. Our inter-related loyalties had been often tried and proven good. Not one had failed, and now we felt the wrench of our parting. The Bhotias and Dotials of west Nepal had both won our lasting respect. They lived in hard country, as free from fear and deceit as any people are likely to be. We had been everywhere welcomed, shown unstinted kindness after assessment, then given help to meet our seen needs. They had natural honesty, maybe symbolised by that empty jail at Bajhang. We liked them.

On first setting out, we had hoped to learn a great deal about the range of Api – to win a detailed knowledge that would be of value both to ourselves and to other mountaineers – a reward we had won. But now I felt that we had learned still more of value from the country's own people. They have lived long in memory, as strongly as their mountains.

The Himalayan magic casts a spell that one seeks to renew. I made some valuable experiments in the sixties and seventies. I accompanied as leader several treks organised by Colonel Jimmy Roberts' Mountain Travel, the first of their kind out of Kathmandu to Sola Khumbu, to Dhaulagiri and Annapurna, and to Darjeeling by the Arun River. With everything laid on – no worries about money, gear, customs, food supplies, route planning or porterage – one could fully relax. This was pure holiday, unadulterated by the hard work, the anxieties and the distractions of business inevitable to the self-mounted expedition. Surely one could live in the present, forgetting all before and after, as never before?

Here I learnt a new lesson, for the answer was No. The relaxation was the wrong kind. One could be happy, enjoy, feel at peace, but the real magic was not experienced. Like Providence, or all the other intangibles that yield little to reason's scrutiny, the magic of the present moment has to be won on initiatives taken by oneself, and in the sweat of one's own brow, with attendant discomforts and dangers. The reward is for him who accepts the penalty.

EVEREST AND THE MUZTAGH TOWER

32 Everest and the Muztagh Tower: The seemingly impossible overcome

When long ago I first thought to write of my life on mountains, I had hopes to regale readers with the more vivid memories, which would naturally include moments of danger, hairbreadth escapes, the suspense of exploration, and their direct opposites when relaxation brings new insights. Always I had tried to keep in mind the principle at the back of Tom Longstaff's words: 'Number your red letter days by camps, not summits.'

Enjoyable as the recall was, I had begun to think near its close that much of it could seem to be a beating about the bush, an evasion of the real issue, which was: what had mountains taught me in the course of a long life? What if anything had I learned of real value – real not just for me but hopefully for others too? I had learned a multitude of things, and have been trying already to set some of them down, both in this book and its predecessors. Two remain outstanding. They are important: enough for a short conclusion to the Himalayan chapters.

The first of these is the value of commitment, and the second, its corollary, that all obstacles are impostors, and none impossible. I will explain these two, but first, let me say that I do know the aphorism, 'Nothing is impossible for the man who doesn't have to do it himself.' The words have a glib ring, spoken perhaps by one who has not yet discovered commitment's secret.

When I began climbing as a young man, one of the first things I had to learn, if only by slow degrees, was a proper irreverence for the pundits of my own country, that is, when they told me, as they did from time to time, that a rock route was impossible, or else 'unjustifiable under snow and ice'. In my early years on Scottish mountains, I began to appreciate the truth of Fridtjof Nansen's words, spoken out of his Arctic travels: 'The difficult is that which can be done at once, the impossible that which takes a little longer.' But I still had to learn their truth more thoroughly.

In 1939 I had found a friend in John Hartog, then a schoolboy of seventeen at Westminster. He told me that ever since he was fourteen his ambition had been to climb one particular peak in the Karakoram – the Muztagh Tower. When he spoke of its awesome obstacles, his eyes shone. Sella's famous photograph – a telephoto at eighteen miles range from the foot of the Golden Throne – hung on his bedroom wall. I took one look at that monolith, nearly 10,000 feet of unbroken rock – impossible! The thought came to me involuntarily, despite the lessons I thought I knew by heart. Mercifully, I held my tongue and swallowed my laughter. I did not want to embarrass the boy. The North Wall of the Eiger, which had just been climbed, looked by comparison stumpy and practicable. Yet John was no wild-eyed youth. He had common sense and an orderly mind. Behind his glasses were quiet eyes and a quality of stillness. I liked him. He knew already that he had a first-class brain, and seemed able to relax in that awareness. When he grew up, he would act with authority without seeming aggressive – and also, I felt sure, grow out of his Muztagh folly.

Even Tom Longstaff whose opinion I respected before all others had written, 'The Muztagh Tower will remain inviolate.'

The war with Germany carried us off. When we were demobbed, John went to Oxford and soon became president of the Oxford University Mountaineering Club. His boyhood dream was still with him. Sella's photograph still hung on his wall at college, and still I discounted all thought of his acting, for he could not climb to my standard on rock and ice, and I reckoned my standard not equal to his Muztagh. I had not seen his collection of photographs, taken at other angles.

Two years later, I was climbing with friends in Garhwal and Kumaon. Within a month of our return, China invaded Tibet. That event sharply reminded Michael Ward and me, and Tom Bourdillon, that the old approach to Everest through Tibet being now closed, a new one might be opening: because Tilman, that same autumn of 1950, had been allowed to go up the Khumbu Glacier from Nepal with Houston's American party. A new reconnaissance of Everest from Nepal seemed to us an urgent need. Tilman had photographed its west side from 18,000 feet on Kala Patar, at six miles' range. I asked him what he thought. His reply was unequivocal, characteristically terse: 'Impossible. No route.' Confounded as I felt, I was not unduly dismayed. I knew that no one could say such a thing of any obstacle without rubbing his nose against it, and Tilman's nose was not six miles long.

I am unable to criticise his opinion. Had I not been saying the same thing, inwardly, of the Muztagh Tower? Meantime, the Himalayan Committee of the Royal Geographical Society and Alpine Club backed Tilman. That was hardly surprising. They had read Mallory's report of the Khumbu side (seen from the col east of Pumori):

> 'I do not much fancy it would be possible, even if one could get up the glacier ... the western glacier and the slopes above revealed one of the most awful and utterly forbidding scenes ever observed by man.'

Tilman's emphatic words therefore came as a clincher. The RGS would grant us no money for Everest. So we each agreed to put up £300 of our own, and on that basis I went ahead and organised. The *News Chronicle* heard of our plan and offered £40,000 on condition that we took along a staff photographer, and a reporter with freedom to write as he chose. We turned that down as likely to generate ballyhoo of a kind we were unwilling to suffer. At the last moment *The Times* gave £5,000 with no strings attached, but too late to be of practical use – it went not to us to buy gear, but to the Himalayan Committee, who later refunded our expenses. Throughout we had good moral support from the RGS.

One month before we set off, Eric Shipton had arrived back from China, where he'd held a consulate. We asked him to lead. No one knew Everest better than he; so it seemed appropriate to give him the position which I happily resigned. He told me that he too had seen Everest's west side from the Pumori Col, and agreed with Mallory and Tilman – no route from the Khumbu – but he would come because he'd love to visit the Sherpas' homeland and here was an expedition already organised and ready to go. I could not help reflecting that if he'd come home from China just a few months earlier, there would have been no British expedition to Sola Khumbu in 1951.

The upshot was, of course, that as soon as we climbed on to Pumori's flank in late September, and looked on to Everest's western flank from 20,000 feet, the route to the south col lay plain before our eyes. Despite the expert's opinions, we had been right.

No less plain rose that major obstacle, the Khumbu Icefall; it looked to us all like a death-trap. Hanging glaciers draped the flanks of both its containing ridges. Judged by alpine standards, the avalanches falling from these must surely rake the icefall from side to side. I could already see that debris scarring the Nuptse wall had shot out to near the icefall's centre. Could we justly ask Sherpas to go there? Doubts filled our minds. But long as we watched and waited, no other ice blocks fell. I then remembered the advice given me by Tom Longstaff when he had first heard of our reconnaissance: 'My guess is that you'll find the ice on the mountain's south-west side much more viscous than that on the north, therefore, less prone to avalanche.'

I mentioned this to Eric. He was naturally uncertain.

We made three probing climbs to search that icy chaos for a safe route through, and in late October began our final ascent of the whole icefall. Nearly a month of dry weather had reduced its snow-cover. It was now in extremely open, rickety condition. The glacier seemed to have been moving down in uncoordinated jerks. Less than two hours up, we came on a badly shattered area, which had greatly changed in the last five days. It looked as if up-heaved and shaken by earthquake. The upper glacier overhung the lower, and between them a great chasm had opened, jammed tight with ice blocks the size of houses. A glassy bridge spanned the nearer part of this chasm. As we roped carefully across, we could feel it trembling beneath our feet. I felt terrified, Shipton too. He muttered to me, 'We shouldn't be here.' I agreed. Quite apart from the blue depth waiting below, we feared still more the threat of the Nuptse flanks above.

The farther we went the more tortuous grew the route. The glacier became badly riven with dark cracks running in every direction. When an ice axe was thrust hard through, it was apt to meet empty space. We were not wearing crampons, and glad of it. At one passage through séracs, a giant pillar, as tall as the Tower of Pisa, leaned so far out that we expected to see it topple at any moment. We crept past, holding our breath. At the last, we faced a final wall of ice. After two abortive attempts, a route to the top was cut by Tom Bourdillon

We had made it – the way ahead looked clear to the south col. But not quite: a vast crevasse, 100 feet broad at its narrowest, barred the full breadth of the glacier. We could go no further. We had won – but hadn't won. It was hard to have come past the difficulties, to be so near the summit ridges and to see the upper mountain clear and beckoning. It looked eminently climbable. We knew now that the mountain would not be ours – not today. But its day would come. I had believed in this way to the summit and we had dispelled the psychological barrier of the inaccessible and the negative attitudes it had engendered. We had climbed up and we had climbed down the impossible! Gainsaying the pundits we had found the route up Everest. This route would 'go'. We could pass it to our successors. To gain the upper glacier and to make a tolerably safe route for porters up the icefall would need long aluminium ladders and much fixed rope. We could not have foreseen the need for these ladders – hardly a usual piece of mountaineering equipment. But it wasn't a usual route and their absence had stopped us. We were disappointed. At the same time we were triumphant at having found the way and the key to the world's highest mountain – I felt vindicated. In the future a party would come this way bringing with it the necessary equipment to bridge these huge crevasses and they would succeed.

In one long day of nervous tension, we had climbed up and down that icefall without incident. Nothing had fallen from Nuptse. No sérac had toppled. Longstaff had been right as usual. Subsequent history has shown the whole obstacle – so intimidating on our first ascent – to be like every other, an imposter, not impossible. Nonetheless, it has been one of the mountain's principal killers – not to be underestimated.

In 1953 a large British party duly arrived and, using assault tactics, climbed Mount Everest for the first time. No previous expedition had ever been so well equipped – a gun for lobbing bombs on to unsafe snow slopes to clear the route, walkie-talkies, extendable metal bridges for crossing crevasses, rope ladders. Oxygen apparatus and clothing were of a calibre hitherto unavailable.

Stores for the expedition weighed 71–2 tons and 350 porters were required to carry it. Colonel Hunt had planned his expedition with thoroughness, learning from the accumulation of knowledge and experience won in adversity by the climbers of ten previous expeditions – but the judgement and efficiency with which he drew on that knowledge were his own.

At last, a man had stood on the world's summit.

THE MUZTAGH TOWER

After that, I ought to have learned my lesson – but my grasp of it still fell short: *We live and learn but not the wiser grow.* Pomfret's one-line shaft might have been aimed straight at me. Thus, when John Hartog told me that he soon hoped to have time and money to make his attempt on the Muztagh Tower, I gave no positive encouragement. In 1956 Hartog was aged thirty-four and working as a nuclear physicist. He invited Tom Patey, Ian McNaught-Davis and Joe Brown to join his team. That they were able to climb the mountain at short notice that summer, with minimum reconnaissance and no hitches, was due entirely to John's twenty-year research. He had in his possession every known photograph of the mountain from ground and air at every angle. Every written report had been collected, filed and analysed. Never before had an unclimbed peak of the Karakoram been so thoroughly studied by a man trained to research from his youth. His was the first attempt from any nation, yet he knew already that his best approach was by the Muztagh and Chagaran Glaciers, and his most hopeful route the north-west ridge.

At his first try, the twin summits were climbed. There has since been a wrong tendency to give all credit to his companions by reason of their great skills and known names. The truth is, while they all had need of each other, the Muztagh Tower had been Hartog's peak, his the chosen route, his the long-term commitment, and so principally his the first ascent. He was the vital initiator, the linchpin and energy source in conception. The route as climbed was thought to be technically the hardest done at that time in Asia.[1] It made history for another and better reason: following the ascent of Everest and eight other 8,000-metre peaks by ponderous expeditions, mounted at high cost and manageable only by use of army-type logistics, the Muztagh came as a pointer to

1 Brown and McNaught-Davis reached the west summit on 5 July. On 7 July Patey and Hartog crossed the west summit and continued to the slightly higher east summit. The south-east ridge to the east summit was also climbed a few days later by a French group comprising Guido Magnone, André Contamine, Robert Paragot and Paul Keller. Hartog noted in his account (*AJ* 61, p.253) the close fraternal ties that developed between the two groups, the French having chosen a different route of ascent rather than compete with the British: 'The kindness of the French remains for me one of the noblest deeds in the history of international mountaineering – the conversion of rivalry into great friendship and affection.'

the future. It seemed to clear the air. It directed the climbing world's attention to the new goal – not height for its own sake as before, but to high standard climbing on lower peaks done alpine-style by small, swift parties and with costs cut from £100,000 or more to £4,000 or less.

The Muztagh story had begun with a schoolboy's dream. John Hartog was so unassuming that I forbore to scoff, but confess I had thought his dream impractical. This is an old, old story, which we all have to keep in mind – that dreams are more potent than reason: that if you can dream a thing you can attain it too, as often as not. The pages of mountain literature through the years give endless testimony. Dreams are for action.

That truth has a universal application, without limit other than needful time for penetration. When I was young, we dreamed that Everest might be climbed one day without oxygen, and were derided by the physiologists. We dreamed of space travel to the moon and planets, and were derided by the physicists. And so it is on every plane. This year, in a debate broadcast from Oxford University, I heard those who dreamed of man's union with Deity derided by the biologist-philosophers. We may all be slow to learn, but slowest of all are the men of science when they lack vision. I do not seek to abrogate reason, but to raise it. A camel cannot pass through the eye of a needle. Vision can. There are many doors closed in this world to a handicapped man or woman. But for mankind, of which we all are part, no doors are closed. Ways through will always be found.

That brings me to commitment. When three friends and I thought to make our very first expedition to the Himalaya, we were dreaming in particular of Garhwal and Kumaon, but were not yet committed. Dearly we wanted to go, yet we wondered: Could we raise the money? Dared we jeopardise our jobs? Did we know enough about Himalayan conditions? We dithered and delayed, but not too long. The great change came when with sudden resolve we put down our money and booked a passage to India. A simple but vital act. We were committed. Our change in fortune was then so rapid, much of it through prompt help from members of the Himalayan Club, that I felt moved at the time to set down this record:

> 'Until one is committed there is hesitancy, the chance to draw back, always ineffectiveness. Concerning all acts of initiative and creation, there is one elementary truth, ignorance of which kills countless ideas and splendid plans: that the moment one commits oneself, then Providence moves too. All kinds of things occur to help one that would not otherwise have occurred. A whole series of events issues from the decision, raising in one's favour all manner of unforeseen incidents, and meetings, and material assistance, which no man could have dreamt would

> have come his way. I have a deep respect for one of Goethe's couplets:
>
> "Whatever you can do, or dream you can, begin it,
> Boldness has genius, power, and magic in it.'"

The Himalaya has finally taught me that man, given single-minded commitment, is in the long run not subject to impossible obstacles.

CONCERNS CLOSER TO HOME

33 Return to Scotland

I returned from the Himalaya to Scotland wondering how I would react to the vastly smaller scale of mountains and rivers and to a life constrained by the need to earn a living. In short, my days instead of being lived wholly outside in a constant state of wonder, fascination, struggle, at one with the world's wildest landscape, would have to be contained in Argyll. I had need to work on my house, lay a floor, patch the roof, re-roof the boat shed, tame the wilderness that had once been a garden, grow vegetables. There was plenty to do – many heavy physical tasks. I didn't mind that. I liked the challenge of being practical. I had some aptitude and fortunately was fit. However, I would also have to 'work', i.e. I would have to write and, while not commercially minded, the writing would have to sell as, in common with other people, I required money to live. Pleasant as it was roaming the Himalaya, I couldn't do this forever. I had to work to live. I liked writing but wondered how I would find settling down again to the necessary disciplined life that this entailed – a different discipline to that from which I had returned. But I needn't have feared. It wasn't so different. Discipline was discipline wherever it was. Soon I was deeply immersed in the activities of home – work both physical and mental and trips to the mountains of Scotland to climb.

I enjoyed being back at Lochwood, its sound and silence, its wildlife. In season the colour and scent of this place could put a spell on me. I discovered the difference between the birds one welcomed as friends and the birds so splendidly coloured which made blossom fall like snow and left trees bare. I came to know bullfinches. I watched and listened for owls in winter dusk. Roe deer occasionally entered the garden and I admired the delicacy of their movements, but also discovered their voracious appetites. My enthusiasm dimmed. However in those days there tended to be room for us both. Today the position is more serious if one wants to have a garden. Those who can manage to, have their properties deer-fenced. I developed marked antipathy to high fencing in prison camps – but soon learned to chase deer on sight like everyone else. Deer love to munch rosebuds while smiling in at the windows of irate gardeners. They enjoy bay leaves also. The Forestry Commission which owns the surrounding land do nothing to control this wildlife which even wanders the village street. Gardeners become desperate.

With the loch bordered my ground I would rest from my labours by swimming in its icy waters. The sea was cleaner in those days. I had a sailing dinghy moored at a buoy in the bay and would sometimes swim out to right the capsized boat or to disentangle the trip line. I acquired a salmon net, put up posts on the shore to dry it on and expected good catches. This didn't materialise but I sometimes had trout. Mackerel would pass in season – leaping, glinting shoals and I would go out at once to bring back a meal. Sometimes when sailing I would trail a line but usually wind and sail took all my attention.

I had friends along the loch who had a Bermudan sloop, *Sybil of Cumae*, and I would sometimes join them to cruise or to race, either on this beautiful slim ship with its sixty-foot mast or on a Scottish Islander. I liked the space of the sea. It was akin to mountaintops and gave me physical involvement with the elements, with water and wind. I liked the tension of racing and learned the difference between the weekend sailor and the real sailor – the devotee of skill with a constant awareness of a boat's being. One such owned the *Sybil* – Miss Edwards, known as Jimmy. She 'could sail a boat' – her own accolade for those who could. She looked frail but was not. A superb sailor, it seemed incidental that she happened to have a Master Mariner's Certificate. I enjoyed many good days on *Sybil*. Storms I enjoyed less. The calm bearing of the crew impressed me, for the sea can be ferocious and like mountains shows little patience for the unwary or inept.

Not all my efforts were successful. My attempts at joinery on the boathouse roof were interrupted when I crashed through the roof to the stones below, landing on my elbow. The roof certainly required attention but now so did I. I sought medical opinion and was told the arm was 'all right'. My respect for this story was scant – I had heard similar before. When I visited my brother-in-law, a dentist, he correctly diagnosed the injury, was duly appalled and arranged for me to go to Glasgow's Royal Infirmary where the badly shattered bones were attended to. In time I regained full use of the arm to my relief; I needed that arm. There was much to do.

My books sold well enough in the 1950s to allow me some breathing space. I remember how at the age of six – almost as soon as I had learned to read and write, I had written a one-act play. Its hero was my school's headmaster, whom I cast as an Admiral, repelling invasion of Britain's shores (more cutlass play than sailing). Looking back on this episode thirty years later, I thought it high time and only sensible to find out if I had in me some latent talent for play writing.

Drama appealed to me. I had read, and now studied, the works of Ibsen, Barrie, Shaw, Somerset Maugham, James Bridie, Tennessee Williams, Terence Rattigan, Arthur Miller and others. The Citizens' Theatre at Glasgow gave much encouragement. Its producer allowed me to attend rehearsals, where

I learned some of the practical problems of stage production. In three years I wrote two plays: the first on the early years of Francis of Assisi, whose wild youth and follies led to the founding of his Order; and the second on Scotland's national leader, Sir William Wallace, whose robust efforts to right wrongs paralleled on the physical plane those of Francis Bernardone on the spiritual. Both earned praise from sharp-eyed critics – Margery Vosper, the London play agent, and R.J.B. Seller of Edinburgh's Gateway Theatre – who both turned down my plays as too expensive in scene change (five and three respectively), and in character number (thirteen and twenty-one). Furthermore, short passages in each were judged likely to offend the religious suppositions of Catholics and Protestants: all (in those days) weighty points against a new playwright.

I did not think of my time as wasted, but decided that talent for stage drama was not mine in sufficient degree to earn a living – a very necessary aspect of writing often overlooked by others.

Around this time I met Anne Clark. I had just spent a good day on the hills. It had been clear and crisp and I had lingered over views of ice-hard ridges tumbling range upon range to the horizon and the sea. I had seen long slate blue lochs cut into the land, seen the notched knife edge of the Arran hills, the peaks of Mull and Jura, heads in the sky. Coming down from the tops in the gloaming of a winter's day I turned to look back. Someone was running lightly down the last slopes out of the day's ebb. It was a woman, hair seemingly on fire. It blazed brighter than the flare of the sinking sun behind her. I stared. Who was this?

We spoke briefly but soon had to go our separate ways. She too had enjoyed the day.

Some weeks later I almost met this unknown woman again – a 'tiger' a climbing friend had warned me, I was curious. I heard that she was due to appear one evening at the Girvans' whitewashed Inverarnan House by Loch Lomond, a climbers' gathering place. Apparently she had been spending the weekend climbing in Glen Coe. But on Sunday evening she didn't come. Instead, news arrived of an accident. There had been an avalanche on a winter climb and a long fall. I knew that the day had been freezing hard for I too had been climbing.

Eventually I traced Anne and heard why she had failed to come back from the hills. There had been a serious accident in which the weight of a sweeping powder snow avalanche had wrenched out a belay and sent her tumbling down the gully. Breaking and stopping with an axe she was pulled off again as the rope tightened around her waist. Then tumbling, avalanche-swimming to stay on top of the smothering, twisting snow, another attempt to stop, another – just holding this time when the weight came on the rope, the snow piling on top. Then a seriously injured companion to dig out, and the six blasts a minute distress signal to give ... Afterwards came the long freezing wait, helping to carry a stretcher down in the dark, wading the river.

Having found Anne, I climbed with her and came to know her – a tall slim redhead with eyes that could glint like peaty pools in sunlight or be deep and unfathomable. She loved hills and all the outside world, its fields, woods, moors. The beauty of things enthralled her. She liked books, was fascinated by the sound of words. She had a keen sense of humour, was intelligent, lively – fiery in fact – and had a hatred of humbug. She liked things to be real – truth was a goal to be reached. She has become a poet of real talent.

I married Anne one December day and she joined me at Lochwood. It was her kind of place too. We lived with the natural scene, simply. Anne's ideas stimulated, were often controversial. I wasn't bored. Often she would see or hear things that I was missing, being absorbed in thought. She helped to keep my feet on the ground, my ears to the wind. It was important to her to hear the grass whisper, to touch the green of spring. I was often bemused but more often glad. She hadn't acquired my way of thinking – my insulation she would call it. This was true and sometimes I couldn't understand how sharp the edges could seem to her. But we had space to learn – we had all the wideness of the sky.

Anne is a very private person and I hesitate to mention her at all but, contrary to her oft expressed view to people interviewing me who wanted to include her for 'human interest', she does exist.

In 1991 she was nearly killed in a car crash but eventually, with determination and the help of several hospitals, recovered. Slightly altered in appearance, and to some, difficult to recognise, she didn't seem different to me – she was still herself and undoubtedly existed.

Although the years following the expeditions were interspersed with shorter trips to the Himalaya or Europe, time was mostly spent in Scotland. Scotland was my home and in it I felt at home. Life was structured by writing, climbing, sailing and practical work and of course the study and practice of mystical religion. Despite having turned my back on the monastic life I had not turned my back on its aim and purpose; study and meditation were an integral part of life and I have continued to receive instruction. Time was well filled. Later, I added conservation work to this programme.

Usually I was tied to work but occasionally, when the weather was good, Anne and I would take off for the hills. On one such day we headed for Glen Coe intent on the pleasure of traversing the *Aonach Eagach Ridge* in sun and snow. In those days it was not a 'trade route'. Fewer people went to the hills. Conditions were iron hard, the way untracked, the snow and ice sparkling, the sky blue against white, gleaming hills. Roped, we traversed west towards the sun and far out, the sea. Absorbed, we eventually found ourselves climbing on a crest of pink snow, the glen a growing blackness beneath us. The sun was setting but we moved in a world of light. Anne had no desire to leave the ridge. She liked pink snow. I should have been warned, remembering a winter sunset on the tops when her enthusiasm to stay high had resulted in hours of steep descent in darkness, torch in one hand, axe in the other, cutting steps. Fortunately she liked cutting. On this occasion, under a scatter of stars, we plunged down the side of the ridge somewhere before Clachaig Gully, still able to see a little way ahead. And of course I knew the way. Soon I was less sure and Anne was very unsure as, egged on by me, she went ahead into what seemed like bottomless darkness. I was aware that the apparent drops when the torch beam hung in space were indeed drops. This hillside was iced and hard, studded with cliffs. The way, supposed to be direct, began to seem long. Eventually we reached a good ledge and took stock of the situation. Lights approached. We saw the Glen Coe road under our feet – a fine ledge on a dark night. We were down. It had been a good day.

In ice and darkness descent should, of course, be made from the col west of Sgurr nam Fiannaidh.

So, days were sometimes stolen from work. Living in Argyll I didn't have to travel far and I offset this advantage against the very real disadvantage of over 100 inches of annual rainfall, plus the summer scourge of the Scottish midge. Dinghy sailing was another escape. Anne would observe that the wind was right, was blowing strongly and, having tempted me away from work, would have the boat rigged and ready to sail. I knew that if I didn't come she would go anyway – but sometimes she needed ballast, and I needed a change from work.

However, writing tended to be the arbiter – or maintenance or gardening – jobs requiring good weather. But if the writing was going well I had to stay with it. If it was going badly I had to struggle, however tempted to escape from a reluctant, motionless pen and bare paper. Writing required application being work like any other. Often I would be oblivious to all but the work in hand. I had to live with it, breathe with it, if pages were to be covered, thoughts deciphered. I have been accused of being present in the flesh only and fear that this was often justified. Writing could be wholly absorbing but was no sinecure. It was my livelihood and, in its own way, an exploration. It was a very large part of my life.

And so the seasons turned. Winter in particular was writing time. Spring, in the west, after the long winter, after darkness, was always especially welcome. It brought light and colour, green growing, absorption in its beauty, a peace – yet at the same time it brought a familiar unrest. Exploring was never far away.

– now, in April
This winter window tapping tree
Is still and starred in white.
It holds my breath along its branches
Holds my mind's seeking
In unaccustomed quiet.
For me
It is enough that there should be
Only this tree
Its black branches lit with white
Its petals bright
Light in the air's blue touch
Enough that there should be
Only this blossoming tree
Belonging not to the dark
But to me.
But at night
The tree has gone
And on the wrong side of the window
Tapping the brittle glass
It is I, now
Who have to seek that other side of night.

34 The Cragsmen of Lewis: How they Climbed the Great Stac of Handa

In the normal course of our lives, some of the lessons we learn are picked up as though inadvertently from other peoples' experience. One such I owe to Dr Tom Patey, and to three Outer Islesmen of the nineteenth century.

Tom Patey was one of the best all round mountaineers that Scotland has bred. After setting up medical practice in Ullapool, he had much fun during the sixties exploring seastacks around the northern coasts. They gave him spectacular climbing, posing rock problems not only in finding ways through their overhangs but in approaching their sea-washed bases. One unusually tricky episode was his Tyrolean traverse to the top of the Great Stac of Handa.

The island of Handa lies close to the Sutherland coast. Once inhabited by a dozen families, until the potato famine of 1848 forced their evacuation, it now belongs to the Royal Society for the Protection of Birds. It owed its fame to its big northern cliffs of Torridon sandstone. They rise sheer out of the sea to 380 feet. Their main feature is the Great Stac, a 350-foot pillar set within a creek of the main cliff, which in May and June gives nesting sites to 100,000 sea birds. Tom Patey knew that in the nineteenth century three Outer Islesmen had made a crossing by rope to the top of the Great Stac. But how had they done it? By what means had they managed to get a rope across? The gap between cliff and Stac is eighty feet at the west side, and more than double that to its south and east. In the Dolomites, isolated pinnacles have often been lassoed from neighbouring cliffs – hence the term 'Tyrolean traverse' – but here on Handa the top of the Stac was a flat grassy oval fifty yards wide at centre and free of projection.

Tom studied the site and solved the problem. On 1 July 1967, assisted by Chris Bonington and Ian McNaught-Davis, he made the crossing. When I heard, I wrote my congratulations and asked how the job had been done. Tom replied with full detail, for he wanted my help. He had used four 150-foot lengths of nylon rope, joined them together, and had the two ends carried outward along the diverging tops of the creek until the rope lay across the nearer part of the Stac's oval top. The rope's western end was secured to a huge boulder, and the south-eastern end to four interlinked pitons driven into cracks in the rock. The fixed rope did not bridge the gulf at its narrowest (west) point, but ran across it obliquely, thus lengthening the western crossing to 120 feet.

Although nesting time was nearing its end, the rocks were still thronged with birds, mainly auks (guillemots and razorbills), which outnumbered the kittiwakes, fulmars and puffins. They would all be gone by August, but meantime had no welcome for Tom Patey.

To make the crossing, he wore a waist harness, to which he attached two jumars – sliding clamps that can be pushed along a fixed rope, but are prevented from sliding back by a ratchet. The upper jumar supported the waist; the lower his left leg by a foot stirrup. The jumars were essential, for the rope sagged a full forty feet when his weight came on it. To these aids were added two more: a safety line to his waist, held and paid out by McNaught-Davis, and a snap-link between his waistband and the fixed rope. His companions could thus lower him quickly away on the sliding snap-link to the midway point of the sag, where his real task began.

He secured his two jumars to the fixed rope so that he could climb up its far side by stepping up on the stirrup, and pushing up the waist-jumar, then lifting up the stirrup-jumar and again stepping up. This process, said Tom, might sound safe and easy, but in practice it cost him forty-five minutes' work, all awkward and nerve-racking. He and the fixed rope could not very well part company, but the jumars were hard to handle at the rope's oblique angle before it became vertical under the Stac. The chasm kept drawing his anxious attention because filled with a multitude of excited sea birds, some of them cannoning into the taut rope, then dropping stunned into the sea surge far below. Two guillemots on top of the Stac were pecking so vigorously at the rope that Tom said if ever he went back again he would want the fixed rope doubled. He added, 'I take off my hat to the pioneers.' At the end, he had a tough fight to get any footing on the Stac, and could not have managed to get up without the jumars. He had time on top only for a brief scout around, and saw no trace of the stakes left by his predecessors. If not blown off by wind, they might have been hidden by thick grass. He could see no nests at the Stac's centre, but innumerable puffins ringed the outer fringes.

He concluded, 'Munro, the ferryman at Tarbet, told us of a visit three years ago by the son of the pioneer cragsman of the Great Stac. He had come to view the scene of his father's famous exploit. His name is Donald MacDonald, formerly headmaster of the school at Dunoon in Argyll only thirty miles away from you. Now retired, he still lives there.' Tom implored me to visit MacDonald, and to ask if he remembered detail of the first crossing. Tom could scarcely believe that the first traverse had been made without aids, for he could not have done that himself – the very thought of trying shook him. So what aids had been used?

My visit to MacDonald proved fruitful, and my report to Tom is of interest on three counts. First, it disclosed an error in the historical record as given by Harvie Brown's *Fauna in the North-West Highlands* (1904). The book is erroneous throughout on the Handa passage, giving the credit to 'two men and a boy from Uist, at the request of the late Evander McIver ... ' In fact it was done by three men of Lewis on their own initiative.

Secondly, it reveals a more advanced state of rock climbing in the Outer Hebrides than mainland climbers had realised. Even Patey, comparing his own hair-raising traverse to that of the previous century, wrote (*SMCJ* Vol. 29, p.310), 'It is even more certain that no mountaineering amateur of that era would have committed himself to such an undertaking.'

He might be right, but thirdly, and more importantly, his words draw notice to a moral ripe for plucking, and for slow digestion. Mountaineers of every period share a common frailty (I too being guilty in past days): we start humbly enough in acquiring new skills – hardly dare to hope to match our exemplars – but humility wanes when the skills are ours. We end in belief that our fellows of an earlier age could not have been as bold and skilful as we. From one century to the next, our self-flattering hearts offer up that much beloved toast: 'Here's tae us! Wha's like us? Gey few and they're a' deid.'

On 26 March, I sent my reply to Ullapool:

> 'Dear Tom
>
> I have at last seen Donald MacDonald. I called on him yesterday at Dunoon. His wife died three years ago, just after his visit to Handa, and he now lives alone. One son is a doctor in Fife, and another I forget where. Donald in his mid-eighties looks fresh complexioned and fit, with all his faculties except for a slight deafness. He's not at all frail, and is mentally alert. He remembers the whole story of his father's crossing to the Great Stac, which had been told to him many times by his father and friends. He can't remember the month, but says the year was 1876, when his father was twenty-six.
>
> His father's name was Donald MacDonald, fisherman and crofter at Ness, near the Butt of Lewis, of mixed Norse and Gaelic stock – like all the other families around, fair-haired and blue-eyed. Donald the son still has strong impression of how hard his father worked. He was out on the sea in all weathers, line fishing, yet still managing to wring a good product from the croft: enough to put sons through universities before the welfare state had been thought of. He remarked that the mainlanders' idea of the islesmen as idlers is quite wrong. The reverse was the truth, and that few mainland farmers or crofters could begin to cope with the work these men did. But they might appear idle if seen after a voyage, when they'd stand around for a brief spell

with hands in their pockets, relaxing. Their one outdoor recreation was rock climbing.

His father at twenty-six was in constant practice on rock, very strong in the arm, and supremely confident in his physical fitness. He and other men of Ness learned their rock climbing initially in hunting the birds on the sea cliffs of Ness, and nearly fifty miles north on Sula Sgeir and North Rona, which islands they never referred to by name, but always in Gaelic as "The Lands out Yonder". This kind of naming seems to be a typically Norse idiom, just as they originally referred to the Scottish Western Isles as *Havbredey* which in Norse meant "The Isles on the Edge of the Sea". Hence the Latin name *Ebudae* picked up in Lewis from Norse seamen by the Roman navigators of AD 129 and rendered thus by Ptolemy. (The Norse longboats traded along Europe's coasts even before that time.)[1]

Donald the son says that the men of Ness did not merely cull sea birds for the pot. They liked birds in the same way as modern bird-watchers. They observed and studied them and could tell you as much about the life of sea birds in detail as any amateur ornithologist today. Hunting the birds for food was another matter, which of course had led to their interest in rock work. But they also had a genuine love of birds and of rock climbing for their own sakes. His father in his twenties would often be working out on the croft, and when the main work was done would suddenly "disappear" off to the sea cliffs just to enjoy the climbing. All his spare time went to the rocks. The best cliffs near Ness were on the east coast between Ness and Tolsta. On the west coast from the Butt to Europe, the cliffs were lower.

In those days, they spent much more time than they do today in culling the birds from "The Lands out Yonder": now only a day or two, but last century at least a fortnight in September. They took the gugas (young gannets) as they "ripened", salting them in the barrel as soon as taken, so that most of them were cured by the time the boats returned to Lewis. They tasted, said Donald, not unlike good kippers. The birds were exported world-wide. The young men enjoyed these expeditions. Hard living but a wonderful change from croft work and deep-sea fishing. They went wild with delight and would throw off some

1 *Havebredey* might be split *Hav* meaning sea; *Bred* meaning edge; *ey* meaning island. The plural is *Havbredey jar.*

feats of daring that would make your hair curl. One of these was the Handa epic.

This was organised not by Donald MacDonald but by his neighbour, Malcolm McDonald (no relation). Malcolm, then in his fifties, was a natural leader, full of resource and bright ideas. He planned the visit to the Great Stac of Handa and decided how it would be done. Donald was the man chosen (or maybe the volunteer) to make the first crossing. He had the needed nerve and strength. The Stac had already been reconnoitred with a full intention of climbing it from the sea upward, but no line had seemed practicable. The idea of nailing rocks had been thought of, and been not acceptable.

Their method of crossing was in general outline the same as yours. A long rope – more than 500 feet – was carried ends outwards to the farther points of Handa until the centre crossed the top of the Stac. The ends were then secured to stakes. It could be that they used the same boulder as you at the western end.

Donald then crossed from the west side hand over fist, bare feet curled round the rope. He used no waist-loop or foot-loop and had no safety line at the waist. He carried nothing at all. The fixed rope was a thick fishing rope normally used for securing the deep sea fishing lines to buoys – he gave it a Gaelic name that I can't remember. There was a tremendous sag in the middle and worse at the outer end. Donald had a hard job getting up the last bit. This was the only time when he thought he was going to fall – it was made especially difficult because he was unable to make his landing where he had hoped. There was a point where the Stac sloped down towards the gulf, and the rope had slipped while he was crossing till it hung over this abruptly sloping ground, which was steep, loose, and gave no firm footing when he tried again and again to make lodgement. Now fighting for his life, he in the end tapped the reserve of strength needed to pull himself up. He collapsed all out on top.

When he was rested, his companions threw him a line, by which he pulled across two stakes, a block-and-tackle, a breeches-buoy, and baskets. Donald fixed the stakes, attached the tackle, and the two others crossed by breeches-buoy. They culled the sea cliff birds and filled the baskets. All were then able to return to Handa by breeches-buoy, leaving the stakes behind on the Stac, where they were seen during the next seventy years.

This ploy became one of the wonders of Ness for many a year; but no one thought that the islesmen's high spirited play would be of interest to mainlanders.

So that's the story. There are details one would like to know more about. How did Donald hammer in his stakes? What was the thickness of the fixed rope? Given a really thick and taut rope, crossing hand over fist is not in itself difficult for a skilled man, as we both know. In western Nepal, the hill men use this method for crossing rivers wider than the Handa gulf but, their grass ropes are one and a half inches in diameter, stretched so tight that little sag comes in the middle, and they lead to easy landings. The rivers below are killers if one falls in, but nothing like so fearsome as the long drop at Handa.

Eight years later, Malcolm McDonald, the prime mover, quarrelled with his Presbyterian minister at Ness. Rather than submit to his rule of the parish, Malcolm chose self-exile to North Rona. A fellow crofter, McKay, went with him. The island had been uninhabited for forty-five years. They arrived early in the summer of 1884, and occupied a ruined house. Their friends at Ness, feeling uneasy about them after a stormy winter, sent out a boat in April 1885, when Malcolm and his friend were found indoors dead of exposure.

Regards, Bill'

This history clearly places the origins of hard rock-climbing in Britain several years earlier than Haskett Smith's ascent of *Napes Needle* (1886) and well in advance of the scrambles of Atkinson (Pillar Rock, 1826), Forbes and MacIntyre (Sgurr nan Gillean, 1836) and Nicholson (various parts of the Cuillin Ridge, 1870s) – to name just three early climbing events. R.M. Barrington's 1883 ascent (with two locals) of Stac na Biorrach on St Kilda may point to an earlier tradition of quite hard rock climbing – it was suggested that the St Kilda stacs had been climbed from as early as 1678 for collection of birds' eggs for food.

It is interesting to reflect that some of the hardest climbs in Britain have recently been pioneered in the Outer Hebrides by visiting climbers, but as yet, as far as I am aware, no local climbers have emerged to continue the ancient traditions of the Hebridean crofters.

35 The Life of Ben Humble – Tribute to a Fighter

In an earlier chapter, I said that handicapped men face closed doors. In this one, I have to add that for them other doors can open. Life has a way of contriving compensations. To the blind, light may be given; to the deaf, an inner ear. They are often able to see and hear and understand more than we with faculties unimpaired. This I first learned from knowing Ben Humble. He was deaf – and one of those eccentric characters to whose self-dedication the mountaineering fraternity, and more besides, owe so much, and to him more than most.

Mountains are dangerous – never trite words to the ears of mountaineers. They lose too many friends. More of my own have been killed before their time than in any other field of action. In my early years, I was naturally drawn to help in mountain rescue. There were no official teams. Rescue parties were called out by telephone from the lowland towns as need arose. Infrequent as occasions were before the war – never more than an average of six a year – after it they grew to a mounting tide. They could no longer be left to ad hoc teams from the few principal clubs. In the late forties and early fifties, I spent much time helping to organise mountain rescue in Scotland, serving on its central committee, for whom I drew up its constitution whereby the rapidly forming district teams might be co-ordinated with those of the RAF and Police.

Ben Humble led me into this latter work from 1946 onwards. His zeal stimulated much of the action in Scotland with far-reaching results. He had been born in Dumbarton in 1904, one of eight brothers. The important thing to know of Ben is that here was a youth of bright mind and vigour, who left Glasgow High School only to have his professional hopes frustrated by a fast growing deafness. The experience induced not only eccentricities but a stubborn will, and a strong force of personality – all turned in time to the service of others.

Ben graduated in dental surgery at Glasgow University. His student years were made harder by his refusal to acknowledge lost hearing. He declined to learn lip-reading. He spent a whole term, said his fellow student Archie MacAlpine, carving his name three inches high on his desk, for he felt obliged to sit out lectures hearing nothing. Undaunted, he duly set up in general practice at Dumbarton. That failed so he moved to Charing Cross in Glasgow, where he specialised in radiology (a dental science new to Scotland), at the same time writing research papers on forensic dentistry. His pioneer work on bite marks greatly extended dental evidence acceptable to judge and jury on criminal trials world-wide. Result: successive convictions, from his own day to the present.

His practice failed in 1935. Dentists then rarely had X-ray machines, but even so found communication with Ben too difficult. He was now stone deaf and by 1937 had to abandon dentistry to earn a living from journalism, photography and the writing of books. His first had been *Tramping in Skye* (1930), when he helped to organise the first Skye Week.

Ben survived with apparent ease. He was a shrewd businessman, who could drive a hard bargain, yet much of his energy went to voluntary interests, profitless in money terms, and far beyond what lesser mortals could sustain. He aroused in me, and in all who knew him, wonder and admiration. We could not imagine how he made the time or kept the pace. One thing is certain, he was driven by deafness into constant communication and involvement in affairs.

Ben had been walking the hills from his youth. He began climbing when he joined the JMCS in 1930. I first met him at a club meeting in 1935. He was short in stature, with alert brown eyes that often held a mischievous gleam, his hair was already thinning to baldness. I was only twenty-two, an age at which men of thirty are believed to have one foot in the grave, yet with Ben this thought never occurred to me. A natural vitality made him ageless. Among his other activities were cross-country running with Dumbarton Harriers (he was an early organiser of the annual race up Ben Nevis); botany, in which he was expert on heathers, photography, including movies; and public speaking through membership of a debating and dining club, so that despite peculiarities of accent caused by deafness, he became a top-class after-dinner speaker. These were just a few of his many interests pursued with infectious enthusiasm.

I had no thought of climbing with Ben until June the following year, when chance brought our tents to the same campsite at Glen Brittle in Skye. I discovered there that the hard headed Ben was a romantic, to whom the mountain ambience was all and physical discomforts nothing – a too rare quality that made him for me instantly congenial company. The first intimation came at ten o'clock one evening, when I stood outside to watch the mist gather and swirl round the Cuillin. His head suddenly thrust out from the door of his tent.

'It would be a fine night for a climb,' he announced, and I knew from his voice that he meant it. The notion startled me. I was a beginner. Night climbing had not yet entered my dreams. 'We'd start right now,' he added, 'up to the main ridge, north along the tops *aaaaaah*!' I protested the need of food and sleep, this to express a merely bodily wish, for the mind was already aloft. We enjoyed the best night and morning we were ever to have in Skye, finishing down at Loch Coruisk.

I revert to Ben's long drawn *aaaaaah* – a habitual expression. By subtle expression of voice, he could use it to signify equally well approval of censure, or to convey from the gamut of emotion any note that he chose – delight, derision, admiration, contempt, laughter, scepticism, wonder, scandal, irony. He did this unaffectedly, since he could hear nothing of his own tone, giving unerring expression to inward feeling. His eloquent *aaaaaahs* could communicate more than other men's innumerable words.

Ben and I climbed often together in 1936 and 1937, but rarely on rock above Very Difficult standard. On Severes his deafness affected balance, and communication became too chancy (unless on a short climb). I found his photography a sore trial of my patience. He was so keen, constantly given to the endless search for dramatic stances, unusual lighting, right composition, revealing effects, that hours would seem to go by while we dilly-dallied. I learned more patience when I viewed the results. The best reward we had, since it yielded his best known and favourite picture, came from one trying hour in June 1936 spent in posing me on the Cioch. It was 9 p.m. and still broad daylight with a cloud-sea below, yet by judicious stopping of the camera he created a splendid sunset photograph, though true to the Cuillin at their best. To me, that seemed good art, and justified. His hunger for good subjects made him sometimes quite unscrupulous, as witness the day I came down from the rocks to our camp in Glen Brittle and found Ben absorbed in photographing a cow, which was munching my pyjamas where they hung on a drying line. I raged. Ben was totally unrepentant. His image stays with me, face gleeful, an imp of mischief.

The real Ben came out in his love of highly uncomfortable howffs. Often he would bicycle up from Dumbarton to Arrochar to sleep in the caves of Ben Narnain, or else at the Narnain Boulder under the Cobbler corrie. Ben was devoted to the Cobbler, and to Arrochar, where he lived for many years, and to the gentle art of howffing for which that district lavishly provides. He wrote of one New Year howff, 1,600 feet up on Beinn an Lochain:

> 'I was particularly anxious to test this one under hard conditions as it had been my own discovery the previous April – still do I remember the sunset over distant Loch Fyne, perfectly framed in the arch which formed the entrance and named the howff "Sunset Arch". We had hoped for really frosty conditions at New Year, but typical Arrochar rain was our reward. When heavy rain came in drips from the roof, it was a queer business sitting round a blazing fire wearing oil-skins. Our preoccupation was such that no one noticed candle grease steadily dripping into the pan of soup hotting up, till at last the candle itself fell in.'

Always he hankered for a cave under real winter conditions, and at last he found both at a Hogmanay howff in the Lost Valley of Glen Coe.

My brightest memory is of sallying forth in the deep snow, returning with two armfuls of icicles, and discovering that porridge made from icicles was much better than porridge made from snow. Conditions that night had been just about as severe as could be experienced in Scotland.

Much of his howffing had been done in Jock Nimlin's company. He used to quote with relish Nimlin's opinion that howffing ought to be an essential part of the climbing game, which might eliminate some of the dross from the mountaineering clubs.

All members of the SMC [Ben had joined in 1936] should be let loose in a high corrie one winter evening, each to find his own howff, those present in the morning to remain members – *aaaaaah*!

Disputes with Ben were frequent and long pursued. Always he had the last word. Nearly all troubles arose from some written note. He kept a notebook for companions to write down thoughts or replies. Ben's advantage then was this permanent record of everything one ever said, often in unwise haste. He could refer back and confound the man who had changed an opinion or a lightly given promise. But the real ground of trouble was that written words so often fail to convey the full meaning of words uttered, the tone if voice is absent. In speech one can say many things that when written would arouse wrath. One may speak frankly if the tone is heard to be friendly, or concerned, or humorous. When young, I would sometimes forget this in the heat of the moment when scribbling a note to Ben – as did most people sooner or later – forget, too, since Ben himself was most outspoken, that he was far more sensitive to our adverse opinions than we were to his, and Ben, misinterpreting, would then feel grossly insulted.

My worst offence came when I was organising in Glasgow an exhibition of mountain photographs. My sister submitted a print of Ben sitting outside this tent in Glen Brittle eating a kipper. To my untold delight, he looked the picture of an old man and the entry was titled 'The Humble Kipper'. I hung it in a prominent position, a riposte for that cow-and-pyjama photo. When Ben came into the room and saw it, he ripped it off the wall. I asked for his notebook and wrote, 'Don't be a bf – please put it back.' His fury boiled over. He would neither speak to me nor see me again for nearly two years, in which time war had broken out. The next time we met was by chance in the summer of 1945 in Sauchiehall Street. He came up to me grinning.

'Three years in prison camps *aaaaaah*! – maybe you've been punished enough,' and held out his hand, which I thankfully took.

In 1945 Ben focused his energies to mountain rescue. From 1936 this had been organised by a First-Aid Committee drawn from the mountaineering clubs (at their own expense). Ben was involved from the start. With his usual clear-headedness, he now foresaw the rise in climbers' numbers and the coming need for locally raised teams to take over the physical task of rescue from the clubs. The central committee could then concentrate on fostering mountain safety by propaganda, and negotiate support from central and local governments. I and others were persuaded by his arguments, most notably of all, Donald Duff, the well known surgeon at the Belford Hospital at Fort William. An excellent mountaineer, he raised the first civilian team in Scotland, and gave it, and the police too, training in mountain rescue techniques.

The clubs' committee had already laid down the basic principles of rescue, sited first-aid posts, and begun recruiting teams. During the next decade, they all worked hard to develop the service. All was not sweetness and light. The task needed endless patience (not Ben's forte – his was applying the spur to our flanks) in dealing with and reconciling the different priorities of the Ministry of Health, Police, RAF, Red Cross, numerous outdoor bodies, local teams and opinionated mountaineers. Between them, they set up the new regime under Donald Duff's chairmanship in 1950. It evolved over the next decade into the Mountain Rescue Committee of Scotland, providing the comprehensive service we know today. Mountaineers are heavily in Ben Humble's debt.

Ben, always a member of the committee, made two most important contributions: first, he made sure that control remained with mountaineers and was not handed to a statutory body and second, he recorded mountain accidents for the next thirty-two years of his life, starting from 1945. No one with less than Ben's strong will, maintained over the years, could have extracted the information required from reluctant teams, until at last their reporting became habitual. The result was an invaluable fund of rescue and safety data, which he was determined to use positively. His theme on committee was that while the teams' job was to save life, the committee's job was to prevent accidents. To that end he pioneered the Duff Memorial Mountain Safety Exhibition, 'Adventure in Safety', held in Glasgow in 1968, and subsequently in London, Edinburgh, Aberdeen and Fort William. It became a permanent, transportable exhibition which showed great numbers of young hill-walkers how best to enjoy mountains. In 1972, he received an MBE.

In achieving his multitudinous ends, Ben became a thorn in the flesh of every dilatory office-bearer, editor or committee man. He was a constant prompter of the most active, and to all his friends a fount of advice that poured out of him in a daily stream of correspondence. We all had to keep a special file for Ben alone. He seemed to know everything and everyone, deafness no handicap at all. In the mountain fraternity, he was the best informed man, to whom everyone could turn for the latest inside information. Being more alert and brighter minded than his friends and (temporary) enemies, Ben could be quite excessively irritating: when we rejected his sage advises he almost always proved to be right. Nor did he fail to remind us of that at the end, when his trumpeted *aaaaaah* rang in our ears.

Ben somehow made time to write six books. *The Cuillin of Skye*, published by Hale in 1952, was by far his best and unique in its subject, a history of the Cuillin with over seventy photographs, of which a third were his own. He had another gift that all might envy, an instinctive rapport with children. They responded, liking him instantly. The best in Ben came out in their company. He sparkled and all his cares fell away. When the first Adventure Centre opened at Loch Morlich below Cairn Gorm, he began to serve as a voluntary leader of children's courses in hill-walking. His accord with the young and his passion for instilling safe practice made him an ideal instructor.

His appearances at Glenmore Lodge, at first infrequent, so greatly increased when the centre moved up hill to its present site, that he sold his Arrochar house in 1970 and moved to Aviemore, where he lived till he died seven years later. When he became unable to lead groups to the hills, he turned his botanical skills to the creation of a heather and alpine rockery at the front of the Lodge. It is still there today, one of several memorials to his energetic loves. Another is the Cuillin book, for he loved the Black Cuillin more than any other mountains. To them he offered his best work, declaring on its first page, 'They have no equal in all the world.' He said it again when he gave me a copy of the book. I knew from his voice that he meant it.

36 A Writer's World

Apart from exploring my thoughts and my own talents what have I learned about writing as a way of life?

Were I able to escape the time capsule and from my eighty years station speak to myself in my twenties when I was wondering whether to risk the plunge to full time writing, I would say – like every author before me, 'Don't!' I would say it knowing that wise as the words might be they would be rejected, for that young man's will had been set too long, deaf to argument and blind to prospects. But still, I would have to say it.

Certainly in some ways writing accords freedom – choice of work place. But it does not give freedom from work, endless free time such as we all think we would enjoy. Nor does it bring free time just when we want it because, when the pen, often so reluctant to start, does stir it behoves a writer to keep the momentum going.

After writing five books on mountains and knowing that I could easily write and sell a sixth on the expedition to Api, I deliberately turned away from this temptation. I wanted to avoid mountain subjects. I didn't want to combine earning my living with mountains, above all not to climb to earn. Mountains were not to me a means to this end. Soon after the war I had turned down the offer of wardenship of the National Outdoor Centre at Glenmore Lodge in the Cairngorms. This was a good offer, a good place to stay, assured income (to back up my writing) and interesting work. But somehow it wasn't right for me. Mountains had to remain recreational and not be mixed up with earning. So I stuck to writing alone.

Then I wondered what else I might write, perhaps better, whether one of fiction's several varieties, or history, biography, travel, topography – all of which attracted me. I wanted to explore other kinds of writing.

I wrote about a score of books, four novels, a collection of short stories, eight books on the landscape and natural history of the Scottish Highlands and Hebrides and a biography of Rob Roy MacGregor.

I found that I enjoyed writing fiction. Thrillers were fun and set in places I knew. They entertained, sold well, were described by some as John Buchanish. They were adventure stories – pure escapism. After writing the short stories I reverted to non-fiction.

ROB ROY MACGREGOR

Rob Roy MacGregor: His Life and Times is a book that gave me a peculiar satisfaction in that justice to a man could be seen to be done. At last I had discovered the real Rob Roy, hitherto a villain of Scottish folklore best known as described by Sir Walter Scott in his novel. After long research of family and historical papers not previously available, I revealed – created – a character wholly different from that cast up on hearsay by his earlier traducers – a man of integrity and that of heroic proportion.

Iverach McDonald, for many years foreign editor and associate editor of *The Times*, wrote to me:

> 'May I say how much I have enjoyed and admired your *Rob Roy MacGregor* – a wholly admirable work. No book has given a clearer or more convincing picture of everyday life and the deeper forces at work in the Central and Southern Highlands of the early 18th Century. You bring out the structure of the clans, the organisation of the Watches, the rules of blackmail, the old unwritten codes in war and peace. No one has better demonstrated exactly what the patronage of a great nobleman meant to Rob Roy and others of his degree or how deep were the divisions within Clan Campbell or how utterly separate were the two worlds north and south of the Highland line. The Highlands have remained my first and keenest interest. My warm congratulations.'

A blockbuster film was made about Rob Roy in 1995 in Glen Nevis, complete with a hero whose integrity of character is its theme. My book, the result of much work and years of research into hitherto unavailable papers, was used: my 'Man of Integrity' was taken for its hero.

The scriptwriter of the film, Alan Sharp, noted:[1]

> 'My own needs in historical writing are to be drawn into the time by a writer who knows the landscape and then engaged imaginatively by narrative.
>
> A necessary element in all successful forays into the past is a binding sense of the real. In Mr Murray's book I had the great good fortune to be introduced to a distant, distorted, historical personage and to catch glimpses, through his steadfast vision, of a man and the events amidst which he had his being. It is a very

1 Letter to Canongate (4 March 1995)

> fine book indeed. The painting of Rob Roy, cleaned and revealed by Murray, was the one I wished to portray.'

In the (Glasgow) *Herald* (13 March 1995) Sharp was reported as saying:

> 'I tried to model the character of Rob Roy on Murray's *Rob Roy [McGregor]* – a poignantly clear, vivid and coherent portrayal, by far the best documented book. I wanted to write something which if Murray read it would not cause me to cringe with embarrassment.'

The star, Liam Neeson, was attracted to the part because, 'The word "honour" goes all the way through it.'[2] The producer, Peter Brougham, stated that my book was 'The staple source of material for the film and of understanding and rounding off Rob's character.'[3] He even offered me £1,000 for a TV option on my book (via my publisher) but the lengthy contract for this princely sum seemed confining and, on advice, I didn't sign. The publisher had been offered a publicity photograph from the film for the cover of the new edition of *Rob Roy MacGregor* – provided I signed. He was disappointed, this being regarded as a good sales gimmick.

Obviously subsidiary rights could earn money for an author. Here surely was an example. But whatever this is, it is not an example of riches earned by writing. Despite the film's £25 million budget no money (apart from the aforementioned 'offer') was accorded to the writer.

How could this be? I don't know. Certainly the lawyers whom I was advised to acquire were at one stage jubilant and wrote that they were about to 'strike' in America by bringing an action against the film-makers on the principle of 'Unjustified Enrichment' – one person gains by using another's work. They even arranged for an experienced journalist from a national newspaper to interview me at home for the exclusive story. However, the hard-working journalist soon found himself in the invidious position of having an editor on one hand clamouring for the scoop and lawyers on the other hand trying to silence him. Apparently, we were given to understand American legal homework hadn't been adequately done. It was all beyond me and quite extraordinary. Suddenly, within hours, there was no case. At least I hadn't counted my chickens. The lawyers said they would pursue the case in Britain but the matter dwindled to an end. Nothing happened. I never did understand this. There were peculiarities. A QC was briefed by the lawyers for an opinion but existing

---

2 *Telegraph Colour Magazine*, 28 January 1995

3 Comments to Canongate, 28 January 1995

relevant facts apparently did not reach him. I didn't understand this either – although I have copies of both facts and briefing.

I have been told that I am naive and this is of course possible. Certainly I felt out of my depths. Iain Fleming of *James Bond* fame, has said:

> 'You don't make a great deal of money from royalties and translation rights and so forth – you could only just about live on these profits – but if you sell the film rights you do very well.'

This might be so, but be warned if you are tempted to a writing career with this idea in mind – subsidiary rights can be illusory as a source of payment for your work. It is well to remember that Fleming compared the author's lot to that of an office cleaner (i.e. hard work, little pay).

THE WRITER'S ART AND BUSINESS

These matters concerning *Rob Roy* bring me to a more general critique of the book business, particularly the contractual and publishing part that attends the actual creative process. While a writer usually enjoys his work, he appreciates fair pay. In writing, the financial reward is usually derisory. [The Society of Authors in the year 2000 noted that half of all writers earn less than the country's minimum wage – only one in ten can earn a living from writing. A.B.M.]

How many full time writers do you know?[4]

Book writing is by its nature a lonely job. An author needs peace and quiet in order to concentrate his mind on his creative act. I had learned in prison camps that this need not be an outer peace. Continuous outer disturbance does not matter if the writer can find the way to retire inwardly. Amid the stramash of barrack room life in the camps, I learned how to concentrate by the very necessity of detachment. Having no other choice, I learned so well that it became ingrained, a permanent trait, causing in later years some social embarrassment to my friends, who would sometimes speak and not be heard.

I imagined on my release that work would be all the easier in the peace of Highland countryside. I was wrong. Country people, spread more thinly on the ground than are townspeople, may seem to be not such close neighbours, but for that very reason can be more so, can be a real community, their sociability enhanced by need of mutual help. An author can be dubbed a recluse if he holds himself apart. Townsfolk are much more inclined to be 'islands'. Today of course, even in the country, community has changed – ceased to exist, some say. Movement of population, a different ethos, the national growth of the 'Me' culture and society's greater consciousness of perceived

4 See Appendix V for *Notes on Publishing and the Practicalities of the Writing Business.*

'rights' rather than of privileges and responsibilities may all have contributed. Of course this change is not seen in all areas. A professional author can work well anywhere, but in town faster with swift access to libraries, book shops, museums, other vital reference points – all this with fewer distractions. I came to Argyll because of the peace and beauty of the country after years in prisons.

A common fallacy is that authors write by inspiration. One who waits for that blessing will starve. Like any businessman, an author works by routine, and writes to set hours if he's wise, a minimum of 1,000 words a day. He hopes for more according to his subject's grade of difficulty. If, in the course of his work, inspiration should indeed arrive, all rules are shed. The pen speeds, the hours fly. Routine abandoned, the writer writes until he can write no more. Elation stays with him through exhaustion. Such inspiration is rare indeed. If genuine, his work will stand more or less as first written. If it has come in fits and starts, it will need hard but pleasurable work in emendation. If it has been false, its purple passages must be struck out – ruthlessly struck if bad. Be wary. Sometimes a purple passage is basically good, and needs only an adjectival pruning, or correction of suspect simile or mixed and overdone metaphor. A good writer should positively strive for apt metaphors and similes. They can add greatly to the force and vitality of his work. But they must be true or else earn derision.

Laboured desk-work is not enough, and especially dangerous in landscape writing. The author must then look, really use his eyes, as efficiently as a landscape painter. Like him, he can retain an after image to which he can work, re-creating a scene to get its essence onto paper. The memory can pigeon hole that image, retain it for years undimmed, just as it can retain a fact, and reproduce it when wanted. A revealing metaphor can be based on such an image. If instead it is desk-constructed on the sound and play of words only, the most likely result is a fake to be blue-pencilled.

Writing is exhilarating for anyone visited by true inspiration. Even its briefest advent can seem a huge encouragement. But no author can wait on it. Waiting turns it off. That having been said, an author should not start writing in earnest until his feeling is aroused, otherwise his words will stay dry, their composition as laborious to himself as to readers, and not worth the trouble. Emotion gives the power drive, its real effect still depending on the mind's control and the will's discipline. An author has to be moved by more than his need to earn a living. Will, heart and mind have to act as one. All obstacles fall to that triad.

That said, yet again there is no 'best time to write.' The prison camps taught me that all times are best, every chance to be seized as it comes. On my return to Scotland I began to forget the lesson. I even came to think that I wrote best between ten o'clock at night and two in the morning. At these hours my mind grew most lucid and work went rapidly. Marriage brought me to my senses. Such hours being impractical, I reverted to normal business routine, promptly finding daylight hours to be no way inferior. Authors in their relative loneliness become prone to illusion. I can recommend as a prophylactic three years in prison. Years thought to be lost can be the most profitable.

MOUNTAINEERING AND WRITING

Although I tried to avoid using mountains and mountain books as a way of earning a living, I found in exploring the field that mountaineering and writing do have a lot in common – heavy penalties for a start. For climber and author alike, there is no big money in the game – that is raked off by the book and equipment dealers. But I think more of the agonies, like 2 a.m. starts in the Alps. The mind is just as lazy as the body when it comes to starting a book. I remember the days spent staring at blank sheets of A4 when I was willing to do anything, virtually anything, except put pen to paper. A spell of nerves before a hard climb is not any worse, for at least one is not normally alone, as one is while trying to write. But to learn any skill well, there is first need to practise as often as possible.

Unusually today, I write my books in longhand. I then go over the words, sometimes changing so many times that the script becomes difficult to read. Sometimes the first writing passes scrutiny, but more usually it does not. Afterwards comes the first typing and usually more changes. The typescript gives distance, sharpens the critical faculty – but this first typescript is never final.

I have sometimes been asked, to my surprise, if I do my own punctuation. Of course I do. I even do my own spelling though I gather that today's machinery can provide this service. I am not into the world's modern technology yet and use pen and paper and my manual typewriter. The physical task of production is changing, becoming easier and more time efficient but no machine will do good writing for you – only lessen the labour.

It has been said that writers live in an ideal world of their own creation from which suffering has disappeared – they view it but are not subject to it. This would store up trouble for a writer if he wanted to get at the truth. If he makes light of the pains he bores by understatement. If he makes too much of the joys he deceives by overstatement. How to get it right? Having tried for fifty years I am tempted to say that it cannot be done. I have made all the mistakes that can be made. Words so often seem fully apposite only to material things. To get the subjective reality at the same time you have to be able to play on words and wring out meaning between the lines. This involves effort but is worth it. The true art is to balance on that knife-edge between the two realities and let them both speak. Poetry is a prime example of this. But prose can also be made to walk this bright edge. It can be done. But it does take a touch of inspiration to get that direct simplicity of expression, that hallmark of good writing which goes straight to the heart of things.

What of the pleasures of writing?

In those all too prevalent half dead times when the mind seems blind, recording nothing, a scene can come alive afterwards stored up in all its splendour – and we write ourselves back to that scene. Descending the Himalayan peak, Hanuman, in bad weather, steering by compass across a desert of writhing snow in a race against night, suddenly, a great shaft opened up through the clouds disclosing a vast, white arrowhead, floating in the upper air, no visible support. It seemed not of this earth. I just had a momentary glimpse, then clouds swirled round and swallowed it up. I could have sworn my mind took no impression being intent on survival. Later, back in camp it was different, that vision of Nanda Devi came back as when first seen. It is those moments that last.

Writing does have its compensations – like recollection. There is also the aspect of sharing the recollection or observation with others – the child's 'look what I've found'. This seems to be a natural instinct. Readers have written in gratitude on finding another voice that shares their feelings, encapsulating them in words and somehow clarifying, increasing perception. It is good to hear from these people. Others appreciate being taken to places, situations which they would not otherwise experience. I have always found that even my mountain books appeal not simply to the mountaineer but to the general reader who wants to see further – as I do. If we were fully rational I think none of us would be writers or climbers at all. I have long recognised that we are daft – 'daft' in the old Scots sense which means unreasonably happy! We enjoy these strange ploys – despite their drawbacks. In climbing there is an elation just in practice of the craft when all is going well. You make the moves surely and swiftly with rhythm. When you are climbing well you know it. The same goes for writing. The two crafts are often akin even though one is mainly physical the other mental. When you are off form you write clumsily, just as you move clumsily; you pick wrong words as you pick wrong holds. You lose the purpose and thread of writing as you lose route – but on mountains and in writing when good form is struck, when it all comes together, when inspiration is caught and held – you rise from the dead. The world is yours.

37 Conservation

Shortly after marriage, I became drawn into conservation. Anne shared this interest. Her attitude to land made caring inescapable. I need to define my terms closely, for the subject is vast and my part small. By conservation, I mean to keep from harm the natural beauty of our countryside, including its wildlife. I do not include towns or their parks, these forming a different subject of conservation.

THE HIGHLAND LANDSCAPE REPORT

In May 1961, the National Trust for Scotland asked me to make a survey of the Scottish Highlands, describe the areas of supreme landscape value, report on their distinguishing characters, and assess recent change or future threat. No one before me had attempted such a survey. The Trust wanted it done now, believing it essential to good management of the land, and to right decisions on the use of natural resources. Right decisions had to keep a balance between mankind's material and spiritual needs – meaning, in down-to-earth terms, money and natural beauty. Preservation of the latter had been a duty laid on the Trust in 1935 by Parliament, in its Act of Incorporation.

The Trust's spur to action had been the intransigence of the North of Scotland Hydro-Electric Board, who were intent on damming the famous gorge of upper Glen Nevis. The Board had already impaired three of Scotland's finest glens – Affric, Cannich and Strathfarrar. The dams with their new roads had dispelled the natural atmosphere of these remote mountain passes; eroded the unusual beauty of their ancient woodlands and rivers, and so too the spiritual quality that wildland conveys to walkers – a refreshment beyond the physical. The proposed addition of Glen Nevis to the list of depredations inflicted was one too many.

To the jab of the Board's spur had been added the whip of the Forestry Commission, whose sitka plantations were spreading a coniferous monotony over the West Highlands. The Trust, in support of their national appeal against the plans of that resolute pair – the Hydro Board, deaf to reason, the Commission, blind to people's need of natural amenities – required full background knowledge.

My pilot survey had (for political reasons) to be completed by autumn, and therefore restricted to what one man could do in four months. We judged this to be the Highlands, excluding the Hebrides and coastal strips, unless where the latter formed a natural bound to a highland interior. For me it was possible in the time only because I already knew the ground through nearly thirty years' travel, walking and climbing. My wife Anne and I spent that 'summer' living in a small tent carried into the wild, looking and learning.

On that basis, I chose fifty-two regions for survey, covered them all on foot, and surveyed each from the lowest ground to its mountain tops. I selected twenty-one as outstanding in point of landscape beauty alone. I chose none for its social or historic interest, or for its recreational facilities, these being no more than additional reasons for commending a choice made on quite another ground.

The beauty of Highland country is that of mountain, loch, moor, glen, river and forest. So diverse is the Scottish scene that the stating of criteria to cover every excellence can become unnecessarily detailed and complex. In the rocky wildland of Fisherfield Forest there is a beauty no less than in rich woodland like Glen Lyon. The two are at opposite poles of the scenic scale, utterly different yet both valued as the best of their kind. So, too, any criterion must be broad enough to reconcile the remote desolation of Loch Avon in the Cairngorms with the populous Tummel Valley. The criterion to cover so wide a range is not complex and exclusive, but simple and universal.

My choice of areas of outstanding beauty was determined, of necessity, on the criterion of beauty itself. Beauty is the perfect expression of that ideal form to which everything that is perfect of its kind approaches. The idea of beauty is innate in our minds, so that outward expression of it can be recognised. Had the mind no idea or criterion of beauty within itself, no number of outward exhibitions would suffice for its recognition. Hence, in my survey, regions were selected on the criterion of beauty as I saw it. In confirmation of this approach, I discovered that no one disagreed with my selection, either on first publication or during the next thirty years. Some disagreed with several of my exclusions: for example, Loch Awe, Glen Tilt, and others, not because I had denied them outstanding beauty, but because I had pitched my standard very high.

In my report's final paragraph, I pointed out that ugliness had crept into many of our towns by slow degrees through lack of over-all control, foresight and direction. I then noted that the same situation was arising in the Highland scene, one of Scotland's great natural assets, whose outstanding beauty had likewise been haphazardly expended and no account kept. The wasting of this asset was bound to continue and accelerate unless control was brought to bear by a statutory body created by government and granted powers, so that checks and safeguards could be set up. If action were not taken now, the people would lose by neglect what remained of their natural heritage.

Another problem of the time was the social revolution that followed the last great war – an earthquake effect that sent tidal waves of humanity rolling into the Highland countryside at weekends and holidays. Good as this might be for the people, it was not good for the countryside, or its mountains, or its wildlife. The troubles thrown up are known to us all. In 1962, I had an informal talk in London with the secretary of the National Parks Commission. We discussed a possible Countryside Commission for Scotland. I asked him to say, out of his own experience, what were the most important points that we, the Scots, should bear in mind if setting up a commission. He had no hesitation:

> 'There are two essentials. In the commission's term of reference, put conservation first and foremost. There is never a lack of developers and their plans. But if you want to keep the best of your landscape, you'll have to fight for it if you don't, no one else will.
>
> Second point: Local Authorities must get 100% grants for amenity work, not 75% as in England, because Local Authorities are always hard up and will not spend ratepayers' money to provide amenities for the nation.'

THE COUNTRYSIDE COMMISSION FOR SCOTLAND

The NTS, having approved my survey, wanted to bring it out in book form (*Highland Landscape*, 1962) to give wider dissemination. There were serious risks to landscape in Scotland and while unprepared to hand a book to the Trust under guise of a report – no working author can afford to do this – I at once agreed to the wider distribution deemed helpful to conservation. It proved to be to good effect. The subject grew topical, snowballed, and government finally assembled the Duke of Edinburgh's Countryside Conference, which reported in 1965. Two years later, the Countryside Commission for Scotland was established by Act of Parliament. I was appointed a commissioner, or member of its board.

I was warned by the Secretary of State in a private talk:

> '*Conservation* is now the name of the game – the old word *preservation* has gone out of fashion – not used now in the jargon.'

The two words, of course, meant exactly the same thing: to preserve or keep from harm. In our society to *preserve* has come to connote to *stultify*.

The new Commission inherited from its Act several weaknesses. First, Parliament had not given it the real powers I had seen to be needed – only a right to advise local and central governments, who ignored as they chose. Second, its powers of grant to local authorities were too low. Third, its double remit was stated in the wrong order: 'to develop facilities for the enjoyment of the Scottish countryside, and to conserve its natural beauty'. Fourth, and not a fault of the Act itself, too few of the commissioners appointed had any intimate knowledge of Scotland's countryside. Also too many were local authority politicians, hence a majority were intent on the first stated task, development, and paid little attention to natural beauty, from which they were blinkered. In short, the essentials for success had not been enshrined either in the Act or in the heart of the responsible Minister.

I noticed at meetings that those who knew least were the most fluently vociferous, feeling able to speak with most confident assurance.

Comic situations could arise. One commissioner, appointed after a lifetime's service at the Ministry of Defence in London, gave eloquent backing to a developer's plan to build a chalet complex on top of the Isle of Staffa. This is the tiny cliff-girt isle renowned for Fingal's Cave and Mendelssohn's attendant *Hebrides Overture*. One mile long and a third of a mile wide, it is situated several miles off Mull's west coast. I opposed his proposal. He upbraided me, telling the commission:

> 'The wretched inhabitants of Staffa have need of these jobs. Here is real employment offered them at last – a chance to make a worthwhile living for themselves and their families – surely more important than preserving wild scenery!'

I asked how many inhabitants Staffa had. He could not, he said, give the precise numbers without notice. When I told him that Staffa was uninhabited, had never been inhabited and was one of 500 others of like kind in the Hebrides, he sat back with a sigh, not a bit abashed, and remarked with a grin, 'This doesn't seem to be my day.'

The commissioners chose excellent members of staff, too many of whom had to come from England, for Scotland lacked countryside planners. They worked hard and built up their knowledge of the Highlands and Islands, but this took time to go deep. When they in turn came to assess the landscape for designation of quality and a park system, they felt that they could not accept my subjective criterion of beauty and instead sought objective criteria 'more logically sited and complex'. I sympathised, having faced the same problem seven years earlier, but felt assured they would fail. The Commission duly appointed a firm of landscape consultants to devise the objective system. They spent years of work at home and abroad, and much public money on wide travel and research, only to come up at the end with a system so elaborate that it proved unworkable in the field.

I thought our own staff vastly superior to the business consultants whom they were often forced to employ (and pay) through pressure of work, and whose jargon was risible (e.g. 'vehicular circulatory systems' instead of roads).

Our staff surveyors in the end had to revert to my simple subjective method, which again worked splendidly. It gave the same results as mine for their final report of 1974. Everyone agreed, as before, that the designations were true. The idea of beauty is innate to people's mind. Logicians who oppose were once again shown to have worked from a faulty premise and therefore to be wrong in practice. But I felt no sense of triumph. We all have to live and learn. Yet to see further and learn faster men must sometimes stand on the shoulders of others.

While the defects of the Act had ensured the Commission's failure to achieve its principal goals, like the creation of parks nationally funded, it did much good work in its twenty-five years. Nearly eighty per cent of recommendations were accepted, but the twenty per cent refused were the more vital ones. The commission's successor of 1992, the Scottish Natural Heritage, has no prospect of faring better in conserving that heritage short of National Park legislation, and a change of heart in central government. The Act must create management boards independent of local authorities, but with full planning powers, full national funding, and full moral support from the government's responsible minister. Senior civil servants, who declare this to be 'impossible' and not practical politics, are misinformed. It has been proven practical, and sustainable long term. It can be made practicable in Scotland too.

OTHER ROLES

Before joining the Countryside Commission, I had become adviser (my advice was taken sometimes) on mountain properties to the National Trust for Scotland, President of the Scottish Mountaineering Club, the Ramblers' Association (Scotland), the Mountaineering Council of Scotland and the Scottish Countryside Activities Council. I founded the latter in 1967 comprising the twenty principal outdoor bodies whose quarter of a million members took recreation in Scotland's countryside. Hence I was well briefed on all the live issues of the day, and made aware of all the differences of opinion that had to be reconciled

My one regret was that while I was embroiled in this work, I was offered (1976) nomination as President of The Alpine Club. I should have liked to accept that honour. I had to say no. The job was no sinecure, but an active office and as such a last straw that would mean sacrifice of conservation work, which I felt just then to be the more urgent. The Alpine Club was not short of better men.

THE SCOTTISH COUNTRYSIDE ACTIVITIES COUNCIL

The daunting task in Scotland was made easier by an important early decision (doctrine) by the Scottish Countryside Activities Council (SCAC). This body embraced the main outdoor groups which lent the decision extra value. The

SCAC decided that in their recreational use of the countryside 'conservation of landscape beauty and wildlife must take priority over any provision of facilities for enjoyment'. In that attitude, SCAC showed more enlightenment than the politicians, or their civil servants, or all but a few landowners, whose exceptions to the general rule were only just sufficient to keep hope alive.

When I first gave attention to the problems of conserving the wildlands, I heard such activity described as selfish by the National Trust's opponents. The Hydro Board's advocates damned objectors who, they alleged, selfishly denied the benefits of electric power to the people of Lochaber. Since their conclusion was so obviously a non sequitur arising out of a false premise, and therefore doubly nonsense, no one took the trouble to counter it. That was a mistake, easy to make. A moment's reflection could show that the Trust and others were not opposing power generation but the siting of a particular dam in Glen Nevis, for which a less harmful site could be found. Few people take the trouble to think – they have always to be told in no uncertain words.

Thereafter, I heard 'selfish' applied to all who opposed afforestation with sitkas of places like Rannoch Moor, or the Trossachs, or the flow country of Caithness, or wherever, on the grounds that they denied a crop and jobs to the people. They denied no such thing, but the same easy sophistry became the plea of every developer of no matter what – chalet and caravan sites, oil-rig platform yards, bull-dozed hill tracks, long distance routes, chair-lifts, quarries – in short of everyone who might find his exploitation of wild land opposed. Taken to its logical conclusion, it could be used to justify a fish factory alongside Glasgow's Burrell Gallery. This *reductio ad absurdam* was ironically matched by its repetition in the 1980s by a few officers of the National Trust for Scotland against mountaineers, who had asked the Trust's executive to honour the Unna Rules.

THE UNNA RULES

Percy Unna was a former President of the Scottish Mountaineering Club, who had headed a successful national appeal for funds to buy Glen Coe for the National Trust (he later funded other acquisitions).

Unna's historic Rules came in the form of a letter, signed in 1937 by Unna on behalf of all contributors to the fund, asking the Trust to allow unrestricted access, while maintaining mountain properties in their primitive condition for all time. Unna was a man of vision and meant 'for all time'. He had envisaged increased pressure on the land and acted accordingly. The Trust accepted the conditions in writing.

By the 1980s, the Trust found itself in the same quandary as the Countryside Commission for Scotland. How to facilitate public enjoyment while conserving natural beauty? The land manager able to fulfil such a task without hitch would earn the biblical greeting, 'Behold, a greater than Solomon is here!'

The hard truth is that when visitor numbers pass beyond a certain point, erosion of ground is bound to occur, wildlife to suffer, scars to appear, and property to be seen to deteriorate. The Trust was no more to be held responsible for such wear and tear than other conservators, in so far as mountain lands become victims of social history. Allowing unrestricted access should have been sufficient, providing nothing was done to facilitate enjoyment and actively encourage use, e.g. by advertising. Even with these restraints wear and tear became apparent.

What then is the remedy? Unna (who died in 1950) framed his Rules because he clearly foresaw (I am informed by those who knew him well) the increase in human pressures. That is why Unna followed his first positive statement on access for all with an equally firm negative: that access should not be made easier or safer by the building of bridges, tracks, signposts, or shelters. It was that very stipulation that had moved the public to contribute. His foresight has since been seen to be justified, for it is precisely where his rules have been breached by persons of lesser vision (e.g. in Glen Coe or on Ben Lawers) that the worst erosion occurred.

Hill-walkers accordingly asked the Trust to honour the Unna Rules by continuing full privilege of access as before, but doing nothing to increase use of impaired ground by directing people to it from reception centres (where the Trust earns needed money), or signposts, or by pamphlets. This request, fully in accord with Unna's twofold policy, led a few of the Trust's own members to think of the policy as selfish, and self-contradictory in putting up barriers (by denying information) to open access. Both these points were Orwellian doublethink. The Unna Rules were ignored by the National Trust to the land's detriment – and ours.

Are mountaineers selfish? There is probably no one alive who is not, since no one is yet perfect. Equally, people can be unselfish. I know Unna was, and so too are his present-day supporters, whose attitudes I find exemplified in that repeated decision of the Scottish Countryside Activities Council, that where access to open country and conservation seriously clash, priority should be given to conservation.

Mountaineers are a small proportion of hill-walkers, but for all of them access is the one thing most needed for selfish reasons – their own enjoyment of wild lands. Despite that fact, and for reasons not selfish, they also want to share that enjoyment with others, including those who come after them. The wish arises from an emotion of fellow feeling natural to humankind, allied to plain logic: we are all able to enjoy the wild lands today because people of the past left them to us unscarred. We can continue to enjoy them only if we continue to conserve them; therefore, if some sacrifice of their use has to be made right now, this will benefit all who come after us.

Those who describe mountaineers as selfish on this score are worse than wrong. They contribute to the bad idea that access to, and use of, wild land may be prompted and indeed encouraged without discrimination, for short-term gains, and with no regard to the interest of the next generation. In this they contribute to a betrayal of trust. I feel sure that is not their real intention, but the potential harm wrought by such seemingly egalitarian thinking is immense.

A SELF-DENYING ORDINANCE

Some sacrifice of land use has got to be accepted when the real need for it comes. The need has appeared. Withholding positive promotion of access is the only restraint that is needed at present. Properties can be held for the enjoyment of all, who will find them for themselves through their love of wild lands. This is an approach endorsed by the John Muir Trust, of which I was a founder member and Trustee. Hill-walkers, in turn, should halt the positive promotion in book and magazine publications of Munro collection for collection's own sake, a manic end in itself. Scotland has 277 mountains over 3,000 feet known as Munros and today erosion seriously affects them. They are scarred and quagmired. People frequently no longer go their own hill ways, widely dispersed, but follow guidebook routes in hordes to the destruction of the scene. This new erosion is not due to wind or weather but to pressure of feet, or even wheels. It is man-made.

Even remote mountain areas now exhibit the effects of people. High camps in the Himalaya and Everest itself are becoming dumps strewn with every conceivable detritus of previous expeditions from discarded oxygen cylinders to discarded bodies. I have to hope that reports are exaggerated ... but I wonder. With expeditions to Everest now continual, in season the mountain has ladders and fixed ropes in place. On the summit ridge to the north a twenty-foot aluminium ladder has been put in place by the Chinese. There can be congestion problems on the mountain as people queue – a serious matter at altitude where slowness can lead to benightment and death.

After the recce of 1951 we advised the Swiss and Everest Committee of the need of ladders to cope with the heavily crevassed ice-fall to allow passage for load-carrying Sherpas – never dreaming what was to follow. Deaths have proportionately increased and some incidents suggest that respect for life can be outweighed by personal ambition.

Today one only has to write of an unspoilt area to put it in danger. This was not always so. Perhaps we writers were slow to perceive the change. Less 'unknown' land, fewer cliffs, climbs even, are left to seek and find – to our diminishment. And of course the old adage to 'leave no sign of your passing' is not followed.

I had to face a similar situation in the middle sixties. David Brower, the Director of the Sierra Club of San Francisco, which had been founded by John Muir in 1892 to conserve American wild land, invited me to write a book on the wild lands of Scotland. It would be heavily illustrated with full page colour photographs of highest quality. The writing had to be descriptive writing at its best. The idea was that readers, their eyes opened to the natural beauty of their own land, would want to preserve it. It was a challenge I would have enjoyed – I was tempted. I liked the idea – the Sierra Club's Exhibit Format series of books on the world's wild lands had been splendid productions. But I knew now that the practical effect would not be what David Brower hoped, for Scotland's wild lands, unlike those of the USA, were unprotected. The better the book, the more tourists would come to see the wild lands portrayed. Quite involuntarily, numbers would destroy them by erosion – 'each the other's blight'.[1] I declined to write.

RIGHTS AND RESPONSIBILITIES

Like the hill-lovers who fought for access long before Unna, those of today want no barriers to access. 'The Right to Roam' – open access for all to moor and mountain – is an ideal worth fighting for. But 'the right' is a paradox, for its ideal can become practical only when 'the right' is seen as a privilege. Those who earn the term selfish are of two groups, each a notorious minority to either side of the land-owning pale. First the outdoor fraternity harbours among its great numbers those who wreck bothies, fire heather and trees and destroy the wildlife that shelter and feed in them, vandalise first aid posts, steal campers' gear and equipment, leave litter, create noise, and among other ills disrupt the rights and activities of others who use land for work or recreation. Such louts have forfeited their right to roam. Worse, they call down curbs that deprive others of the rights that might otherwise be theirs. Therefore we should all talk less of rights than privileges, which entail responsible action until the day comes when we have learned the lesson.

The second group are those who, holding land, whether in trust or in public or private ownership, would expend the qualities that make the hills worth knowing, their beauty and peace, for expedient motives, or money, or for other quick convenience of our time. Beware the exploiters! Easy presumptions like 'the mountain properties exist for public enjoyment', if wrongly interpreted, lead to misconception. It implies that the wild lands and wildlife are there to minister to our needs for recreation. That becomes true only as a

1 Wordsworth's 'Cave of Staffa'

secondary function. The primary fact is that land and wildlife have their own being in their own right and our true interest is bound up with theirs. Thus our recreation on wild land is an incidental gain, not an end in itself to be reached by exploiting land when that means degrading it.

The human privilege is to take decisions for more than our own good; our reward, that it turns out to be best for us too.

38 Tomorrow

All my life my curious fingers have turned the pages of time with interest, sometimes with trepidation, but more often eagerly, anticipating desired days. Where there has been doubt about future events I have usually managed to do the best I can and, after due consideration, forget the doubts which would only fog the present and be content to leave events in the hands of Providence. I could do no more than this. I have been fortunate in being able to 'simply control my mind' (not easy, as Anne would tell me when urged to do likewise). It takes practice; I don't brood on dire outcomes over which I have no control. Such is counter-productive. Single-mindedness can cut a swathe where blunt instruments fail.

The world and man have always had problems and too few easy answers. Struggle is endemic. The young of today have challenges to meet, much to do if our world is to be retained. It must be held sacrosanct, not regarded as a commodity to be used and abused – a process roundly detrimental and ultimately destructive.

For myself, and for all of us, however much we strive to see, tomorrow is a closed door. Even when opened to allow us through to a new day, we will find that day has layers beyond our eyes' curious viewing, invisible still, sensed but not seen. We may seek the holds under its surface, strange to our touch, exult in their roughness and firmness in the firmament's space – try to fathom the route, find the way, understand more – and perhaps we will. We must foresee as competently, as intelligently as we can and act accordingly for good.

As I end this book I believe that it will be my last. With the exception of *Mountaineering in Scotland,* written in prison camps, I have written all my books here at this cottage on the loch's shore. This is my twentieth book and if I do write another I hope that it will be here – the loch and hills beyond my window, the still heron on the shore intent on waves, a seal pulling up on to the jetty – quietness.

I have found my way through the years, not always easily and certainly not affluently, but I have had riches and there has always been a thread to follow.

I am aware now of not being young. Time may be limited. But the past was a good age to live in. I was lucky to view the world earlier when more was unspoiled, untouched. Looking back over a wide landscape, cloud shadows racing over the mountain, sun, wind – I know that I have known beauty.

All the days light was ours ...

We walked the heights that day
The sky a blue sea around us;
Strode with the sun the arched ridges
Of the earth's bare rim
Rejoicing that the globe's white spinning held us there
Against the pull and spill of space

So slight were we
Who walked the edge

So brief our hold
Who had the world beneath our feet

Epilogue

Bill died before seeing his book published. He knew he still had much work to do on it but basically it was finished and passed to me for first editing. I was the reader, having the distance an author lacks when his book is newly off the typewriter. We were collaborating on the editing when events took matters out of his hands.

At Easter [1995] he fell while repairing the roof of the house. I heard a slither and a fall and found him on rocks at the edge of the loch. Not being in the habit of falling he was more concerned about this aberration than about his injuries.

Hospital examination revealed a problem with an artery below the heart – an aortic aneurysm – which could have caused him to black out when bending over the roof's edge.

Despite the potentially serious nature of this illness Bill enjoyed the best summer weather we ever had at Loch Goil. Even the midges were in abeyance and days were lived outside, loving the colours of the garden, the loch and the surrounding hills, and working. Bill even insisted on balancing precariously on ledges on the cliff in the garden to cut overgrown heather. His fall had not deterred him from heights.

He appeared to have recovered but in December a hospital check-up revealed the need for surgery. We were taken aback, especially as the proposed operation in three days' time, had, at best a fifty-fifty chance of success.

Bill felt fine. He had a book to finish and wanted to get on with it.

'You'll be out in a week,' the surgeon said. 'You are very fit.'

I doubted both statements. I wondered about his chances of surviving surgery and after that the uncertainties of NHS after-care.

In the event, the complications I had feared materialised. After the operation there were indeed follow-up problems including hospital infection and pulmonary oedema – the latter regarded by Bill as a hazard of altitude and Himalayan climbing and not as a hazard of the NHS. Moreover in hospital he would have expected early diagnosis and treatment.

Finally, about to be discharged despite laboured breathing, he suffered a serious cardiac arrest.

By February 1996 he had recovered sufficiently to return home. He saw the hills again, walked in his garden by the water's edge. He even picked up his pen – he was going to write again. He was very glad to be back.

Four weeks later a relapse forced me to take him back to hospital. 'Just a slight set-back,' he assured me.

He seemed to improve, even discussing this book with me.

Two days later he died.

Giving the address at Bill's funeral service his friend, Professor Donald McIntyre remembered the previous time Bill had been ill in hospital:

> 'He had little strength to speak but he told me he was going to die, indeed the doctors thought this very likely. Bill looked on death, and indeed on every eventuality, with quite extraordinary composure. He knew no fear. As an experienced mystic he was confident that through death he would arrive at a higher level of perception and adoration.
>
> *Integer Vitae Scelerisque Purus*
>
> The man whose life is characterised by moral integrity and whose heart is pure needs not the weapons of lesser mortals.
>
> Bill exemplified the truth of Horace's words. He trained himself to develop Purity, Fearlessness, Truthfulness, Selflessness, Humility and Love of all fellow creatures. Again and again Bill advised us that "Our search for beauty has to be a conscious one – wings do not grow of their own accord".
>
> "May it not be possible" he wrote, "by some practical method to help one's mind to grow in awareness of beauty, to develop that faculty of perception, which we frustrate and stunt if we do not exercise? The answer is that growth may be given to the body by awakening it from slumber, providing nourishment then giving hard exercise. In this work there is no static position; one goes on or one drops back. Therefore and above all persist."
>
> Bill persisted.'

I came out of that crematorium on a hill into the cut of spring sunshine. The wide expanse of the Firth of Clyde, water glittering, stretched northwards to the high hills, rugged against the winded sky …

Anne B. Murray

APPENDIX I: Murray's Books, Plays and Articles plus a selection of relevant articles and books by others

Books and ***Plays*** are in emboldened italics, '*articles*' are in italics with inverted commas, *magazines, journals* and *booklets* are in italics, * indicates fiction; *AJ* – Alpine Journal; *SMJC* – Scottish Mountaineering Club Journal; *MC* – Mountain Craft

(N.B. There are various additional newspaper and magazine articles that are not recorded here.)

Mountaineering in Scotland (Dent, London, 1947, new edition 1962; paperback: Aldine, London, 1967) Rock and ice-climbing adventures in winter and summer. An acknowledged classic. Reprinted since 1979 as part of an omnibus edition with *Undiscovered Scotland.*

Rock Climbs: Glencoe and Ardgour (Scottish Mountaineering Club, Edinburgh, 1949) A guidebook.

Undiscovered Scotland (Dent, London, 1951) Post-war Scottish climbing and walking adventures but with more far flung areas. Reprinted since 1979 as part of an omnibus edition with *Mountaineering in Scotland.*

The Scottish Himalayan Expedition (Dent, London 1951) An account of a wide-ranging expedition to the Garhwal/Kamaon region of the Indian Himalaya. Abridged as part of this book.

The Story of Everest (Dent, London/Dutton, New York, April, 1953) 193pp; revised and reprinted in May, July, August (218pp), November 1953; Second edition, February 1954 (230pp). A comprehensive commentary on all Everest attempts published just as the successful expedition reached Base Camp. The early editions contain discussions on how the climb might be conducted and how oxygen might be employed. Later reprints and the second edition covered the unfolding story of the successful ascent. An authoritative and up-to-date book in print at a time of huge national interest in the subject (*The Ascent of Everest* being published in November 1953). The book received 'The Literature Award of the United States Education Board' in 1954.

'For the first time a complete and reliable account … excellently done.' *The Times.*

Five Frontiers* (Dent, London/Dutton, New York, 1959) A spy thriller ranging from the Hebrides, the Maritime Alps and Nepal. The American title was *Appointment in Tibet.*

'A prodigious adventure … the story races along.' *The Herald.*

The Spurs of Troodos* (Dent, London, 1960) A sequel to *Five Frontiers* – set mostly in Cyprus.

Maelstrom* (Secker and Warburg, London, 1962) A novel with sailing and climbing based on the Western Highlands.

'A rousing tale of pursuit … unhesitatingly recommended.' *The Guardian.*

Highland Landscape (National Trust of Scotland, 1962) Murray's landscape report published (once only, by special permission) in book form for greater political punch. The book highlights twenty-one areas.

The Craft of Climbing (Kaye and Ward, London, 1964) Written jointly with J.E.B. Wright. Part technique, part descriptive and part polemical. Murray indulged in a rare ethical comment:

> 'When pegs are used on climbs of severe standard or less, the time has come to pronounce "anathema". The nailing of new routes that are only severe is a mean practice. There was a time when action so poor-spirited was unheard of. Men who could not force a new route without a piton turned back and left it for someone who could. The writer has been lucky enough to climb many new routes but would have climbed few had his predecessors had chosen to nail the cruxes. If we cannot make a route go it is reasonable humility in us if we reckon that a better climber than ourselves somewhere exists. Who is the best climber in the land? The slam of hammer on piton cries Me, Me, Me!'

It is not clear what had prompted this warning. Bell and MacInnes were not averse to using the odd piton and by the mid-sixties piton use was becoming more prevalent on the big rock problems of Scotland by a range of leading climbers. Standards were rising but protection techniques were not keeping pace.

Dark Rose the Phoenix* (Secker and Warburg, London/Mackay, New York, 1965) A spy story set in Paris, the Rhineland and Andorra.

The Hebrides (Heinemann, London, 1966, 2nd Edition 1975) General description and culture.

Companion Guide to the West Highlands of Scotland (Collins, Glasgow, 1968, reprinted until 1985).

'Almost every paragraph evokes its own memory of the varied West Highland landscape.' *Times Literary Supplement.*

The Real Mackay* (Heinemann, London 1969) 'A comedy of highland life in twelve stories.'

The Islands of Western Scotland (Eyre Methuen, London, 1973) General description, geology and culture but in far greater depth than *The Hebrides.*

The Scottish Highlands (Scottish Mountaineering Trust, Edinburgh, 1976) A title in the SMC's long running series of District guides.

Mountaineering in Scotland/Undiscovered Scotland (Diadem, London 1979, reprinted 1980, 1982 and 1986) and in trade paperback (Diadem, London, 1992); new trade paperback edition (Bâton Wicks, 1997, reprint 1999).

The Curling Companion (Richard Drew, Glasgow, 1981) A commissioned book on the history and culture of the sport. Murray commented about this to Sheriff David Smith (an expert Curling writer): 'I have spent much of my life writing about vertical ice so I didn't find it too difficult transferring to horizontal ice for a period.'

Rob Roy MacGregor: His Life and Times (Richard Drew, Glasgow, 1982; paperback edition: Canongate, Edinburgh, 1993, reprinted 1995).

Scotland's Mountains (Scottish Mountaineering Trust, Edinburgh, 1987) A companion title to the District Guide series with a strong geological, ecological and cultural stress.

Journal and magazine articles by W.H. Murray, plus two plays and essays or chapters in other books:

Pre-war *SMCJ* articles: *'Defeat (A December Night on the Crowberry Ridge)' SMCJ* 21, 1937. The *Garrick's Shelf* epic; *'The Great Gully of Sgor nam Fiannaidh' SMCJ* 21, 1938. The *Clachaig Gully* climb; *'Hogmanay on Ben Nevis' SMCJ* 22, 1940; *'Notes on Blood and Glucose Diet' SMCJ* 22, 1940. Concerning the Greater Cuillin Ridge (including Blaven) traverse; *'Last Day on the Buachaille' SMCJ* 23, 1942; *'The Evidence of Things Not Seen' SMCJ* 23, 1946.

'Review' of ***The Island of Skye*** (SMC Guidebook) *AJ* 57, 1949.

'The Scottish Himalayan Expedition' SMCJ 24, 1951.

'The Scottish Garhwal and Kamaon Expedition' AJ 58, 1951.

'The Reconnaissance of Mount Everest, 1951' AJ 58, 1952. Murray's fullest account of this trip ... very comprehensive. The article ends with a summary of the difficulties and advantages of the Nepalese route in comparison to that from Tibet. Murray makes no mention of the incident in Tibet that Ang Tharkay resolved.

> 'It is worth recording that this is the first instance where the members of an Everest expedition have chosen themselves, chosen their leader, and initiated the expedition. It is unlikely to happen again.'

'Review' of J.H.B. Bell's ***A Progress of Mountaineering***. *SMCJ* 24, 1951

The Game of Love (a three-act play concerning St Francis of Assisi) and ***William Wallace*** (a three-act play). Two plays that were never produced – see comments in Chapter 33 – written during the early 1950s.

'British Mountains', a chapter in ***The Age of Mountaineering*** by James Ramsey Ullman (Collins, London, 1956).

'Review' of ***White Fury*** by Raymond Lambert and Claude Kogan (Hurst & Blackett, London, 1956) *AJ* 61, 1956.

> 'The book as a literary work reveals a most successful experiment in padding ... Mme Kogan makes some recompense by offering (p. 84) a most excellent thumb-nail sketch of true love in action ... [They were stopped at 26,500ft on Cho Oyu] by bad weather – hence the book's title. Since they [had in their supplies] ... no less than thirty-five quarts of whisky, the storm

> must have been very terrible indeed – or the whisky not Scotch. ... The translation is well done [but] ... our ears seem to catch, from a distant valley, the bark of a shaggy dog.'

'Slings and Pegs' (*MC* 42, 1959); *'Axe and Crampon'* (*MC* 51, 1961); *'The Rope in Rock Climbing'* (*MC* 54, 1962) – three discursive articles on technique (with historical examples and anecdotes) written for the magazine *Mountain Craft* at a time when Murray was much involved with the Mountaineering Association.

'The Country of the Blind' SMCJ 27, 1963. A call to protect the mountain landscape.

'The Last Twenty-Five Years' SMCJ 28, 1964. An overview of Scottish climbing – made at the end of Murray's period as SMC President.

'Wild Scotland – a priceless asset in danger' An article for *The Scots Magazine* February, 1968.

'A Traveller's Tale: There was this Englishman and this Scotsman' An account of the events and pressures that led to the secession of Scottish climbers from the BMC and the setting up of the Mountaineering Council of Scotland. *Mountain Life* 8, June 1972.

'The Formation of the JMCS: The Glasgow Section, 1935–1940' SMCJ 30, 1975.

'J.H.B. Bell as a Climber' The main section of a comprehensive obituary record for the great Scottish climber. A valuable historical commentary. *SMCJ* 31, 1976.

'The C.I.C. Hut – 1930s' Part of a decade-by-decade history of the role of the hut. *SMCJ* 31, 1976.

'Reconnaissance, 1951' an essay in ***The Book of Modern Mountaineering*** (Arthur Barker, London, 1968):

> 'Every mountain instinct I possessed revolted at the thought of going into it [the Khumbu Icefall] ... we finally made the climb to the top. For my own part, I had to climb while suppressing a sense of impending disaster. Our ascent therefore was peculiarly useful, not only in proving the icefall climbable, but in breaking the psychological barrier and showing that the sense of heavy menace was illusory.'

'Tower Ridge' An essay in ***Classic Rock*** (Granada, London, 1978).

'The High Tops' The first chapter in ***The Wildlife of Scotland*** by Fred Holliday (Macmillan, London 1979). Murray was one of eleven invited authors.

'New Year on Ben Nevis' An essay in ***The Winding Trail*** (Diadem, London, 1981).

'Buachaille Etive Mor' An essay in ***Classic Walks*** (Diadem, London, 1982).

'Prisoner of War' An essay in ***Mirrors in the Cliffs*** (Diadem, London, 1983).

'Newspeak in the Hills' An article in *Wild Land News* 3, Spring 1984.

'Writing and Climbing' The BMC speech reprinted in Appendix III. *Climber*, November, 1984.

'A Question of Intent' An article in the *John Muir Trust Newsletter* 1, August 1985

'My Cairngorms' An article in *'Cairngorms at a Crossroads'* (Scottish Wild Land Group, Edinburgh, 1987).

'The Perfect Rock Climb' An essay in ***Mountains*** (John Murray, London). Concerns an ascent of the Rosa Pinnacle.

'John Hartog' An obituary note. *SMCJ* 33, 1987.

'Peculiarities of a High Climber' SMCJ 35, 1993. Here Murray presents a questionnaire about high-altitude climbing sent to him (as SMC President) by Eugene Gippenreiter (of the Mountaineering Federation of the USSR). This was clearly bureaucratically inspired – an official attempt to pinpoint aspects of high-altitude performance. John Hartog and Tom Patey provided most of the answers.

'Leyton Johnstone's Resurrection' SMCJ* 34, 1990. A climber reappears six months after being lost on *Tower Ridge*.

Reviews of ***North West Highlands*** by Donald Bennet and Tom Strang, and ***One Step in the Clouds*** compiled by Audrey Salkeld and Rosie Smith. *SMCJ* 34, 1990. The latter (dealing with a mountain fiction anthology) is interesting in revealing Murray's tastes and opinions on the genre.

'The Old Loch Lomond Road' An article in *Friends of Loch Lomond Newsletter*, Autumn 1992.

'Archie MacAlpine' An obituary note. *SMCJ* Vol. 35, 1995.

Articles and books by others that are relevant to this book:

Robert Aitken Obituary notice: *'Bill Murray's work in Mountain Conservation' SMCJ* 36. 1996.

Robert Aitken *W.H. Murray – Mountain Conservationist* (Scottish Countryside Activities Council, 2000) A booklet summarising Murray's conservation work (reprinting much that was in his *SMCJ* obituary) with valuable additional information, contacts and reference sources.

Anon 'The accident on the Col de la Coste Rouge' *AJ* 56, 1947.

J.H.B. Bell *'Valhalla' SMCJ* 22, 1940. The 1939 *Tower Ridge* ascent with Murray and Laidlaw.

J.H.B. Bell *'A Ben Nevis Constellation of Climbs' SMCJ* 22, 1941.

J.H.B. Bell ***A Progress of Mountaineering*** (Oliver and Boyd, Edinburgh, 1950). This contains numerous small references to Murray and full accounts of Bell's 1939 winter ascents of *Tower Ridge, Observatory Ridge* and *North-East Buttress* with the Murray and others.

Sandy Cousins and others '*The Coruisk Affair' SMCJ* 29, 1969. A detailed account of the exchanges, meetings and correspondence attending the now notorious plan to establish a road to the head of Loch Coruisk thereby penetrating and thus despoiling one of the finest tracts of wild mountain country in Britain.

Ken Crocket ***Ben Nevis – Britain's Highest Mountain*** (Scottish Mountaineering Trust, Edinburgh, 1986). Reference to several climbs involving Murray and his friends and particularly valuable in explaining the *Orion Face* events and complexities.

Al Gore ***Earth in the balance; Forging a new common purpose*** (Earthscan, London, 1992). Gore quotes a Murray dictum in his introduction:

> 'I hope you, too, will make a commitment to bring the earth back to balance, for as W.H. Murray has said: "'Until one is committed there is hesitancy, the chance to draw back, always ineffectiveness. Concerning all acts of initiative ... there is one elementary truth, the ignorance of which kills countless ideas and splendid plans: that the moment one commits oneself, then providence moves too."'

M.A. Douglas Hamilton 'Review' of ***Mountaineering in Scotland*** *AJ* 56, 1947. Complimentary comments noting the book's importance in revealing the fine sport to be had in Scotland.

Arnold Heim and August Gansser ***In the Throne of the Gods*** (Morgarten, Zurich, 1938; Macmillan, London, 1939). Early explorations in the Api Massif.

B.H. Humble ***The Cuillin of Skye*** (Robert Hale, London, 1952).

A.G. Hutchison and others *'The Formation of the JMCS' SMCJ* 30, 1975.

W.M. Mackenzie *'Fourteen Hours on Observatory Ridge' SMCJ* 21, 1938. An account of the February 1938 ascent with MacAlpine and Murray.

Donald McIntyre Obituary notice: *'Tribute to W.H. Murray, OBE., Honorary President'* plus additional tributes by Douglas Scott and W.M. Mackenzie.

Kenneth Mason *Abode of Snow* (Rupert Hart Davis, London, 1955; Diadem, London, 1987).

Wilfrid Noyce 'Review' of ***The Scottish Himalayan Expedition*** *AJ* 58, 1952. An approving notice that finishes with a paragraph discussing religion in which the reviewer misinterpreted the author's intentions. This prompted the following letter from Murray to the Editor (*AJ* 59, 1953):

> 'Dear Sir,
>
> I have to thank Wilfrid Noyce for his kind review of my book ... but am outraged by his perverting the meaning of an important passage. He ascribes to me a 'sense of oneness with the mountain universe around whose "name men call God ..."'. Let me say at once that I wrote no such nonsense. The reviewer would foist on to me a pantheism that I detest, and which I hold in less honour than a relatively healthy agnosticism. The passage to which it refers occurs on page 50. It is not the mountain universe, but the integrating principle of the universe, whose name men call God, etc. Since the passage states this fact in English that could hardly be more clear, I feel justified in asking you to publish my disclaimer.
>
> Yours truly W.H. Murray'

A.H. Savage Landor ***Tibet and Nepal*** (A. and C. Black, London, 1905). The first Api explorations.

Eric Shipton ***The Mount Everest Reconnaissance Expedition, 1951*** (Hodder and Stoughton, London/Dutton, New York, 1952). The main book of the expedition – comprehensively illustrated.

John Tyson *'Exploring the Api and Nampa Group'. AJ* 59, 1954. The main account of the expedition.

Walt Unsworth ***Everest – the mountaineering history*** Alan Lane, London, 1981; Oxford Illustrated Press, Yeovil, 1989; The Mountaineers, Seattle/Bâton Wicks, London, 2000.

Michael Ward ***In This Short Span*** (Gollancz, London, 1972). With Ward's account of the Dauphiné accident, the Everest Reconnaissance and other adventures with Murray and others.

Michael Ward *'The Yeti Footprints: Myth and Reality' AJ* 104, 1999. A debate over the tracks found below Menlungste in 1951.

Michael Ward *'The Great Angtharkay: A Tribute'*[1] *AJ* 101, 1996. Here Ward discusses the Sherpa's role in the incident in Tibet after the Menlungste reconnaissance. (This was not mentioned in either Shipton's book or Murray's *AJ* article.)

> 'As the Tibetans approached us the shouting started. Not to be outdone our Sherpas replied, Angtharkay leading the onslaught with messianic vigour. After about ten minutes he came over to us and suggested that we poor Europeans should retire for a suitable distance. … Later he returned … "Everything is settled he said … At the time the incident was treated light-heartedly … but it was potentially rather more serious because Shipton had just left the Foreign Office, I was in the army and Tom Bourdillon was a rocket scientist. Only Bill Murray was a free agent. In others words three of us were connected to the British Government."' (See also Chapter 25 of this book.)

Adam Watson *'The Vanishing Wilderness' Mountain Life* 11, 1974.

Tom Weir ***The Ultimate Mountains*** (Cassell, London, 1953). A more 'chatty' account of the 1950 Garhwal trip.

1 The author's spelling is preserved in this item though Ang Tharkay is the norm elsewhere in the book. The Sherpa's headed notepaper in 1951 was inscribed 'Ang Tarke Sirdar' but his letter was signed Ang Tharkay.

APPENDIX II: Sundry Correspondence

ENLISTMENT AND LIFE IN THE ARMY
Letters written to Murray's sister Margaret and his brother-in-law, Archie MacAlpine.

68 Westland Drive, Glasgow W4
19.6.1940

Dear Margaret,

Very many thanks for your letter. You may be right about me and the army – we'll see. Anyhow I'll get along ok and it can't be much worse than the bank, which I loathed but tolerated for the sake of my mountaineering. So far as the war goes either we'll lose this summer or we'll win any time between winter 1940 and 1950. If the former, I reckon I've got a good chance of survival under unpleasant conditions; if the latter, I entertain no hopes. You yourself should be all right with reasonable luck whatever happens. Don't worry about the war or about Archibald. I calculate that we'll win this war because Germans hate flying across water, and Archibald is fairly adept at looking after himself.

Meantime the JMCS still goes on, there were sixteen at the meet last Sunday in Glencoe (mostly on the Buachaille). This was done by hiring a bus for £10 for two days.

As a last climb I did the Chasm of the Buachaille. Dry as a bone, party – Redman (an Englishman) and Douglas Laidlaw. Tell Archibald that Ogilvy has done the Girdle Traverse of Rannoch Wall. There are now twenty-six routes on Rannoch Wall. A year ago there were two.

For some months I have had no news of Mackenzie, Dunn, Higgins and Co. But I phoned up Mrs Higgins and found that the 2nd HLI are in Essex and have not been abroad.

Tonight I go to Roganos & the Whitehall for a final feast with Roger, Marshall, MacKinnon etc – I am already due to depart.

Yours, Bill

Platoon 3, Bay, Clackmannanshire
13.7.1940

Dear Margaret,

Here I am at last. I have written a great number of letters since arriving here, but somehow one always writes to one's relatives last of all. However I can at least say that as far you are concerned the prospect fills me with no dismay, but even with pleasure. I propose to tell you more or less exactly what I think of the army life and how I react therefore and how I'm getting on. Viewing the matter detachedly I should think this may interest you.

The general opinion of most people I knew, especially Kenneth Dunn, was that I'd be the world's worst soldier and would hate the life. I accepted this as a compliment (unintentional so far as K.D. was concerned, but intentional from you and Archie) and I agreed that you were probably right. My good opinion of myself has been growing in recent years, however reprehensible such an attitude or development may be. And in regard to social life I'm more or less a self-contained unit.

Perhaps this is because I'm lazy. A large number of acquaintances involves too much work and hassle – out of proportion to their value, and I find I'm more favourably placed than most people. But on the whole I did not look forward to conscription and was properly horrified at the idea of army discipline, red tape, coarse living and separation from mountains not to mention the reduction of thought-life to the brute level.

On arriving here I soon found that the company was hopelessly uncongenial. There was no one whom I had the slightest desire to have as a friend either now or later, there was no one, in fact, to whom one could talk intelligently. As a matter of interest I have actually had to write letters home for a Manchester man who can neither read nor write. He dodged all schooling and can only sign his own name. Such things as mountain climbing, philosophy or psychology, art of any kind and so on, are considered too exotic even to be mentioned without embarrassment.

Life in barracks is dull and noisy. I have spent a good part of my life in the company of men, and thought I should hear little new of swearing and filthy language, but I was wrong. The style of conversation has truly been a revelation to me. I didn't think it possible. It is interesting to note that although I've been here a month I haven't heard one bawdy song or dirty joke. The normal life is too "coarse" to bother with attempted witticisms on the subject, any more than one troubles to crack jokes about banking or dentistry.

The pleasures of army life are entirely sensual and conform exactly to the six main pleasures of life as laid down by Feuchtwanger – eating, drinking, sleeping, excrementing and fornicating.[1] No one can deny that all these undeniable

1 Lion Feuchtwanger 1884–1958 – prolific German/Jewish playwright, novelist, biographer and historian from Munich. His works include *Jud Süss* 1925 (published as *Jew Suss* in the UK) which was highly praised

pleasures are enjoyed by most people on earth at some time and that therefore they must be the principal pleasures of the human race. Or can you?

The food is usually lousy, but dinner is not a bad meal. The suppers are always two slices of white bread and one teaspoonful of jam. At dinner one gets all one can possibly eat, stew, beans or cabbage and dough pudding; it never changes.

The actual outside work – eleven hours a day for seven days a week – is as hard as it can be without people cracking up.

I have now stated the background of existence at Tillicoultry. Your prognostications about my reactions therefore are at once partly correct and hopelessly wrong.

(a) I loathe the food, but I have the money to buy my evening meals either in the canteen or in Tillie hotels.
(b) I can't forget the mountains.
(c) At first I missed companionship and all intimacy and privacy. But now I get along excellently as a sort of solo or isolated unit. I maintain first class relations with everyone from the uneducated oaf who can't read or write, from the razor slasher to the Company Commander, and off the field I don't give a damn for anyone and find plenty to do in my spare time. Besides I have a lot of correspondence – mainly Donaldson, Mackenzie, Bell and Garrick.
(d) The work is very hard and discomforts not inconsiderable. But I find that I can stand the physical strains better than most people here. The strains I've had in mountaineering are greater than any I'll ever have at Tillie. The only point is that here the strain never slacks off. As a consequence I'm fitter than I've ever been in my life. The sense of physical well-being is simply intense.

Discomforts at Tillie are just trifling compared with those of mountaineering. To everyone else they were new. Through mountaineering I've had a big advantage over everyone else. For example some of the men on guard duty this week had to stand for four hours (two hours on – four hours off – two hours on) in high wind and rain. They came in nearly dropping with cold and exhaustion – none of them had ever spent such a terrible night before – literally never before! The fuss that they made was terrific. Visions of Garrick's Shelf, Observatory Ridge, Tower Ridge, Crowberry Gully, S.C. Gully and my Chasm climb last month flitted through my mind.
(e) The toughness of the men is entirely superficial. It sounds good in the barrack room and is quite valueless in action. Thus I have the advantage of most of the conscripts for the physical and mental aspects of army work.

---

by Arnold Bennett, and *Erfolg*, 1930 (one of a series of four novels) – a satire on the Munich putsch. Targeted by the Nazis he moved to France in 1933 and visited Russia, was interned by Vichy in 1940 but escaped to the USA where he linked up with Brecht and other emigres.

(f) The training is absorbingly interesting. We have the usual dull parade ground drill, which I accomplished with ease so that the sergeants never knew I existed – the best way of earning their gratitude.

We have parade drill for an hour each morning. Its only purpose is to get us to act quickly on command and to be on the alert to hear offensive types of orders. The training is interesting because we are being pushed so fast. Six months training has to be done now in two months. They do this by making us do three times as much work per day as formerly. But in consequence there is so much variety and change in relatively short times that the work never seems dull nor monotonous.

Even on our first day we started not with drill but with Bren guns (anti-tank rifles). We have to be able to take them all to pieces which are innumerable, and put them up again in quick time, to know exactly how all the parts work and the theory of them working; we have loading, unloading, shooting, selection of the best defensive positions in the field etc. We have bayonet fighting, fencing, ordinary rifle shooting, field craft and gas work etc. The latter two afford much entertainment.

One could write volumes on field craft – i.e. fighting across open country and the countless dodges thereof. This includes camouflage. One can hide a platform on a perfectly flat field so that no one can be seen from the end of that field. By lying down and using minor depressions and tufts of grass, one can approach within ten yards of a man also lying and not be seen. One learns how to use shadow as a perfect camouflage, the gentlest undulations of ground for effective concealment and all manner of natural obstacles, trees, streams, gorse, boulders as defensive and offensive points. We also have practice shooting tanks.

All this is as yet elementary. Night work will start soon. The gas instruction is just deadly. We try all the gases used in warfare. Firstly with respirators then without so that we can recognise them by their smells and first effects. The latter are most unpleasant. We even get phosgene which drowns the victim in his own lymph and is worst gas yet known. The chloropicuim feels worse being a tear gas as well as a choking gas. All this is very vague but I mention it to show you that life is far from dull. I can honestly say that I am enjoying the 'poor bloody infantry' very much indeed, outside of barracks. Inside barracks I get along OK through a technique that seems peculiar to me.

Last Monday I was up at Stirling Castle being interviewed by some brass hats for a commission that I have been recommended by my company commander. This second interview went off okay and I was again recommended, in consequence thereof I am booked for an OTC sometime this summer. I have still to get a final OK from a general of the Scottish command but I'm told that this is a formality unless I make a bloody fool of myself. Again I may fail to pass the OTC exams but I don't think so. It would mean four more months training.

Air raids, all by night, are quite frequent hereabouts. One of them was most spectacular. We lay out in ditches and watched a great search light display, while AA guns got into action with a roar and the sky was alight with exploding shells and the glow of bursting bombs. I counted eleven of the latter. One German plane was caught in searchlight cross beams and was brought down in flames. We saw all this of course. Last night they tried again but missed us and hit Dollar instead which is two miles away. Two people were killed. We could feel the blast in the barracks which may seem incredible but is true.

Just now I'm reading Leslie Stephen's *Agnostics Apology* and a comparison between yoga and psycho analysis (both lent to me by Donaldson). I have also read Joad's *Philosophy For Our Times* which I recommend. What are your opinions on Christian ethics in general? I'd like to know what you think without leg-pulling please. Please give my regards to Archie. It might be an idea if you sent him this letter – after replying to it if I can persuade you to do that. I wrote to him after getting here but haven't had a reply yet.

How do you like your new house and how is Roderick getting on?

Yours, Bill

The Highland Light Infantry,
Maryhill Barracks, Glasgow
7.1.1941

Dear Margaret,

I write very belatedly to thank you for the *The Seven Pillars of Wisdom*. It was exceedingly good of you giving me such a magnificent present for a war-time Xmas. I have been reading it here in my spare time and simply didn't realise before how good it was. I read your own copy once rather hurriedly, but failed to do it justice beyond feeling that I should like to have the book for future reference. Although I am late in acknowledging the present, I can now say more emphatically how much I really enjoy it, through have read chunks.

How are Roderick & Euan and yourself, have you any news of Archie? I have heard only that he is now at Aldershot. I was sorry to miss seeing you all at New Year, but it can't be helped, for the present I collected that afternoon from Donaldson made all the difference to the climbing at Bridge of Orchy.

The meet was most successful – plenty snow and ice, hard frost, blue sky and brilliant sun. With Donaldson, McCarter I did Laoigh Gully, the Upper Couloir of Stob Ghabhar, Centre Gully of Bidian and the Crowberry by

Naismith route. The latter was very hard and was brilliantly led by Donaldson. The upper Couloir ice-pitch was as big and icy as I have ever seen it – led by George Roger!

Charlie Hampton is here, I see him daily in the Mess. He expresses great anxiety to see you and asks for you every day. He is now a Captain but in a different company from myself. He is going to join Sandy Wedderburn at Loch Ailort.

Best Wishes

Yours, Bill

Maryhill Barracks,
Glasgow
13.2.1941

Dear Margaret,

I write in great haste, this morning I received your criticism and my article. Very many thanks. It is all exceedingly valuable.

I can realise now how much time it must take you, and obviously I have no time to correct the articles before I leave. Therefore: please take your time, make your criticising at leisure, and afterwards send the whole works to R.G. Donaldson, Clare College, Cambridge. He is very anxious to see what you think of them and how you criticise such things. If you finish before I leave the country, send them to me. Although I am warned to be all ready to leave next week, they may quite well keep me waiting another week, fortnight, or month – you know what the army is like!

I only wish I had given you the MSS long ago. If I leave at short notice I shall either phone you or get mother to do so.

It is exceedingly good of you bothering to put in so much work for me and I appreciate it greatly.

Yours, Bill

2nd Lt W.H. Murray, Highland Light Infantry
Middle East Forces, Egypt
7.7.1941

Dear Margaret,

I enclose an article on Crowberry Gully and a letter to Gordon Donaldson, Clare College, Cambridge. Please criticise article, read letter to G, and send him the whole issue at the end of the Cambridge summer vacation, which I think is the end of September. If you know his home address, which I don't since he left

Bearsden, you can send the stuff to him sooner. You have only yourself to thank for all this trouble. I was living quite peacefully on the shores of the Bitter Lakes when I received your postcard containing the following passage:

> The lilac is in bloom, cuckoos are calling, Arran is clear of snow and mostly purple in the evening haze, and Roderick has had his first bathe. Four years ago yesterday you were in the Crowberry Gully with A. and Mackenzie. It was pouring rain – I stayed in the tent at Coupall Bridge and you returned wet and slimy and covered in mud. I trust you were not in a similar condition this weekend.

I would have given 5,000 piastres to be back there in the same condition. In all this heat, dust and sweat and barren desert your postcard nearly made me frantic, your reference to Crowberry Gully put me in the mood to make up my last climb there. So now everything has recoiled on your own head. I am pleased to hear about Roderick's progress. It is a help when a person can talk. And if he uses this precious gift to express a desire to go up mountains, I regard it all as a very good omen. In another twenty years he may even be a Secretary of the JMCS which would be a great honour and no little credit to his family. You can tell him I accept the dare for going "up high" among the snow. Nothing would please me more. He may yet have to support his aged relatives.

Archie is lucky still to be in Wales. So are Kenneth and Ross lucky even though they don't believe it. However, I was in Cairo three weeks ago (mid June) for a few days. I had a hectic time during which I climbed the east face of the Great Pyramid of Giza (451 ft.) and came down the north-east ridge. I visited the Sphinx which was well worth seeing, and in Cairo I went round cabarets, mosques, bazaars and other places of renown.

While at the Pyramids we went inside and crawled along passages to the tombs. Three days cost £10. I sent an account of the Pyramids to Bell for his SMC abroad notes if these latter still exist.

The summer is now at its height and the heat sometimes reaches 135 degrees. We have no snakes here, but there are some scorpions (not much in evidence), vultures, storks, camels, flies of every kind and enormous insects. I live in a hut 15 feet by 20 feet by 10 feet which I share with one other officer. We use camp beds, over which mosquito nets are suspended. The floor is carpeted with canvas and there is piles of room. The mess is pretty comfortable and the food fairly good. I may leave here anytime for anywhere except home. I don't require any books, thank you. It might be an idea if you sent this letter on to Archie, or tell him of the contents.

Yours, Bill

P.S. Your postcard of 2 June arrived on 28 June

2nd Lt. W.H. Murray, Cyprus
8.10.1941

Dear Archie and Margaret,

Your letter of 1 June has just arrived! Before replying I had better also acknowledge just a few other letters and cards which you posted just before going to Wales. Actually I have replied to these by Air Mail letter but I think that this aircraft may arrive first though it left a week later.

I do hope you get a really comfortable home in Wales. Wales seems to be a grand place if one has a car to get about in, and if only Archie can get petrol you ought to reach the Welsh mountains occasionally … I shall be most interested to hear what you think of the C.G. article. If by any chance Bell publishes abbreviated version in the *SMCJ*, please say whether you think the short version is better. I think, however, that even the abbreviated version would be too long for the Journal (2,500 words).

I am keeping very well. If my correspondence is not bright it is mainly because I never seem to have a chance to write until about 2200 hrs, at least not for the last month. However I am getting back again to more reasonable hours in fact I have little excuse for this scrawl except the trials of travels. Best wishes for Xmas and New Year. Tell Marshall that Gordon Donaldson and George McCarter are presidents of the CUMC and OUMC respectively.

Yours, Bill

4.12.1941

Dear Archie and Margaret,

I'm still in the best of health, although my usual winter cough has started again. I can say nothing of where I am except that I am no longer in Egypt. Our main trouble is cold for a change. The weather is rather like Autumn days in Britain, with a cold wind, and a bitterly cold starry sky at night. It is very difficult to keep warm although I wear battledress and two sweaters. The trouble is that I had become thoroughly acclimatised to the extreme summer heat of Egypt and Iraq. I had a letter from Ben Humble last week still moaning about Hardstill's refusing to repudiate my old letter, but otherwise cheerful and chatty.

Ross Higgins has a commission RASC. I had a long and interesting letter from Bell recounting some climbs he has done recently on Lochnagar and Nevis. His direct route on Tough-Brown Ridge is terrific (I've done that ridge by the ordinary route with Bell and some small variation). His Girdle traverse of Nevis is an epic which [I] envy him exceedingly. My Crowberry Gully article goes into the April journal. Bell thinks it is my best one so far. He asks me when I return (a) to write the Central Highlands Guide, (b) to edit the *SMCJ*.

I should be obliged however if you would not mention this to anyone in the SMC. It would involve my joining the SMC (in which B & W wish to place me on committee!) of which you can well imagine I am more than doubtful. I hear from mother that you have settled down in Wales, somewhere on a farm. I hope you like it and are getting to the hills. What is your address? I hope to have turkey for Xmas. Tell mother that all mail between 5 Aug and 6 Sept was sent, i.e. her Xmas present to me would go then.

Yours, Bill

Two letters about mysticism written while in captivity:

31.7.1944

Dear Margaret,

Philosophy points the same way, for materialism is exploded. Great art, music, literature – they too indicate the ultimate reality. Observe all forms of beauty, in Nature, in virtues of man, in moral law. They too point but one way – examine the world's greatest religions, behind creed the care is the same Science, Arts, Philosophy, Nature, Religions, all buttress a mountain at whose summit is Beauty, Truth, God, Brahman – choose a name – it is one and the same. People are hasty enough to call this peak unscalable. I seem to have heard that tale before! At first they seem right – philosophy ends in theory, science in speculation, art in intuition, institutional religion in faith – nowhere direct knowledge. They stop one with an overhang. But there *is* a route winding through the overhangs to the summit. The peak has been often climbed. The route is old but the start is hard to find. I have been shown the start and I find that it goes.

The purpose of life and the goal and the way have become for me clear as crystal. I have learned more in four months than during the last thirty years. The point is that the summit may be reached in *this* life. To refuse the ascent is to deny the lessons of life, and to deny the development of the only part of you that is enduring. Result frustration. If you wish I'll describe this route – which has nothing to do with formal religion, creed or dogma – on my return. It involves no renunciation of life nor asceticism, for one must be practical and retain one's common sense. In a letter no more can be said. I keep well, my health was never better.

Yours, Bill

22.9.1944

Dear Margaret,

The philosophy I follow is the idealism best described as "mentalism", which backs the Vedas and the Mahyana of Buddhism. The works of Plato fall within its border, those of Hegel, Kant, etc, whom I have not read in full, seem more vulnerable efforts at same goal. They peter out at a point of solipsism. Thereafter must one either be content with faith – or undertake the mystic training and let reason follow perception. The latter course is scientific, practical and practicable. What type mysticism? There only is one true mysticism. This is at the core of all great religions. The nature of reality does not vary. Everywhere and in all ages the doctrine is the same. Upon it having been built creeds and dogmas to meet national temper and tradition. The creeds have value but are not important to the mystic.

Therefore, the mysticism I follow is that of Sankara's Vedanta-Sutras, of Lao Tse, Christ, Buddha, Plato, etc. These are one and the same, but frequently stress different aspects of reality, which confuses men of narrow vision. Re. literature: get *Bible of the World* (Balhu) and read Vedas, Bhagava Gita, St. John's Gospel, Sri Ramakrishna; *Theosophy* (Muller), *Grey Eminence* (3rd Chpt. Huxley), *Diagnosis of Man* (Walker), *Signature of All Things* (Boehme), *Way of Initiation* (Steiner), *Dialogues* – Plato, Eckhert, etc.

Of the training I shall say nothing. The goal is service of mankind and not withdrawal. The fruits are an undivided mind, inner stillness, self-realisation and a fullness of life that I have believed possible. Fulfilment of life's purpose will be found in oneness with reality.

Yours, Bill

Letters from the famous mountaineer/author whose writing Murray greatly admired. The first is a response to Murray's letter on the circumstances of the death of John Barford (the first Secretary of the recently established BMC). The forthcoming publication of *Mountaineering in Scotland* was also mentioned. The second letter follows the publication of the book and also has observations on two major alpine accidents in 1947 (that to Murray, Ward and Barford in the Dauphiné and the fatal accident to H.E. (Nully) Kretschmer and John Jenkins who fell whilst descending the *Old Brenva* Route). The third letter was written in the aftermath of GWY's visit as a guest to an SMC dinner in Scotland. All the letters were poorly typewritten by Young which explains the errors and lack of fluency.

LETTERS FROM GEOFFREY WINTHROP YOUNG

12 Holland Street, London W8
23.10.46

My Dear Murray,

I have been deeply moved by your letter, and by your thought in writing it.

It is difficult to tell you how much an unexpected word, like yours, can help as one nears the end of a long – and certainly not easy – pilgrimage.

Pain is an extraordinary educator, in real values or life.

I would rather give a helping hand to another mountaineer than have been able to lengthen my own climbing by a year. And you have given me that assurance.

Indeed I shall await your book with very special pleasure and interest.

Geoffrey Winthrop Young

London W8
26.8.47

My dear Murray,

Your book has just come out. And damnably spoilt my morning's writing. I have not resisted dipping twice, and deep into Cir Mhor and Sron na Ciche. Then I shall read it really.

Oh, thank heaven at last – for someone who can write!

I've been writing my 50-years-ago attempt on the Cir Mhor buttress with Sandy Mackay, and a climb on Cioch Slab with Norman Collie, and it has been like opening a book of coloured revelation, only to dip into your chapters on the same cliffs, but such a glorious advance in the knowledge that opens up the innermost of these great cliffs.

I am going to have enormous pleasure, I see, out of it. I feel safe, with you, straight off, and that means a lot, after all the sympathetic reading I do of climbers' efforts-to-record!

I see at once that you've written a book – and the first book – worthy of the subject, that is of Scottish climbing of the high order. I am glad that it was left until you did it!

I'll probably write again, when I have read, and digested ... but here's my first burst of delight – Glory be! – a climber's book, and yet a writer's too!!

I think folk have the facts about John [Barford] correct. I've seen most of his close friends. I shall state them again at the BMC Com. this week and we'll have them written. The reports from all over Alps multiply minor accidents and major, from the same, usually rare, cause ... It was sheer accident, unavoidable, and desperately sad ...

Kretschmer's death and Jenkins' seem to me in a different category; avoidable.

My warmest wishes for your complete recovery, at once.

G. Winthrop Young (not Mr!)

The Two Queens, Cambo, Northumberland
22.2.50

Dear Bill Murray,

Difficult to tell you, how deeply we appreciated all the thought that had gone to making that evening wholly delightful – and surprising!

Every minute was a new glow, realising all those fine young climbers, and their undying idealism ...

Your own words moved me much. Thought, feeling, and graceful presentation, are rare gifts: I had not thought our mountain world still held anyone who had them to such a degree.

I believe I had rather talk to you than to anyone now in the mountain world.

Which means you are to be extra careful, on far cries [difficult climbs?].

Indeed we could not spare you.

Come here when you can ... Yours gratefully

Geoffrey Winthrop Young

THE EVEREST RECONNAISSANCE AND ITS AFTERMATH

Loch Goil
12.6.1951

Dear Archie and Margaret,

Michael Ward, being driven to distraction by the army, decided three weeks ago that his only way out was to start an Everest Expedition. He therefore rang up Campbell Secord of the AC Committee and gave them hell for sloth and idleness. He impressed upon Secord to act.

Secord and Michael then invited me to lead an expedition to explore and recce the South Face, sending me air maps from the RGS. The summit sends a long South Ridge into Nepal. That ridge ends on Lhotse (27,890 ft.). Between Everest and Lhotse is a col – the South Col – at 26,000 ft. Running west from the South Col is the great Khumbu Glacier, called the "West Cwm". No one has ever explored it. (Tilman saw it from a very great distance and thought it looked harder than the old North Col).

Everest also has a West Ridge, which might be accessible from the Khumbu glacier if the South Col route fails. The West Ridge was seen by Mallory (from the other side) who thought it very direct but harder than the North Ridge – nonetheless climbable. If the South Col is accessible, then the last 3,000 feet up the south ridge is probably much easier than the old north route.

I agreed to act. Secord then saw Kirwan (Director of the RGS) and Claude Elliott (President of the Alpine Club). They gave encouragement. Secord then invited the AC to summon the Himalayan Committee (i.e. the old Everest Committee). This was done on 12 June. Secord urged that it was high time the Committee demonstrated effectively that it still had an interest in the Everest region. He proposed the Expedition to recce the South Col, produced the arguments for it, and pointed out that it had advantages over the old route (i.e. if it went at all) in that the difficulties would be between 23 and 26,000 ft., whereas the crux of the north route was between 28 and 29,000 ft. Moreover since Tibet was now closed we were morally bound to assume the only other approach. One door had closed, but another had opened. We ought to look in.

Result: The committee took it like lambs and had agreed to vote funds to cover part of costs. Basil Goodfellow and Peter Lloyd have been selected to help us. The party is to consist of Michael and I, plus two or three of the following; Secord, Tissieres, Tom Bourdillon, Peter Nock, Chas Evans, Dan Stewart (JMCS). Party not fixed.

Meantime Goodfellow has commended the Foreign Office to cable the ambassador at Kathmandu for permission to enter at mid August. This has been done. But we may be refused. A French expedition was refused entry earlier in the year. However, things may be quieter now.

If it's on, then we have the calm, clear weather of mid September to end October in which to cope with Everest. November will be too cold, and the monsoon is still going strong in August. We shall have to go by air through lack of time.

On Saturday morning I arrive London to meet Secord, Goodfellow, Lloyd, Michael etc and get the organisation laid on and decisions made. Probably I return Monday. I may not see you. But if possible I may call on Monday and stop overnight. If that does not suit, please write me c/o Campbell H. Secord, 4 Carlton Mews, London SW1.

All this letter is confidential. Please don't tell the boys or it will leak. After all Nepal may say no. Hope you are all well now. Look forward to seeing you.

Yours, Bill

Loch Goil
11.7.1951

Dear Archie,

I should probably be in London about 20 July to see to the shipping of all gear, which goes on the *Strathaird* – sailing 2 August.

You would see from the press that there has been further developments in the composition of the party. A few days after I left you Shipton arrived in the country from China. Secord wrote me about this and asked if I'd give him permission to sound Shipton, to see if he'd come too. Since Shipton's knowledge of the Everest region is unrivalled by anyone else on this earth, and his judgement of snow conditions would have high value, I said yes. Secord sounded him. Shipton was keen to come, but reluctant to 'gatecrash' at the last moment. So I wrote to Shipton and welcomed him into the fold. He, then, naturally became official leader of the expedition for no other situation could be appropriate. I myself continued the work of organisation, for the stream of correspondence was too complicated to permit a change of horse midway.

Shipton is very pessimistic about our prospects on the Khumbu Glacier. He once reached the Lho La from the Rongbuk Glacier and looked down on to the icefall of the great bend. It looked steep and tricky but he thought it could be made to go. The snag was that above the icefall the glacier continued level, or fairly level, not rising above 20,000 ft. to the farthest point he could see, which was within four miles of the South Col. That final four miles was invisible. But within that distance the rise to the col is 6,000 ft. That is it rises the same height in the same distance as does the Matterhorn above the Schwarzsee. When this has sunk in, also reflect that we only start that climb 7,000 feet above the top of the Matterhorn, and that all snow that has fallen on the upper 3,000 feet will not have consolidated, but is of necessity bound to remain in powder form. However, he agrees we must go and look.

Michael commands me to call on you and have my teeth looked at! He wants to know if you have an old multiple-purpose forceps to save carrying the two forceps.

Shipton has at least spared me excessive pestering by the press. As it is, he complains that they are putting into his mouth all sorts of things that he never said at all especially regarding equipment and stores.

This will probably be his last visit to the Himalaya. Next year he goes as adviser to the Queen of the Tonga Islands in the South Pacific Ocean.

Tilman has retired from Himalayan climbing as from last year.

My regards Yours, Bill

Namche Bazar, Nepal
25.9.1951

Dear Archie and Margaret,

We have arrived at the Sherpa HQ fifteen days late. We started from Mailhead [Jogbani] 27 August.

Rain, swollen rivers, porter trouble held us off. The Sherpa country is the size of an average English county. Namche is approached by an enormous ravine (the Dudh Kosi river) from which one climbs steeply 2,000 feet to Namche which is set in a sort of amphitheatre of grassy hills, backed by a bigger amphitheatre of 20/21,000 feet snow peaks all spiky – a most splendid position. There are 70/80 houses all double-storied, walls of stone, covered with mud and white washed. Roofs and floors of wood. The better houses have glass in the windows. The Sherpas are most delightful. They report that Tibet is quiet [under the then new Chinese occupation] and that life there goes on as usual. The Tibetan tea is excellent (butter, salt & tea churned up). We have been joined by two New Zealand climbers, Hillary and Riddiford who were in Garhwal this year. The president of NZ Alpine Club cabled Shipton (in London in August) asking if they could join us.

The monsoon ended 20 September. Weather now good but very cold. Today we set off for Everest. Three days from now our base camp should be established.

If we get home by Xmas Michael says he would also come and visit the Well Cottage and asks if you could get in some Dubonnet (the apperitif) of which he is especially fond. I have promised to pass on this message. He is serious, he can't get it at home. The larger the quantity the better. ...

I hope that the Dent's proofs have not been troublesome. We were very sorry about the bad Alpine weather. Were you able to climb anything?

Yours, Bill

The following two letters were written at the time when Murray was completing *The Story of Everest* (Dent, 1953), the second Swiss Expedition was on the mountain (the first having reached the South Col and climbed much of the final pyramid) and the British 1953 team was being selected.

Loch Goil
7.10.1952

Dear Margaret,

Thank you very much for the *Swiss Alpine Club Journal*, which I shall read today. I've just got back from a lecture trip Inverness/Yorkshire. F........ has replied to my letter [name illegible – possibly Marcel Kurz], in which I had asked permission to write 2,000 words on his expedition detailing one or more lively incidents and illustrated with two Swiss photos, agreeing quite cheerfully to their propositions and saying that he is delighted to hear that I have this book coming out. But he is 'leaving the details of this arrangement with you to my chief press agent, Mr Guntner.' [spelling not clear, he may be referring to Othmar Gurtner] has not yet written. The expedition is much criticised in Switzerland as being excessively commercialised. It remains to be seen whether Guntner is going to try to drive a hard bargain on whether F........ has issued orders that he has to deal gently with me.

I agree with all you say about the Everest icefall, much the same situation arises near the summit in the risk of these storms out of blue sky. Smythe in 1933, turning back at 28,100 ft. through deep powder, would, had he enjoyed clean rocks, have been killed by the storm that [later] caught Eric Shipton [during his descent to Camp 5]. However, there is a great difference between accepting unseen risks, like that and accepting them when they are plain and obvious down on the icefall.

On 22 October, and again on 24 October, I am lecturing on Everest at the Hoare Memorial Hall, Church House, Westminster. On 23 October I am at Lord Wandsworth College, Surrey, then I come north. I now hear that Shipton is not leading next year. I do not even know if Roberts is the man.

Dent is pushing up price of book to 15/- and using twenty-four photos, not sixteen. It was my typist Mrs Mackay who proposed changes in book. In Chapter 13, approach words, I have cut all personal details such as the Sherpa women, the Treasurer of the Him. Com., myself as organiser etc.

Regards, Bill

P.S. Roderick just wrote to ask if I were going to Everest next year!

Loch Goil
13.10.1952

Dear Margaret,

The Mountaineering Association Lectures [Murray was on an Everest lecture tour] are open to the general public. I enclose a ticket for Mrs Dell for Friday 24 October.

I can give her one for Wed 22nd if she'd prefer that but the house will be packed for the first night and she'd have to be there early to get a decent seat, i.e. all tickets have been used. The second night should be easier. If she wants the 22nd she'd have to contact me before Friday next, because I'm then off to Leeds, Ackworth, Birmingham, Sale, London, Keswick.

I don't know John Hunt personally, although I know of his ascents in the Himalaya and the Alps. His attempt on Peak 36 in the Saltoro Karakorum with Waller was a very good effort. He has climbed with John Hartog, in the Dauphiné and I'll get more information from that source. Bill Mackenzie met him in the Cairngorms during the war when he (Hunt) was a Major in the Commandos. Bill thought he was a very good man. I was climbing with Bill on Sunday. He described John Hunt as physically powerful and a fine leader who "would stand no swash from the Himalayan Committee". (The Himalayan Committee are tougher gentlemen than honest William realises). However it sounds as though he had a forceful personality. Bill remarked that Mrs Hunt was an amazing woman and every bit as tough as her husband. She was with him in the Cairngorms. He thought her age was then 30. Hunt, he thought was now 45 or 46. Mrs Hunt when she came to a river like the Dee or Spey, didn't bother making long detours in search of bridges. She just swam across fully clothed. This, said Bill, would be done in high summer or dead of winter. It made no difference. She was a good climber. Hunt has climbed a great deal in the Near East – Greece, Cyprus, Egypt, Sinai. I assume that you know (from the press?) that he was on Eisenhower's staff in Paris recently, at least I think so. All who know him have a high regard for him. He writes often in the *AJ* and *HJ* and his articles are well written, although not outstandingly good.

I wrote Goodfellow recently about candidates for Everest, especially re. Dick Meyer, who ought to be taken. He sent my letter straight to John Hunt, as he himself was flying to India immediately on business. Hunt is at Esher and I gather is going to choose his own teams with no more than advice from all and sundry.[2]

The statement that Shipton 'disagreed' with the Himalayan Committee is just a dish out for the press. It is true that he did favour a party of six. But the Him. Com. decided unanimously (this is an off-record report) not to have Shipton as leader, because while he excels at running small expeditions which set out without plans to cover a wide area and to seize chances as they come, he is no leader for a big party employing siege tactics. This is no discredit to Shipton. He is unrivalled as a Himalayan mountaineer and his is a truer mountaineering than laying siege to one big peak. However, it could not be said publicly that Shipton was not fitted to run a big expedition to Everest. Therefore the disagreement about size of party was given out as the reason of Shipton

2 Murray had also commended Tom Patey for consideration. According to his own account in *The Ascent of Everest* Hunt was preoccupied with team selection at this point and resisting a variety of team proposals. The highly charged atmosphere in the aftermath of Shipton's withdrawal from the leadership (described in Chapter 13 of *Everest* by Walt Unsworth) had created a new situation to which all had to adjust. Tales of Joy Hunt crossing the Dee and Spey were apocryphal.

retiral! The fact remains that Shipton deserves to command greater respect as a mountaineer, than Hunt. But I have no doubt that Hunt is the better leader for Everest.

The Himalayan Committee declare that the team will be finally chosen at the end of October.

I agree about the Swiss attempt. The odds are very heavily against the success ....

I met Kurt Hahn the other day and put the icefall problem to him. His reply was instant and vehement:

> It is my lifelong experience that the discarding of first principles never yet led a man to the end he deserved. During the war our designers of aircraft, oppressed by the urgent need to produce faster planes, tried again and again to break through the limitations imposed e.g. principles of aero-dynamics. The results were disastrous. Success came to them only when they accepted the limitations and worked to the principles. Likewise in mountaineering. You have been trained to accept certain principles, acknowledged e.g. British mountaineers. On no pretext should they be discarded on Everest, for you will not in that way arrive at the end you desire.

This sounded very impressive when delivered with all the force of Kurt Hahn's overwhelming personality.

Yours, Bill

FROM TOM PATEY

Inverurie Hospital, Aberdeenshire
24.10.1957

Dear Bill,

Thanks for your last letter. I am afraid that after some thought I've had to give up the idea of committee membership as my future in the services is so uncertain. Thank you very much however for proposing me.

You are a bit off the mark when you say that *Mountaineering in Scotland* is overwritten. I think it gives a very true picture of the climbs it describes. There is nothing more deplorable than the present day tendency (originating from the Oxford and Cambridge [University Mountaineering Club] Journals) to underwrite climbs. Such accounts are neither interesting, humorous or informative.

You might be interested to know that in a discussion on the Muztagh Expedition as to why we all started rock climbing, in two cases (Joe Brown and myself) it was reading your book that did the trick!

All the best and do let me know if you can fit in a weekend's climbing in these parts.

Yours, Tom

TO ROBERT AITKEN REGARDING CONSERVATION

Loch Goil
31.8.1985

Dear Bob,

I am very glad to have your Footpath report. Very many thanks for sending it.

On a first skim through it I can see that I'll learn a lot I didn't know before or had overlooked, or hadn't taken aboard in sufficient detail like the psychology of visual impact etc. The CCS [Countryside Commission for Scotland] is quite unused to reading such good English composition in reports. The freedom from jargon amazed me. I still remember a report (on Culzean) in which roads were 'vehicular circulatory systems'. This firm charged the CCS the better part of £10,000 for that specimen, which would have been in the early 1970's. A rip-off, so blatant that I lost all respect for the CCS staff who accepted it. I could have written it myself in a few days, minus jargon but then so brief that they would not have wanted to pay for it, except for travel costs to Culzean and back. You at least have given them value for money! I am impressed by the solid work that has gone into it and the clarity of the writing.

I've still to read it properly, for I'm not yet clear of the Boardman/Tasker Award. Among the latest entries is a most beautifully produced book by Alfred Wainwright: *Wainwright on the Pennine Way* with superb photos by Derry Brabbs.

The Question of Intent will not go down well with Trustees. I will be astounded if they consent to strict rules and if they do not I will be getting out. I wasted years of time on the NTS [National Trust of Scotland] and on CCS playing games with men who never were in earnest about conservation of wild land and who did not in reality give a damn what happened to it. I was so slow in leaving that I now feel guilty (of my own stupidity). You are right about the need of a bigger following for the Unna-type approach. CCS staff have no time for that, nor NTS either. Both feel they are there 'to facilitate access and public enjoyment' and have a mental block on the question 'enjoyment of what?' – for how can people enjoy wild land if the wild aspect is removed?

The Wildland Group have a lot of work to do. Meantime I am asking myself, in what way is the JMT [John Muir Trust], as at presently composed, superior to the NTS, as a prospective holder of mountainous property? I am still waiting to find out. I have not yet abandoned hope, although I'm mentally prepared for that. Another question is whether the NH Fund [National Heritage Fund] are sufficiently enlightened to part with money on Unna-approach terms? Or are they convertible?

Perhaps compromise cannot be avoided. I remember Morton Boyd saying to me (after a CCS meeting) 'On conservation, never compromise'. I learned that he was right.

Best Wishes
Yours, Bill

APPENDIX III: Writing about Climbing and Mountain Landscape

A speech given in 1984 to the British Mountaineering Council at Portinscale, Cumbria.[1]

I have long since discovered that the human race is composed of just two species, those who climb and those who don't. Or, as a more rational man might phrase it, the daft and the sober. Which means, for example, that the BMC has spent the last forty years fostering insobriety. As a writer, by trade, I have shared that ministry. It consoles me to feel that I am not alone, and that, we are each and all keeping such bad company.

Writing and climbing have a lot more in common than that – heavy penalties for one. For a start there is no loot in it – at least not for you and me. Yet still we do it. Think too of all the agonies, like 2 a.m. starts in the Alps. Well, the mind is just as lazy as the body when it comes to starting a book.

But enough about pains. What of pleasures? In climbing, there's an elation just in practice of the craft when all is going well. You make the moves surely, or swiftly with rhythm. When you are climbing well you know it. It's the same in writing. The two crafts are often akin, even though one is mainly physical, the other mental. When you are off form too, you write clumsily, just as you move clumsily; you pick wrong words as you pick wrong holds; you lose the thread and purpose of writing as you lose a route. But when good form is suddenly struck, you rise from the dead.

We must, of course, be wary of analogies. You cannot press them too far. In climbing you are living. In reading or writing about climbing you live at second hand. That might seem a truism, yet life does not always happen to work that way.

We can all think of days on the mountains when we have felt half dead. Apart from pre-dawn starts, there is altitude, or too heavy loads, or the morning after … or just plain pain – like a bad bivouac, or hours of icy waiting

1 Murray was the chief guest at the Annual Dinner. He had previously (1968–1971) served as Vice-President, the last to officially represent Scotland before the establishment of the Mountaineering Council of Scotland. The author deals more fully with this subject in the second part of Chapter 36 (with some overlap) and this speech is therefore slightly abridged.

between pitches, frozen to the bone. But when it comes to recollection, after some decent interval, what a different tale is often told! The pains have gone as, if they had, never been, or … certainly not lasted. Whereas the day as a whole lasts in the mind. Are pains unimportant? We joke about them. But we had not felt like joking at the time. So where is the truth?

As for those half dead occasions, when the mind itself seems blind, recording nothing, afterwards the scene can come alive. … A foremost example … was on the first ascent of the Everest icefall. We were far too frightened to pay attention to any quality of scene. After all, the walls were just half a mile apart, some 5,000 feet high and bursting with hanging glaciers: by alpine standards, ripe to avalanche. Yet the mind stored up that splendid scene, while we were unaware.

Maybe a better example … [was when we] were trying to get down from Hanuman. … We were steering by compass across a desert of writhing snow … when a great shaft opened up through the clouds of the Rishi. It disclosed a vast white arrowhead floating in upper air with no visible support. It seemed not of this earth, just a momentary glimpse, then clouds swirled round and swallowed it up. I would have sworn the mind took no impression … but later, back in camp, that vision of Nanda Devi came back, fair as when first seen. It is those moments that last. All the sharp anxieties of the situation, so much more prolonged and more real at the time, have in time proved to be less real.

So, you can see that one reward of writing is ableness to live in a kind of ideal world, from which suffering has disappeared – one may regard the suffering of others, and even oneself, yet not be subject to it. Writing does have its points. But now you can see too how much trouble this stores up for the writer. Trouble, that is, if he wants to get at the truth. If he wants to be free of humbug, then he's faced with dilemmas. If he makes too light of the pains, he bores by understatement. If he makes too much of the joys, he deceives by overstatement.

How to get it right? Having tried for fifty years to get it right, I am tempted to say it cannot be done – were it not that climbing has taught me never to say *that.* While trying, I have made all the mistakes that can be made. The true art is finding words to express what you really mean, so that you can balance on that knife-edge between two realities, and let both speak. But words, so often, seem fully apposite only to material things. To get the subjective reality at the same time you have to be able to play on words and wring out meaning between the lines. It can be done. But it does need a touch of inspiration, which is why I feel a bit frustrated. Few of us are ever able to say fully what we want to say. We are then tempted to give up trying. I think that is a mistake. We have to accept the errors we make for the sake of the few times we get it right.

By 'a touch of inspiration' I do not mean at Shakespearean level. A lesser gift will do. I do not even mean fine writing, rather than a direct simplicity of expression, which is very hard to get, but is the hallmark of good writing. It goes to the heart of the matter.

Most of us who are given to writing can sometimes come away with a sentence or two that is just right. A few can get a whole paragraph, or even a scatter of paragraphs through a book-length work. Men who can do that rank high. For me, Mummery could sometimes do it. He first brought me to see that climbers and writers (in fact most humans) have this in common, that we are not rational beings ... we are usually moved to act less by logic than feeling. This stands out clear in the best mountain writing. Some early writers chose to forget this, and without ill intention dressed up climbers in sheep's clothing. They threw around them a cloak of scientific record, and with it an air of Victorian respectability. As for the writing, that fell flat. Stripped of subjective realities, it gave no expression to the climbers' real motives or experience. It was rescued by what I have heard miscalled a romantic movement – miscalled, that is, if 'romantic' is misinterpreted as meaning sentimentalising or in any way falsifying personal experience, instead of presenting it more roundly. Among its early writers were Whymper and Leslie Stephen (1871). But for me, Mummery (1895) was its leading exponent. His words rang true. They gave the spirit of the game. In this century they were followed (in Britain) by Young, Smythe, Shipton, Tilman, and Longstaff.

In the 1950s, came a reaction. The fashion-pendulum swung back to rational report. A gambit of understatement, overused, came close to humbug. Writing as reflected in journals and magazines fell to an all-time low. I thought the pendulum had stuck at that. To my delight and surprise, it was swung free ... starting with Chris Bonington's *I Chose to Climb* – an impetus since given by many, as witnessed by Jim Perrin's anthology *Mirrors in the Cliffs*. The quality of the new writing in book-form had a creative liveliness in Dennis Gray's *Rope Boy*, and Tom Patey's *One Man's Mountains*.

That quality has since peaked in two books, which have made me ask myself, 'If I were once again a beginner, who would I choose today as my writing and climbing paragons?' I have no hesitation. They are Peter Boardman and Joe Tasker. They do really say directly and simply what mountains mean to them. *The Shining Mountain* (1978) and *Savage Arena* (1982) deal with extreme climbing. They might seem to be for the hard men, not for hill-men in general. In fact, I find that all who read are enthralled. That is because Pete and Joe re-lived their climbs in the writing. They re-created them, and the mountains too – more still, they brought each other intensely alive. Single-minded as they were, some might think fanatical, they kept balance between the two worlds, the subjective and the objective, and made each real, the one between the lines, the other in plain words. Therefore I honour them. That chosen blend goes to the heart of full living or writing. The fact is that if we were all fully rational none of us would climb at all. When we raise a head of steam for action, the fuel has to be a mix – emotion with reason – to give spark. If we left climbing to cold reason, we would all be afflicted by that occupational disease that Tilman used to call Mountaineer's Foot – the inability to put one foot in front of the other. So, I am glad of this chance to express my own heavy debt to the climbers and writers of Britain. I have long recognised that they are all daft. I use daft in its old Scots sense, which meant 'unreasonably happy'. It would seem, despite all, that climbing is good for us.

APPENDIX IV: The Rob Roy Affair

The matters noted in Chapter 36 were attended by media comment and legal activity.

> 'This weekend US lawyers for Murray are studying papers for a potential multi-million dollar battle against United Artists and stars Neeson and Lange unless a settlement can be reached.' (*Sunday Times*, 11 Dec. 1994)

The author was warned that a 'strike' was scheduled for the following day – and *The Sunday Times* given (by the lawyers) an exclusive on the story.

Murray's book *Rob Roy MacGregor* was first published by Richard Drew, in 1982, and then by Canongate in 1993. It revealed Rob Roy's true status as an upright Highland chieftain protecting those in his care from noblemen preying on the clans in the aftermath of the 1715 Uprising. It was this heroic characterisation that had been portrayed so effectively by Liam Neeson in the 1995 film *Rob Roy*.[1]

The issue was whether the filmmakers had exceeded their rights in basing their characterisation of Rob Roy on the author's scrupulously researched biography. Prior to Murray's researches and *his* portrayal of Rob Roy as a hero, this man had been considered a brigand and a criminal. This earlier image had resulted from Sir Walter Scott's *Rob Roy* – long required reading in Scottish schools in the study of Scott's work and filmed in 1953.[2]

Peter Broughan, the 1995 film's producer, suggested to the *Herald* that Alan Sharp (a noted screenwriter) could have written the same story without having read Murray – yet Sharp (in Jack Webster's *Herald* article of 13 March 1995) said:

---

1 *Rob Roy* United Artists 1995 Screenplay written by Alan Sharp, directed by Michael Caton-Jones, produced by Peter Broughan and Richard Jackson. Starring: Liam Neeson, Jessica Lange, John Hurt, Tim Roth and Eric Stolz.

2 *Rob Roy the Highland Rogue* Walt Disney 1953 Screenplay written by Lawrence Watkin, directed by Harold French, produced by Perce Pearce. Starring: Richard Todd, Glynis Johns and James Robertson Justice.

> 'There is no doubt that the painting of Rob Roy revealed by Murray was the one I wished to portray. I had no intention of repeating the Walter Scott version.
>
> Mr Murray demonstrates both a keen knowledge of historical landscape and an ability to imaginatively engage the reader in his narrative. I would happily place W.H. Murray's book amongst the finest examples of historic writing I know.'

Filmmakers and the public like heroes. A fine portrayal of Rob Roy was before them, the research done, a story told and a hero created – ideal for attracting both stars and the necessary financial backing for the film – which could go ahead without delay.

The fact remains that Murray died having received nothing from a highly profitable film venture – a film that might never have been made without his painstaking researches, fine writing and creation of a hero figure. Yet no credit was given: the hero, created in the book – Murray's 'man of honour' – was lifted for a multi-million pound film.

There is no copyright on historical facts but copyright can exist on conclusions drawn from facts – here seen as Murray's Rob Roy MacGregor, the hero and the man of honour.

This tawdry affair seems to demonstrate that 'honour' is a concept with no place in our modern, acquisitive society – at least in the rarefied world of filmmaking.

APPENDIX V: Publishing and the Practicalities of the Writing Business

Britain, complacently civilised, has the worst royalty rates for writers in Western Europe. Scandinavia has a standard royalty of 16.5% with 20% [of the recommended selling price] guaranteed on a proportion of every new work of imaginative literature – riches compared to British rates. A writer here is more likely to be offered 7.5% – 10%, or less, particularly if he is young and keen to have his book published.

The British public apparently want to read but do not want to pay, having been brain-washed into regarding free books as their right. They read at the expense of their authors. Guided by governments, usually caring little for minorities or literature, the public are conned. They are ignorant of the true situation, happy to pay highly for other pleasures or interests but not to pay for books. Eleven books are borrowed from libraries for every one bought. Libraries of course do sterling work on low funding – ever decreasing – and are particularly appreciated by authors who need constant access to books. However, despite the advent of Public Lending Right (PLR) few authors are much richer. This payment is parsimonious. Out of about 25,000 authors registered in the scheme the majority get less than £100 per annum from PLR. A thousand of them get between £1,000 and £6,000, which is the maximum allowed. Only about a hundred bestselling authors attain to this sum. The rate to the author is two pence for borrowings, estimated on samples.

It is often forgotten that a writer gives employment. He supports the publishing and book selling industries, libraries, education, and of course enhances leisure and culture. His books would be missed if they ceased to be.

A potential business hazard for the author is the publishing contract. It can conceal much from the unwary or inept. One such hazard is the practice of discounting sales to booksellers, calling almost all the sales 'bulk' (the term bulk not being defined) and thereupon reducing the authors royalty i.e. paying it on the sum the publisher receives (a net sale) rather that on the advised retail price of the book (gross) as is (or rather was) normal. An author can find to his horror that on a book selling well his royalty income has been halved owing to his failure to notice a few simple words inserted in a familiar and usually harmless clause.

Of course some call this sort of thing sharp practice – designed to mislead – but if the author has signed the contract he can have a problem unless his publisher acknowledges an error, perhaps in the clarity of his phrasing. Of course no author in his right mind would sign a contract in which his negotiated royalty rate, his income, is somehow halved in the next paragraph. Would you do this, knowingly? Of course not – but authors do it – albeit unknowingly. Publishers rarely explain this caveat in advance.

Do not assume that because you are intelligent this sort of thing can't happen to you, despite years of experience I too have fallen prey to the kind of punitive contract that no good agent would permit his author to sign. I give you only the tip of an iceberg and like the iceberg, it is chilling.

Of course the situation varies from publisher to publisher. Fortunately there are good publishers – but they have to be found. Part of a publisher's side of the deal is book promotion, advertising, distribution – selling your book. Will he do it well? The publisher, having produced the book, receives most of its selling price, about 50%,[1] apart from the author's percentage, say 10%. The bookseller receives the rest, about 40%. Of course they have upkeep. Does your publisher prefer short sales, no storage or advertising costs? Will there be an advance?

To deal with the world he finds himself in an author should endeavour to get professional help – a good literary agent who knows both books and business. The 10% commission on sales will save the author money, time and worry (provided the agent is indeed good). This is the best advice I can give an author today.

THE PUBLISHING SCENE

The literary scene has greatly changed in these last fifty years. When I began to write full-time in the late 1940s, it was possible for an author to earn a living from books alone. Even I did that without trouble. The bigger London publishing houses were happy to accept books that might sell up to 5,000 copies to cover their costs, while hoping for bigger sales in the longer run. The UK's book production was a fraction of its present 68,000 titles per year. High Street booksellers, then numerous, were able to display new books on their shelves over much longer periods.

Authors' incomes have since been decimated by a series of ills. These include competition, but not of the kind to stimulate good writing.

Though book production has multiplied, publishers have shrunk in number. The old family firms, which upheld literary traditions, have been taken over by huge, international conglomerates, whose primary aim is commercial, not literary; profit, not quality. Be wary of dulcet tones – wolves still graze in sheep's clothing. Good writing, drowned in the flood of trash, can still bob to

1 From this the publisher must recoup the cost of manufacturing the book.

the top if the media throw it a publicity life belt. Such occasions of mercy are rare, more usually stimulated by some newsworthy investment of 'real money' by the publisher.

Secondly, the High Street booksellers have also dwindled in number, afflicted by supermarket competition, soaring local rates, lack of parking space at their own doors, and sometimes recruitment of shop assistants lacking literary interest or knowledge – multiple ills exacerbated by the publishers' over-production, so that new titles are allowed too short time on the shelves, where the public can see them and sales grow. All too soon they are replaced by still newer titles that pour in from distributors.

The sorry tale could be greatly lengthened. The hub of it is that the author of today, unless he has an established name, must have a second, money-earning occupation. His job is, like that of a crofter, not viable in itself. When his secondary occupation is the better paying, it becomes the principal, and the now amateur author then more easily succumbs to the publishers' ruthless policy of royalty reductions – to the detriment of professional authors. The literary seas are infested by sharks.

Since I had started off with a top-class publisher in J.M. Dent & Sons, who paid fair royalties without argument – 10% on the selling price of the first 2,500 copies, 12.5% to 5,000, and 15% thereafter (rates now recommended by the Society of Authors in their Minimum Terms Agreement), I imagined that I might need no agent when I moved to commissioned work for other leading publishers. I lived to regret that mistake, both for the snares and delays of negotiation, and the lower rates won. No new author should attempt to deal alone with publishing contracts.

An author faces long delays in receiving his money, more especially in writing nonfiction. First come the delays of research – possibly a few years; then the writing, anything from months to years; then the publisher's reading delay, followed by delay in settling the business agreement, perhaps three months without an agent; then the printing delay, usually a year if the subject is not of topical urgency, for publishers' lists are planned in advance, and the author's manuscript has to wait in the printer's queue – not all time lost, for it must be remembered that each book is sold thrice, first from author to publisher, second from publisher to book seller through his trade journals and representatives, and third by the booksellers (or distributor) to the public through reviews, press advertisements and display. Finally comes the payment delay of nine months from publication date, unless an advance (deducted from royalties) has first been granted. This can add sometimes up to the better part of three years before any money is won. A budding, full-time author, without private means, is therefore in financial trouble until he has built up a body of published work yielding annual income. I had in part escaped that dilemma, most ironically, by writing my first book under the favour of three years' sustenance from my country's enemies. Without such adventitious help, all aspiring authors must now start part time.

ADVANCES

While press publicity tends to suggest that a gold mine awaits the budding author it rarely does. It is a less likely happening than winning the lottery. Huge advances don't always pay their way for the publisher. They do not always relate to the book's earning potential – and an advance is an advance on earnings.

The attraction of commissioned work is that publishers' money is put down at early stages. But if an author falls to that temptation too often, he tends to become the publisher's employee, and to lose his freedom to develop an individual talent in new ways. The publisher likes the old way, the set formula, from which he can better see his way to win profit. New departures imply risk. The truth is that publishers have no better idea than the author what books will sell. The crass mistakes they make are notorious. Potential best sellers can do rounds of publishers before being taken and failures can be taken immediately. Publishers feel the need to play safe more especially with young or new authors, who should not be so bound.

The author as a schoolboy, *c.*1923.

Pupils of Glasgow Academy *c.*1925. Murray is second from the left on the back row.

Prison camp near Brunswick, 1944.

Lochwood by Loch Goil, Argyll, *c.*1948.

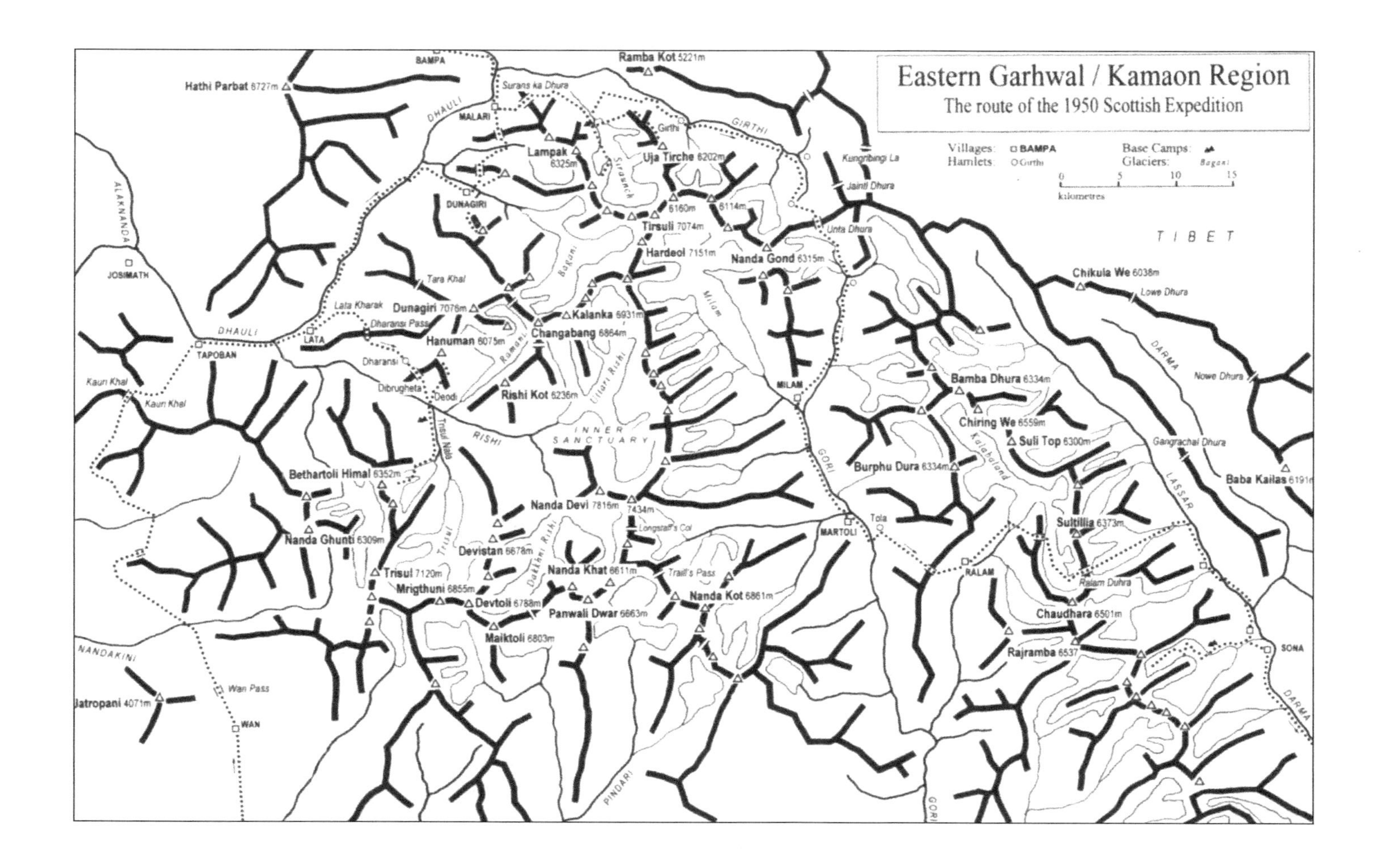

Eastern Garhwal / Kamaon Region
The route of the 1950 Scottish Expedition
Villages: BAMPA
Hamlets: Girthi
Base Camps:
Glaciers: Bagani
0 5 10 15
kilometres
TIBET
Hathi Parbat 6727m
BAMPA
Ramba Kot 5221m
Surans ka Dhura
MALARI
DHAULI
Girthi
GIRTHI
Lampak 6325m
Uja Tirche 6202m
Siraunch
Kungribingi La
Jainti Dhura
Unta Dhura
DUNAGIRI
6160m
6114m
Tirsuli 7074m
Hardeol 7151m
Nanda Gond 6315m
ALAKNANDA
JOSIMATH
Tara Khal
Bagani
Chikula We 6038m
Lowe Dhura
Lata Kharak
Dunagiri 7076m
Kalanka 6931m
Milam
Dharansi Pass
Changabang 6864m
DHAULI
LATA
Hanuman 6075m
TAPOBAN
Ramani
Uttari Rishi
DARMA
Dharansi
Rishi Kot 6236m
MILAM
Bamba Dhura 6334m
Nowe Dhura
Kauri Khal
Dibrugheta
Deodi
Kauri Khal
Chiring We 6559m
Trisul Nala
INNER SANCTUARY
RISHI
Suli Top 6300m
Gangrachal Dhura
GORI
Kalabaland
Burphu Dura 6334m
Bethartoli Himal 6352m
Baba Kailas 6191m
LASSAR
Nanda Devi 7816m
7434m
Tola
MARTOLI
Longstaff's Col
Sultilia 6373m
Nanda Ghunti 6309m
Devistan 6678m
Trisul
Dakkhni Rishi
RALAM
Ralam Dhura
Trisul 7120m
Nanda Khat 6611m
Traill's Pass
Mrigthuni 6855m
Devtoli 6788m
Nanda Kot 6861m
Chaudhara 6501m
Panwali Dwar 6663m
Maiktoli 6803m
NANDAKINI
Rajramba 6537
SONA
Wan Pass
Jatropani 4071m
WAN
DARMA
PINDARI
GORI

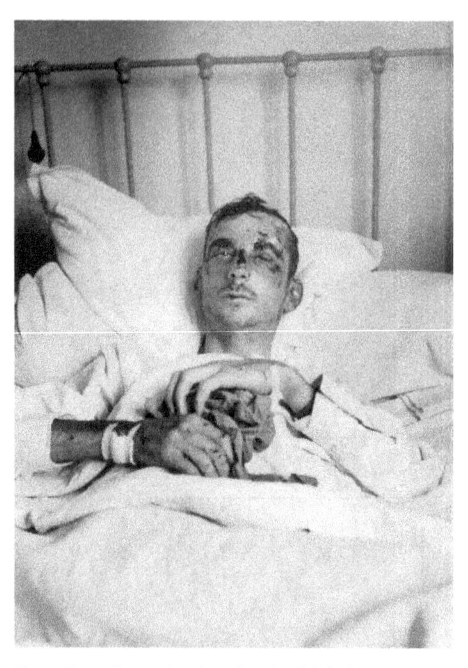

The author in hospital in Gap after the Col de Coste Rouge accident.

After the first Everest (Khumbu) icefall probe Murray, Ward, Earle Riddiford and Tom Bourdillon crossed the Changri La, west of Pumori. This gave access to the glacier basins south of Gyachung Kang from where they attempted (unsuccessfully) to reach the Nup La. This photo shows the Changri La camp, looking to Pt. 6853.

The Everest group from the Sonang Ridge.

Tom Bourdillon.

Bill Murray (clad as a monk at Namche).

In the Menlung Chu.

Everest Reconnaissance 1951 – Conceived by Michael Ward and planned by Bill Murray, this rapidly organised venture 'kick-started' Everest attempts from Nepal after the earlier doubts of experts. A full study of the problems of the huge Khumbu Icefall *(above)* was made, and the previously hidden Lhotse Face was visually assessed.

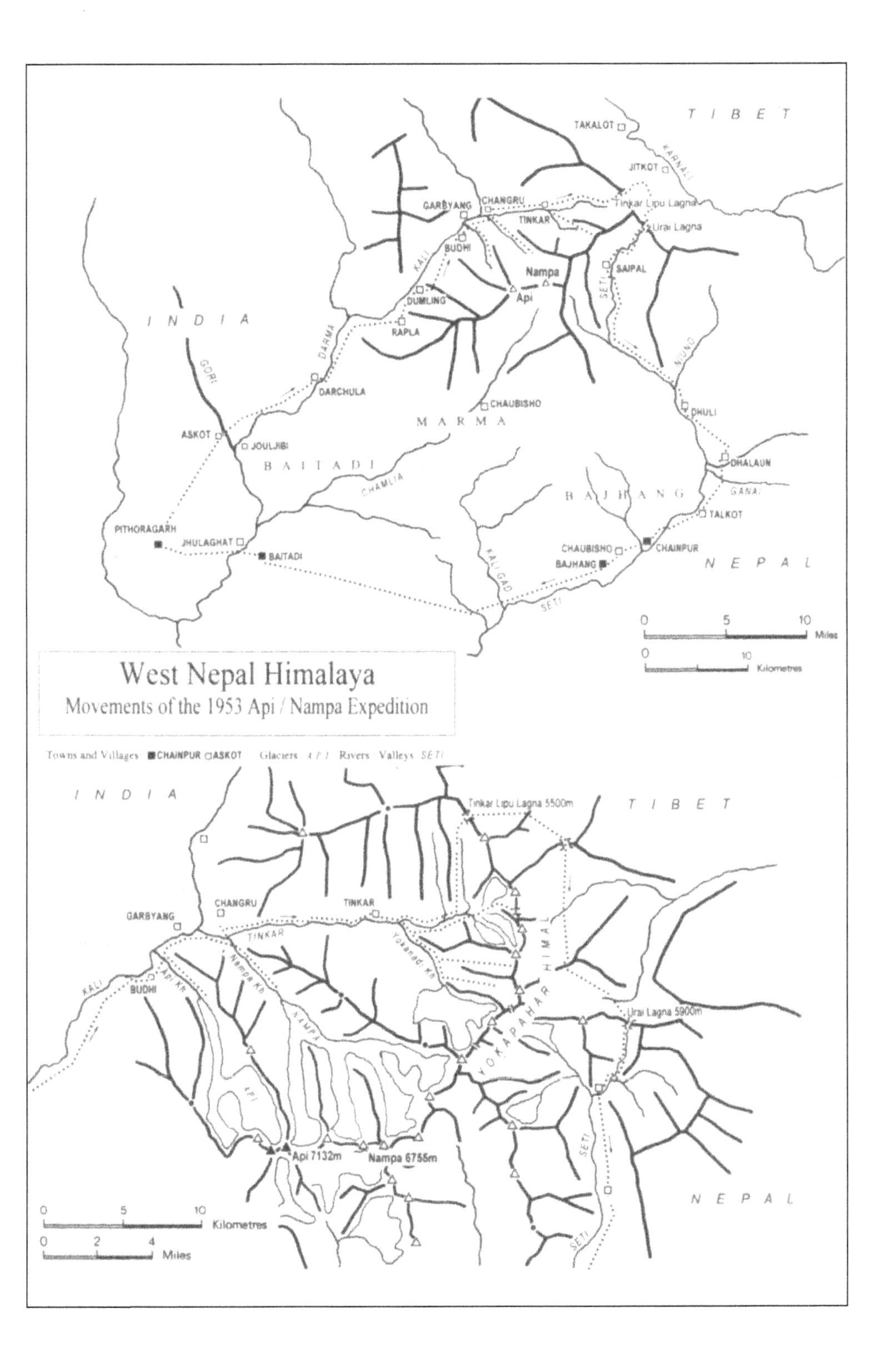
TIBET
TAKALOT
KARNALI
JITKOT
Tinkar Lipu Lagna
GARBYANG
CHANGRU
TINKAR
Urai Lagna
BUDHI
KALI
SAIPAL
SETI
Nampa
Api
DUMLING
RAPLA
INDIA
DARMA
GORI
DARCHULA
NIUNG
CHAUBISHO
DHULI
MARMA
ASKOT
JOULJIBI
BAITADI
DHALAUN
CHAMLIA
GANAI
BAJHANG
TALKOT
PITHORAGARH
JHULAGHAT
BAITADI
CHAUBISHO
CHAINPUR
BAJHANG
KALI GAD
NEPAL
SETI
0 5 10 Miles
0 10 Kilometres
West Nepal Himalaya
Movements of the 1953 Api / Nampa Expedition
Towns and Villages CHAINPUR ASKOT Glaciers API Rivers Valleys SETI
INDIA
Tinkar Lipu Lagna 5500m
TIBET
CHANGRU
TINKAR
GARBYANG
TINKAR
Yokanadi Kh
HIMAL
KALI
BUDHI
Api Kh
Nampa Kh
NAMPA
Urai Lagna 5900m
YOKAPAHAR
API
SETI
Api 7132m
Nampa 6755m
0 5 10 Kilometres
0 2 4 Miles
NEPAL
SETI

Expedition members (left to right) Eric Shipton, Bill Murray, Tom Bourdillon, Earle Riddiford (and seated) Michael Ward and Ed Hillary.

In the boat house at Lochwood.

Everest and Lhotse from Pumori.

Anne Murray.

At the launch of paperback edition of *Rob Roy* in Callander in 1995 – the town being a centre of Rob Roy linked cultural matters. Murray poses for press photos with Pat Greenhill the Provost of Stirling.

Printed in the USA
CPSIA information can be obtained
at www.ICGtesting.com
JSHW012013140824
68134JS00025B/2400